Bankruptcy of Empire

This book incorporates recent, rich literature on the history of the fiscal organization and financial dynamics of the Spanish empire within the broader historical debates on rival European imperial states in the eighteenth and early nineteenth centuries. The focus is on colonial Mexico because it served as a fiscal and financial submetropolis that ensured the capacity of the imperial state to defend itself in a time of successive international conflicts.

Whereas the monarchy of Charles III (1759–1788) was able to successfully meet the challenges of reinforcement of empire, the finances of the Spanish state began to sink under Charles IV (1789–1808). This collapse was caused by the enormous expense of waging successive wars in the Americas and Europe. In each war, colonial Mexico was the most important source of resources for the Crown, but these demands gradually outstripped the tax base of the viceroyalty despite the extraordinary silver boom of the late eighteenth century. The bankruptcy of the Spanish monarchy and its empire was the inevitable consequence.

Carlos Marichal was born in Baltimore, Maryland, and has dual nationality of both the United States and Mexico. He earned his B.A. and Ph.D. from Harvard and has taught history at the university level in Mexico since 1979. Since 1989, he has been a professor of history at El Colegio de Mexico, the leading social science university institute in Mexico. He is the founder and former president of the Mexican Association of Economic History and has served on the executive committee of the International Economic History Association since 2003. He is the author of *A Century of Debt Crises in Latin America, 1820–1930* (1989), and is the editor or coeditor of fifteen books in Spanish and English, published over the last twenty years, the majority on the fiscal and financial history of Mexico, as well as numerous texts on the economic history of Latin America.

CAMBRIDGE LATIN AMERICAN STUDIES

General Editor
Herbert S. Klein
Gouverneur Morris Emeritus Professor of History, Columbia University
Director of the Center of Latin American Studies, Professor of History, and Hoover Senior Fellow, Stanford University

91
Bankruptcy of Empire

Other Books in the Series

1. *Ideas and Politics of Chilean Independence, 1808–1833*, Simon Collier
2. *Church Wealth in Mexico: A Study of the "Juzgado de Capellanias" in the Archbishopric of Mexico 1800–1856*, Michael P. Costeloe
3. *The Mexican Revolution, 1910–1914: The Diplomacy of Anglo-American Conflict*, P. A. R. Calvert
4. *Britain and the Onset of Modernization in Brazil, 1850–1914*, Richard Graham
5. *Parties and Political Change in Bolivia, 1880–1952*, Herbert S. Klein
6. *The Abolition of the Brazilian Slave Trade: Britain, Brazil and the Slave Trade Question, 1807–1869*, Leslie Bethell
7. *Regional Economic Development: The River Basin Approach in Mexico*, David Barkin and Timothy King
8. *Economic Development of Latin America: Historical Background and Contemporary Problems*, Celso Furtado and Suzette Macedo
9. *An Economic History of Colombia, 1845–1930*, W. P. McGreevey
10. *Miners and Merchants in Bourbon Mexico, 1763–1810*, D. A. Brading
11. *Alienation of Church Wealth in Mexico: Social and Economic Aspects of the Liberal Revolution, 1856–1875*, Jan Bazant
12. *Politics and Trade in Southern Mexico, 1750–1821*, Brian R. Hamnett
13. *Bolivia: Land, Location and Politics since 1825*, J. Valerie Fifer, Malcolm Deas, Clifford Smith, and John Street
14. *A Guide to the Historical Geography of New Spain*, Peter Gerhard
15. *Silver Mining and Society in Colonial Mexico: Zacatecas, 1546–1700*, P. J. Bakewell

(*Continued after index*)

Bankruptcy of Empire

Mexican Silver and the Wars Between Spain, Britain, and France, 1760–1810

CARLOS MARICHAL
El Colegio de Mexico

CAMBRIDGE
UNIVERSITY PRESS

CAMBRIDGE UNIVERSITY PRESS
Cambridge, New York, Melbourne, Madrid, Cape Town, Singapore,
São Paulo, Delhi, Dubai, Tokyo

Cambridge University Press
32 Avenue of the Americas, New York, NY 10013-2473, USA

www.cambridge.org
Information on this title: www.cambridge.org/9780521142359

First published 2007
This digitally printed version 2010

A catalog record for this publication is available from the British Library

Library of Congress Cataloging in Publication data

Marichal, Carlos.
Bankruptcy of empire : Mexican silver and the wars between Spain,
Britain, and France, 1760–1810 / Carlos Marichal.
p. cm. – (Cambridge Latin American studies ; 91)
Includes bibliographical references and index.
ISBN-13: 978-0-521-87964-4 (hardback)
ISBN-10: 0-521-87964-7 (hardback)
1. Spain–History, Military–18th century. 2. New Spain–Economic conditions–18th century
3. Finance, Public–New Spain–History–18th century. I. Title. II. Series.
DP78.M27 2007
946′.057–dc22 2007017750

ISBN 978-0-521-87964-4 Hardback
ISBN 978-0-521-14235-9 Paperback

To Soledad, with love and admiration

Contents

List of Tables and Figures

Tables

Figures

Acknowledgements

The late eighteenth century may be considered the greatest age of silver of the Spanish empire and, without question, Mexico was the tax jewel of the monarchy, providing it with the fiscal and financial resources to function on a world scale. This book documents and analyzes the enormous extraction of Mexican silver that was used mainly to finance an extraordinary succession of wars between Spain, Britain, and France that marked the crisis of the *ancien regime* in Europe and the Americas. The intention of this work is therefore to contribute to transatlantic history, a field so extensive that I owe a great deal to the work carried on by a great number of researchers from different countries.

The approach adopted here has its roots in comparative history, a fact related to my personal intellectual trajectory. After working in the 1980s on the comparative history of Latin American debt crises in the nineteenth and twentieth centuries, I turned my attention to the history of colonial finance and debts because I found it to be a field on which work had just begun and was flourishing. I published a series of articles and directed a number of doctoral theses, learning much from the work on Mexican colonial finance by Luis Jáuregui, Guillermina del Valle, Matilde Souto, and Antonio Ibarra as well as Iván Escamilla, Gisela von Wobeser, Pilar Martínez, Leonor Ludlow, and Ernest Sánchez Santiró, among others. At the same time, I benefited from discussions with colleagues from Spain who had worked on the history of the transition from empire to nation, as aptly phrased by Leandro Prados de la Escosura; other Spanish historians who contributed to ideas in this book are Pedro Tedde, Francisco Comín, Nicolás Sánchez Albornoz, Pablo Martín Aceña, Gabriel Tortella, Albert Carreras, Josep María Fradera, and Jordi Maluquer de Motes, whom I thank for their collaboration in many things, large and small. At the same time, my research was nurtured by the research of a broad cohort of cosmopolitan historians who have contributed to the great edifice of historiography on Bourbon Mexico and Spanish America: among those who provided initial guidance on colonial finance and economy were Pedro Pérez Herrero, Juan Carlos Garavaglia, and our dear and lamented friend, Juan Carlos Grosso.

Also fundamental have been the contributions of Herbert Klein, José Carlos Chiaramonte, John Coatsworth, Richard Garner, Richard Salvucci, Linda Arnold, John TePaske, Stanley Stein, Eric Van Young, and David Brading – through both their writings and intellectually stimulating visits to Mexico.

Among the many persons who provided assistance in archives and libraries, I wish to single out Juan Manuel Herrera, Armando Rojas, and Eutiquio Franco at the Archivo General de la Nación, Teresa Tortella, director of the archives of the Banco de España, Micaela Chávez, and the personnel of the library of El Colegio de México, who have assisted me consistently for many years. In addition, I must thank the collaboration of Carlos Rodríguez Venegas who assisted me in many stages of the research; Irasema Infante who helped with tables and figures; Anthony Tillet who swiftly translated first versions of Chapters 3, 5, 6, and 7; and Lorena Murillo who translated Chapter 4. I am also grateful to the editors of diverse academic journals in which preliminary research of this volume appeared, as well as for the permission to translate previous versions of materials contained in a work published by the Fideicomiso de las Américas at El Colegio de Mexico, whose director, Alicia Hernández Chávez, is a dynamic promoter of the comparative history of Latin America.

Finally, I wish to thank the professional and enthusiastic support of Herbert Klein, general editor of *Cambridge Latin America Studies*, the courteous attention of editor Frank Smith and his assistant Kate Queram, as well as the two anonymous readers from Cambridge University Press for their penetrating observations. Last, but certainly not least, my thanks go to Navdeep Singh and his team in Delhi who have done the work on the electronic version of the manuscript that was necessary to transform virtual reality into the physical book!

Introduction

From before the time of Gibbon, historians with a global perspective have been discussing the rise and fall of empires. Today political scientists frequently speak of hegemonic *states*. If we review some of the best-known studies conducted over the last forty-odd years, it is possible to identify a variety of theoretical approaches adopted by those working on the history of imperial or hegemonic states. The literature is vast and includes traditional geopolitical studies with a focus on the roots of military superiority,[1] the sweeping propositions of the *world-system school*,[2] as well as the interpretations of historical sociologists who offer explanations based on the changing capacities of states to exercise power through manipulation of capital and coercion.[3] While all raise important questions, these quite general approaches do not necessarily provide convincing answers to the issue of explaining the specific reasons for the rise and/or decline of a given state or empire.[4]

Fortunately, in recent years, numerous historians have adopted a more focused approach, analyzing specific features of the historical evolution of states that can be studied in considerable depth, both empirically and

1 The number of historical studies on the role of the military in the evolution of great powers is legion. Two classics are William H. McNeill, *The Pursuit of Power: Technology, Armed Force and Society since* A.D. *1000* (Chicago: University of Chicago Press, 1982) and Paul Kennedy, *The Rise and Fall of British Naval Mastery* (London: Macmillan, 1983). A more recent and widely read contribution is that of Nial Fergusson, *Empire: The Rise and Demise of the British World Order* (New York: Basic Books, 2002).

2 Standard works of this school include Immanuel Wallerstein and Christopher Chase-Dunn, *Rise and Demise: Comparing World Systems* (Boulder, Colo.: Westview Press, 1997).

3 A pioneering collective work is Charles Tilly, ed., *The Formation of Nation States in Western Europe* (Princeton, N.J.: Princeton University Press, 1975). A subsequent study is Charles Tilly, *Coercion, Capital and European States,* A.D. *900–1990* (Cambridge, U.K.: Basil Blackwell, 1990).

4 More satisfactory and informative than some of these historically applied social science models are diverse classic historical studies. For example, on the rise of the Spanish empire in the sixteenth century, two superb examples are Fernand Braudel, *La Méditerranée et le Monde Méditerranéan à l'Epoque de Philippe II* (Paris: Armand Colin, 1949) and John H. Elliott, *Imperial Spain, 1469–1716* (New York: Mentor, 1963). The most recent contribution of Elliott is the magnificent *Empires of the Atlantic World, Britain and Spain in America, 1492–1830* (New Haven, Conn.: Yale University Press, 2004).

theoretically. One of the most fruitful of these is the analysis of the fiscal and financial structures of *ancien regime* monarchies and/or empires as well as modern states. The advantage of such an approach is that it allows for major insights into the specific links between economy and polity. This is because the resources made available by taxes and credit have always constituted the basis of long standing military and hence political power. The study of fiscal organization and dynamics can therefore contribute to clarify key aspects of the *different anatomies and trajectories* of states (whether imperial or not) under consideration.

Particularly illuminating has been the work of a generation of contemporary scholars who have carried out studies and provoked debates on the historical origins of the fiscal and military bases of modern states in Europe, prior to the nineteenth century. Comparative analysis of fiscal history for the medieval and modern eras became possible from the 1980s and 1990s as a result of the construction of long series of tax data by more than a score of European historians – a selection of their work published in a set of volumes edited by Richard Bonney.[5] But perhaps the most innovative discussion has centered on the relation between the rise of the modern *tax state* and the consolidation of the military and naval power of Great Britain in the eighteenth century, put forth forcefully by Patrick O'Brien and John Brewer.[6] Their hypotheses galvanized a broad set of ongoing historical debates on great powers, focusing primarily on the comparison of the relative fiscal, financial, and military success of Britain as opposed to the more problematic experience of France during that same century.[7]

Among the provocative hypotheses to emerge from this debate was the proposition that parliamentary regimes, such as that of Great Britain, could prove more effective at systematically raising taxes: in a seminal study, Philip Hoffman and Kathryn Norberg explicitly argued that "representative institutions, not absolute monarchy, proved superior in revenue extraction."[8] Other researchers focused on public debt policies,

5 See Richard Bonney, ed., *Economic Systems and State Finance* (Oxford: Oxford University Press/The European Science Foundation, 1995) and Richard Bonney, ed., *The Rise of the Fiscal State in Europe c.1200–1815* (Oxford: Oxford University Press, 1999).

6 John Brewer, *The Sinews of Power: War, Money and the English State, 1688–1783* (London: Unwin Hyman, 1989); Patrick O'Brien, "The Political Economy of British Taxation, 1600–1815," *Economic History Review*, 2nd series, 41 (1988), 1–32; Patrick O'Brien, "Power with Profit: The State and the Economy, 1688–1815," Inaugural Lecture, University of London, 1991.

7 See, for example, Hilton L. Root, *The Fountain of Privilege: Political Foundations of Markets in Old Regime France and England* (Berkeley: University of California Press, 1993) and, more recently, David Stasavage, *Public Debt and the Birth of the Democratic State: France and Great Britain, 1688–1789* (New York: Cambridge University Press, 2003).

8 Philip T. Hoffman and Kathryn Norberg, eds., *Fiscal Crises, Liberty and Representative Governments, 1450–1789* (Stanford, Calif.: Stanford University Press, 1994), pp. 306–310.

explaining in detail the relation between financial and political revolution in late-seventeenth-century England and its lasting consequences.[9] Barry Weingast and Douglass North published a much-cited essay based on a variety of historical monographs to demonstrate that the establishment of credible public debt policies contributed notably to institutional reform and the creation of deep and stable capital markets: "the financial revolution played a critical role in England's long-run success."[10]

But was Britain so singular? The debates have deepened as a result of a full-scale research campaign to reevaluate the history of taxes, credit, and debt under the French absolute monarchy, on which there now exists a broad range of studies that reveal the extraordinary complexity of *ancien regime* finance.[11] On the one hand, a thorough revision of the policies of French finance ministers during the eighteenth century reinforced the contrast between relatively stagnant revenues and the rising costs of war.[12] Yet, as Eugene White has argued in a series of incisive essays, there was nothing inevitable about the financial collapse of the monarchy, and it is possible to identify major mistakes that contributed to the buildup of a deadly deficit before the outbreak of revolution in 1789.[13] On the other hand, a number of researchers began to reconstruct French fiscal and debt policies by focusing on regional estates, revealing that provincial parliaments played a significant role in the finances of the Bourbon regime, in contrast to the traditional view of virtual centralization of the absolutist state.[14] Nonetheless, there is consensus that the costs of war and of rapidly rising debt surpassed the fiscal and financial capacities of the French monarchy and impelled its final bankruptcy and downfall.

While the ensuing discussions have been vigorous and stimulating, they would appear to follow in the path of the traditional Britain/France dichotomy which has been prevalent in the discussion of power politics during the apogee and final crisis of the European old regime. Such a markedly

9 The pioneering and still indispensable study is P. G. M. Dickson, *The Financial Revolution in England, a Study in the Development of Public Credit, 1688–1756* (New York: Macmillan, 1967).

10 Douglass C. North and Barry R. Weingast, "Constitutions and Commitment: The Evolution of Institutions Governing Public Choice in Seventeenth Century England," *The Journal of Economic History*, 44, 4 (December 1989), 803–832.

11 For a detailed overview, see Richard Bonney, "What's New about the New French Fiscal History," *The Journal of Modern History*, 70, 3 (September 1998), 639–667.

12 Two representative studies are James C. Riley, *The Seven Years War and the Old Regime in France: The Economic and Financial Toll* (Princeton, N.J.: Princeton University Press, 1986) and Robert D. Harris, "French Finances and the American War, 1777–1783," *The Journal of Modern History*, 48, 2 (June 1976), 233–258.

13 See, for example, Eugene Nelson White, "The French Revolution and the Politics of Government Finance, 1770–1815," *The Journal of Economic History*, 55, 2 (June 1995), 227–255.

14 Marc Potter and Jean Laurent Rosenthal, "Politics and Public Finance in France: The Estates of Burgundy, 1660–1790," *The Journal of Interdisciplinary History*, 27, 4 (Spring 1997), 577–612.

binary focus has the disadvantage of leaving out most discussion of the parallel trajectories of other rival, imperial states, most notably Spain and Portugal, which continued to govern vast territories on a world scale during the eighteenth century.[15]

Indeed, it is important to recall that before the Napoleonic wars, the Spanish imperial state remained the *third* most important state in Europe in terms of fiscal income and naval power, and first in size of territorial empire.[16] Due, in good measure, to the rise in colonial fiscal income during the second half of the eighteenth century, the Spanish monarchy was able to compete actively with its principal and more powerful rivals, Britain and France, and succeeded in building a fairly centralized fiscal-military administration throughout its extensive empire. This allowed it to regain stature as a colonial and naval power, participating in naval wars against Great Britain in 1762, 1779–1783, 1796–1802, and 1805–1808, while it also engaged in a major land war against France in 1793–1795 before the devastating invasion and occupation of the Iberian peninsula by Napoleon's armies from 1808 to 1814.

Surprisingly, in the western hemisphere, the Spanish empire proved more resilient – in many ways – than the colonial regimes of Great Britain or France. The French lost effective control of Canada and the vast territory of Louisiana after 1763 and of their richest Caribbean colony, Haiti, in 1803. The British were forced to let go their most important North American colonies (the United States) in 1783. In contrast, the huge Spanish American empire remained in place until the wars of independence, 1810–1825. This resiliency – in an era of revolution and war in the Atlantic world – undoubtedly merits more historical analysis and debate in the future. In any case, it bespeaks the capacity of the Spanish Bourbon administration in transforming the tax structure in the colonies into an effective engine of imperial defense.

This book focuses on the viceroyalty of New Spain, because in terms of colonial tax productivity, it is hard to find examples in history that surpass Mexico in the eighteenth century. Mexican tax silver not only covered the costs of its colonial administration and military forces but also served to finance deficits of Spain itself and of large parts of the empire. As the richest tax colony of the eighteenth century, the viceroyalty of New Spain served as

15 A broader approach can be found in R. Bonney, ed., *Economic Systems and State Finance* and in the recent compilation by Manuel Lucena Giraldo, "Las tinieblas de la memoria: una reflexión sobre los imperios en la Edad moderna" *Debates y Perspectivas, Cuadernos de Historia y Ciencias Sociales*, vol. 2 (Madrid, Fundación MAPFRE, Instiuto de Cultura), September 2002, which compares the Spanish, Portuguese, British, French, Dutch, and Ottoman empires.

16 A recent major work is Stanley J. Stein and Barbara H. Stein, *Apogee of Empire: Spain and New Spain in the Age of Charles III, 1759–1789* (Baltimore: The Johns Hopkins Press, 2003).

a *fiscal submetropolis* that assured the capacity of the imperial state to defend itself in a time of successive international conflicts.

But how did the Spanish crown coerce or convince its colonies to pay for the empire? The analysis of Bourbon tax policy in Spanish America provides us with a striking example of the successful rebuilding of a fiscal military state *without* a parliamentary government. A combination of coercion, fiscal and administrative efficiency, and colonial pacts allowed for an extraordinary tax revolution in the Spanish empire. The success in imposing a highly extractive tax regime in Bourbon Mexico contrasts markedly with the failure of the British government in establishing new taxes in the thirteen colonies in North America after 1765. In this case, the European historical debate on political regimes and finance in the eighteenth century is turned upside down: legislatures in colonial British America impeded tax reforms, while in colonial Mexico absolutist policy successfully rebuilt a formidable fiscal machine that financed not only the defense of the viceroyalty but also of other colonies of the Spanish Caribbean as well as the metropolis itself in a time of a succession of international wars.

Taxes, however, were not the only factor in this story. In colonial Mexico ordinary revenues provided much of the money required by the Bourbon monarchy to revitalize its defenses and yet were not sufficient to cover all the extraordinary expenses provoked by each new war. At the behest of Madrid, the viceregal administration turned increasingly to raising loans and donations. As metropolitan deficits skyrocketed, especially from the 1790s, taxes were increasingly complemented with a policy of indebtedness – including an extraordinary succession of loans and forced contributions – in both metropolis and colonies, which would eventually have catastrophic consequences for the monarchy and empire.

In short, by looking *from* the colony *toward* the metropolis, we argue that it is possible to gain a new perspective on the complex dynamics – military, fiscal, and financial – of the Spanish *imperial state* in the successive wars with Britain and France between 1780 and 1810. Such an approach feeds into the current debate on the antecedents of globalization in one of the many paths suggested by A. G. Hopkins in a recent seminal study aimed at stimulating more comparative history.[17] It also speaks to the need for more *transatlantic* history, linking the already rich historiography of eighteenth-century Spanish America with that of Europe and North America.[18]

17 Anthony G. Hopkins, ed., *Globalization in World History* (New York: W. W. Norton & Co., 2002).

18 A recent examplar is Horst Pietschmann, ed., *Atlantic History: History of the Atlantic System, 1580–1830* (Gottingen, Germany: Vandehoek & Ruprecht, 2002).

The *Longue Durée* of the Spanish American Empire: Military and Fiscal Resurgence in the Eighteenth Century

Historians have argued in many different studies that of all European empires, the Spanish empire was long the most productive in strictly fiscal terms. The tax and financial surpluses obtained from Spanish America that were transferred to the metropolis from the mid-sixteenth century onward have been described in classic works by Earl Hamilton and Michel Morineau as well as more recent studies by María Emelina Martín Acosta and Carlos Alvarez Nogal, among others.[19] During the late sixteenth and early seventeenth centuries, the great transfers of volume of silver (and gold) were used in good measure to finance the military forces of the Habsburg administration in Italy and Flanders, engaged in almost constant war from the 1570s until the late 1640s.[20]

The historiography on the second half of the seventeenth century tends to emphasize the decline of the Spanish empire after 1648 and, indeed, many historical works go as far as to suggest that there was *never* any recovery.[21] This is a serious mistake which long misled much European historiography. It is true that in the second half of the seventeenth century, the Hapsburg monarchs of Spain proved singularly ineffectual. It is also true that during the first half of the eighteenth century, the new Bourbon regime was relatively slow in materializing reform in both metropolis and the colonies. But it should also be recognized that in the last four decades of the same century (1760–1800), the Spanish empire in the Americas experienced a remarkable resurgence, visible in the recuperation of naval strength and land defense and, equally so, in the notable increase in fiscal income of most colonies (which allowed for greater military strength). The Spanish imperial state was, therefore, neither static nor condemned to permanent decline.

19 Earl Hamilton, *American Treasure and the Price Revolution in Spain, 1551–1650* (Cambridge, Mass.: Harvard University Press, 1934); Michel Morineau, *Incroyables gazettes et fabuleux métaux: les retours des trésors americains d'après les gazettes hollandaises, xvie-xviiie siècles* (Paris/London: University of Cambridge Press/Maison des Sciences de l'Homme, 1985); María Emelina Martín Acosta, *El dinero americano y la política del imperio* (Madrid: Mapfre, 1992); Carlos Alvarez Nogal, *El crédito de la monarquía hispánica en el reinado de Felipe IV* (Avila: Junta de Castilla y León, 1997).

20 Classic works on the Spanish possessions in Italy are Helmut G. Koenigsberger, *La práctica del imperio* (Madrid: Alianza, 1969) and Antonio Calabria, *The Cost of Empire: The Finances of the Kingdom of Naples in the Time of Spanish Rule* (Cambridge, U.K.: Cambridge University Press, 1991) and those on Flanders and the Low Countries are Geoffrey Parker, *The Army of Flanders and the Spanish Road, 1569–1659: The Logistics of Spanish Victory and Defeat in the Low Countries' Wars* (Cambridge, U.K.: Cambridge University Press, 1972) and Jonathan Israel, *The Dutch Republic and the Hispanic World, 1606–1661* (Oxford: Clarendon Press, 1982).

21 A typical example of this view of irremediable decline can be found in Carlo M. Cipolla, *The Economic Decline of Empires* (London: Methuen, 1970) but is also adopted by most of the "great power" theorists.

To use a metaphor, the Spanish empire may have been slumbering but it reawakened in the late Bourbon era. David Brading has eloquently illustrated this point:

> If in the reign of Philip II, the mines of Potosí rescued the monarchy from bankruptcy and paid for Spanish hegemony in Europe, during the reign of Charles III, in contrast, the silver mines of New Spain provided the funds for the reconstruction of the Spanish navy and the resurgence of the American empire.[22]

But the road to imperial recovery was paved with enormous difficulties. The wars of Spanish Succession (1702–1713) reflected the military decadence of the Spanish state as many European powers fought in the peninsula for the spoils of an ancient power. After the accession of the Bourbon dynasty, nonetheless, there was a gradual transition to a more modern and powerful military and fiscal state. The Spanish imperial state regained strength progressively during the eighteenth century, although this did not imply that – in the long run – it was able to match its chief competitors, in particular Great Britain, which had begun its extraordinary march forward as the first industrial power and the leading naval power in the world.

Despite the naval superiority of Britain in the Atlantic, the Spanish empire responded and restructured during the second half of the eighteenth century and therefore retained control of most trade and military dominion in its extensive colonies overseas. The process of imperial renovation was driven by the fact that Spanish America continued to fulfill an absolutely critical function for the world economy: the viceroyalties of Peru and New Spain provided the bulk of silver, which served as the basis of the metallic currencies of virtually all countries in the world. In particular, the steady increase of silver production in Mexico during the eighteenth century contributed to its increasingly important role in the dynamics of world money and trade at the same time that it provided a fundamental stimulus to the economy of the viceroyalty and created the conditions for a spectacular rise in tax revenues of the colonial administration. The Bourbon reforms in Spanish America were a notable example of the capacity to use the silver boom to forge an increasingly productive and efficient tax state, on an imperial scale.[23]

From the perspective of the comparative history of the eighteenth century in the Atlantic world, the present book raises a simple question: did

22 David Brading, "Balance crítico," in Oscar Mazín, ed., *México en el mundo hispánico*, vol. 2 (Mexico: El Colegio Mexiquense, 2000), p. 656.

23 This hypothesis is developed at length in the major quantitative study by R. Garner and S. E. Stefanou *Economic Growth and Change in Bourbon Mexico* (Gainesville: University of Florida Press, 1993).

Spain and Spanish America matter? Our answer is loudly affirmative and argues for the need to incorporate the recent, rich literature on the history of the fiscal organization and financial dynamics of the Spanish American empire (metropolis and colonies) within the broader historical debates on the destinies of the diverse and rival European imperial states in the eighteenth and early nineteenth centuries. For, it is important to emphasize that the hypotheses advanced in this book are based on a vast, collective effort of recent historical research realized over the last two decades. The labors of a diverse cohort of scholars from Latin America, Europe, the United States, and Canada have progressively illuminated large parcels of the vast and complex fiscal structure of the Spanish monarchy both in the metropolis and in its overseas possessions.[24] Particularly important strides have been made in the reconstruction of the tax system and finances of colonial Mexico in the eighteenth century.[25] These studies lay the basis for a deeper understanding of the common dynamics of financial administration over the vast mosaic of

24 Miguel Artola, *La hacienda del antiguo régimen* (Madrid: Alianza Editorial, 1982); Herbert S. Klein, *The American Finances of the Spanish Empire: Royal Expenditures in Colonial Mexico, Peru and Bolivia, 1680–1809* (Albuquerque: University of New Mexico Press, 1998); John J. TePaske and Hebert Klein, *Ingresos y Egresos de la Real Hacienda de Nueva España*, 2 vols. (Mexico: Instituto Nacional de Antropología e Historia, 1987–1989); John J. TePaske and Herbert S. Klein, *The Royal Treasuries of the Spanish Empire in America*, 3 vols. (Durham, N.C.: Duke University Press, 1990); Herbert Klein and Jacques Barbier, "Revolutionary Wars and Public Finance: The Madrid Treasury, 1784–1807," *The Journal of Economic History*, 41, 2 (1981), 315–339; Jacques A. Barbier, "Peninsular Finance and Colonial Trade: The Dilemma of Charles IV's Spain," *Journal of Latin American Studies*, 12, 1 (1980), 21–37; Jacques A. Barbier and Hebert Klein, "Las prioridades de un virrey ilustrado: el gasto público bajo el reinado de Carlos III," *Revista de Historia Económica*, III, 3 (1986), 473–496; Javier Cuenca, "Ingresos netos del Estado español, 1788–1820," *Hacienda Pública Española*, 49 (1981), 183–208; José P. Merino Navarro, "La Hacienda de Carlos IV," *Hacienda Pública Española*, 18, 69(1981), 131–181; Renate Pieper, *La Real Hacienda bajo Fernando VII y Carlos III, 1753–1788* (Madrid: Instituto de Estudios Fiscales, 1992).

25 For an overview of the recent literature on colonial fiscal history in Mexico, see Luis Jáuregui, "Vino viejo y odres nuevos. La historia fiscal en México," *Historia Mexicana*, lii, 3 (January–March 2003), 725–773; also see references in Carlos Marichal, "La historiografía económica reciente sobre el México borbónico: los estudios del comercio y las finanzas virreinales, 1760–1820," *Boletín del Instituto de Historia Argentina y Americana Dr. E. Ravignani (Buenos Aires)*, tercera serie, 2 (1990), 161–180. Among the numerous studies on colonial Mexican taxes and finance, see the overviews by the following authors: Luis Jáuregui, *La Real Hacienda de Nueva España: su administración en la época de los intendentes, 1786–1821* (Mexico: UNAM, 1999); John J. TePaske, "The Financial Disintegration of the Royal Government of Mexico during the Epoch of Independence, 1791–1821," in Jaime Rodríguez, ed., *The Independence of Mexico and the Creation of the New Nation* (Los Angeles: University of California Press, 1989), pp. 63–84; John J. TePaske, José Hernández Palomo, and Mari Luz Hernández Palomo, *La Real Hacienda de Nueva España: la Real Caja de México, 1576–1816* (Mexico: Colección Científica INAH, 1976); H. Klein, "La economía de la Nueva España, 1680–1809: Un análisis a partir de las cajas reales," *Historia Mexicana*, xxxiv, 4 [136] (1985), 561–609; Carlos Marichal, *La bancarrota del virreinato. Nueva España y las finanzas del imperio español, 1780–1810* (Mexico: Fondo de Cultura Económica and El Colegio de México/Fideicomiso Históricos de las Américas, 1999).

multiethnic territories under Spanish rule. They also provide a huge amount of reliable, quantitative data for the detailed study of the income and expenditure of most parts of the Spanish American empire. This represents a major step forward in our understanding of the eighteenth-century world.

Atlantic Wars, Mexican Silver, and Colonial Debts in the Second Half of the Eighteenth Century

In the first chapter of this book, the principal objective is to illustrate the military and especially the fiscal resurgence of the Spanish empire in the second half of the eighteenth century. We argue that from the end of the Seven Years' War (1756–1763), the finances of imperial defense in Spanish America depended to a great degree on Mexican silver tax remittances. We propose a model for analysis of the *fiscal logic* of imperial *expenditures* and look particularly at how they contributed to sustaining the defense of both Mexico and the Spanish colonies in the greater Caribbean. Special emphasis is placed on the description of the complex network of tax transfers from one colony to another – known as *situados* – which financed the military and naval infrastructure of the empire. In this sense, our study demonstrates how Spain increasingly shifted many of the costs of imperial defense and of war to Mexico, precisely as the viceroyalty experienced a great silver boom that allowed royal functionaries to implement a rigorous campaign to increase extraction of taxes. In order to facilitate estimates of the relative importance of the data presented, we include in the appendix at the end of the book basic information on the colonial monetary system and several key indicators of the colonial economy.

In the second chapter we analyze the fiscal *income* structure of the administration of the viceroyalty of New Spain during the decades 1760–1800. We extend the concept of national tax state developed by historians of eighteenth-century Europe and propose that, in the case of Spain and Spanish America, it can be useful and appropriate to think in terms of an *imperial tax state*. Despite the vast extension of the empire, the Bourbon reforms allowed for the development of a relatively homogeneous fiscal administration, particularly in the colonies. The operation of the almost one hundred different regional treasuries in the western hemisphere is illuminated by a case study of those of New Spain, the wealthiest viceroyalty. The recent and rich historical literature on colonial taxes provides the foundation for this analysis of what Herbert Klein has described as one of the most complex and, in many ways, efficient tax machines of the eighteenth century.[26]

The emphasis in this chapter is on the anatomy of the fiscal system in the viceroyalty of New Spain in the final decades of colonial rule. The review

26 H. Klein, "La economía de la Nueva España," 592.

of the trends of major tax branches raises many questions as to the relation between the fiscal and the general performance of the colonial economy. To obtain a more complete view of overall trends, it is recommended that the reader complement our analysis with the broad historical literature on the Mexican economy in the eighteenth century. While major overviews have been published by such historians as John Coatsworth, Eric Van Young, and particularly Richard Garner, researchers have not yet reached a consensus view on the nature of economic growth in this era.[27] It is clear that Mexico then experienced the greatest silver boom in colonial history, but also that the colonial economy modernized slowly in a period that one historian has baptized the "age of paradox."[28] What our first two chapters demonstrate is the enormous weight of the official extraction of silver from the economy and society and the large percentage of it shipped abroad.

The remaining chapters are devoted to analysis of two major questions: (1) How many loans and *donativos* (forced contributions) were raised in Mexico to assist in the finance of the wars of the Spanish crown in the second half of the eighteenth century? These financial instruments gave rise to a steadily rising volume of colonial debts that have been seldom analyzed in depth. (2) How important were the Mexican silver remittances in the wars between Spain, Britain, and France in the final decades of colonial rule? Silver was a crucial means of payment for armies and navies, and therefore all the European powers were acutely interested in these flows of coins and precious metals, the greatest amounts coming from New Spain.

Chapter 3 focuses on the first issue, namely the methods by which the Spanish imperial administrations were able to raise an astonishing volume of donations, forced loans, and interest-bearing loans in Mexico to pay for successive wars in the 1780s and 1790s. Fundamental in this strategy of raising loan capital for the Crown Wars was the collaboration of colonial privileged corporations: wealthy merchant guilds, the silver miners, royal officers, landowners, and rentiers. The loans reflected the increasing sophistication of colonial financial markets but at the same time proved to be essentially a mechanism of extraction of funds for the royal coffers rather than a method of establishing a new public credit system.

Surprisingly, neither Spanish nor Mexican historiography has paid much attention to the problem of colonial debt despite its importance. In a classic study of the economy of colonial Mexico in the eighteenth century, Richard Garner stated: "The history of the colonial public debt remains

27 John Coatsworth, *Los orígenes del atraso* (Mexico: Alianza Mexicana, 1990); Eric Van Young, *La crisis del orden colonial: Estructura agraria y rebeliones populares de la Nueva España, 1750–1821* (Mexico, Alianza Mexicana, 1992); and R. Garner and S. E. Stefanou, *Economic Growth and Change in Bourbon Mexico.*

28 See E. Van Young, *La crisis del orden colonial*, first subtitle of Chapter 1.

to be written."[29] In the present work we have attempted to remedy this situation by providing the essential data on the royal loans issued in the viceroyalty. The analysis of colonial loans is not only of interest for the history of colonial Mexico, but it is also fundamental to the broader historiographical debate on the relation between state finance and war in the eighteenth century.[30] In this regard, it is important to keep in mind that historians working on the eighteenth century have devoted much time and energy to compare the different financial policies that the two leading powers of the era, Britain and France, adopted to deal with the huge accumulation of war debts.[31] The discussion can be enriched by consideration of the case of the Spanish empire, which presents the peculiar case of a monarchy that raised loans not only in the metropolis but also in the colonies for the prosecution of wars with its rivals, especially at the end of the century.

While colonial loans increased in the early 1780s, the debt explosion came later. The multiplication of wars in both Spain and the Caribbean led to the transfer of almost ten million pesos per year from the treasuries of Mexico in the 1790s. As a result of the war launched against Spain by the revolutionary French Assembly (1793–1794), the Madrid government faced a much graver challenge as military expenditures in the land war in northern Spain increased exponentially. After the conclusion of this major conflict, there came a brief peace, but by 1796, the Spanish monarchy was at war again, with Britain, in what is known as The First Naval War (1796–1802), causing a steep increase in expenditures in both the Atlantic and the Caribbean.

As military expenditures and debts spiraled upward, the demands for Mexican tax silver increased year by year, although, inevitably, the colonial administration was hard-pressed to meet the growing demands of the Crown only with ordinary tax receipts. When the regular tax resources of Bourbon Mexico were found inadequate to finance both defense in the Americas and war in the metropolis, the Madrid government instructed successive viceroys of New Spain – Revillagigedo (1791–1794), Branciforte

29 R. Garner and S. E. Stefanou, *Economic Growth and Change in Bourbon Mexico*, p. 238.

30 Some illuminating pages can be found in the classic work by Lucas Alamán, *Historia de México*, particularly vol. 1 (Mexico: Fondo de Cultura Económica/Instituto Cultural Helénico, 1985) [facsimile of the first edition of 1849–1852], pp. 304–344. The founding father of Mexican historiography reviewed a few of the loans raised between 1808 and 1810, but, significantly, he did not mention the numerous royal donations and loans obtained in New Spain between 1780 and 1808. A major recent work that reviews many of the loans managed by the Mexico City Merchant Guild in the eighteenth century is Guillermina del valle, "El Consulado de Comerciantes de la Ciudad de México y las finanzas novohispanas, 1592–1827," Ph.D. thesis, El Colegio de México, 1997.

31 For a stimulating interpretation, see Jean Laurent Rosenthal, "The Political Economy of Absolutism Reconsidered," in Robert H. Bates et al., *Analytic Narratives* (Princeton, N.J.: Princeton University Press, 1998), p. 65, which argues that "the French and British experience had their roots in the different outcomes of domestic conflicts over fiscal policy."

(1795–1797), Azanza (1798–1802), and Iturrigary (1803–1808) – to raise new combinations of voluntary and forced loans from the population of the viceroyalty. Chapter 4 illustrates the fact that the financial collaboration of the Catholic Church proved to be of special importance in the financial campaigns both by providing great amounts of money in the way of donations and loans to the Crown and by convincing the population at large to do so as well. Among the most important contributors to state loans were colonial convents and monasteries, bishops and cathedral councils, and even the fiscal branch of the Inquisition.

The Second Naval War against Britain (1805–1808) accentuated the financial difficulties faced by the treasuries of the Spanish empire, particularly after the decisive naval battle of Trafalgar, as royal transatlantic transfers hence were abruptly reduced. New, indirect methods had to be implemented to sustain the financial machinery of the empire and avoid total bankruptcy. Among these was a radical financial reform adopted by the ministers of Charles IV, known as the Consolidation Fund, which led to the first process of disentailment of church assets and properties in both the metropolis and the colonies. Inevitably, the tensions between church and state increased acutely.

While the intensification of the Napoleonic wars had a serious impact on the Spanish empire, equally grave financial problems were faced by Britain and France as the army and navy expenses of these two great contenders rose spectacularly. Chapters 5 and 6 explain why the leaders of the two leading powers of Europe looked to Spanish America and especially toward silver-rich Mexico to obtain sources of hard currency with which to finance war. Napoleon Bonaparte and William Pitt each authorized a set of extraordinary stratagems aimed at procuring Mexican silver in the midst of Atlantic war during the years 1804–1808.

Even after the invasion of Spain by Napoleon in 1808, the colonial administration in Mexico continued to send an astonishing volume of tax funds and silver loans to Spain. These flows are analyzed in Chapter 7. The Mexican silver was destined to support the patriot armies and the Cádiz Parliament (1810–1812) in the prolonged struggle against the French invaders. As a result, however, the colonial government in Mexico became ever more indebted. By early 1812, colonial debts had surpassed thirty-five million pesos and weighed heavily on the local exchequer. The largest debts were owed to many of the wealthiest members of colonial Mexican society and to the most powerful and privileged corporations, including the Catholic Church. Estimates of the loans outstanding by sector presented in Chapter 8 offer new material for researchers interested in the subject of the financial costs of colonialism.

The colonial debts taken between 1780 and 1810 constituted something quite different from *domestic* public debts and must be considered a special category of finance since the loans raised in New Spain were not used to cover deficits generated inside the viceroyalty. What took place was different and more complex: the metropolis transferred a part of its deficits to the richest colony. The Madrid government did not promise to pay back the loans. On the contrary, Mexican tax branches were mortgaged indefinitely to pay the king's debts. The same occurred in the case of loans raised in other viceroyalties in Spanish America, although on a smaller scale – all of which can be considered examples of almost *pure financial colonialism*.

At the same time, it is important to keep in mind that colonial elites, led by privileged corporations, collaborated in all the royal financial campaigns. In this regard, it should be noted that the debt policies applied in the Spanish American empire had no counterpart in the British colonies in North America. In the case of the thirteen colonies, for instance, it would have been unthinkable for the British Parliament to demand that the colonists provide loans to cover deficits of the metropolis. The degree of power exercised by the British authorities in North America was but a pale shadow of the fiscal control and financial influence of the Bourbon administration in Spanish America.

Comparative Issues in Colonial Finance in the Eighteenth Century

Exploring fiscal and financial dynamics in the colonies can help in evaluating whether empires involved fiscal costs or benefits for the respective metropolis, and vice versa.[32] However, most recent historical studies on the major European powers of the eighteenth century – in particular Britain and France – have tended to focus quite strictly on success or failure in *domestic* tax reforms and their impact on the fiscal military state. According to a large number of historians, for example, the success of fiscal and administrative reforms put in place in Britain during the *long century* from 1688 to 1815 was key to the military and naval preeminence of the first industrial nation.[33] Such an approach, however, tends to leave out a significant chunk

32 A recent comparative survey focusing on the different metropolises is Patrick O'Brien and Leandro Prados de la Escosura, "The Costs and Benefits of European Imperialism," *Revista de Historia Económica*, 16, 1 (1998), 29–89.

33 The hypotheses were first advanced by P. O'Brien, "The Political Economy of British Taxation" and J. Brewer, *The Sinews of Power*. For additional studies and bibliographical references, see Lawrence Stone, ed., *An Imperial State at War: Britain from 1689 to 1815* (London: Routledge, 1994) and Leandro Prados, ed., *Exceptionalism and Industrialisation: Britian and Its European Rivals, 1688–1815* (Cambridge, U.K.: Cambridge University Press, 2004).

of history, considering that Britain had an extensive, if quite scattered, empire. Similarly, French historiography has devoted insufficient attention to the costs of colonial wars in the gradual weakening of the finances of the absolute monarchy during the second half of the eighteenth century.

Our study suggests that it may prove useful to add a *colonial dimension* to this debate, developing comparative studies of the colonial finance of Spain, Britain, and France in the eighteenth century. One clear contrast was the difference in tax reforms in the American colonies. British authorities faced stiff opposition to new taxes in the thirteen colonies in North America and to the expansion of the royal army forces there. As a result, the defense of empire in North America proved to be a fiscal and political burden for Britain in the 1760s and 1770s.[34] In contrast, the Spanish monarchy – a major imperial rival of Britain in the western hemisphere – did not have to expend funds for overseas defenses, as these were paid for almost entirely by colonial administrations in Spanish America. Modern historical research demonstrates that the tax burden was, in fact, much lighter in the Anglo-American colonies: colonial Mexicans paid perhaps ten times more per capita than taxpayers in the thirteen colonies.[35] Nonetheless, and paradoxically, it was in the lightly taxed Anglo-American colonies that independence would triumph first, whereas in Spanish America the royal administration applied increasing fiscal and financial pressures until the critical year of 1810.

But what was the fiscal situation of colonies in other regions at the end of the eighteenth century? The questions are numerous, and most are still unanswered. How costly were the British colonies in the West Indies? Did they pay their way? Similarly, one may ask: how was the colonial administration financed in Canada in this period? Michael Bordo and Angela Redish have provided some recent answers, but many other questions remain open.[36] And, finally, how fiscally profitable was British India as a colony in

34 Nonetheless, explaining the success of this tax rebellion presents a challenge to current historical interpretations, which have drawn attention to the notable domestic success of the government in Britain in constructing a strong fiscal/military state during the eighteenth century. Major studies by J. Brewer, *The Sinews of Power* and P. O'Brien, "The Political Economy of British Taxation" do not fully explain social response to taxation nor do they explore the contrast with the tax revolt in the United States.

35 The first historian to propose comparative studies in this realm was John Coatsworth, "Obstacles to Economic Growth in Nineteenth Century Mexico," *American Historical Review*, 83, 1 (1978), 80–100. Coatsworth used as one of his sources Robert Paul Thomas, "A Quantitative Approach to the Study of the Effects of British Imperial Policy upon Colonial Welfare," *The Journal of Economic History*, 25, 4 (1965), 615–638, which provides some estimates for comparative analysis. For further details see our estimates in Chapter 2 of this book.

36 Michael D. Bordo and Angela Redish, "The Legacy of French and English Fiscal and Monetary Institutions for Canada," in Michael D. Bordo and Roberto Cortes Conde, eds., *Transferring Wealth*

the late eighteenth century? Recent monographs by Javier Cuenca-Esteban have demonstrated that the financial contribution of India to the English balance of payments was critical and helped avoid bankruptcy of the British government during the Napoleonic wars, but more comparative research is needed.[37]

And what of France? Its richest colony, Saint Domingue (Haiti), certainly required considerable military expenditures, particularly naval, but there were also indirect fiscal benefits for the metropolis. Nonetheless, we know little on this score because historians working on French finance have been perhaps overtly domestic in their research preoccupations. They have incisively explored the rising costs of the debt of the monarchy, but only a few historians, such as James Riley, have paid sufficient attention to some of the key external causes of the deficits, which included colonial wars and the great expenses of the rebuilding of the French navy in the eighteenth century.[38]

Our research and that of a score of other historians who have worked on royal finances in eighteenth-century Spanish America suggests the crucial importance of *colonial* taxes and loans for the resurgence of the Spanish empire as a whole in the decades 1760–1790 and then to finance the monarchy in its final wars. It is true that despite the enormous and sustained financial contributions of the colonies, these were not sufficient to avoid imperial collapse. This contradictory process is precisely the subject of the present book, which focuses on a case study of New Spain, the most productive tax colony in the eighteenth-century world. We do so by placing colonial Mexico in the context of the geopolitical and military conflicts of the age, as shifting alliances led the Spanish monarchy into an extraordinary sequence of wars with, alternatively, Britain or France. In sum, analysis of the finances of the viceroyalty of New Spain in the last decades of the *ancien regime* is significant for comprehension of comparative colonial history and of contemporary imperial rivalries among the European powers. And it is precisely for this reason that we are inclined to think that the view from the capital of colonial Mexico or from the port of Veracruz can prove to be singularly illuminating for an understanding of the increasingly complex nature of war finance in the age of Atlantic revolutions.

and Power from the Old to the New World: Monetary and Fiscal Institutions in the 17th through the 19th Centuries (Cambridge, U.K.: Cambridge University Press, 2001), pp. 259–283.

37 Javier CuencaEsteban, "The British Balance of Payments, 1172–1820: India Transfers and War Finance," *Economic History Review*, 54, 1 (2001), 58–86; by the same author, "India's Contribution to the British Balance of Payments, 1757–1812," unpublished paper in *Session 106 of the XIV International Economic History Conference*, Helsinki, 2006.

38 J. C. Riley, *The Seven Years War and the Old Regime in France.*

1

Resurgence of the Spanish Empire: Bourbon Mexico as Submetropolis, 1763–1800

When the great explorer and scientist Alexander von Humboldt visited colonial Mexico in 1803, he was witness to one of the final and most brilliant periods in the history of the viceroyalty. Eloquent proof could be found in the capital of Mexico which, with its more than 100,000 inhabitants, was the largest city in the western hemisphere. It was also one of the most prosperous to be judged by its many magnificent palaces, by the display of luxurious carriages along its broad avenues, by the great number of mercantile establishments, and by the activity of its popular markets. The heart of political, financial, and social life revolved around the royal palace, cathedral, and stores in the main square known as the *zocalo*. In the palace were the grand offices of the viceroy of New Spain and of many high-level functionaries, and there they received the members of the privileged corporations of colonial society: the ancient and venerable merchant guild, the miner's association, the great landowners, the church prelates, and military officers. But in late afternoons and evenings, the palace was also seat to a number of social events, including games of gambling.

Behind the royal palace, there was a large building with patio which also had enormous economic and political importance: the royal mint. In his classic work, *Political Essay on the Kingdom of New Spain*, Humboldt noted that it was the greatest and richest mint in the world, and added:

> It is impossible to visit this building . . . without recalling that from it have come more than two billion silver pesos in the space of less than three hundred years and without reflecting on the powerful influence these treasures have had on the destiny of the peoples of Europe.[1]

The well-informed German scientist emphasized the fundamental contribution of Mexican silver to the sustenance of the Spanish empire as a whole, providing large annual tax subsidies in silver to the Spanish colonies

1 Humboldt actually used the expression "two thousand million pesos": see Alexander von Humboldt, *Ensayo político sobre el reino de la Nueva España* (Mexico: Ed. Porrúa, 1991), p. 457. The work was originally published in Paris in 1809 and a more complete edition in 1811.

throughout the Caribbean, to the Philippines, and to the metropolis itself. He added, based on his detailed calculations, that the Madrid General Treasury received in net tax receipts from Mexico more than double what Great Britain received from India.[2]

But for how long would it be possible for colonial Mexico to continue to export such a large amount of its tax revenues? Humboldt felt that the viceroyalty could continue to make its huge annual contributions to the empire without grave difficulties because of the great output of its silver mines and the considerable productivity of its economy, as a whole. This was an overly optimistic assessment, however, for as we now know, by the end of the eighteenth century both the public and private economy of New Spain were confronting severe strains.[3]

The inordinate ability of the Spanish monarchy to extract fiscal revenues from its colonies had long been the cause of envy by its rivals. In his classic work on *The Wealth of Nations* (published in 1776), Adam Smith underscored the extraction capacity of the Spanish empire as compared to the pronounced failures of the British authorities to increase taxes in the thirteen colonies.[4] Other contemporaries coincided with the famous Scottish economist. The fiscal surplus produced by the Spanish American colonies attracted the attention of the Spanish General Francisco Saavedra during a prolonged military mission to the Caribbean in the midst of war with Great Britain in the years 1780–1783. He wrote:

> Among the European possessions in the New World only those of the Spanish and Portuguese have contributed immediately to enlarge the public treasuries of their respective metropolises, aiding them in peacetime with sums of money more than sufficient to defray expenditures made on their behalf and maintaining in wartime the great armaments needed for their defence. The other nations (France and Britain) have required of their colonies only the necessary costs of sustaining their civil government and the small military establishments calculated as indispensable for their *domestic* tranquility.[5]

2 Humboldt affirmed that in the year 1804 British India produced a net tax transfer of 3.4 million dollars to England, while in the years 1802–1804 Mexico transferred an annual average of 8 million dollars in tax funds to Spain (1 silver peso = 1 dollar): A. Humboldt, *Ensayo politico sobre el reino*, pp. 553–554. For recent estimates, see J. Cuenca, "The British Balance of Payments," 58–86.

3 Considerable consensus now exists in the historical literature on this issue: see summaries in R. Garner, *Economic Change*, Chapter 7 and Richard Salvucci, "Mexican National Income, 1800–1840," in S. Haber, ed., *How Latin America Fell Behind, Essays on the Economic History of Brazil and Mexico, 1800–1914* (Stanford, Calif.: Stanford University Press, 1997), pp. 232–234.

4 Adam Smith, *An Inquiry into the Nature and Causes of the Wealth of Nations*, fifth edition (London: Methuen and Co. Ltd., 1904) (First published, 1776), IV. 7. 9.9.

5 See Francisco Saavedra de Sangronis, *Journal of Don Francisco Saavedra de Sangronis during the Commission Which He Had in His Charge, 1780–1783* (Gainesville: University of Florida Press, 1989), pp. 90–91.

Saavedra noted that in all major interimperial conflicts in the Americas since midcentury, the British and French metropolitan governments had been forced to expend huge sums on their overseas army and naval forces, transferring monies from metropolis to colonies. Spain, on the other hand, relied on American taxes to provide the bulk of monies for its military garrisons and fortresses throughout its vast empire. During the second half of the eighteenth century, for instance, the treasuries of colonial Mexico not only paid for the buildup of a large army and militia force in the viceroyalty but also transferred great amounts of tax monies to the Spanish colonial garrisons throughout the greater Caribbean.[6] The annual silver subsidies sent from Mexico to Cuba, for example, paid for the construction of almost 100 warships at the shipyard of Havana between 1720 and 1790. Furthermore, during numerous European wars, the richest Spanish American colonies provided taxes and loans for defense of the metropolis, when the monarchy so required.

The tax funds transferred out of colonial Mexico between 1760 and 1810 surpassed 250 million pesos, which made it the true, fiscal jewel of the Spanish crown in this period.[7] For comparative purposes it may be observed that the sum mentioned was huge, being equivalent to ten times the average annual peacetime expenditures of the Spanish government at Madrid in the second half of the eighteenth century; alternatively, this figure was equivalent to the total expenditures of the British government during three and half years in the same time period.[8] It should be noted that at the time the silver peso was equivalent to one U.S. dollar as can be seen in the dollar bills issued from the early 1780s, which stipulated that they were payable in "Spanish milled dollars," in other words, Mexican silver pesos. (For additional details, see Appendix 1.)

In short, New Spain distinguished itself as a viceroyalty that produced an annual fiscal surplus in what we could call the consolidated accounts of the colonial royal treasury.[9] This situation contrasted with other territories of the Spanish empire such as Cuba, Puerto Rico, Santo Domingo, or the Philippines, which – during centuries – were unable to produce sufficient internal tax resources to meet the total civil and military costs of their own

6 For a detailed quantitative analysis, see Carlos Marichal and Matilde Souto, "Silver and Situados: New Spain and the Financing of the Spanish Empire in the Caribbean in the Eighteenth Century," *Hispanic American Historical Review*, 74, 4 (1994), 587–613.

7 For data on tax remittances, see sources cited in Figures 1.1 and 1.2. This estimate does not include loans and forced loans which are analyzed in subsequent chapters of the present book.

8 For comparative data on Spanish and British government expenditure between 1764 and 1799, see Rafael Torres Sánchez, Rafael "Possibilities and Limits: Testing the Fiscal Military State in the Anglo-Spanish War of 1779–1783," paper presented at *Session 69, XIII International Economic History Congress*, Helsinki, August 2006; see our Appendix, 1.5.

9 In Chapter 2 we explain this concept. For data from the 1790s, see Table 2.1.

administrations. To cover their considerable and regular deficits, the latter were obliged to rely on remittances of silver from other parts of the empire, and most particularly from New Spain. The transfers of tax silver from rich to poor colonies were known as *situados*, a term which usually referred to monies dispatched to cover the expenses of military or naval garrisons in different parts of the empire. The complex network of these tax transfers was one of the great fiscal secrets of the longevity of the Spanish empire in the Americas since the metropolis did not have to cover most overseas defense expenses as they were financed by the silver-rich colonies.

The fact that colonial Mexico did count upon a plethora of fiscal income placed it in a special position within the global structure of Spanish imperial finance – as was also the case of the viceroyalty of Peru.[10] From the mid-sixteenth century, the chief officers of the royal treasuries of New Spain and Peru had been instructed by the Crown to send surplus funds abroad, in part to the metropolis and in part to military and naval garrisons in the rest of the hemisphere that were of strategic importance to the Crown but had insufficient funds for all their defense expenses. Both viceroyalties thus fulfilled the role of *fiscal submetropolis*. As Herbert Klein has demonstrated in a magnificent study, Peru was the leader in exporting silver revenues during the late sixteenth and early seventeenth centuries, while Mexico came to exercise a dominant role during the eighteenth century.[11]

During the years 1720–1800 there was a notable increase in current values of the remittances by the royal treasuries of colonial Mexico to *both* Spain and military garrisons in the greater Caribbean. The funds were collected in numerous tax districts throughout the viceroyalty and sent to Mexico City, whence the bags of silver pesos were transported by mule to Veracruz, to be shipped abroad. Until 1740 these *situados* did not usually exceed two million pesos per annum, but subsequently they increased as a result of the outbreak of wars, which impelled a surge of financial demands for the defense of the Spanish empire. The preeminence of New Spain as fiscal bulwark of the empire was reinforced after the Seven Years' War (1756–1763), as can be observed in Figure 1.1 and in the Appendix, Table 1.1

10 The extraordinary fiscal series collected by Klein and Tepaske for the viceroyalties of New Spain, Peru, and Buenos Aires can be consulted in Excell format at the database "Estadísticas Históricas de México" in the general Web site of El Colegio de Mexico, www.colmex.mx, where a link will be found in "Biblioteca" under "Bases de datos" from July, 2007.

11 The classic study is Herbert Klein, "El gran viraje: ascenso de México y decadencia de Perú en el imperio colonial de la América colonial, 1609–1808" in Herbert Klein, *Las finanzas americanas del imperio español* (Mexico: Instituto de Investigaciones "Dr. José María Luis Mora,"/Universidad Autónoma Metropolitana, 1995), pp. 133–162. Also see Hebert S. Klein, "Origin and Volume of Remission of Royal Tax Revenues from the Viceroyalties of Peru and New Spain," in Antonio Miguel Bernal, ed., *Dinero, moneda y crédito en la monarquía hispánica* (Madrid: Fundación ICO/Marcial Pons, 2000), pp. 269–292.

Table 1.1. *Wars in which the Spanish Monarchy was engaged in 1762–1814*

War of Spain against	Years
Great Britain[a]	1762–1763
Great Britain[a]	1779–1783
France	1793–1795
Great Britain[a]	1796–1802
Great Britain[a]	1805–1807
France[b]	1808–1814

[a] In the wars against Great Britain, Spain invariably was allied with France

[b] In the war against Napoleonic France, Spain was allied with Great Britain.

The statistics speak of certain peaks in the royal remittances from New Spain which correspond with periods of military conflicts: the Seven Years' War (1756–1763), the war against Great Britain (1779–1783), and the war against the French Convention (1793–1795). It was in these times that the military and financial demands of the metropolis and of the empire, as a whole, intensified. (See Table 1.1 and Figure 1.1.) Nonetheless, it should also be kept in mind that after the conclusion of hostilities, remittances to the metropolis did not necessarily diminish but could actually expand because of greater safety at sea. Hence, the years following armistices, generally, were witness to the shipment of large quantities of transfers of royal silver to other colonies as well as to the metropolis.

The contributions of the treasuries of New Spain to the rest of the empire increased most markedly in the final decades of the eighteenth century. Never in the history of New Spain, or for that matter of Spanish America, had so great a volume of monetary resources had been extracted to assist in the defense and survival of the empire as a whole. By that time, the remittances exported by the royal treasury from Veracruz were equivalent to approximately 40 percent of the total annual silver production of the viceroyalty – a clear indication of the enormous weight of the state within the economy.[12]

In this chapter we explore the complex strategy of the administrators of the Spanish empire in exporting such voluminous tax resources from New Spain that, according to contemporaries, they constituted "a river of silver"

12 The decennial totals of government fiscal silver exports are impressive from any point of view: in 1771–1780, forty-eight million pesos were exported by the royal treasury; in 1781–1790 the figure increased to seventy-five million pesos; and in the decade of 1791–1800 reached the extraordinary level of almost ninety million pesos. See our Appendix 1.3.

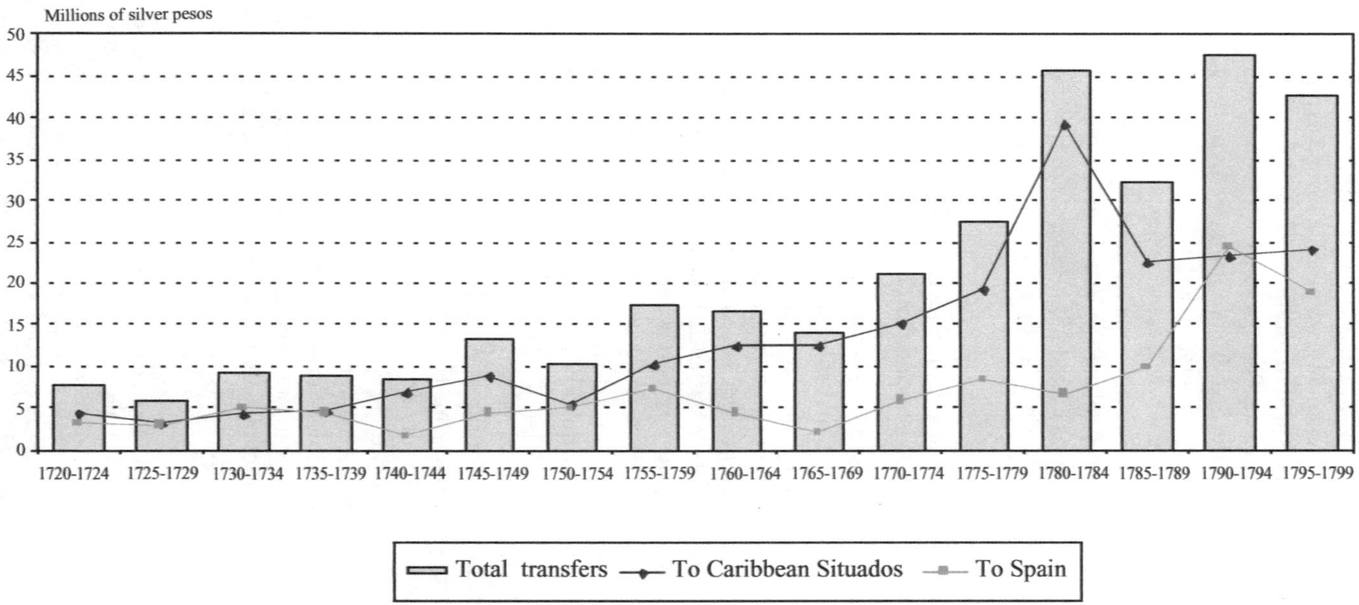

Figure 1.1. Fiscal Transfers from New Spain to the Caribbean and Spain, 1720–1799.
Source: Carlos Marichal and Matilde Souto, "Silver and Situados: New Spain and the Financing of the Spanish Empire in the Carribbean in the Eighteenth Century," *Hispanic American Historical Review*, 74, 4 (1994), 587–613.

flowing from Veracruz to Havana and thence to Cádiz.[13] By focusing on the richest Spanish American colony, we propose several explanations as to how the Spanish empire operated in military and fiscal terms during an age of Atlantic wars and revolutions. We begin with a summary of the impact of the defeats suffered by the Spanish empire in 1762 at the hands of the British, which led the Bourbon state to design and adopt a vast set of new strategies of overseas defense. How these were financed is the second major theme of this chapter, focusing on the fiscal logic of imperial expenditures and, in particular, on the key role of the *situados* of colonial Mexico, which came to operate financially as a kind of *submetropolis* of the Spanish empire in the last third of the eighteenth century.

The Military and Financial Consequences of 1762 for the Spanish Imperial State

The occupation in 1762 of the port cities of Havana and Manila by British military forces was an event that shook the Spanish monarchy to its foundations. For over two and a half centuries, no foreign power had seriously attempted to take control of Cuba, fundamental locus of Spanish power in the Caribbean and the point from which all the great armadas had arrived and departed. The bulk of transatlantic Spanish American trade depended on Havana as entrepôt, the key port where the flotillas of both warships and private merchant vessels concentrated for the voyages in and out from the western hemisphere. When British troops seized this great Caribbean port city, the news spread quickly through Spanish America, provoking considerable commotion. Equally, galling had been the occupation in the same year by British naval forces of the port city of Manila, the key outpost of the Spanish empire in Southeast Asia. Great relief was felt after the exit of the British troops, following the Treaty of Paris in 1763, but clearly the Spanish crown (and its ally France) had suffered a major setback in the international power struggle.

The effectiveness of the contemporary British military machine was based on its notable amphibious capabilities. From early in the eighteenth century the British Navy had outdistanced all competitors in number of ships, firepower, and skill of officers and mariners.[14] In addition, it had the faculty of being able to transport large numbers of troops to attack rival

13 This was an expression frequently found in contemporary Spanish documents and reports.

14 See two recent overviews: Patrick K. O'Brien, "Fiscal Exceptionalism: Great Britain and Its European Rivals from Civil War to Triumph at Trafalgar and Waterloo," London School of Economics, Working Paper No. 65/01, 2001 and Daniel A. Baugh, "Naval Power: What Gave the British Navy Superiority?" in Leandro Prados, ed., *Exceptionalism and Industrialisation: Britain and Its European Rivals, 1688–1815* (Cambridge, U.K., Cambridge University Press, 2004), pp. 235–257.

empires overseas. When the British Navy attacked Havana, over 12,000 infantry disembarked and, after two months of persistent siege, eventually overwhelmed the relatively small contingent of Spanish troops defending the Cuban port.[15] Much as the American marines of the twentieth century, these amphibious British forces were capable of traveling long distances, disembarking, and seizing key enemy fortresses and ports with considerable speed.

Historians posit that the conclusion of the Seven Years' War (1756–1763) "marked a fundamental turning-point in the eighteenth century balance of power."[16] As a result of the war and the Treaty of Paris (1763), France suffered significant territorial losses, ceding complete control over Canada to Great Britain and temporary control of Louisiana to Spain. But the Spanish monarchy was also hard hit, losing Florida to the British and being put on the defensive in the Caribbean. The clear victor was Great Britain, although, paradoxically, increased defense requirements in North America would generate fateful tensions with the thirteen colonies.

The response of the two Bourbon monarchies to the defeats suffered in the Seven Years' War was to adopt a common set of defensive policies against Britain.[17] The alliance between France and Spain is known in diplomatic history as the *Third Family Compact* and would last for thirty years, until just after the outbreak of the French Revolution in 1789.[18] Both monarchies based their alliance fundamentally on a joint naval policy, funneling huge amounts of money into the rebuilding and expansion of their sea forces. The results of such investments were not long in bearing fruit: as of 1765, the British Navy outdistanced the combined fleets of Spain and France in number of ships, but in the 1770s barely held parity; by 1780 the Bourbon navies had overtaken their great rival.[19] (See Table 1.2.)

15 The classic work is Allan J. Kuethe, *Cuba, 1753–1815, Crown, Military and Society* (Knoxville: University of Tennesese Press, 1986), particularly Chapter 1.

16 Richard Bonney, "Towards the comparative fiscal history of Britain and France during the long eighteenth century," in L. Prados, ed., *Exceptionalism and Industrialisation*, p. 197. For recent studies on this war, see Fred Anderson, *Crucible of War: The Seven Years' War and the Fate of Empire in British North America, 1754–1766* (New York: Vintage, 2000) and Juan Ortiz Escamilla, ed., *Guerzas militares en Iberoamérica, siglos xviii y xix* (Mexico: El Colegio de Mexico, 2005).

17 Perhaps the most perceptive analysis of the traditionally defensive strategy of the French and Spanish naval forces as opposed to the more aggressive British *imperial navy* is that by John Robert McNeil, *Atlantic Empires of France and Spain, Louisbourg and Havana, 1700–1763* (Chapel Hill: University of North Carolina Press, 1985), pp. 75–78.

18 See the classic study: Francis Paul Renault, *Le pacte de famille et l'Amérique: la politique coloniale franco-espagnole, de 1760 à 1792* (Paris: Leroux, 1922). For an overview and new interpretation, see Allan J. Kuethe and Lowell Blaisdell, "French Influences and the Origins of the Bourbon Colonial Reorganization," *Hispanic American Historical Review*, 71, 3 (August 1991), 579–607.

19 Jan Glete, *Navies and Nations: Warships, Navies and State Building in Europe and America, 1500–1860*, vol. 2 (Stockholm: Almquist and Wiksell International), pp. 256, 263, and 271.

Table 1.2. *The Atlantic Navies, 1720–1790*

	1720	1730	1740	1750	1760	1765	1770	1775	1780	1785	1790
Great Britain	174	189	195	276	375	377	350	337	372	447	473
France	48	73	91	115	156	175	219	199	271	268	324
Spain	22	73	91	41	137	124	165	198	196	211	253
Netherlands	79	62	65	62	62	66	79	68	70	124	123
Portugal	(37)	(29)	(28)	(28)	(32)	(32)	(36)	41	37	34	43
				—	—	—	1	6	—	—	
TOTAL	360	426	470	522	762	774	849	844	952	1,084	1,216

Note: Total displacement in 1,000 tons. The figures for Portugal (1760–1770) are more approximate than the others.

Source: Jan Glete, *Navies and Nations: Warships, Navies and State Building in Europe and America, 1500–1860*, vol. 2 (Stockholm: Almquist and Wiksell International), 1993, pp. 256, 263, and 271.

Less well known are the economic bases of the *Family Compact*, which underlay the alliance during wars but also in peacetime. A growing and perhaps dominant portion of the trade with Spanish America came to be managed by French trading firms, which exercised an increasingly preeminent role in the great port city of Cádiz, entrepôt for colonial commerce. The ties between the two monarchies were also strengthened by the active role of French merchants and merchant bankers in Spain during the second half of the eighteenth century as they took a leading role in the financing of much Spanish foreign trade and a prominent role in Spanish government finance during the 1780s.[20]

Nonetheless, Spanish authorities were not willing to allow the French to have any say in direct, colonial rule. Quite to the contrary, Spain had the upper hand in the Americas. After 1763 France only retained control of three Caribbean islands, sugar-rich Saint Domingue (Haiti), Martinique, and Guadeloupe. Spain, in contrast, continued to rule over a vast, continental empire, stretching 10,000 miles, from Texas and California to Cape Horn. Such extensive imperial responsibilities implied considerable costs for defense, but most especially after the defeats suffered at the hands of the British military forces. It was then that the government of Charles III decided to launch a set of major military, administrative, and fiscal reforms, which were intended to fortify the whole of the empire in Spanish America.[21] While the reforms were eventually implemented in all the colonies,

20 An outstanding study is Michel Zylberberg, *Une si douce domination. Les milieux d'affaires français et l'Espagne vers 1780–1808* (Paris: Comité pour l'histoire économique et financière de la France, 1993).

21 In a classic work, David Brading called the Bourbon reforms "A revolution in government": David Brading, *Miners and Merchants in Bourbon Mexico, 1763–1810* (Cambridge, U.K.: Cambridge University Press, 1971), Chapter 1. Most subsequent studies have followed his interpretation, in the sense of emphasizing the profound nature and impact of these reforms: much of the recent bibliography

the costs were covered unequally. Those tax districts which produced most revenue – especially those in New Spain and upper Peru – were forced to cover deficits in other regions of the empire, ostensibly for military defense.[22]

Bourbon Reforms and Grand Strategies of Imperial Defense

One of the most astonishing facts of imperial rule in the Americas was that for over two centuries the Spanish monarchy had not been obliged to cover *major* land expenses for the defense of its many colonies. The noted historian John Parry argued in a series of classic works that prior to 1760s the Spanish royal administration kept remarkably small military forces in the western hemisphere.[23] Subsequent research has demonstrated that the reinforcement of army forces began in the first half of the eighteenth century, but it is abundantly clear that the reforms adopted after 1763 were crucial in the establishment of a much larger military establishment throughout the colonies. Equally striking was the fact that most defense expenses were covered by local treasuries.

The army and navy buildup had begun in the metropolis in the 1760s but was promptly applied in Spanish America. The new military policies were based on a three-pronged strategy: (1) building colonial armies and militias, (2) rebuilding the Spanish naval forces, and (3) strengthening a great number of military fortresses in the Caribbean and, to a lesser degree, in South America. The emphasis clearly was on defense against attacks by the British Navy and/or possible invasions of key ports by British troops. Practically all these expenses were financed with colonial taxes: in the greater Caribbean, mostly with Mexican silver remittances while in South America, most were financed with fiscal funds from upper Peru.

The main objectives of the military reforms in Spanish America were designed by a secret committee of imperial defense, appointed by the monarch, Charles III, meeting in Madrid on a regular basis during late 1763 and early 1764 until they came up with a general plan. One of the first measures adopted was to send General Alejandro O'Reilly to Cuba to

is reviewed in Alfredo Casillero Calvo and Allan Kuethe, eds., *Historia General de América Latina*, vol. 3 (Paris: UNESCO, 2000).

22 The royal treasuries at Lima and Potosi produced tax surplus that was remitted to cover external military expenditures, mainly in Chile and Buenos Aires. Treasuries in New Granada helped finance military and naval garrisons at Cartagena. See Herbert S. Klein and John TePaske, *Las cajas reales de la real hacienda de la América española (siglos xvi a principios del xix)* CD (Mexico: Asociación Mexicana de Historia Económica/El Colegio de México, 2004).

23 Parry wrote: "It is curious that the Spanish Indies – reputedly so rich, so envied, so repeatedly attacked – possessed, until the Seven Years War, no standing army." John Parry, *The Spanish Seaborne Empire* (New York: A Knopf, 1966), p. 325.

reorganize both the regular army forces and a new militia. The Spanish crown had established the first of the American fixed battalions in Havana in 1719, in Cartagena in 1736, in Santo Domingo in 1738, and in Veracruz in 1740, but after the military defeats of 1762, it had become clear that they were insufficient to meet the British threats of invasion. O'Reilly was successful in building up a relatively effective defense establishment in Cuba in the years following. Equally important, in 1767, Julián Arriaga, minister of the Indies, ordered a faithful but ambitious technocrat, José Gálvez, to travel to New Spain as royal envoy (*Visitador General*) with instructions to carry out a thorough report on the defense conditions and the fiscal administration of the viceroyalty. Not surprisingly, the Viceroy marquis de Cruillas was surprised by the Gálvez mission as he arrived with extraordinary military and political powers. After Gálvez had presented his first reports, the Crown authorized a broad-ranging set of administrative, fiscal, and military reforms to be put in practice in New Spain.[24]

The innovations of O'Reilly and Gálvez proved to be models for the rest of Spanish America in the last decades of the eighteenth century. Their introduction should not, however, be seen as positively modern nor as an undisputed success. They were based on a combination of traditional absolutist coercion and a series of complex negotiations with local elites. While formally proposing to eradicate fiscal corruption, the new Bourbon functionaries (many of whom arrived from Spain) did not overlook opportunities for enrichment and the forging of alliances with local, wealthy families.[25] Nonetheless, the aim of the reforms was clearly to make for a more efficient fiscal machine and a larger and proficient army in each of the colonies.

Several historians have analyzed the army buildup in various colonies. Allan Kuethe has described in detail the military plans put in place in Cuba, which were perhaps the most successful.[26] Initiated by General O'Reilly, they were continued by his allies, the O'Farrill clan of Spanish officers, who virtually came to rule the island in the second half of the eighteenth century and the first decades of the nineteenth century. Paradoxically, as historians Kuethe and Marchena have demonstrated, the Spanish army reforms led to an expansion of the number of native-born Cubans who became officers. The new military elite, moreover, was closely bound to the rising sugar slave-owning oligarchy as well as to the wealthiest Havana merchants.

During the same decades, military reform proceeded apace in colonial Mexico. Christon Archer has analyzed the expansion of the Bourbon army in

24 The classic study is Herbert Ingram Priestley, *José de Gálvez, Visitor-General of New Spain 1765–1771* (Philadelphia: Porcupine Press, 1963).

25 Linda Salvucci, "Costumbres viejas, 'hombres nuevos': José de Gálvez y la burocracia fiscal novohispana (1754–1800)," *Historia Mexicana*, 33, 2 (1983), 224–264.

26 A. J. Kuethe, *Cuba, 1753–1815*.

New Spain.[27] The colonial forces grew to be a significant force: by the turn of the century, they were composed by more than 10,000 regular infantry and perhaps 30,000 militia. The former were concentrated mainly in the region of Veracruz since this was considered the most likely zone for possible British invasions in the future. The militia forces, on the other hand, were organized in practically all cities of the viceroyalty, being financed mainly by local, commercial elites; actually, most of the officers of the militia were themselves merchants. Finally, under the careful and rigorous supervision of Gálvez, a special effort was made to reinforce military garrisons of cavalry and infantry in the garrisons (*presidios*) in northern territories, including Sonora, Chihuahua, and Texas.

Also important was the growth of the regular army and the militia in the viceroyalties of New Granada and Peru as well as in upper Peru (modern-day Bolivia), in the viceroyalty of the Río de la Plata (modern Argentina and Uruguay), and in Chile.[28] At the end of the eighteenth century, the total strength of the Spanish royal armies in the western hemisphere surpassed 30,000 regular infantry and cavalry and there were perhaps as many as 80,000 men in the different colonial militias.

Simultaneous to the expansion of land forces was the launching of an ambitious and expensive series of investments in great fortresses in many Spanish American ports. The 1760s and 1770s were the greatest age of construction of major defensive works throughout the Americas, but particularly in the Caribbean. Huge amounts of tax funds were funneled into building of defensive walls and bulwarks as well as imposing fortresses at the entrance to the ports of Havana, San Juan, Cartagena, Santo Domingo, and Veracruz. These were equipped with great numbers of cannon, placed strategically at the entrance to bays and ports to impede any new British invasions.[29]

Equally important was the process of rebuilding of the Spanish Navy, which soon became the third most powerful in the Atlantic, although this development has only recently begun to be studied.[30] Whereas British and French historians have devoted much time and energy to analyze the expansion of their navies in this "age of the admirals," researchers have

27 Christon I. Archer, *El ejército en el México borbónico, 1760–1810* (México: Fondo de Cultura Económica, 1983).

28 See Leon Campbell, *The Military and Society in Colonial Peru, 1750–1820*, (Philadelphia: The American Philosophical Society, 1978) and Allan Kuethe, *Military Reform and Society in New Granada, 1773–1808* (Gainesville: University of Florida Press, 1976).

29 The fundamental work is José Antonio Calderón Quijano, *Las fortificaciones españolas en América y Filipinas* (Madrid: MAPFRE, 1996), but the bibliography on the subject is vast.

30 The most important work is J. Glete, *Navies and Nations*, 2 vols., 1993. Also the review article by N. A. M. Rodger, "Recent Books on the Royal Navy of the Eighteenth Century," *The Journal of Military History*, 63, 3 (July 1999), 683–703.

been slow to recognize the simultaneous and surprising renovation of the Spanish Navy. However, the recent monumental study by Jan Grete has forcefully demonstrated that, already quite early in the eighteenth century, the Spanish naval forces became the third most important in the world, after those of Great Britain and France. The maritime contest for world power intensified from the 1740s onward as both France and Spain pushed forward with new construction of warships and frigates. Although the Seven Years' War led to major defeats at sea for both Bourbon monarchies, this did not discourage them. The Bourbon allies were bent on establishing parity with their more vigorous, naval rival, Great Britain. As a result, the French and the Spanish governments plowed enormous amounts of money into warship construction during the last four decades of the eighteenth century.[31]

In the case of metropolitan Spain the three naval ports of Cartagena, Ferrol, and Cádiz were sites of construction of a large number of warships, particularly in the second half of the century.[32] But, the most important naval shipbuilding arsenal was, in fact, that of Havana, where there were built a grand total of 114 ships for the Spanish Navy during the eighteenth century, including fifty-four warships as well as sixteen frigates and many smaller armed vessels. The Havana-built warships carried a total of 3,642 cannon and the frigates 684 cannon, altogether a formidable force.[33] The enormously expensive naval construction program in Cuba, however, was not financed from Spain but mainly from colonial Mexico. A review of imperial finance demonstrates that it was New Spain that financed the bulk of construction of the great warships built in Cuba during the century by sending large annual silver subsidies to Havana as well as basic provisions.[34]

All these military projects – army, navy, and fortresses – were extremely costly and required the financial support that only a strong *tax state* could provide. The tax reforms (which financed the military buildup) are analyzed in detail in the next chapter, but here we wish to reiterate that the greater part of military and naval expenditures for the defense of empire was covered *by the colonies themselves*. Metropolitan Spain did not have to finance more than a fraction of the expenses in the Americas. The colonial administrations

31 For data on construction of warships, see numerous charts in J. Glete, *Navies and Nations*, vol. 2.

32 The essential study on building of warships in Spain is José Patricio Merino Navarro, *La armada española en el siglo XVIII* (Madrid: Fundación Universitaria Española, 1981) but, unfortunately, this work provides no information on the Havana naval arsenal.

33 The detailed notes by J. S. Thrasher provide the information on each of the ships built in Havana. These notes are found in Alejandro von Humboldt, *Ensayo político sobre la isla de Cuba* (Havana: Archivo Nacional de Cuba, 1960), pp. 114–117. J. S. Thrasher was translator into English of Humboldt's essay that was published in New York in 1856.

34 A recent study is Andrade Muñoz, "La búsqueda española de suministros, víveres y pertrechos navales en Nueva España (siglo XVIII). Los intereses coloniales frente a los problemas imperiales," Master's thesis, Instituto Mora, Mexico, 2002.

took charge of the military salaries of rapidly growing armies and militias in the western hemisphere, of the finance and building of the numerous great and small fortresses, and of the construction of close to half of the warships of Spanish royal Navy. In addition, they provided victualling of the Spanish warships in American waters, which included provisioning of ships in the greater Caribbean, in the River Plate, as well as the few warships on the Pacific coast and the famous Manila galleon that yearly crossed the largest ocean in the world. In order to understand how these vast requirements were financed, it is essential to focus attention on the vast network of interimperial fiscal transfers. In the section that follows, particular attention will be focused on the contributions of the richest tax colony – the viceroyalty of New Spain – to the defense of the Spanish empire.

The Fiscal Logic of Imperial Expenditures

The fiscal and military system of the Spanish empire in the Americas was older, quite different, and more complex than that of its imperial rivals. This vast imperial organization had its fulcrum in Spain, yet it spanned a great part of the western hemisphere as well as the Philippines and was based to a large degree on a complex network of tax transfers between the different treasuries of the different viceroyalties and captaincy generals. But how centralized was the fiscal administration in the empire? This is a hotly debated issue among historians today with a confrontation between two points of view. On the one hand, there is a traditional view that emphasizes the success of the Bourbon monarchy in establishing a professional fiscal bureaucracy, a modern accounting system, and an increasingly centralized tax machinery.[35] On the other, there is a growing school of historians who emphasize the active role of local elites in the control of transfers of silver taxes from one treasury to another and in management of supply contracts derived from much local expenditure in the military sphere.[36]

35 L. Jáuregui, *La Real Hacienda de Nueva España*; C. Marichal, *La bancarrota del virreinato* (1999), Chapter 2; Linda Arnold, *Burocracia y burócratas en México, 1742–1835* (Mexico: Grijalbo/Consejo Nacional para la Cultura y las Artes, 1991).

36 Alexandra Irigoin has argued: "Thus, private merchants largely ran the system and made handsome profits out of it.... But funds were also employed in various other purposes, in addition to the expected naval and military defence.[36] These ranged from funding shipbuilding or tobacco purchases in Cuba, to the support of religious missions or colonisation ventures in other islands, to stipends for clergy and civil officials": Alexandra Irigoin, "Bargaining for Absolutism: A Spanish Path to Nation State and Empire Building," unpublished manuscript, October 2005, p. 16. Similar arguments have been advanced forcefully by Pedro Pérez Herrero, "Los beneficiarios del reformismo borbónico: metrópoli versus élites novohispanas," *Historia Mexicana*, xii, 2 [162] (1991), 207–264 and by Allan Kuethe and Juan Marchena F., eds., *Soldados del Rey. El ejército borbónico en América colonial en vísperas de la Independencia* (Castellon: Universitat Jaume I, Colección América, 2005).

In any case, it is clear that the dynamics and logic of expenditure of funds in Spanish America were based on a secular *three-tiered* system of management of imperial finance. This system can be defined in terms of the operation of basic principles that explain the disbursement of public monies as well as the logic of expenditures of the multiple treasuries of the empire. A first, basic and secular principle of imperial finance (applied since the sixteenth century) was that the largest number of expenses should be covered in situ with the tax income collected on a regional level and accumulated in a local *caja real* (treasury).[37] However, when a local treasury district produced a fiscal surplus, part of this money would be transferred to another tax district which had a deficit or, alternatively, to one of the principal treasuries of the respective viceroyalty. These remittances, nonetheless, were not necessarily limited to the viceroyalty itself; they frequently were also shipped abroad to different points of the empire, as we will see.

In the case of New Spain, we can observe the dynamics of this tridimensional fiscal system in the transferences regularly realized (in the late eighteenth century) among the different twenty-four regional treasury offices of the viceroyalty, in most cases to cover military expenditures. For example, certain regional treasuries such as that of Veracruz and Yucatán (that regularly accumulated fiscal surpluses) were responsible for the payment of a substantial part of military expenses of districts that had scarce tax income such as Campeche, located in the Gulf of Mexico, which had an important military and naval garrison. Similarly, the revenue-poor military forts and garrisons (*presidios*) of northern Mexico depended heavily on the remittances of funds collected by the more proximate regional treasuries of Guadalajara and Bolaños that accumulated a regular surplus of funds from taxes on local silver production as well as on trade.

A second level of expenditures were the transfer of surplus fiscal funds from one colony to another which were known as *situados*, those from New Spain being directed principally to the Greater Caribbean, including Cuba, Santo Domingo, Puerto Rico, Florida, Louisiana, and Trinidad. These constituted a broad network of tax transfers between the different colonies, the quantitative importance of which suggests that historians should rethink many fundamental aspects of the way that imperial finance operated in Spanish America.[38] In addition, it should be noted that the viceroyalty of

37 José Patricio Merino Navarro, *Las cuentas de la administración central española, 1750–1820* (Madrid: Instituto de Estudios Fiscales, 1987), pp. 11–28 offers a preliminary outline of the operating principles of the Spanish Treasury administration.

38 In the latter half of the eighteenth century, New Spain covered approximately 75% of the costs of administrative and military costs of the government of Cuba and a large portion of the other Caribbean colonies mentioned. For information and estimates, see C. Marichal and M. Souto, "Silver and Situados" and C. Marichal, *La bancarrota del virreinato* (1999), Chapter 1.

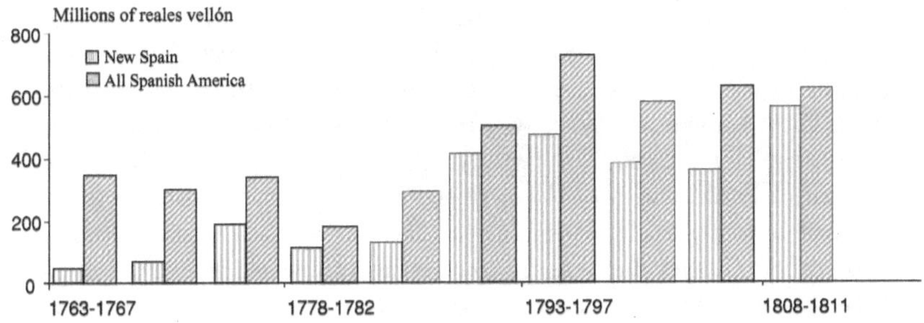

Figure 1.2. General Treasury of Spain, 1763–1811: Remittances from Spanish America and New Spain.
Source: Appendix Tables 1.1 and 1.3.

New Spain also provided regular fiscal subsidies for the Phillipines and occasional sums for Guatemala and Central America in times of emergencies.

A third and important set of *intraimperial* tax transfers were remittances to the metropolitan treasury.[39] Analysis of shipments to Spain suggests that in the early decades of the century (1720s to the 1750s) the contribution of Mexican royal silver to the metropolitan fiscal regime was important but limited in scope. (See Figure 1.1.) During this thirty-year period fiscal transfers to Spain did not ordinarily surpass one million pesos per year but in the 1750s average remittances increased to close to two million pesos a year.[40] Then, after the two-year war with Britain (1762–1763), royal remittances from Mexico to Spain declined as a result of the huge expansion of expenditures in reinforcement of the defensive infrastructure in the greater Caribbean. By the 1770s the shipments of royal silver from New Spain to Cádiz had returned to the levels of the 1750s, and from that date until the 1780s the fiscal remittances by Mexico and Peru provided an average of approximately 15 percent of the ordinary revenues of the General Treasury at Madrid.[41] Then, in the last-quarter century of empire – 1785–1810 – the percentages rose, reaching extraordinary levels, as is seen in Figures 1.1 and 1.2.

Whether we look at expenses within the viceroyalty or at fiscal transfers abroad (to other colonies or to the metropolis), the bulk were destined to cover military requirements. A recent monograph demonstrates with clarity

39 These transfers were registered under the category of "Indias" in the metropolitan treasury accounts.

40 Compare the data on Spanish American remittances in our Appendix, Tables I.1 and I.3 with series in Jacques Barbier "Towards a New Chronology for Bourbon Colonialism: The 'Depositaría de Indias' of Cádiz, 1722–1789," *Ibero-Amerikanisches Archiv*, N.F. Jg. 6, H 4 (1980), 335–353.

41 Carlos Marichal, "Beneficios y costes fiscales del colonialismo: las remesas americana a España, 1760–1814" *Revista de Historia Económica*, x, 3 (1997), 475–505.

that the expenditure of funds for military objectives in the viceroyalty of New Spain increased throughout the eighteenth century.[42] Under Phillip V (1726–1746), total disbursements of the branch of the royal treasury of Mexico City, known as "War" (*Guerra*), increased from 1 million pesos a year in the mid-1720s to over 3 million pesos by 1745. Under the succeeding reign of Ferdinand VI (1746–1759) military expenditures rose to an average of almost 4 million pesos a year, and during the reign of Charles III (1759–1788), this level rose again to reach an annual average of 6.3 million pesos a year, which represented over 60 percent of total disbursements of the Mexico City central treasury. These sums included both military expenses effected within the viceroyalty and certain transfers for the defense of other colonies. These transfers bespeak the highly complex nature of the financial integration of the empire and reflect the fiscal interdependence of its different parts.

A review of the long-term trends in the export of tax monies from Mexico, however, indicates that in toto more funds were actually shipped to other colonies than to Spain itself, between 1720 and 1800. This phenomenon is relatively little-known and rarely appears in the traditional historiography but its analysis helps explain why we argue that New Spain operated as a fiscal submetropolis during the Bourbon era.

The Richest Colony: Mexico as Submetropolis

It may be presumed that, as historians continue to work on the extensive statistical series of Spanish royal finance in the eighteenth century, a full description of the fiscal and financial geography and dynamics of the empire will eventually emerge. But such an ambitious purpose must be restricted at the present stage to more limited objectives. Our aim here is quite simply to demonstrate that during the eighteenth century a major part of the costs of maintenance of the Spanish civil and military administration in the greater Caribbean fell upon large and rising transfers of silver from the royal treasuries of New Spain.[43]

42 Carlos Rodríguez Venegas, "La sociedad novohispana y las guerras imperiales a la luz del donativo y préstamos de 1781," B.A. thesis (Philosophy and literature), Universidad Nacional Autónoma de Mexico, 1996, Figure 3.2 and Table 2, pp. 75–76.

43 The statistical series of the real hacienda of New Spain (and especially that of the real caja of Veracruz) published by Herbert Klein and John TePaske make possible a year-by-year reconstruction and analysis of the financial transfers from the viceroyalty to the metropolis and to different parts of the American empire. We have complemented this data with additional archival information on the "Situados" from New Spain, among the most important of which were financial remittances established from the end of sixteenth century for the support of military and administrative bastions in the Caribbean.

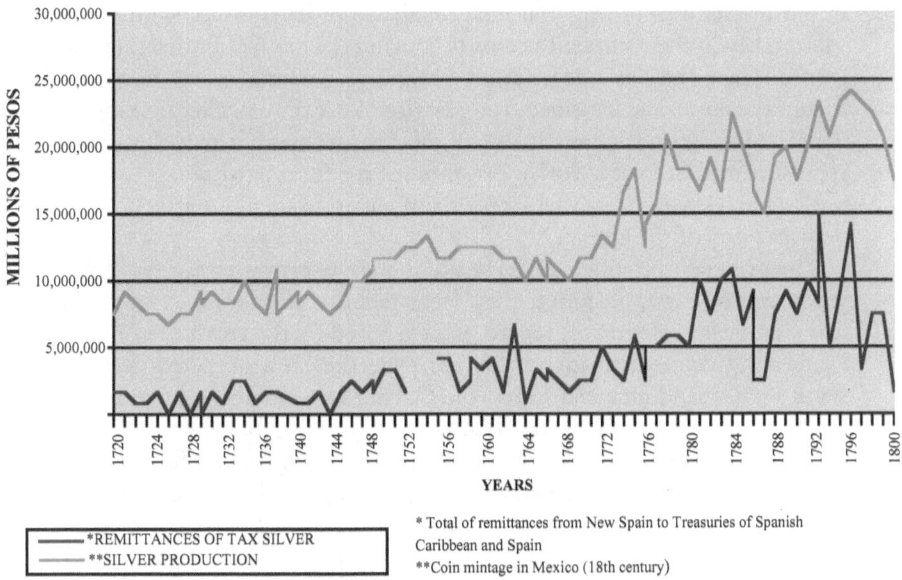

Figure 1.3. Silver Coin Mintage and Remittances by the Royal Treasuries of New Spain. *Source:* Data from Richard Garner, Economic History Data Desk, http://home.comcast.net/~richardgarner04/ and C. Marichal and M. Souto, Silver and Situados: New Spain and the Finances of the Spanish Empire in the Carribbean in the Eighteenth Century, *Hispanic American Historical Review*, 74, 4 (1994).

That these remittances could have increased so notably during the eighteenth century has drawn the attention of historians who have been struck not only by the great volume of tax silver exported but also by the quite close correspondence with the trends of silver production and mintage in New Spain.[44] (See Figure 1.3.) Despite the close correlations, it would be a mistake to think that remittances were simply derived from the mines, for as we will have occasion to see in Chapter 2, the tax system of the colonial regime in the late Bourbon period was quite broadly based, and only one-quarter of the monies collected by the royal administration came from mining taxes. On the other hand, there is no question that without the great silver mining boom of the late colonial era, there would not have been possible such high volumes of fiscal transfers to the other Spanish American colonies and to Spain itself.

The remittance of royal silver from the richest colonies to support military defenses in South America, the Caribbean, and the Philippines was

44 See, in particular, R. Garner and S. E. Stefanou, *Economic Growth and Change in Bourbon Mexico*, Chapter 7.

an old mechanism of imperial finance, although its significance increased enormously in the eighteenth century. During the reign of Philip II (1556–1598), when the basic legislation governing commerce and navigation within the empire was ratified, the practice of tax transfers became institutionalized and came to constitute a regular part of royal finance throughout Spanish America. Not surprisingly, most of the fiscal remittances (*situados*) were sent to key ports with fortresses and garrisons or, alternatively, to key frontier posts of the empire.[45]

The principal providers of these funds were the royal treasuries of New Spain and of Peru, although they were not the only ones. A lesser but still significant role in this regard was exercised by the treasuries of Tierra Firme and Caracas. Already in the year 1584 the Crown ordered that New Spain should send financial support to Cuba, Santo Domingo, Puerto Rico, and Florida and hence Havana became the key redistributing point for the fiscal transfers sent from Mexico to the greater Caribbean.[46] Since foreign shippers and pirates (particularly British, French, Dutch) also used the same sea-routes, the Spanish authorities found it necessary to create a defensive system that was based on the protection of the most vulnerable and strategic ports and channels of passage, and it was there that the major fortifications and garrisons were established.[47]

The costs that such a defensive system required could not be covered by the Caribbean provinces and, as a result, recourse was had to remittances from the more prosperous American possessions of the Spanish crown – a tendency that was accentuated progressively as military expenses rose over the seventeenth and eighteenth centuries. Thus, it became established practice that the viceroyalty of New Spain would send large, annual sums of royal funds to pay for a large part costs of the garrisons and fortifications

45 Although the term "situado" means salary or rent paid or remitted, within the Spanish empire it was used specifically to refer to the remittance or transfer of royal funds from one "caja" of the royal treasury to another in order to cover expenses of strategic importance. For a definition, see José Canga Arguelles, *Diccionario de Hacienda*, vol. 2 (Madrid Imprenta de Don Marcelino Calero y portocarrero: 1834), p. 509: "Llevaban este nombre ("Situados") las cantidades que anualmente se remitían desde las cajas reales de América a otras provincias, para suplir con su importe la falta de los productos de sus rentas y atender al pago de las obligaciones del erario en ellas."

46 Julio Le Riverend Brusone, "Relaciones entre Nueva España y Cuba (1518–1520)," *Revista de Historia de América*, 37–38 (1954), 90. The exact date of the establishment of the first *situados* to the islands of the great Caribbean has not yet been established. According to the references cited by Le Riverend, more or less regular remittances were made to Havana from the 1570s. But the only precise date for a royal order in this respect – September 18, 1584 – is that provided by Manuel Villanova, "Economía y civismo," *Revista cubana* (1892), 157–190 (reprinted in Havana: Ministerio de Educación, 1945), p. 43.

47 A suggestive analysis is found in Paul E. Hoffman, *The Spanish Crown and the Defense of the Caribbean, 1535–1585* (Baton Rouge: Louisiana State University, 1980).

throughout the greater Caribbean and in the Gulf of Mexico. Furthermore, New Spain was charged with the financial support of the *Armada de Barlovento*, a naval squadron created to protect the main sea-lanes used by Spanish shipping in the Caribbean.[48]

The original objectives of the *situados* in the Caribbean were closely tied to naval priorities and especially to the need to defend the annual flotillas on the initial or final stages of their transatlantic journeys. The main predators in the Caribbean were pirates and privateers of different European nationalities that flourished in the mid- and late seventeenth century. By the early eighteenth century, it was British warships that came to represent the greatest danger. As a result, the Spanish monarchy reinforced its networks of intraimperial financial transfers, the economic and strategic importance of which is essential to understand key aspects of the military and financial administration of the empire in the Americas.

But were the Mexican *situados* unique? Clearly not. While our focus is on the remittances from colonial Mexico, it should not be forgotten that both the viceroyalty of New Granada and that of Peru provided monies to a large number of military garrisons and ports in South America. From the royal treasury at Santa Fé de Bogotá, capital of New Grenada, and from that of Quito, tax monies were sent to support the military garrisons at Cartagena, Santa Marta, Rio Rancha, Isla Margarita, and a part of the costs of the *Armada de Barlovento*.[49] The royal treasuries of Lima, for their part, annually sent monies to sustain the military and naval garrisons at Panama and Portobello as well as to Valdivia and Chilhoé on the southern coast of Chile. In addition, it should be noted that the great treasury at the silver-rich city of Potosi (in modern Bolivia) financed additional garrisons, including that of Buenos Aires and, through it, those of Montevideo, Patagonia, and the Malvinas Islands.

The analysis of these remittances speaks to the complexity of intraimperial tax structures and dynamics.[50] Since the Mexican *situados* were the

48 Bibiano Torres Ramírez, *La Armada de Barlovento* (Seville: Escuela de Estudios Americanos, 1981), Chapter 8 and pp. 221–226; Manuel Alvarado Morales, "El cabildo de la ciudad de México ante la fundación de la armada de Barlovento, 1635–1643," Ph.D. thesis, El Colegio de México, 1979, pp. 11–17.

49 On the evolution of the remittances from New Granada in the seventeenth and eighteenth centuries, see Hermes Tovar Pinzón, "Remesas, situados y real hacienda en el siglo XVII," in Antonio Miguel Bernal, ed., *Dinero, moneda y crédito en la monarquía hispánica*, pp. 241–267. José Manuel Serrano Alvarez, *Fortificaciones y tropas. El gasto militar en Tierra Firme, 1700–1788* (Seville: Universidad de Sevilla/CSIS/Diputación de Sevilla, 2004).

50 There are several historical studies of the "Situados," including John J. TePaske, "La política española en el Caribe durante los siglos XVII y XVIII," in Antonio Acosta and Juan Marchena, eds., *La influencia de España en el Caribe, la Florida y La Luisiana (1500–1800)* (Madrid: Instituto de Cooperación Iberoamericana), pp. 61–87; John J. TePaske, "New World Silver, Castille and the Philippines, 1590–1800," in J. F. Richards, *Precious Metals in the Later Medieval and Early Modern Worlds* (Durham, N.C.:

most important in the period under consideration, we now turn our attention specifically to the analysis of the problems associated with the financial transfers by the royal treasury at Veracruz for the sustenance of the civil and military administrations in Cuba, Santo Domingo, Puerto Rico, Florida, Louisiana, and several other Spanish colonies in the Antilles.[51] A brief review of the origins of the military objectives of this kind of intraimperial remittances is followed by summary analysis of the volume of remittances to the different colonial territories. We underline the importance of the financial transfers in times of international war, in particular the huge contribution of the royal treasuries of Mexico and Veracruz to cover the costs of the military operations conducted by the Spanish crown in the years 1779–1783 against Great Britain throughout the greater Caribbean – including Florida and Louisiana – precisely as the war of independence of the thirteen colonies reached its apogee.

Imperial Expenses Covered by the Mexican *Situados*

Military expenditures were the principal items financed by the *situados*, although they were not the only ones. The payment of salaries of troops and officers (infantry and artillery) stationed in the different garrisons and the costs of fortifications in the principal ports and of the various naval squadrons absorbed a large volume of funds, which tended to rise through most of the eighteenth century.

The strategic importance of these fiscal transfers in sustaining the naval "life-lines" of the empire in the Caribbean and the Gulf of Mexico can be judged by their contribution to the costly reinforcement of the great fortifications of Havana, Cartagena, San Juan, and Veracruz,[52] as well as in the maintenance of the ships of the royal Armada (when on mission in the region) and the expenses of the Havana shipyards. While the construction of ships at the Cuban capital was financed mainly with the royal remittances

Duke University Press, 1983), pp. 425–445; Juan Marchena Fernández, "La financiación militar en Indias: introducción a su estudio," *Anuario de Estudios Americanos*, 36 (1979), 93–110; and Juan Marchena Fernández, "Financiación militar y situados," in *Temas de historia militar*, Ponencias del 2o. Congreso de Historia Militar, vol. 1 (Madrid: Servicio de Publicaciones del EME, 1988) (Colección Adalid), pp. 263–307.

51 To determine the levels of remittances on account of the royal treasury from New Spain to Spain and to the American *situados*, we consider that the series from the "real caja" of Veracruz are the fundamental and most complete source of data. We follow here J. J. TePaske in his essays "New World Silver" and "The Financial Disintegration."

52 A description of the fortifications constructed during the colonial period can be found in J. A. Calderón Quijano, *Las fortificaciones españolas*. Also by the same author: *Historia de las fortificaciones de Nueva España* (Seville: Escuela de Estudios Hispanoamericanos, 1953).

from New Spain, there were also private contributions to the Armada. In the 1780s, for example, two of the largest battleships the *Regla* and the *Mexicano* (both with 114 cannon) were built in Havana shipyards with a half-million peso contribution by two of the wealthiest silver miners of New Spain.[53]

During the reign of Carlos III (1759–1788) a considerable portion of the Mexican fiscal transfers was also used to reinforce fixed garrisons composed mostly of infantry in the principal Caribbean ports. These military forces grew in size as is confirmed by the increase in number of local units (both regular troops and militia), provoking a parallel rise in expenditures in salaries, provisions, and equipment.[54] Feeding thousands of troops as well as providing them with tobacco and alcohol, supplying them with uniforms, arms, and munitions required considerable resources. To which was added the maintenance of the small and great fortresses with cannon and powder as well as materials for regular repairs.

Although the tax monies sent from Mexico were employed principally to cover costs of the defensive apparatus of the empire, this was not their only function. From an early date, funds were also used for additional purposes such as the support of religious missions charged with the submission and indoctrination of rebel Indian tribes, as was the case both in northern New Spain and in different parts of the greater Caribbean.[55] In addition, the *situados* were not infrequently utilized to provide for salaries of civil functionaries and for ecclesiastical authorities on the frontiers of the empire.[56] Occasionally they even were of assistance in financing certain specific colonization projects such as was the case in Santo Domingo, whence a considerable number of peasant families from the Canary Islands were transferred with

53 The silver miners in question were the Count of Regla and the Count of Valenciana. These donations were also common in France. See Martine Acerra and André Zysberg, *L'essor des marines de guerre européennes, 1680–1790* (Paris: Editions Sedes, 1997), p. 71, which notes that fourteen warships of the French Royal Navy were financed by donations from French wealthy contributors between 1763 and 1766.

54 For the increase in military expenditures and the expansion of military forces in Spanish America in the eighteenth century, see J. Marchena, "Financiación military y situados," 271–273. On Cuba, see Allan J. Kuethe and C. Douglas Inglis, "Absolutism and Enlightened Reform: Charles III, the Establishment of the Alcabala, and Commercial Reorganization in Cuba," *Past and Present*, 109 (1985), 118–143.

55 Engel Sluiter, *The Florida Situado: Quantifying the First Eighty Years, 1571–1651* (Gainsville: University of Florida Libraries, 1985), pp. 5–6. As late as the eighteenth century the *situados* were used to cover these expenses as can be seen in the "reales cédulas" of November 20, 1741; October 13, 1756, and April 6, 1763: Archivo General de la Nación (hereafter AGN), Mexico, *Reales Cédulas Originales*, vol. 61, exp. 91, f. 334; vol. 76, exp. 123, f. 290; and vol. 86, exp. 66.

56 See, for example, AGN, *Reales Cédulas Originales*, vol. 62, exp. 60, f. 185; vol. 76, exp. 144, f. 331; and vol. 63, exp. 60, f. 159, *Historia*, vol. 570, f. 57, and *Archivo Histórico de Hacienda*, leg. 1210, exp. 1.

support of the royal treasury, or the case of Trinidad, where the Spanish government promoted agricultural colonies.[57]

Last but not least, important remittances not related to imperial defense were those managed by the royal tobacco monopoly. In order to help pay the costs of the annual tobacco harvests in Cuba, the Madrid Cabinet instructed the tobacco monopoly of New Spain to send a fixed annual sum to the royal treasury in Cuba to assist with annual payments due to local tobacco farmers. In 1723 the sum sent to Havana on this account was of 200,000 pesos, but by 1744 the figure had risen to 500,000 pesos per year, at a time when the money destined for the military garrison of the Cuban port was but 400,000 pesos. Both the tobacco and military remittances were ratified in 1768 and continued to be sent annually from New Spain until the beginning of the nineteenth century.

The significance of the tobacco *situado* was underlined by Ramón de la Sagra in a classic study which pointed out the strategic importance of the Mexican silver transfers in greasing the wheels of the royal tobacco monopoly, probably the largest state enterprise in the eighteenth-century world.[58] According to de la Sagra, more than 100 million pesos worth of tobacco leaf were sent from Cuba to Spain during the five decades of 1760–1810.[59] The Cuban leaf was processed by the great Seville tobacco factory, helping to generate almost 25 percent of total revenues of the metropolitan treasury by the end of the century.[60] As a result, Mexican and Cuban fiscal subsidies were key factors for the solvency of the monarchy.

Geographic Distribution of the *Situados*

The increase of the volume of tax remittances from colonial Mexico to the Spanish Caribbean during the eighteenth century was of such significance

57 See AGN, *Reales Cédulas Originales*, vol. 64, exp. 33, f. 103, *Historia*, vol. 570, f. 25, and Eduardo Arcila Farías, *Comercio entre México y Venezuela en los siglos XVI y XVII* (Mexico: IMCE, 1975), p. 218.

58 Ramón de la Sagra, *Historia económico-política y estadística de la isla de Cuba* (Habana, 1831), pp. 240–266. That the Spanish tobacco monopoly was an enormous enterprise can be judged from the fact that from 1770 its production sphere included factories in Spain (that at Seville employed over 5,000 workers in 1800), in Mexico City (over 8,000 workers in 1800), as well in many other parts of the empire. At the same time, thousands of persons were employed in official tobaccionist sales points throughout the empire. Finally, several thousand tobacco farmers in Cuba and Mexico as well as a fewer number in Louisiana, Puerto Rico, Santo Domingo, New Granada and the Phillipines depended for their living upon the royal monopoly. For details, see Laura Nater, "El tabaco y las finanzas del imperio español: Nueva España y la metrópoli, 1760–1810," Ph.D. thesis, El Colegio de México, 1998.

59 R. de la Sagra, *Historia económico-política y estadística*, pp. 264–266.

60 By the 1780s the tobacco monopoly was contributing close to a quarter of annual ordinary revenues of the Spanish Treasury. The estimates are to be found in C. Marichal, "Beneficios y costes fiscales del colonialismo. Also see data in Appendix I.

that the distinguished Cuban historian Le Riverend called this period the "golden age of the situados."[61] As previously indicated, the bulk of the silver pesos were normally sent in ships of the Spanish Navy from Veracruz to Havana and hence redistributed to other points in the greater Caribbean, although some royal tax transfers were sent via other routes. (See the map on page 40.) The amount of money sent annually to the diverse ports, fortresses, and garrisons was, generally speaking, a function of the relative, strategic importance of each.[62] Although fixed yearly amounts (to each destination) were ratified by different royal orders, the actual sums sent varied considerably from year to year, depending on a variety of factors. Variations in troop strength of the various garrisons as a result of deaths and desertions or, alternatively, as a result of the outbreak of military conflicts in the region had an impact on financial demands. Likewise, the requirements of naval squadrons could change dramatically as a result of battles or storms: the loss of a large number of ships, inevitably, implied extraordinary expenditures as much new ship construction became obligatory.

Throughout the eighteenth century the Havana "Situado" was made up of three principal items: "tierra", "marina," and "tabaco," the former two categories being essentially defense expenditures. The first royal order that refers to the ordinary annual "Situado" to Havana is that of August 2, 1744, in which it was established that 500,000 pesos should be sent from New Spain to cover the annual expenses of the Cuba royal treasury offices in the acquisition of the tobacco harvest.[63] Archival sources indicate that during the 1750s the remittances of Mexican tax funds for infantry in Havana averaged 400,000 pesos a year as well and additional 500,000 pesos for naval forces and shipbuilding.[64]

61 J. Le Riverend, "Relaciones entre Nueva España y Cuba," 92 and 143–144 is one of the first historical studies to have underlined the significance of the *situados*; his estimates of remittances to Cuba from New Spain appear to be based on R. de la Sagra.

62 Each American province was obliged to send documents that justified the level of defense expenditures, and this explains why in the AGN of Mexico there are numerous reports of the regiments in each garrison and of the number of deaths and deserters. See, for example, reports on garrisons in Puerto Rico, AGN, *Archivo Histórico de Hacienda*, leg. 1210.

63 E. Arcila Farías, *Comercio entre México y Venezuela*, p. 203 confirms the figure of 500,000 silver pesos, but J. Marchena, "Financiación military y situados," registers only 400,000 pesos. R. de la Sagra, *Historia económico-política y estadística*, p. 277 indicates that in 1756, 436,000 pesos of the Mexican remittances were annually spent to maintain the four battalions of infantry, one of cavalry, and one of artillery in Havana.

64 AGN, Caja Matriz, *Libro manual de cargo y data de la Real Caja de Veracruz* for the year 1758 and J. Marchena, "Financiación military y situados." It should be noted that the category of "marina" is one of the most difficult to specify since some of the funds went for the salaries of sailors and officers and other sums for provisions and ship repair or construction. For example, a report of October 19, 1758 indicated that of 1,016,094 pesos sent to Havana for "marina," 407,123 pesos were to be used for expenses of the naval squadron, 100,924 pesos for ship construction, and 508,047 for urgent naval disbursements. AGN, *Historia*, vol. 570, f. 204.

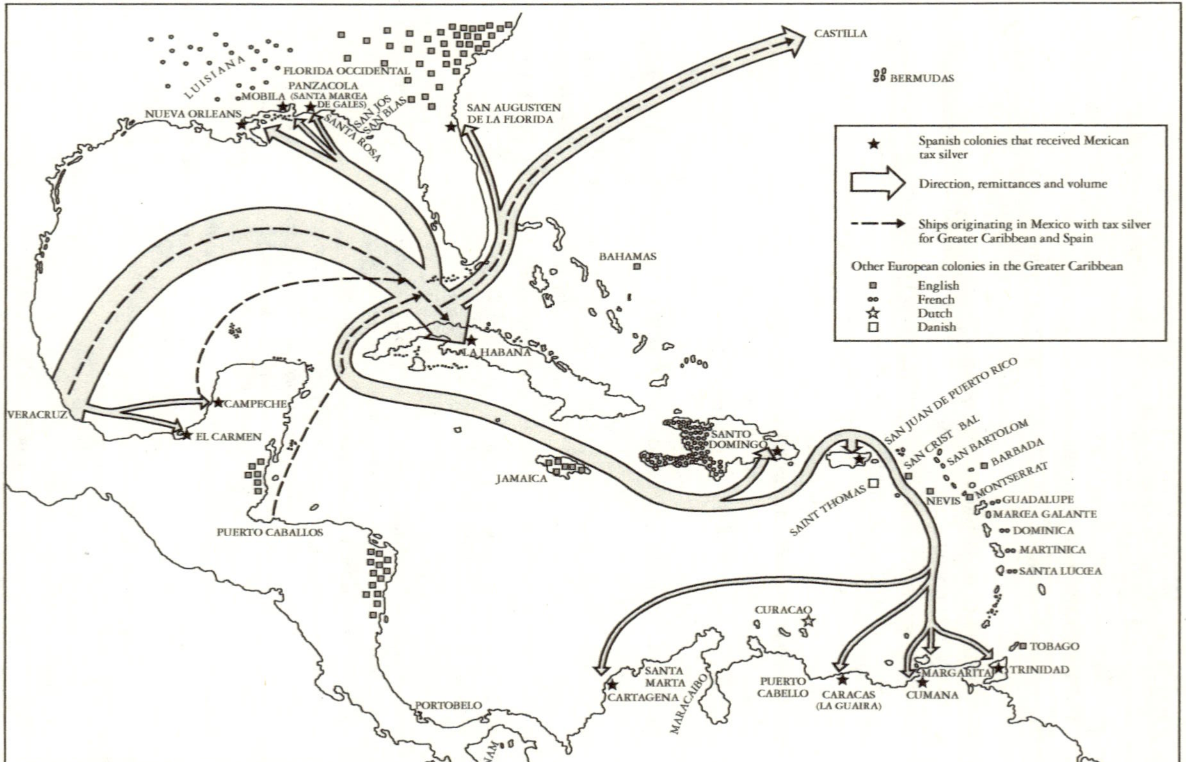

Silver Remittances from Treasuries of Mexico to Spanish Colonies in the Caribbean and to Spain (circa 1790)

Source: Drawn by Araceli Serrano, based on Carlos Marichal and Matilde Souto, "Silver and Situados: New Spain and the Financing of the Spanish Empire in the Caribbean in the Eighteenth Century," *Hispanic American Historical Review*, 74, 4 (1994), 587–613.

After the British invasion and occupation of Havana in 1762, during which local shipyards and forts were seriously damaged, royal officers stationed in Cuba called for increased financial assistance. In 1765, orders were sent from Madrid, instructing the treasuries of New Spain to annually send 300,000 pesos for fortifications in Havana and 100,000 pesos for those in Santiago de Cuba. Three years later in 1768 the remittances to Havana were increased, reaching the sum of 1,900,000 pesos, of which 700,000 pesos were to be used for naval purposes, 400,000 for army troops, 300,000 for fortifications, and 500,000 for the tobacco harvest.[65]

According to the expert statistician Ramón de la Sagra, between 1766 and 1788 Havana received fifty-eight million pesos in fiscal transfers from Mexico, and another fifty-seven million pesos in the years from 1789 to 1806.[66] These figures must be considered estimates since there are considerable differences in the data provided by other contemporary sources but they suggest the enormity of the fiscal contribution of colonial Mexico to the Spanish colonies in the greater Caribbean.[67] Significant differences are also found when comparing the extraordinary sums registered at times of war in the Caribbean, particularly in the 1760s, early 1780s, and 1790s. In order to provide an idea of the complexities involved in these fiscal transfers, we briefly analyze the remittances from New Spain during the war of 1779–1783 when the Mexican *situados* to Havana and the rest of the Spanish Caribbean reached their highest peak in all of colonial history.

The Financial Contribution of New Spain to the War against Great Britain, 1779–1783

Both the French and the Spanish monarchies took advantage of outbreak of the war of independence of the thirteen North American colonies (1776–1783) to launch their own offensives against Great Britain in Europe and in the Caribbean. The central objectives of the military campaigns initiated in the western hemisphere by the Spanish crown in 1779 included the

65 AGN, *Reales Cédulas Originales*, vol. 92, exp. 48, f. 88.

66 R. de la Sagra, *Historia económico-política y estadística*, pp. 280–281.

67 The eighteenth century administrative experts Fonseca and Urrutia calculated the average annual value of Mexican remittances for military expenses to Havana at 1,285,000 pesos between 1785 and 1789 (this obviously did not include the tobacco subsidy) whereas their equally expert colleague Maniau proposed a figure of 2,674,213 pesos as the average between 1788 and 1792. On the other hand, the accounting book of the royal treasury of Veracruz for the year 1791 gave a total of 1,050,000 pesos but did not include the category of naval expenses. See Fabián Fonseca and Carlos de Urrutia, *Historia general de la Real Hacienda*, XIII–XXVII (Mexico: Imprenta de Vicente G. Torres, 1845–1853); Joaquín Maniau y Torquemada, *Compendio de la historia de la Real Hacienda de Nueva España escrito en el año de 1794*, notes by Alberto María Carreño (Mexico: Sociedad Mexicana de Geografía y Estadística, 1914), pp. 43–46; AGN, Caja Matriz, *Libro Manual de cargo y data de la Real Caja de Veracruz para el año de 1791*.

reconquest of Florida, the reinforcement of Spanish positions in Louisiana, (mainly along the southern Mississippi), and attacks upon British positions in the Bahamas, Jamaica, and Honduras.[68] The costs of the war implied great expenditures. These were incurred by Spanish military forces operating in various points in the greater Caribbean, although the requirements were greatest in Havana where the bulk of troops and ships were concentrated from early 1780 onward. In order to finance this great military effort, the Crown made demands on the treasuries of New Spain that went far beyond the standard levels of remittances to Cuba. So considerable were these charges that by the early 1780s they surpassed the capacity of the tax structure of New Spain to provide sufficient funds and obliged the viceroy to call for a series of forced and voluntary loans from all sectors of the Mexican population.[69]

The official correspondence between Viceroy Martín de Mayorga from New Spain and military commanders in Havana illustrates the extraordinary volume of financial support and other types of assistance sent to Havana from Veracruz, including large amounts of provisions and manpower.[70] As historian Melvin Glascock argued, during the war (1779–1783) New Spain "was virtually the sole support of Spanish arms in the Americas . . . and made for the mother country and her allies a contribution unmatched in the history of colonial Spanish America."[71] The estimates by Glascock and fellow historian James Lewis of the huge shipments of silver from Veracruz to Havana during the war are similar despite the fact that they used different primary sources: Lewis estimated that thirty-four million silver pesos were sent from Mexico as *situados* to the Caribbean during the military conflict, while Glascock argued that these remittances reached thirty-seven million pesos (or dollars) in the same five years.[72]

68 The first three objectives were successful, whereas the raids on Honduras were a failure and the naval campaign of Jamaica proved a major failure as a result of the sea victories obtained by the British Navy under the command of Admiral Rodney. On the Bahama campaign, see James A. Lewis monograph *The Final Campaign of the American Revolution. Rise and Fall of the Spanish Bahamas* (Columbia: University of South Carolina Press, 1991).

69 A previous study of these loans can be found in Carlos Marichal, "Las guerras imperiales y los préstamos novohispanos', 1781–1804" *Historia Mexicana*, xxxix, 4 [156], 881–907.

70 The information on the shipments is found in a variety of sources in the AGN as well as in two excellent and infrequently cited doctoral theses by James Lewis and Melvin Glascock, which provide an abundance of data on the crucial role of New Spain in the war. See Melvin Bruce Glascock, "New Spain and the War for America, 1779–1783," Ph.D. thesis, Lousiana State University, 1969 and James A. Lewis, "New Spain during the American Revolution, 1779–1783: A Viceroyalty at War," Ph.D. thesis, Duke University, 1975.

71 M. Glascock, "New Spain and the War," p. 285.

72 The source used by Glascock is a very detailed document titled "Decretos, Planos Certificaciones sobre el Costo de la Guerra," Archivo Histórico Nacional (Madrid) *Consejo de Indias*, leg. 20721, cuaderno v., fs. 77–109, cited in M. Glascock, "New Spain and the War," pp. 265–274. The estimates of

The contribution that these remittances represented for the overall war effort of the Spanish crown can only be judged indirectly, but their importance is manifest. This financial subsidy was worth over 750 million reales (one silver peso was equal to twenty reales de vellón, the monetary unit most used in the treasury accounts in Spain). This was an extraordinary sum for the period if we consider that it was equivalent to twice the annual peacetime defense expenditures of the metropolitan treasury at Madrid.[73]

A difficult problem is to find out exactly how these monies were spent since only a part remained in Cuba while the rest was remitted for various military operations throughout the greater Caribbean. It should be noted, however, that the majority of the funds went to finance three types of military expenditures: (1) the expeditionary army under the command of Bernardo Gálvez, the headquarters of which was at Havana, but operated in the Floridas and Louisiana; (2) the Armada, under the direction of Admiral José Solano, that carried out various naval operations against the British throughout the greater Caribbean; and (3) the military garrisons in Cuba, headed by Captain-General Juan Manuel Cacigal, which included thousands of Spanish, Cuban, and Mexican troops. While there are a number of historical studies that analyze aspects of the military campaigns undertaken by these forces, there are only a few studies of the precise disbursement of funds.[74]

The financial documents generated by the war are abundant but dispersed and are sometimes contradictory. The official correspondence of the viceroys in the Mexican archives includes the confidential reports sent by Viceroy Martín de Mayorga to the Minister of Indies José de Gálvez including much information on the silver remittances sent to Havana on Spanish warships. Mayorga frequently complained that the Cuban functionaries rarely acknowledged receipt of the shipments and that he therefore had insufficient information on effective disbursements in the island; he even went so far as to suggest to Gálvez that he believed that important sums

J. Lewis, "New Spain during American Revolution," 146 are from AGN, *Hacienda*, vol. 395, exp. 7. Despite being derived from different archival sources, these figures also agree with those in the treasury summaries of Veracruz, published by Klein and TePaske: the total amount registered as leaving Veracruz for Havana between 1779 and 1783 is 37.8 million pesos. See Veracruz data in J. TePaske and H. Klein, *Ingresos y egresos de la Real Hacienda*: these can be consulted in Excell format at the database "Estadísticas Históricas de México" in the Web site of El Colegio de Mexico, www.colmex.mx, where a link will be found in "Biblioteca" under "Bases de datos" from July, 2007.

73 This estimate is based on the exchange rate of 20 reales vellón to each silver peso. For comparative financial data on metropolitan finance, see Pedro Tedde, *Política financiera y política commercial en el reinado Carlos III*, Actas del Congreso Internacional sobre Carlos III y la Ilustración (Madrid: Ministerio de Cultura, 1989), vol. 2, p. 143.

74 An exception is Johanna von Grafenstein Gareis, *Nueva España en el Circuncaribe, 1779–1808: revolución, competencia imperial y vínculos intercoloniales* (Mexico: UNAM, 1997), which provides excellent data. Also very useful is J. A. Lewis, "New Spain during the American Revolution," pp. 130–159.

were used for illicit purposes. In October 1781 the viceroy informed Gálvez that he should not pay attention to the complaints of the top royal official at Havana who said that he had not received enough money. Mayorga added that, in fact, enormous sums had been sent in the previous months from Veracruz to Cuba to assist in the war effort: Mexican tax remittances had surpassed 12 million silver pesos, plus 1.5 million pesos in provisions (flour and hard tack, ham, bacon, salt meat, powder, etc.) and the transfer of a force of 1,913 Mexicans who were to be employed by the Spanish naval squadrons operating out of Cuba.[75]

That the viceroy of New Spain was responsible not only for sending funds and supplies but also for evaluating the scale of the financial effort required to sustain the war in the Caribbean is confirmed by his correspondence with a variety of royal functionaries. In October 1782, the chief treasury officer of New Spain informed Mayorga that he had constructed a provisional estimate of war expenditures in the previous year and was using it to calculate future disbursements. On the basis of the correspondence between Admiral Solano, General Bernardo Gálvez, and the Intendant of New Spain Pedro Antonio de Cosío he was able to calculate that the Armada operating out of Havana had absorbed 5,600,000 pesos in the last three years, whereas the expeditionary armies in Florida and Louisiana as well as the garrisons in Cuba had required 7,000,000 pesos.[76] The same treasury officer noted that all of these funds had been sent punctually to Havana on various warships, surpassing all previous expectations of the financial resources that could be obtained in New Spain for this costly war.

Despite assurances from Mexico, the Minister of the Indies at Madrid, José Gálvez, remained profoundly concerned that all military expenses be covered punctually as the war intensified. In 1780 he had dispatched a high-ranking official, General Francisco Saavedra (later minister of finance under Charles IV) to supervise and speed up the remittances of funds from Veracruz to Havana, as well as to coordinate the provisions of additional funds and supplies to the allied French fleet in the Caribbean. In a letter to Gálvez, dated September 1782, Viceroy Mayorga made a point of noting that when Saavedra arrived with royal orders to remit ten million pesos for the war, everyone had thought this impossible. Nonetheless, the task had been fulfilled as one warship after another left Veracruz, carrying silver for Havana. The first to leave was the battleship *San Francisco de Asis* that carried Saavedra on board and one million pesos to Havana, followed by another ship with two million pesos a few days later. Subsequently, the *San Agustín* took more than four million pesos to Cuba and, on a second journey, the *San Francisco de Asis* loaded another two million pesos. Mayorga argued

75 AGN, *Correspondencia de Virreyes*, vol. 129, exp. 1317, fs. 181–283.

76 AGN, *Marina*, vol. 12, fs. 144–149.

that this effort constituted "an increase never before seen in shipments of silver on account of the royal treasury" and he added that this had been possible in part because of his success in raising a combination of forced and voluntary loans from all sectors of the population of the viceroyalty.

Although the transfer of silver was the most valuable contribution of New Spain to the war waged in the Caribbean against Great Britain, other important contributions included food provisions for the troops and other war supplies. Large amounts of gunpowder from the royal powder factory in Mexico City were sent to military forces at Havana, New Orleans, Campeche, Tabasco, and El Guarico. Other important war supplies sent from Veracruz were copper sheets for ship repairs and cargos of lead. Food provisions sent from Mexico included flour, dried vegetables, and ham. The amount of flour (from the region of Atlixco/Puebla) was considerable, totaling 3,983,400 pounds sent to Havana between 1779 and 1783.[77] On the other hand, it is also important to note that even larger quantities of supplies (particularly flour) came from the United States, as Philadelphia shippers plied their wares most actively and were paid in return with Mexican silver.[78]

The provisions sent out from Mexican ports to Cuba were destined not only for the sustenance of the Armada and for the garrisons at Havana but also to supply the several thousand troops operating out of Mobile and Pensacola which successfully carried out the reconquest of Florida and reinforcement of Spanish garrisons in New Orleans. It is interesting to note that a considerable portion of the soldiers and sailors who participated in the diverse battle campaigns in Florida and Louisiana were Mexican: in 1780 some 2,000 seamen were sent from Veracruz to reinforce the naval squadrons at Havana, and in 1782, 3,000 men of the Crown Regiment from Mexico City and 1,000 troops of the Puebla Regiment were incorporated into the infantry in Cuba, Louisiana, and Florida. Finally, hundreds of Mexican convicts were sent out each year to fulfill their sentences, doing forced labor in Cuban shipyards and fortresses.[79]

77 M. Glascock, "New Spain and the War," pp. 265–273, provides detailed lists of provisions sent year by year.

78 Linda Salvucci has written extensively on this subject: see, for example, "Atlantic Interesections: Early American Commerce and the Rise of the Spanish West Indies (Cuba), *Business History Review*, 79 (Winter 2005), 781–800. For additional analysis of this, see essays in Jacques Barbier and Jacques y Allan J. Kuethe, eds., *The North American Role in the Spanish Imperial Economy, 1760–1819* (Manchester: Manchester University, 1984).

79 For information on the soldiers of the Mexican Crown Regiment, see C. Archer, *El ejército en el México borbónico*; M. Glascock, "New Spain and the War," pp. 265–273, provides annual information on the transfer of seamen from Veracruz. Finally, according to Lucas Alaman, *Historia de México*, vol. 1, Appendix, Document 1, the principal police court of New Spain, the Tribunal de la Acordada, condemned 10,244 men as convicts to do hard labor at military garrisons between 1782 and 1808.

Apart from covering strictly military expenditures, the remittances of Mexican silver to Cuba were also used to cover a set of international debts of the Spanish government of Charles III. For example, a total of three million pesos were paid at Havana between 1781 and 1783 to the agents of the French–Spanish syndicate of bankers headed by Francisco de Cabarrús, who was instrumental in the establishment of the Bank of San Carlos in 1782.[80] This bank was charged with handling the new Spanish internal debt (*vales reales*) of the administration of Carlos III and with service of the external debt, mostly held in Amsterdam. The Mexican silver was used for repayment of loans advanced to the Madrid administration to guarantee the success in issue of government bonds, known as *vales reales*, and for the launching of this first Spanish banking institution.

Last but certainly not least, Mexican funds delivered to Cuba indirectly contributed to the most important military victory of the thirteen colonies against the British in 1781. This little known chapter in the early history of the United States merits more research but can be briefly summarized. As of early 1781 a great French naval flotilla, headed by Admiral Count De Grasse, was stationed in the port of Cap François in Saint Domingue (Haiti) but needed one million silver pesos from their Spanish allies. The money was to be used for sailors' pay but more importantly to pay the thousands of French troops, led by Count Rochambeau, who were already heading with American forces under George Washington to blockade Cornwallis in the Chesapeake. The viceroy at Mexico, Martín de Mayorga, received orders to send the silver at all speed. On July 11, hundreds of bags of silver were loaded on mules and wagons and "moved from the capital to Veracruz by forced marches to be loaded on two warships from Havana."[81] The treasure ships traveled to Havana where they were instructed to rendezvous with the French naval forces under De Grasse off the coast of Matanzas, at which point the treasure was transshipped on August 17. The French Armada then immediately headed north and on August 31 arrived in Chesapeake Bay and successfully cut off Cornwallis from a sea exit. In this way, Mexican silver contributed to the decisive surrender of the British army at Yorktown and the victory of the American and French land forces under generals Washington and Rochambeau.

In summary, during the war years of 1779–1783 the fiscal contributions of New Spain proved to be of strategic importance for imperial policy for a combination of military and financial reasons. Our study indicates that the administration of Carlos III was able to meet rising expenditures in the 1780s without risking bankruptcy in large part because of the remittances

80 This operation is reviewed in detail in Pedro Tedde "Los negocios de Cabarrus con la Real Hacienda, 1780–1783," *Revista de Historia Económica*, 3 (1987), 527–551.

81 M. Glascock, "New Spain and the War," p. 187.

of Mexican silver. This suggests that it is necessary to revise the hypotheses of researchers such as historian Pedro Tedde who has argued that the Spanish financial success in the 1780s (in striking contrast to the financial failure of its ally France) was due to the ability of the government of Charles III in covering steeply rising wartime expenditures by intelligent handling of the debt policy of the Spanish monarchy.[82] Our analysis, however, indicates that such an argument – focusing almost exclusively on the metropolis – tends to leave the contributions of colonial Mexico largely out of the picture and therefore makes it virtually impossible to understand the complex course of imperial finance. The fact is that the bulk of the war expenses in the Caribbean and North America were not covered with funds from Spain, but by Mexican silver.

Both during the war and after the conclusion of hostilities, the remittances of silver – raised by taxes and loans in Spanish America – proved to be essential pillars of the fiscal and debt policies of the administration of Charles III as well as of his son Charles IV, who became monarch in 1789. In the last years of the eighteenth century, however, as war became an almost permanent state of affair, large military deficits became a characteristic feature of royal finance. The Bourbon monarchy therefore required more and more money to pay army and navy as well as to cover service on the ballooning public debt. As a result, the fiscal and financial demands of the metropolis upon the Spanish American colonies and, in particular, upon Mexico increased dramatically. In the chapters that follow, we focus, first, on the analysis of the colonial tax system that provided the greatest volume of revenues for the empire and, secondly, on the increasing number and complexity of colonial loans for the metropolitan government.

82 P. Tedde, *Política financiera y política comercial*, pp. 139–217.

2

An Imperial Tax State: The Fiscal Rigors of Colonialism

> The colonies of Spain and Portugal only have contributed any revenue towards the defense of the mother country, or the support of her civil government. The taxes which have been levied upon those of... England in particular, have seldom been equal to the expense laid out upon them in time of peace, and never sufficient to defray that which they occasioned in time of war.
>
> Adam Smith, *Wealth of Nations*, IV. 7. 9.9

In the summer of 1763, the British Cabinet, headed by Lord George Grenville, announced the introduction of the first of a series of new taxes in the thirteen British colonies in North America.[1] After signing the Treaty of Paris,[2] the British government had resolved to assure its multiple victories by increasing its standing military forces in North America, a strategy which inevitably implied considerable expenditures.[3] According to Richard Bonney, "the need after 1763 for a permanent military establishment in the American colonies at a likely cost of some £224,000 per annum (civil administration had cost a mere £50,000) meant that new tax revenues had to be found in the colonies to meet the bill."[4] The fiscal innovations were soon confronted with strong protests. The rejection of the Navigation Acts, the Sugar Act, and the Stamp Act by the colonists was one of the major

1 Grenville was First Lord of the Admiralty "and at the time of its passage (Navigation Act of 1763), head of the Ministry in which he occupied the positions of First Lord of the Treasury and Chancellor of the Exchequer." George Louis Beer, *British Colonial Policy, 1754–1765* (New York: Macmillan, 1922), p. 230.

2 The Treaty of Paris was signed on February 10, 1763 between Great Britain, France, Spain, and Portugal.

3 Early in 1763, it became known that it was the intention of the British government to keep an army of 10,000 men in America and that the colonies were expected to contribute to its support. For an overview, see William R. Nester, *The First Global War: Britain, France, and the Fate of North America, 1756–1775* (Westport, Conn.: Praeger, 2000).

4 Richard Bonney "The Struggle for Great Power Status," in R. Bonney, ed., *Economic Systems and State Finance* (Oxford: Oxford University Press/The European Science Foundation, 1995), p. 341.

catalysts of revolution and of the war of independence (1776–1783) by the new United States, according to most standard historical interpretations.

The protests and political conflicts provoked by imperial taxes in the thirteen colonies were not unique. In Spanish America, tax reforms introduced from the 1760s also spurred a series of popular revolts, some of which eventually became major social and political rebellions. In Mexico, a series of localized protests were repressed quickly and bloodily: over 80 men were executed by royal officials in the late 1760s and many hundreds deported or imprisoned and forced to do hard labor for life.[5] In Peru and New Granada, resistance to fiscal reforms translated into massive mobilizations and the formation of informal armies that threatened colonial rule in both viceroyalties during the years 1780–1782. In Peru the repression of these movements led to imprisonment and execution of thousands of peasant Indians, who had risen in arms to follow their leaders Tupac Amaru and Tupac Catari. In New Granada, in contrast, church officials were able to negotiate a settlement with the rebels, known as *comuneros*, avoiding the fall of Bogotá by means of a series of political and fiscal concessions.

Tax revolts in Spanish America, however, did not lead to independence as in the *emerging* United States, and the viceroyalties remained under control of the Spanish monarchy for almost another half century. In this sense, the Spanish empire in the western hemisphere proved surprisingly durable. Clearly, the persistence of the colonial regime implied high fiscal, political, and economic costs for the inhabitants of Mexico, Peru, New Granada, Chile, Buenos Aires, Venezuela, and the other territories under the sway of the Catholic monarchy. The most striking contrast that can be established is that between the fiscal costs covered by the Spanish colonies and the thirteen colonies in British America: already by 1770, colonial Mexico alone provided the vicerregal administration with three times more tax funds than did all thirteen colonies to their British administrations. Historians have reconstructed the tax trends in Spanish America in the eighteenth century but have not yet adequately explained how the Crown was able to extract increasing amounts from their subjects. Fiscal coercion was certainly a necessary factor but not a sufficient one. At the same time, there is no doubt that social elites and corporations, such as the church and merchant guilds, benefited from the stability and prosperity of the colonial administration from which they derived secular economic privileges and control over official appointments. Indeed, whether one looks to the monarchy or to colonial elites, it would appear that the introduction of new taxes, a more rigorous state administration, and the expansion of colonial armies during the second

5 For details on tax revolts and repression in Mexico in the 1760s, see Felipe Castro Gutiérrez, *Nueva ley y nuevo rey: reformas borbónicas y rebelión popular en Nueva España* (Zamora, Mich.: El Colegio de Michoacán, 1996).

half of the eighteenth century contributed to a conservative *revolution in government.*[6]

In short, it is our argument that the durability of the Spanish empire was due, in great measure, to the success of Bourbon reformers in reforging an *imperial tax state*, albeit of a quite complex character. By the decade 1790–1800, the Spanish colonies generated more revenues than any other colonies in the eighteenth-century world. The joint tax income of all colonial administrations in Spanish America at this time can be placed in the range of thirty to thirty-five million pesos a year.[7] This figure was somewhat more than the total ordinary income of the government in metropolitan Spain: adding them together made for a total of close to sixty million silver pesos.[8] As a result, circa 1790, the Spanish imperial state – metropolis plus colonies – produced a sum total of tax income which was equivalent to approximately 70 percent of peacetime revenues of the metropolitan government of Great Britain and also almost 70 percent of the taxes collected annually by the government of France, the largest and richest nation in continental Europe, at the end of the old regime.[9]

Furthermore, as Herbert Klein has demonstrated, the growth rates of tax receipts throughout Spanish America were among the highest in the world between 1760 and 1790.[10] The establishment of new fiscal monopolies, the rise in tax rates, the elimination of most tax farming, and the establishment of a proficient tax-accounting system throughout the vast empire bespoke considerable state dynamism under the administration of Charles III (1759–1788). The introduction of such policies implied a degree of modernization of the state bureaucracy and appear to be comparable, in many regards, to those underscored for other eighteenth-century European nations. Numerous parallels can be found with the studies by historian Patrick O'Brien and John Brewer which have demonstrated that the British state increased its revenues with great rapidity as a result of a combination of tax reforms

6 See D. Brading, *Miners and Merchants*, Chapter 1, titled "Revolution in Government."

7 Our estimates are considerably lower than those proposed in Herbert S. Klein, *The American Finances of the Spanish Empire*, p. 28.

8 The ordinary tax income of the Spanish government in the year 1790 was 516 million reales, approximately 25.8 million silver pesos. (The average for 1785–1790 was 500 million reales per year without including remittances from the colonies.) See data in J. P. Merino, *Las cuentas de la Administración*, pp. 51–54.

9 For French and British tax revenues in 1785, see Eugene White, "France and the Failure to Modernize," in R. Bonney, ed., *Economic Systems*, p. 64. By 1790–1794, British tax income had reached a level of around seventeen million pounds sterling per year, equivalent to more than eighty-five million silver pesos (or dollars). For Spanish revenues, see annual series in J. P. Merino, *Las cuentas de la Administración*. For the Spanish American treasuries the most important source is H. Klein and J. TePaske, *Las cajas reales de la real hacienda* and J. TePaske and Herbert S. Klein, *Royal Treasuries of the Spanish Empire in America, 1580–1825*.

10 H. S. Klein, *The American Finances*, Chapter 2.

and the growth of a more efficient and rigorous administration of thousands of clerks and tax collectors. These fiscal improvements provided the funds for a striking increase in the size and strength of the British Navy and of the armed forces, in general.[11] A similar set of fiscal, administrative, and military reforms were applied by the Spanish crown in the metropolis and extended to all its colonies; but what made this strategy distinctive is that it could have been carried out so systematically by the absolutist regime of Charles III throughout his vast overseas domains, stretching from California to Chile and Cape Horn.

That the Bourbon monarchy of Spain should have been able to reforge a *fiscal military state* on an *imperial scale* and obtain a growing amount of tax revenues from its colonial subjects despite the lack of representative political institutions may seem surprising. Such a capacity to raise taxes in an absolutist regime seems to run counter to the idea – prevalent in much current historical and political science literature – that representative governments are the best at raising taxes, as well as in contracting public debt.[12] Much has been made of the fact that some of the greatest absolutist monarchies – such as that of France, particularly in the eighteenth century – faced severe problems in expanding tax revenues on a sustained basis.[13] Actually, the same problems besieged the Bourbon monarchy inside Spain itself, since attempts from the 1730s to modernize the tax regime in the metropolis met with rather limited success.[14] However, history offers many examples of authoritarian regimes – whether imperial or not – that were able to extract great amounts of monies from their subjects.

Recent historical research has demonstrated, in fact, that the implementation of Bourbon tax reforms was more effective in the Spanish American colonies than in the metropolis.[15] Coercion was an indispensable tool to increase extraction of monies from colonial subjects, but other instruments were also used to improve collection and diversify tax resources. Bourbon administrative reform proved fundamental in this regard as an empire-wide campaign was launched to increase the number, professionalism, and efficiency of fiscal bureaucrats. The detailed studies by Luis Jáuregui and Linda

11 P. K. O'Brien, "The Political Economy of British Taxation, 1600–1815," *Economic History Review*, 2nd series, 41 (1988), 1–32 and John Brewer, *The Sinews of Power*, Chapters 1 and 2.

12 The classic statement is Philip T. Hoffman and Kathryn Norberg, eds., *Fiscal Crises, Liberty and Representative Government, 1450–1789* (Stanford: Stanford University Press, 1994). More recent is D. Stasavage, *Public Debt*.

13 For an overview of debates, see R. Bonney, "Towards the Comparative Fiscal History," in L. Prados, ed., *Exceptionalism and Industrialisation*, pp. 191–215.

14 R. Pieper demonstrates the limitations of tax reform in metropolitan Spain in the eighteenth century. See Renate Pieper, *La Real Hacienda bajo Fernando VII y Carlos III, 1753–1788* (Madrid: Instituto de Estudios Fiscales, 1992).

15 The fundamental reference work is H. S. Klein, *The American Finances*.

Arnold, among others, illustrate the increasingly professional character of the colonial fiscal administration – branch by branch – transforming it into a complex and highly structured state apparatus.

But to collect more taxes without generating major protests, it was not enough to have a more professional and more rigorous bureaucracy. As we have already mentioned, in the viceroyalties of Peru and New Granada, royal officials initially provoked extreme reactions by tens of thousands of irate, mostly poor taxpayers, although eventually the new taxes were put in place. In New Spain, on the other hand, royal functionaries were more careful in dealing with the privileged corporations that characterized the colonial *ancien regime*. They negotiated specific terms of fiscal innovations with the great miners and merchants as well as the church – and after 1770 managed to avoid major conflicts with the artisan guilds and the Indian peasant communities (known as *repûblicas de indios*). Historian Alejandra Irigoin has argued in this regard: "In a political system in which the underlying nature of the relationship between the crown and its subjects was understood to be one of consensus, negotiation was a necessary and continuous process."[16] Nonetheless, negotiation was also accompanied by coercion and rigor as applied by the Bourbon colonial administrations to all taxpayers, whether Indian peasants or wealthy silver miners.

From a geopolitical perspective, it is clear that the colonial fiscal regime had a differential impact in the various regions of Spanish America, as we have already suggested in our analysis of tax transfers: for example, the silver-rich colonies tended to subsidize other colonies that benefited from the considerable transfers of funds. But overall, the fiscal statistics suggest a general rise of government income as a result of the introduction of new taxes and fiscal monopolies in all the viceroyalties, New Spain, Peru, New Granada, and the Río de la Plata, as well as in the captaincy generals of Chile, Venezuela, Guatemala, and Cuba, particularly during the reign of Charles III.

Tax Reforms and the Construction of an Imperial Tax State

The historical reconstruction of royal income in the different regions of colonial Spanish America has advanced leaps and bounds in the last two decades. The statistical sources collected by Herbert Klein and John TePaske and other historians provide basic guidelines. The detailed series of tax receipts in almost one hundred royal treasuries in Spanish America demonstrate a rising trend from mid-eighteenth century onward. In the early 1780s, there was a temporary drop in tax income in much of the empire as a result of

16 Alejandra Irigoin, "Bargaining for Absolutism: A Spanish Path to Nation State and Empire Building," forthcoming in the *Hispanic American Historical Review*.

agrarian and demographic crises and popular revolts, but from the later part of that decade, a general recovery of receipts can be identified, with the result that the 1790s were witness to the age of greatest fiscal revenues in the history of Spanish America.[17]

In terms of ordinary income, there were vast differences from one colony to another. Further research is necessary to be able to have a detailed evaluation of the fiscal accounts of each of the many treasuries of the Spanish empire, but general estimates can be offered that suggest some problems of scale. Three viceroyalties led the way: circa 1790, colonial Mexico produced between 18 and 20 million pesos annually in *ordinary* revenues; New Granada, approximately 3 million pesos; Peru and upper Peru together more than 6 million pesos. The other Spanish American colonies produced somewhat lesser sums: Cuba, close to 2 million pesos; Venezuela, between 1.5 and 1.8 million pesos; Guatemala and Chile each with over 300,000 pesos; and the viceroyalty of the Rio de la Plata with a regional tax collection of perhaps one million pesos.[18]

The most successful case of fiscal reform was unquestionably that of New Spain which experienced the greatest increase of tax income. The question is how and why this was so. As already established in Chapter 1, colonial Mexico produced such large revenues that it could export a great portion to cover the administrative and military costs of empire in the greater Caribbean as well to Spain itself, in the second half of the eighteenth century. According to Herbert Klein, by 1800, residents in Bourbon Mexico paid

17 This is the conclusion of H. S. Klein, *The American Finances*, Chapter 1. Much of the data can be found in an Excell format in H. Klein and J. TePaske, *Las cajas reales de la real hacienda*, which can be consulted in the Web site at El Colegio de México, "Estadísticas Históricas de México." There are numerous accounting problems in this data (particularly after 1787), and it is therefore obligatory to confront with many other primary sources in the Spanish and Spanish American archives.

18 Our specific source for government income in New Spain in the 1790s is from *Memoria instructive del estado comparativo de los productos de la Real Hacienda* (México, 1813), Biblioteca Nacional (Mexico), ms. 1282; for a summary, see Table 2.1. On Peru, see H. S. Klein, *The American Finances*, Chapters 3 and 4. On New Granada, see Jaime U. Jaramillo, Adolfo R. Meisel, and Miguel M. Urrutia, "Continuities and Discontinuities in the Fiscal and Monetary Institutions of New Granada, 1783–1850," in M. Bordo and R. Cortes Conde, eds., *Transferring Wealth and Power*, pp. 414–424 but compare with Alvaro Jara and John J. TePaske, "El virreinato de Nueva Granada: la caja central de Santa Fé de Bogotá, ingresos y egresos, 1700–1808," ms., Universidad de Chile, 1994. On Cuba, see R. de la Sagra, *Historia económico-política y estadística*, p. 291 and Nadia Fernández de Pinedo Echevarría, *Comercio exterior y fiscalidad (1794–1860)* (Bilbao, Spain: Universidad de País Vasco, 2002), p. 172. On Central America, Miles Wortman "Rentas públicas y tendencias económicas en Centroamérica, 1787–1819," *Hispanic American Historical Review*, 55, 2 (May 1975), 251–286. On the viceroyalty of the Río de la Plata, see H. Klein, "Structure and Profitability of Royal Finance in the Viceroyalty of the Río de la Plata in 1790," *Hispanic American Historical Review*, 54 (August 1973), 440–469 and the critique by Samuel Amaral, "Public Expenditure Financing in the Colonial Treasury: An Analysis of the Real Caja de Buenos Aires Accounts, 1789–1791," *Hispanic American Historical Review* 64 (May 1984), 287–295.

70 percent more taxes per capita than Spaniards in the metropolis.[19] While this is evidently an estimate, it would appear to be pretty much on the mark, as we shall see. There is no doubt that Mexican taxpayers were making a striking contribution to the imperial administration.

If we extend the comparisons further, the high levels of fiscal pressure in New Spain are confirmed. By 1790, colonial Mexicans were paying a yearly average of 3.6 pesos (3.6 dollars) per capita in taxes to the royal government, which was more than paid by the average taxpayer in absolutist Spain (approximately 2.5 pesos per annum) or in pre-Revolutionary France (3.2 pesos per capita).[20] On the other hand, Mexicans paid less than taxpayers in Great Britain who provided their government with the equivalent of 9.5 pesos per capita, but this was in the richest nation of Europe and that with the highest tax rates in the late-eighteenth-century world.[21]

The Bourbon fiscal regime was certainly rigorous, considering the poverty of the majority of the population of New Spain, but also diverse. To begin with, it is important to note that the colonial tax system was quite broadly based: taxes on silver directly produced close to one-quarter of total revenues, while the remaining three-quarters came from a fairly wide range of exactions, of which sales taxes, Indian tribute, and the receipts from state produced monopoly goods were most important. For comparative purposes, one possibility would be to calculate tax payments in relation to average, individual income. According to Richard Salvucci, a review of the existing historical estimates indicates that two-thirds of Mexican families (mostly peasants) received no more than sixty pesos in income at the end of the eighteenth century.[22] If we calculate that each average working family had four members, we can estimate that their tax burden may have been as high as eight pesos per year.[23] This implies that they would have to contribute

19 Hebert S. Klein, "La economía de la Nueva España, 1680–1809: Un análisis a partir de las cajas reales," *Historia Mexicana*, xxxiv, 4 [136] (1985), 598.

20 According to the fiscal data in J. P. Merino, *Las cuentas de la Administración*, by 1790 the ordinary revenues of the Spanish government were averaging 520 million reales (26 million silver pesos), which, divided by a population estimated at 10.2 million (Floridablanca Census of 1787) gives us a figure of 2.5 pesos per capita per year. On the other hand, in Mexico the ordinary income of the colonial administration was close to 20 million pesos per year, which divided by a population of approximately 5.5 million gives us a figure of 3.6 pesos per capita per annum, 69% more than the Spanish figure.

21 The data for France and Britain is in current prices of 1790. See Peter Mathias and Patrick O'Brien, "Taxation in Britain and France, 1715–1810. A Comparison of the Social and Economic Incidence of Taxes Collected for the Central Governments," *Journal of European Economic History*, 5, 3 (Winter 1976), 611. The silver peso was worth between 5.6 and 6.0 French *livres*. However, an accurate comparison would require comparison of real per capita income in each country as well.

22 R. Salvucci, "Mexican National Income, 1800–1840," 220.

23 We here use an estimate of 2 pesos taxes paid per capita, a lower figure than the 3.6 pesos per capita (which is the result of dividing total fiscal income by total population) for several reasons. In the first

to the state close to 15 percent of their extremely limited income, a high level for an *ancien regime* society.[24]

What were the reasons for extraordinary efficiency of the tax machinery in New Spain in terms of extraction capacity? To answer this question it is necessary to turn attention first to the overall fiscal strategy and secondly to the precise nature of tax reforms. This can help us understand how Bourbon reformers extracted money from all sectors of colonial society, both rich and poor.

Bourbon Fiscal Strategies in the Americas: Reforms and Varying Degrees of Resistance

Despite the changes that were introduced in the second half of the eighteenth century, the colonial tax structure in Spanish America was not a modern fiscal system, for it retained many typical features of secular ancien regime tax structures. It was modeled in part on the old fiscal regime of Castile but also had pronounced differences as is demonstrated by the fact that there existed a number of direct taxes that were not applied in the metropolis, in particular Indian tribute and taxes on silver mining. Generally speaking, the tax system in the Americas was oriented toward revenue-raising, since the colonial administrations were not as inclined as the government in the metropolis to offer much flexibility with regard to the interests of tax-paying groups. It is true, of course, that there were some significant exemptions for privileged groups (landowners, churchmen, military officers), which might suggest that the fiscal system was regressive. Nonetheless, a number of taxes, such as those on silver mining, were not regressive – a fact which suggests that the interpretation of the entire range of taxes should be analyzed with attention to nuance. Fiscal administration was also a matter of political negotiations between the state and diverse social corporations, as can be also observed in the case of the Indian communities that also received certain fiscal exemptions.

From the mid-eighteenth century, Bourbon reforms made for a more centralized and efficient tax machine throughout Spanish America. The basic model was that established by royal envoy, José de Gálvez, during his mission in New Spain (1765–1771). His vigorous reform campaign consisted in the introduction of a complex set of administrative, accounting,

place, it is extremely difficult to calculate average tax payments because it is necessary to differentiate between peasants of Indian towns (repúblicas de indios) who paid tribute but were exempt from the *alcabalas* and other workers who did not benefit from exemptions. Moreover, any calculation should eliminate silver taxes which did not directly affect workers.

24 According to Brewer, in Great Britain, the most advanced economy (and the most heavily taxed) of the eighteenth century, "the share of per capita income appropriated as taxes reached 23% in 1783 . . . almost twice the comparable French figures. . . ." J. Brewer, *The Sinews of Power*, p. 91.

and tax instruments aimed at increasing revenues. Gálvez also proceeded to eliminate most tax farming in the viceroyalty, particularly that exercised by the powerful Mexico City Merchant Guild, which had become accustomed to administrating extremely profitable contracts for the collection of sales taxes (*alcabalas*) throughout the viceroyalty. The result of greater state control was to generate a great increase in the revenues generated by these indirect taxes, which were collected in every rural and urban market in the viceroyalty.

At the same time, Gálvez and a generation of high-level functionaries of the Spanish monarchy pressed for the establishment of a larger, more hierarchical, and professional fiscal administration.[25] This was not a unique trend. As John Brewer has demonstrated in the case of eighteenth-century Britain, the activity of thousands of well-trained clerks was key in improving state administration.[26] In the case of Spanish America this is also verified by the high quality of the Bourbon accounting records of taxes and expenditures from 1760 onward.[27] The improvement was visible in the records of the majority of the regional colonial treasuries and the principal branches of the royal tax administration, including the state monopolies and the royal mints. But it should be noted that since the colonial regime was absolutist and there were no local legislatures, there was little publicity given to the tax records. In fact, the summaries of the revenues of the colony were normally known only by the viceroy and his closest advisers, as well as by the Spanish Cabinet. The original documents were kept in the government archives in each colony, and copies of most of the documentation were remitted annually in warships to Cádiz and Seville.[28]

Another innovation of the Bourbon was the reinforcement and modernization of fiscal monopolies.[29] The production and sale of key commodities tobacco, powder, and mercury was now thoroughly controlled by the royal administration. This was accomplished by the transformation of the old monopolies into large and relatively efficient state companies, as we shall

25 L. A. Jáuregui, *La Real Hacienda de Nueva España* and L. Arnold, *Burocracia y burócratas en México, 1742–1835* provide the essential analysis and description of the Bourbon fiscal bureaucracy.

26 J. Brewer, *The Sinews of Power*, particularly Chapter 3.

27 Scores of historians who have worked in the archives of Bourbon Mexico and Spain attest to the high quality and detail of the colonial fiscal accounts. For detailed observations, see the introduction to J. TePaske and H. S. Klein, *Royal Treasuries of the Spanish Empire*.

28 The enormous volume of documents has proved invaluable for scores of contemporary historians. The richest sources are to be found in the Archivo General de Indias in Seville and in the Archivo General de la Nación in Mexico, but there are also major repositories in all the capitals of the Spanish American nations.

29 A thorough analysis of the administrative innovations in the fiscal regime of New Spain can be found in L. A. Jáuregui, *La Real Hacienda de Nueva España*.

have occasion to comment in greater detail in pages following. At the same, an additional revenue source, state lotteries, was introduced in the Spanish American colonies, following in the steps of the ancient lottery of the Kingdom of Naples, where Charles III had been monarch previous to assuming the Spanish throne.[30]

The Gálvez tax reforms as applied in New Spain were extended to the rest of the Spanish American empire and the Phillipines in the 1770s with considerable speed and homogeneity. Other *visitor-generals* (royal inspectors with great powers) were sent from Madrid to Peru, New Granada, and other parts of the Spanish American empire with the same end. However, opposition to tax reforms in the diverse colonies varied notably. In colonial Mexico, for example, the Visitor-General Gálvez responded to initial tax protests by summary executions of almost a hundred workers in the late 1760s and the imprisonment of many more; afterward, there were few protests.

Royal functionaries found greatest resistance in the Andes. The most extensive and violent opposition in the early 1780s to the tax reforms took place in two viceroyalties, New Granada and Peru. According to numerous historians, the catalyst of rebellion in 1780 and 1781 in many towns and cities in the valleys and mountains of southern Peru and, later, in upper Peru (modern-day Bolivia), were "the fiscal reforms initiated by the Visitor-General, José Antonio de Areche and implemented in the viceroyalty from 1777 onwards."[31] The popular disturbances that broke out in early 1780 in Arequipa, Huaraz, Cerro de Pasco, La Paz, and Cochabamba were the prelude to full-scale social rebellions headed by Indian nobles Tupac Amaru and Tupac Catari. Soon, tens of thousands of inhabitants of the Peruvian sierra – rich and poor – were engaged in a revolution which devolved in a regional civil war. The internecine struggle among the leaders of rival Indian lineages contributed to the final defeat of the rebels by Spanish forces. The repression was fierce as thousands were persecuted and executed.

Although much traditional historiography has tended to focus attention on the great Peruvian revolts of 1780 and 1781, more recently researchers have argued that there were many important antecedents that demonstrate

30 The Real Lotería de la Nueva España began operations in 1771 and was used to obtain funds for the government as well as to finance poorhouses, including the Hospicio de Pobres de la ciudad de México. Subsequently, lotteries were established in the late eighteenth century in Peru, Chile, and Cuba.

31 David Cahil "Taxonomy of a Colonial "riot": The Arequipa Disturbances of 1780," in John Fisher, Allan J. Kuethe, and Anthony Mcfarlane, eds., *Reform and Insurrection in Bourbon New Granada and Peru* (Baton Rouge: Louisiana State University Press, 1990), p. 257.

the resistance to tax reforms, long before the arrival of Areche to Peru. The magnificent book by Scarlet O'Phelan Godoy on the successive eighteenth-century rebellions in the viceroyalty of Peru clearly demonstrates the long-standing opposition of great swaths of colonial Andean society to fiscal innovations that negatively affected local trade and also weighed heavily on peasant towns.[32]

Almost at the same time as the Peruvian rebellions were being bloodily dissolved, in the viceroyalty New Granada, a revolution broke out that also was spurred by rejection of the Bourbon tax reforms. Colonial elites allied with popular sectors and organized a rebel army in central regions of the viceroyalty that marched by stages to the capital to protest the increase in sales taxes, the imposition of new duties on alcoholic beverages (*aguardiente*), and the imposition of the tobacco monopoly. The Visitor-General Juan Francisco Gutierrez de Piñeres was forced to flee from Bogotá to the coastal port of Cartagena. Eventually, the rebels (known as *comuneros*) put down their arms in exchange for a wide range of concessions, including temporary reductions in certain taxes.[33]

In colonial Mexico, as we have noted, initial social protests in the late 1760s were rapidly crushed and, subsequently, there is little documentary evidence of tax rebellions before 1810. Why this was so is a major question which historians have not yet resolved since the intensity and breadth of the Bourbon fiscal offensive in colonial Mexico was unmatched. There was undoubtedly much disguised local resistance to hikes in taxes as is confirmed by archival research on the numerous protests to be found in the *alcabala* (sales tax) documentation, every time rates were raised or the base extended.[34] But it is also true that there is scarce testimony of full-blown tax riots in the late colonial period in the viceroyalty. Indeed, the lack of systematic opposition to the tax reforms surely contributed to the extraordinary large volume of receipts from virtually all taxes and state monopolies. The result was that New Spain became the tax jewel of the Spanish empire during its final decades, and more specifically between 1780 and 1810.

32 The resentment was directed at the *mita*, the traditional form of forced labor recruitment imposed by the Spanish regime in the Andes, against hikes in the rates of *alcabalas*, *aguardiente* (alcoholic beverages), and tobacco as well as opposition to reforms of the *repartimiento* system of trade. Details on the many rebellions of the eighteenth century can be found in Scarlet O'Phelan Godoy, *Un siglo de rebeliones anticoloniales. Perú y Bolivia, 1700–1783* (Cuzco, Peru: Centro Bartolomé de las Casas, 1988). An excellent analytical discussion can be found in Juan Garavaglia and Juan Marchena, *América Latina: De los orígenes a la independencia*, vol. 2 (Barcelona: Crítica, 2005), pp. 132–143.

33 The standard study is John L. Phelan, *The People and the King: the Comunero Revolution in Colombia, 1781* (Madison: University of Wisconsin Press, 1978). For more recent contributions, see essays in J. Fisher, A. J. Kuether, and A. Mcfarlane, eds., *Reform and Insurrection*.

34 I thank Richard Salvucci for drawing my attention to this point.

Table 2.1. *Net Income of Royal Treasuries of New Spain, Consolidated Accounts, 1795–1799 (annual average income in silver pesos)*

Fiscal Branches	Gross Income	Collection Costs	Net Income
Mining taxes	4,512,191	524,096	3,988,095
Trade taxes	4,174,124	444,086	3,730,038
Indian tribute	1,247,861	87,910	1,159,951
State monopolies	8,852,943[a]	4,033,311[a]	4,819,632
Church fiscal transfers	6,88,186	29,932	658,254
Administrative income	94,476	2,861	91,615
Other income	233,778	8,939	224,839
Forced loans	652,625	300	652,325
Sum	20,456,184	5,131,435	15,324,749

[a] The costs registered are those involved in production costs of tobacco and powder. In the case of the state tobacco monopoly, collection costs include the payment of sums to tobacco leaf producers, to workers in the state factory and for other costs of production.

Source: Memoria instructiva y documentada del estado comparativo de los productos de la Real Hacienda desde el año de 1809 (México, 1813), ms. 1282, Biblioteca Nacional (México).

The Tax Structure of New Spain: Microcosm of the Spanish Empire in the Americas

The tax structure in colonial Mexico was made up of a combination of direct and indirect taxes. As can be seen from Table 2.1, there were four main sources of fiscal income: taxes on trade, taxes on mining, Indian tribute, and state monopolies. Close to a quarter of the royal receipts came from sales taxes (*alcabalas*) and a series of port taxes (*avería* and *almojarifazgo*), which had long been applied by the monarchy in both Spain and in the colonies.[35] Equally important were the fiscal monopolies, which also had their origins in Spain, such as the mercury, tobacco, and powder monopolies as well as that of playing cards. On the other hand, the direct taxes applied in the colonies had no counterpart in the metropolis, the most notable being the taxes on silver mining (which provided around 25 percent of net fiscal receipts) and the Indian tribute tax (which contributed somewhat less than 10 percent).

Another distinguishing feature of the tax regime in colonial Mexico was that it was more homogeneous than tax systems in the different regions of Spain where fiscal diversity was common, particularly in Navarre, the Basque country, and Aragon. In the viceroyalty of New Spain the same set of taxes were levied throughout the realm and accounting methods tended

35 For a complete list of all tax branches, see H. S. Klein, *The American Finances*, Appendix 3. For Mexico, see Archivo General de la Nación, *Caja Matriz, Libro Común de la Tesorería de Ejército y Real Hacienda año de 1810*.

to be more consistent, particularly after the mid-eighteenth century when the farming out of taxes was eliminated. Nonetheless, there were marked differences in the productivity of diverse taxes according to each region of Mexico. Hence, the only adequate method to understand the functioning of the colonial fiscal system is to review the productivity of different tax branches overall and then to do so on a regional basis.

One important propertied sector that had to pay direct taxes was that composed by the owners of silver mines. The tax rates on silver production had fallen from 20 percent in the sixteenth century to 10 percent in the eighteenth century, but still represented a most significant portion of royal revenues in Mexico. While the *direct* tax on mine production (known as the mining *diezmo*) was the single most important item among the varied list of exactions that fell upon silver, a close runner-up was income derived from seignoriage, as shown by the data on minting revenues *(amonedación de oro y plata)*. (See Table 2.1.) Additional income was derived from the sale of the products of the state-owned mercury monopoly, an essential ingredient for colonial silver refining processes, but the bulk of the income thus generated could not be disposed of by the local treasuries: it was shipped off to Spain to buy more mercury. The net annual revenues obtained from mining taxes – directly and indirectly – approached four million pesos in the 1790s, approximately a fourth of total *net income* of the viceregal government.[36] (See Figure 2.1.)

The mining guild fought for some reductions and exemptions, but these were established only in some regions. Most significant was the struggle by the corporation of silver miners (known as the *Tribunal de Minería*) to obtain preferential prices on mercury, which was a state monopoly. Regular shipments of mercury from the Almaden mines of Spain were indispensable for an efficient process of silver refining. Throughout the eighteenth century, silver miners fought to obtain more and cheaper supplies and in this they were largely successful: as economic historian Rafael Dobado has demonstrated, the extraordinary boom in silver mining in Bourbon Mexico was closely correlated with the rise in imports of mercury supplies.[37]

Richard Garner has demonstrated that the increase of silver production – as measured by the data of the Mexico City mint – approached 1.3 percent a year during the eighteenth century, a figure superior to all other economic

36 These calculations are higher than the relevant percentages offered by Klein (1995), but it should be noted that Klein did not use consolidated accounts nor did he discount costs of fiscal administration nor does he take into account seignorage of the mint. Our source is *Memoria instructive del estado comparativo de los productos de la Real Hacienda* (México, 1813), Biblioteca Nacional (Mexico), ms. 1282.

37 Rafael Dobado González, "El trabajo en las minas de Almadén, 1750–1855," Ph.D. thesis, Universidad Complutense de Madrid, 1989, 2 vols.

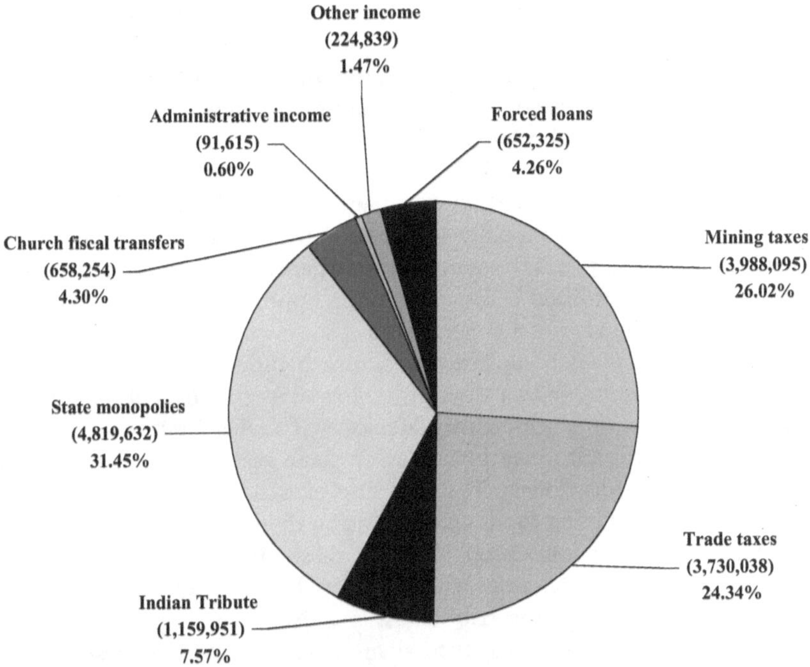

Figure 2.1. Net Income of Royal Treasuries of New Spain, 1795–1799.
Source: Memoria instructiva y documentada del estado comparativo de los productos de la Real Hacienda desde el año de 1809 [Mexico, 1813], Nacional Library of Mexico, ms. 1282.

sectors.[38] This has led other authors to speak of the phenomenon of "mining-led growth" in colonial Mexico. The real and relative increase was notable: "By 1800, New Spain's production represented almost two thirds of world silver output."[39] But silver mining was not simply an extractive sector: it was the most modern sector of the colonial economy in terms of technology, finance, and labor relations, production in the mines being exclusively based on free labor. Moreover, it stimulated innumerable backward linkages to a notable variety of manufacturing and agricultural enterprises.[40] In any case, we have already remarked on the fact that there was certainly a close

38 Richard Garner and S. E. Stefanou, *Economic Growth and Change in Bourbon Mexico* (Gainesville: University of Florida Press, 1993), p. 109.

39 Rafael Dobado, "El crecimiento guiado por la minería, el papel del Estado y el costo económico de la independencia," unpublished paper presented at El Colegio de Mexico, May 9, 2006.

40 The classic study on this subject is Carlos Sempat Assadourian, *El sistema de la economía colonial: el mercado interior. Regiones y espacio económico* (Mexico: Grijalbo, 1983).

correlation between the production of silver and tax receipts and remittances during the eighteenth century.[41]

The most archaic and "sui generis" of the colonial fiscal exactions was the tribute tax (*tributo*) levied on all heads of households in the Indian towns (the so-called Indian republics or communities).[42] The rate was slightly more than two silver pesos (two dollars) to be paid yearly by every *tributario*, being charged uniformly on Indian peasants who lived and cultivated their own land and only occasionally on peasants who worked on haciendas or plantations. In the 1790s the annual income generated from this source was slightly over one million pesos, making up approximately 7.6 percent of net income of the viceregal government.

The *tributo* was levied on the heads of each Indian peasant households in each of the 4,400 Indian towns (designated as *repúblicas de indios*) that existed in late-eighteenth-century Mexico.[43] This head tax was generally collected by local authority figures or, in some cases, by the local parish priests or a royal functionary. The governors of each peasant village or town took charge of receiving funds and depositing them in the local communal treasuries (*cajas de communidad*).[44] Part of these monies were later handed over to the royal functionaries who visited each village and town annually to ensure collection of the tribute. As can be seen in Figure 2.2, there was a marked trend upward in total revenues – a fact that bespoke the demographic recovery in most of the century. While the amounts exacted were considerable for a poor peasantry, they remained stable and there were relatively few major protests against this poll tax, perhaps because it was seen as payment for royal protection of Indian townships, local schools, and communal lands. It should be noted that a part of the money deposited in the communal treasuries were used in the second half of the eighteenth century to pay for the many schools set up in peasant villages and towns as well as to cover expenses of town government.[45] In addition, the payment

41 See the Appendix, Table and the correlations based on a methodological proposal communicated to the author by Richard Garner.

42 This tax was originally derived from the tribute paid to the Aztec emperors by all subjects and therefore can be considered to be an "American" tax with no European legacy. For detailed information on the institutional description of each of the taxes, the fundamental source is the multivolume work by the functionaries of the colonial treasury, F. Fonseca and C. de Urrutia, *Historia General de la Real Hacienda*, a work originally written in the late 1780s.

43 See the extraordinary atlas by Dorothy Tanck de Estrada, *Atlas ilustrado de los pueblos de indios: Nueva España, 1800* (Mexico: El Colegio de México, 2005).

44 The fundamental studies are by Dorothy Tanck de Estrada: "Escuelas y cajas de comunidad en Yucatán al final de la colonia," *Historia Mexicana*, xliii, 3 [171] (1994), 401–449 and "Protesta indígena al rey en contra de las cajas de comunidad, 1793–1806. Cultura política en torno a los reglamentos para los pueblos de indios," unpublished paper, 1995.

45 For information on the comunal treasures and schools, see Dorothy Tanck de Estrada, *Pueblos de indios y educación en el México colonial, 1750–1821* (Mexico: El Colegio de México, 1998).

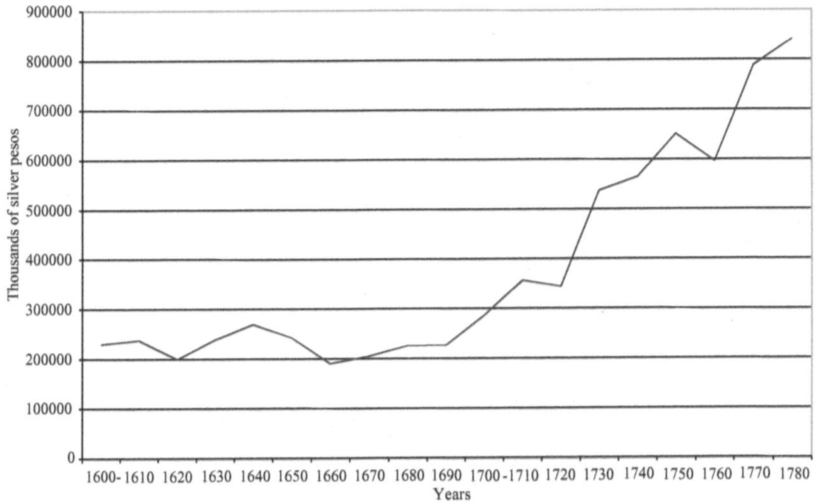

Figure 2.2. Revenue from Indian Tribute in New Spain, 17th and 18th Centuries (average annual income per decade).

Source: Daniel Marino "El afán de reacaudar y la dificultad en reformar. El tributo indígena en la Nueva España tardocolonial," in C. Marichal and D. Marino, eds., *De colonia a nación, Impuestos y política en México, 1750–1860*, Mexico, El Colegio de México, 2001, pp. 76–78.

of tribute was linked to the paternalistic judicial system that had its axis in the General Indian Court, which assisted Indian peasant communities in land disputes, as demonstrated by Woodrow Borah in a magnificient historical study. .[46]

A third branch of income was that derived from taxes on trade, most of which were duties on internal commerce (*alcabalas*) and on native alcoholic beverages (*pulques*), producing 24 percent of net receipts in the 1790s. The *alcabalas* were actually a medieval fiscal instrument of Arabic origin, which was introduced into Spanish America from early in the sixteenth century. These sales taxes were levied in the colonies in almost identical form to counterparts in Spain and France.[47] The entire population of New Spain normally paid the *alcabalas* at all local markets and fairs as well as in urban stores at a rate of 6 percent on the market value of most products sold; but during times of international wars, rates were frequently jacked up. These taxes were popular with royal administrators, largely, because of the large

46 Woodrow Borah, *El Juzgado General de Indios en la Nueva España* (Mexico: Fondo de Cultura Económica, 1985).

47 In Spain, these sales taxes were known as *consumos* but figured under the fiscal category of *rentas provinciales*. For a precise discussion, see Miguel Artola, *La Hacienda del antiguo Régimen*, pp. 336–355.

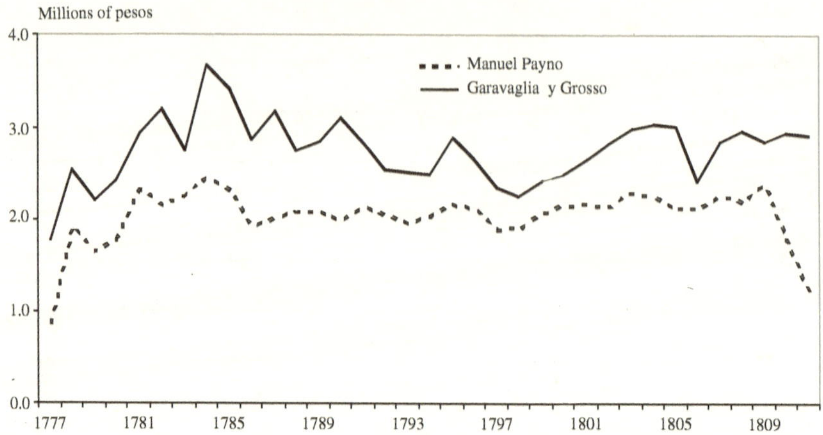

Figure 2.3. Sales Taxes (*Alcabala*) Revenue in New Spain, 1777–1811.
Source: Appendix II, Table I.

volume and relative stability of their yield, although in times of agrarian crises (like the terrible calamity that devastated rural Mexico in 1784/1785) revenues fell drastically. (See Figure 2.3.)

According to the detailed studies of Garavaglia and Grosso, the gross product of these sales taxes increased from the 1760s until the mid 1780s because of growing commerce in countryside and in towns but also as a result of increasing pressure exerted by collectors.[48] A complement to the *alcabalas* was the *pulque* tax, charged on the most popular alcoholic beverage consumed by the Indian and popular sectors. The impact of a severe agrarian crisis such as that of 1785 – which caused an estimated 300,000 deaths – was translated directly into a decline in revenue collection; in fact, after the crisis, pulque tax receipts never recovered previous levels, but rather tended to decline. (See Figure 2.4.)

Another set of indirect contributions were port taxes, paid on warehousing of imported goods and other port services, although these were generally set at low rates and were apparently not considered extortionate. While there existed specific taxes on external trade and such as the *almojarifazgo* (a toll on ships using the harbor), port customs were not of great importance. Merchants who imported goods did not have to pay customs duties in the colonial era, although as in the case of domestic commodities, they were obliged to pay the *alcabala* at rates that ranged from 6 percent

48 On alcabala trends, see Juan Carlos Garavaglia and Juan Carlos Grosso, *Las alcabalas novohispanas, 1776–1821* (Mexico: Archivo General de la Nación, 1987).On pulque collections, see José Jesús Hernández Palomo, *La renta del pulque en Nueva España, 1663–1810* (Sevilla: Escuela de Estudios Hispanoamericanos, 1980).

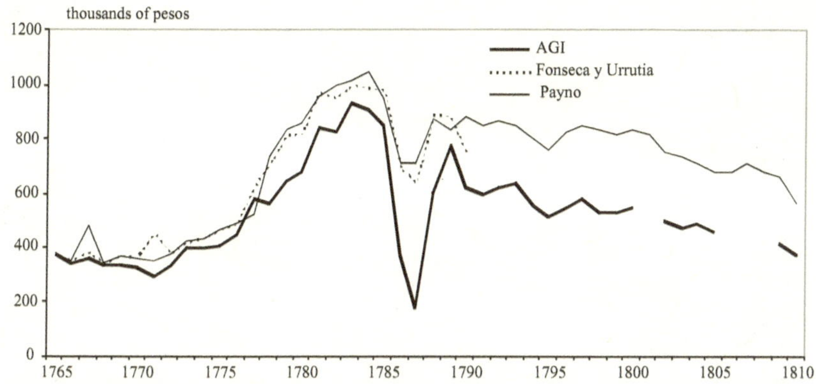

Figure 2.4. Pulque Tax Income in New Spain, 1765–1810.
Source: Appendix II, Table II.2.

in the 1770s, 8 percent in the 1780s, 6 percent in the 1790s, rising subsequently during the wars of independence (1810–1820), to as much as 15 percent.

The highest growth in revenues in late-eighteenth-century New Spain came from various state monopolies, the most important being the tobacco monopoly. Established in New Spain in 1767, it had become the single largest source of public revenues by the end of the century, then providing almost 30 percent of the viceroyalty's net income.[49] Sales of tobacco increased prodigiously in the second half of the century and so did monopoly receipts. The state-owned tobacco factory in Mexico City employed over 8,000 workers by 1800, although this was only a part of the total number of people who depended on the monopoly for their livelihood: these also included some two thousand administrative and commercial employees and several thousand tobacco farmers.[50] However, net income tended to stabilize at around three million pesos a year in the 1790s as a result of the increasing costs of key imported supplies such as paper. (See Figure 2.5.)

The tobacco monopoly was the greatest individual enterprise in New Spain, but it was not autonomous: it maintained close financial, commercial, and productive links to the tobacco monopoly in Cuba, Louisiana, and

49 Also important were the powder and salt monopolies as well as those on playing cards and on cockfights. The state lottery also provided additional income. A detailed description of the different fiscal branches can be found in the various volumes of F. Fonseca and C. Urrutia, *Historia General.*

50 Susan Deans-Smith, *Bureaucrats, Planters and Workers: The Making of the Tobacco Monopoly in Bourbon Mexico* (Austin: University of Texas Press, 1992) is an excellent study of the Mexican state tobacco enterprise in this period.

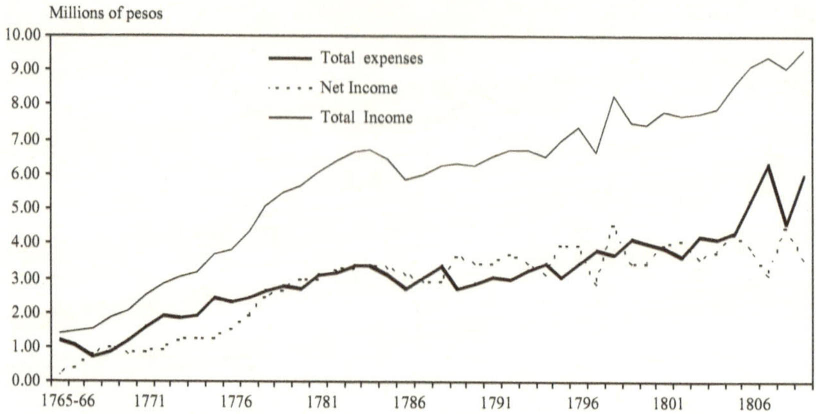

Figure 2.5. Tobacco Monopoly Income and Expenses in New Spain, 1765–1809.
Source: Appendix II, Table III.

Spain.[51] More tenuous were relations with the state tobacco establishments in other colonies of the empire, including Venezuela, Peru, New Granada, Costa Rica, and the Phillipines.[52] In any case, this extended royal firm was a vast and multiregional royal company, perhaps the largest of its kind in the eighteenth-century world.

Other public revenues were obtained from a mosaic of fiscal instruments. For instance, the colonial government received a number of ecclesiastical fiscal transfers, including the *media anata*, *bulas*, and a percentage of the tithes collected from peasants and landlords. These arrangements, dating back to the sixteenth century, bespeak the fact that the Catholic Church was closely linked to the Crown not only ideologically but also in fiscal terms.

In diverse and complementary essays, Herbert Klein has described the fundamental trends of tax income in eighteenth-century colonial Mexico:

51 On relations between the Mexican tobacco monopoly and that of Cuba, see Laura Nater, "El tabaco y las finanzas del imperio español: Nueva España y la metrópoli, 1760–1810," Ph.D. thesis, El Colegio de México, 1998.

52 On the operations of the tobacco monopoly in Venzuela, Peu, and the Phillipines, see Eduardo Arcila Farias, *Historia de un monopolio. El estanco del tabaco en Venezuela (1779–1833)* (Caracas: Universidad Central de Venezuela, Instituto de Estudios Hispanoamericanos, Facultad de Humanidades y Educación, 1977); Catalina Vizcarra and Richard Sicotte, "El control del contrabando en el Perú colonial: el caso del monopolio del tabaco, 1752–1813," in Carlos Contreras and Manuel Glave, eds., *Estado y mercado en la historia del Perú* (Lima: Pontificia Universidad Católica, 2002), pp. 184–211; Josep M. Fradera, *Filipinas, la colonia más peculiar: la hacienda pública en la definición de la política colonial, 1762–1868* (Madrid: CSIC, 1999); Luis Alonso Alvarez, "Los problemas de Hacienda filipina y el estanco del tabaco, siglos xvi-xviii," in Agustín González Enciso and Rafael Torres Sánchez, eds., *Tabaco y economía en el siglo XVIII* (Pamplona, Spain: EUNSA, 1999), pp. 89–112.

tribute tended to move with population, increasing or falling as demographics did. Mining taxes diminished in relative importance because of lowered rates, but were still enormously important.[53] *Alcabalas* and port taxes tended to increase regularly until the 1790s and came to provide approximately 25 percent of total income. Tobacco revenues grew steadily until right down to the wars of independence and also contributed around a quarter of the colonial administration's ordinary revenues. But was there a direct relation between and tax receipts economic growth? Mathematically inclined economic historians raise grave doubts about the possibility of proving this proposal.[54]

For a more nuanced view of tax trends, it is worthwhile taking a brief look at regional revenues in the second half of the eighteenth century. Such a perspective allows us to see that tax revenues reflected some aspects of the varied structure of regional economies. In this regard it is necessary to be cautious rather than deterministic. In order to grasp the difference in dynamics of revenue collection on a regional basis, a summary review of the regional tax evolution can prove instructive: we focus on the royal treasuries at Guadalajara Zacatecas, Mérida (Yucatán), and Veracruz between 1760 and 1810.[55]

In the case of Guadalajara, a predominantly agricultural and ranching zone with a fair number of small silver mines, the latter still produced most state income (54 percent of total) in 1760. In contrast, by 1810, mining taxes represented only 17.6 percent of total receipts. The bulk of receipts now came from taxes on trade, mainly *alcabalas* on agricultural and manufacturing commodities plus duties on *mezcal* (a popular alcoholic beverage), together providing 46 percent of gross royal income of the regional treasuries.[56] (See Table 2.2.) The reasons for the shift from mining taxes to sales taxes can be found in changes in the regional economy. The research of both Eric Van Young and Antonio Ibarra demonstrates that the growth of capital of Guadalajara and secondary cities stimulated an increase in rural

53 For tax trends, see H. Klein, *Las finanzas americanas*, Chapter 5 and C. Marichal, *La Bancarrota del virreinato*, Chapter 2.

54 The arguments of Herbert Klein may be found in *The American Finances of the Spanish Empire*. A very strong logical critique is Mónica Gómez, "El debate sobre el ingreso fiscal y la actividad económica. El caso de la Nueva España en el siglo XVIII," in Carlos Marichal and Daniel Marino, eds., *De colonia a nación: la transición fiscal en México, 1750–1850* (Mexico: El Colegio de México, 2001), pp. 115–134.

55 The tax categories increased in the respective intendancies as follows: in Zacatecas from six main branches in 1760 to fifteen in 1810; in Guadalajara from twelve in 1760 to twenty-five in 1804; in Mérida from eleven in 1760 to twenty-two in 1800.

56 Our estimates are based on fiscal series in J. TePaske and H. Klein, *Ingresos y egresos de la Real Hacienda*. For purpose of obtaining net income, we eliminated the categories of *existencias*, *depósitos*, *otras tesorerías*, and *extraordinario*.

Table 2.2. *Royal Treasury at Guadalajara: Income, 1760, 1790, 1800, and 1804*

	Absolute Values (Pesos)				Percentages			
Tax branches	1760	1790	1800	1804	1760	1790	1800	1804
Mining taxes	142,957	155,721	100,857	160,102	53.7	23.8	15.7	19.3
Sales taxes	22,630	275,583	256,399	382,034	8.5	42.2	40	46
Indian tribute	36,708	61,104	92,311	100,436	13.8	9.4	14.4	12.1
Taxes from eclesiastical resources	27,018	119,201	134,880	132,007	10.2	18.3	21	15.9
Taxes on bureaucrats	5,702	21,874	12,300	9,857	2.1	3.4	1.9	1.2
State monopolies	6,611	17,184	31,066	35,818	2.5	2.6	4.8	4.3
Other fiscal sectors	24,686	2,466	13,523	10,301	9.3	0.4	2.1	1.2
TOTAL INCOME	266,312	653,133	641,336	830,555	100	100	100	100

Source: J. J. TePaske and H. Klein, *Ingresos y egresos de la Real Hacienda de Nueva España*, (Mexico, Instituto Nacional de Antropología e Historia, Colección Fuentes, 1986–88), vol. 1, "Sumario general de carta cuenta de Guadalajara."

production while mining stagnated.[57] As a result, the expansion of rural and urban markets offered excellent opportunities for increased taxation.

In contrast, in a mining region such as Zacatecas, the relative changes in tax revenues were almost imperceptible during the second half of the eighteenth century. In 1760, of nineteen tax categories, those on silver mining produced 83 percent of the total; half a century later, in 1810, there were thirty fiscal branches but mining still contributed 75 percent of gross income. (See Table 2.3.) The continuity in the tax base was also visible in the tax records of the royal treasury of Mérida, Yucatán, where the largest source was taxes on Indian peasant communities. In 1760, Indian tribute produced 43 percent of total receipts while in 1808, the local treasury continued to rely mainly on this source, receiving 35 percent of its income from contributions of the peasant communities.[58] (See Table 2.4.)

A quite different fiscal structure can be observed in the case of Veracruz, a region that had the largest port in the viceroyalty and much comercial agriculture. In 1760, net tax income was 265,000 pesos but by 1810, the total had climbed quite spectacularly to 1.5 millon pesos: much of this was derived from expansion of external trade. Duties on imported goods, known as *alcabalas del mar*, provided 32 percent of total revenues, while harbour duties on ships known as *almojarifazgos* supplied 36 percent of total fiscal receipts.[59] (See Table 2.5.) These figures indicate that the liberalization of commerce impelled by the Bourbon reforms successfully stimulated the expansion of both internal and external trade and thereby provided new sources of tax revenue.

The analysis of regional fiscal trends suggests that royal administrators were well aware of both continuity and change in local economies. When the traditional bases of a regional economy did not change, the old, direct taxes remained the source of most revenues, as can be seen in the case of silver mining in Zacatecas and peasant agriculture in Yucatán. On the other hand, in regions that experienced more rapid economic transformations such as Guadalajara or Veracruz, tax dynamics shifted quickly and indirect taxes came to the fore. In a word, the fiscal officers managed to capture the essential trends of economic expansion without trying to measure or

57 Eric Van Young, *Hacienda and Market in Eighteenth Century Mexico: The Rural Economy of the Guadalajara Region, 1675–1820* (Berkeley: University of California Press, 1981) and Antonio Ibarra, "Mercado urbano y mercado regional en la Guadalajara colonial, 1790–1811," Ph.D. thesis, El Colegio de México, 1995.

58 If we deduce income obtained in Yucatán through the war donation of 1808, the proportion of the Indian tribute in Merida remains the same as in 1760. For details, see D. Tanck de Estrada, "Protesta indígena al rey."

59 Our estimates are based on fiscal series in J. TePaske and H. Klein, *Ingresos y egresos de la Real Hacienda*. We do not include in local Veracruz income the transfers from other treasuries such as that of Mexico which were to be remitted abroad.

Table 2.3. *Royal Treasury at Zacatecas: Income, 1760, 1790, 1800, and 1810*

	Absolute Values (Pesos)				Percentages			
Tax branches	1760	1790	1800	1810	1760	1790	1800	1810
Mining taxes	197,738	340,443	329,930	478,555	82.9	77.9	64.1	75.4
Sales taxes	26,237	41,833	107,134	74,357	11	9.6	20.8	11.7
Indian tribute	7,509	7,754	12,745	24,061	3.15	1.8	2.5	3.8
Taxes from ecclesiastical sources	5,639	5,526	13,541	19,448	2.4	1.3	2.6	3.0
Taxes on bureaucrats	717	1973	2,976	1,030	0.3	0.45	0.6	0.2
State monopolies	793	39,404	45,113	33,698	0.3	9.0	8.8	5.3
Other fiscal sectors		99	3,141	3,626		0.02	0.61	0.57
TOTAL INCOME	238,633	437,032	514,580	634,775	100	100	100	100

Source: J. J. TePaske and H. Klein, *Ingresos y egresos de la Real Hacienda de Nueva España*, Mexico, Instituto Nacional de Antropología e Historia, Colección Fuentes, 1986–88, vol. 2, "Sumario general de carta cuenta de Zacatecas."

Table 2.4. *Royal Treasury at Merida: Income, 1760, 1790, 1800, and 1808*

	Absolute Values (Pesos)				Percentages			
Tax branches	1760	1790	1800	1808	1760	1790	1800	1808
Mining taxes	5,974	8,533	25,002	43,336	4.18	7.80	11.36	14.85
Indian tributes	61,390	65,739	83,102	101,561	42.99	60.07	37.76	34.80
Taxes from ecclesiastic sources	6,172	13,507	27,489	30,209	4.32	12.34	12.49	10.35
Taxes on bureaucrats	15,013	3,923	197	9,802	10.51	3.58	0.09	3.36
State monopolies	2,487	14,234	15,405	29,251	1.74	13.01	7.00	10.02
Other fiscal sectors	51,754	3,509	68,856	77,644	36.24	3.21	31.29	26.61
TOTAL INCOME	142,790	109,445	220,051	291,803	100	100	100	100

Source: J. J. TePaske and H. Klein, *Ingresos y egresos de la Real Hacienda de Nueva España*, Mexico, Instituto Nacional de Antropología e Historia, Colección Fuentes, 1986–88, vol. 1, "Sumario general de carta cuenta de Mérida."

Table 2.5. *Royal Treasury at Veracruz: Income, 1760, 1790, 1800, and 1805*

	Absolute Values (Pesos)				Percentages			
Tax branches	1760	1790	1800	1805	1760	1790	1800	1805
Mining taxes		4,210	6,532			0.21	0.98	
Sales taxes	232,191	1,569,521	490,296	1,389,587	87.50	80.13	73.30	90.94
Indian tribute	8,610	43,647	60,219	50,096	3.24	2.23	9.00	3.28
Taxes from ecclesiastical sources		125,000	705	4,095		6.38	0.11	0.27
Taxes on bureaucrats	2,363	35,966	3,971	11,243	0.89	1.84	0.59	0.74
State monopolies	2,802	87,238	37,044	19,926	1.06	4.45	5.54	1.30
Other fiscal sectors	19,402	93,132	70,128	53,119	7.31	4.75	10.48	3.47
TOTAL INCOME	265,368	1,958,714	668,895	1,528,066	100	100	100	100

Source: J. J. TePaske and H. Klein, *Ingresos y egresos de la Real Hacienda de Nueva España*, Mexico, Instituto Nacional de Antropología e Historia, Colección Fuentes, 1986–88, vol. 2, "Sumario general de carta cuenta de Veracruz."

assess it directly – a near impossibility at that time. An additional aspect that underlines the fiscal sharpness of the royal officials was their emphasis on taxing tobacco and alcohol: this was indicative of an awareness of the positive returns to be obtained from taxing goods for which demand was relatively inelastic, but not compulsory.[60] In any case, the high growth rates of tax revenues throughout the viceroyalty were most visible in the period 1760–1785, being followed later by a slower expansion in the two following decades.

The Fiscal Burden of Colonialism for the Inhabitants of New Spain

Beyond measuring revenue trends over time, it is also important to raise the issue of impact and incidence of taxes, although this is a subject that awaits much future research. In recent years, a few studies have begun to probe into some aspects of the social consequences of tax policies in colonial Mexico, analyzing tax shifting and incidence and also the economic effects of the Bourbon monarchy's efficient but heavy tax machinery.[61] Such analysis can prove of interest for an evaluation of the costs of colonialism for specific social groups, but also sheds light on future debates on what may be termed the *fiscal constitution* of the colonial regime in Spanish America.[62]

In the case of Indian tribute, for example, the burden for Indian peasant families in Mexico was significant since it represented two and a half pesos on a small income (which would be, at best, some twenty to twenty-five pesos a year for a nuclear family).[63] It was also hard on those Indian peasant families which produced little in the way of agricultural or ranching commodities that could be exchanged for money, and particularly hard on those who had no land or were in dire poverty, of which there were many. On the other hand, it is also true that Indian peasant communities were largely exempt from other taxes such as the *alcabalas* on the maize and beans that

60 I am grateful to Richard Salvucci for this and several other observations on the implicit logic of the Spanish fiscal system at this time.

61 See C. Marichal, *La bancarrota del virreinato*, Chapter 2 and C. Marichal and D. Marino, eds., *De colonia a nación*, Chapters 1–3.

62 On the concept of a fiscal constitution in eighteenth century Britain, see R. Bonney, "Revenues" (Chapter 13), in R. Bonney, ed., *Economic Systems*, pp. 431–438 and P. O'Brien, *Fiscal Exceptionalism: Great Britain and Its European Rivals from Civil War to Triumph at Trafalgar and Waterloo*, pp. 13–14 and 19–20.

63 The estimate of 25 pesos would be wage earnings of an Indian who had regular work on a ranching or agricultural "hacienda." For estimates of rural wages and income, see R. Garner and S. E. Stefanou, *Economic Growth and Change in Bourbon Mexico*, pp. 81–84. However, many Indian peasants simply lived off a small piece of their own land, and their income was largely nonmonetary, consisting basically of subsistence food products, mostly maize and beans.

they produced mostly for sustenance but a small percentage of which they regular marketed.[64]

A very different case was that of taxes on silver mining, a tremendously important economic sector. This direct tax of 10 percent on the production of all silver fell directly on the mine owners. It does not appear that there could be much shifting forward of this tax, although some shifting backward was possible insofar as miners might pay less for certain inputs of essential supplies, but this subject has not been studied in depth. In any case, the complaints of miners with respect to rising costs were sufficiently strong from the late 1770s as to force the Crown to reduce various taxes related to mining, including mercury prices (a state monopoly) and *alcabalas* on key supplies for the mining sector such as mules and horses, leather, salt, and powder.

The *alcabalas*, which were the most important of indirect taxes, affected all consumers, rich and poor.[65] The sales taxes fell clearly on the final consumer who bought food or textiles. However, it is hard to evaluate exact incidence because it is necessary to study different types of commodities as well as taxpayers. Since the *alcabalas* were charged on the basic staple goods acquired by a majority of the population (food, textiles, alcohol), it was a clearly regressive tax, although the wealthier sectors paid more *alcabalas* per capita because of greater consumption. It may be calculated that average urban Mexican working families paid in indirect taxes somewhere between 8 and 15 percent of their income, whereas propertied groups generally contributed a marginal percentage of their income on this account.[66]

An important question remains unanswered, namely, was there a clear perception that the taxation had become a greater economic burden than in the past? The impression gained from a review of studies by Klein and Garner is that the multiplication of new taxes and the more rigorous collection resulted in a greater tax burden in colonial Mexico from the time of the reforms of Gálvez. However, this impression must be treated with caution, for there are indications that from 1785 several important sources of

64 Juan Carlos Garavaglia and Juan Carlos Grosso, "Estado borbónico y presión fiscal en la Nueva España, 1750–1821," in Antonio Anino, coord., *América Latina: del Estado colonial al Estado nación*, vol. 1 (Turin, Italy: Franco Angeli Libri, 1995) pp. 92–93.

65 An excellent case study which analyzes local sales taxes is Juan Carlos Garavaglia and Juan Carlos Grosso, *Puebla desde una perspectiva microhistórica. La villa de Tepeaca y su entorno agrario: población, producción e intercambio (1740–1870)* (Mexico: Claves Latinoamericanas, 1994).

66 While much additional research is needed on consumer trends in eighteenth-century Mexico, Van Young has opened the field. He offers various estimates on income by different social groups and argues that circa 1800, poor Mexicans spent close to 63% of their total income on corn (basically for tortillas), a substantially higher percentage than European working poor spent on bread, their staple of life. See the essay by Eric Van Young, Los ricos se vuelven más ricos y los pobres más pobres in the book by the same author, *La crisis del orden colonial: Estructures agraria y rebeliones populares de la Nueva España, 1750–1821* (Mexico: Alianza Mexicana, 1992), pp. 51–123.

tax income stagnated, such as the sales taxes known as *alcabalas* and *pulques*. It is also possible – as historians John TePaske and John Coatsworth have suggested – that inflation might have reduced the impact of the Bourbon state's fiscal offensive and diminished their effects.[67] If price increases were greater than tax contributions and were accompanied by stagnation in wage levels (as argued by Van Young), then it is possible that the tax system might not have been considered as the *principal* cause worsening the economic situation for the lower strata.[68] There may have been greater discontent at price increases and the relative fall in wages, although there is a scarcity of historical monographs on popular response to these trends. Instead of a fiscal rebellion, it would appear that discontent led colonial Mexican taxpayers to carry on what one author has described as disguised resistance to tax payments.[69]

Fiscal Pacts in Colonial Society

In all discussion of tax systems, a major issue concerns the contemporary social perception of the relative fairness of the fiscal charges. Today tax systems are described as regressive or progressive: in the former case, exactions fall unequally on sectors with less income, while with the latter, taxation rates increase proportionally with income. New Spain's tax system was, in many regards, regressive since the preponderance of indirect taxes – especially on *pulque* and the sales tax – fell heavily on items of popular consumption; furthermore, certain direct taxes like the tribute were only paid by the poorest social groups. However, these terms and concepts were not used in the *ancien regime*; the underlying idea was that of fiscal justice.

Fiscal justice was associated with tax exemptions or immunities granted to specific social groups. When New Spain is compared to a number of European societies, it becomes clear that tax exemptions were more common in European Catholic monarchies than in Spanish America. In the Spain of Charles IV, for example, the greatest fortunes rarely paid taxes; while in New Spain, significant proportion of the richest men – among them the owners of silver mines – were obliged to make important payments to the government. In fact, most individuals in colonial Mexico had to contribute

67 See John TePaske, "Economic Cycles in New Spain in the Eighteenth Century: The View from the Public Sector," in Richard Garner and William Taylor, eds., *Iberian Colonies, New World Societies: Essays in Memory of Charles Gibson* (Pennsylvania: State College, 1985), pp. 119–142 but compare with R. Garner and S. E. Stefanou, *Economic Growth and Change in Bourbon Mexico*, pp. 34–35.

68 E. Van Young, *La crisis del orden colonial*, Chapter 2, offers the most complete and penetrating discussion, to date, on income levels and wage trends in Bourbon Mexico.

69 See the suggestive essay discussing disguised opposition to taxes at a time of growing fiscal pressure by Ana Lidia García Peña, "El impacto popular de las reformas fiscales en la ciudad de México, 1780–1820," in C. Marichal and D. Marino, eds., *De colonia a nación*, pp. 85–133.

taxes to the colonial administration – a fact that tends to reveal a degree of fiscal uniformity even though tax rates proved markedly different for different social groups.

The regressive character of New Spain's fiscal system was possibly reduced by this greater uniformity and by relative efficiency in collection of revenues.[70] When compared to Spain's disjointed tax system at the end of the eighteenth century (with very marked differences in terms of norms and collection methods) or the French fiscal system, which offered a great many selective exemptions to privileged corporations, that of New Spain appears more transparent.[71] It may be an exaggeration to claim, as Herbert Klein did, that the Bourbon reforms had achieved "perhaps the most modern tax system in the Atlantic world," but his argument calls attention to the considerable efficiency in tax collection in New Spain during the late Bourbon regime.[72] On the other hand, Humboldt himself considered that there were too many corrupt tax collectors in colonial Mexico.[73] But, possibly, these features caused less rejection than the traditional tax systems in Spain or France where the continuous use of tax farming submitted taxpayers to multitudes of small injustices that were considered as injurious as the tax collection itself.[74]

In any case, it is worth rethinking how the tax system functioned in legal and political terms in a colonial society. The fact that there was neither legislature nor popular press in colonial Mexico implies that discussions about the tax system were limited. This situation clearly contrasts with the intense debates on taxes in societies with a parliamentary tradition.[75] Therefore, it is important to keep in mind that in New Spain the juridical formulation of many taxes responded to a *corporative concept* of the functioning of colonial society. Quite a number of traditional taxes were applied to a group, guild, or corporation and these were considered to be the counterpart

70 Both H. Klein *Las finanzas americanas*, p. 129 and Luis Jáuregui "La anatomía del fisco colonial: la real hacienda de la Nueva España, 1784–1821," Ph.D. thesis, El Colegio de México, 1994, pp. 170–189, calculate relatively low costs for tax collection, and so it may be presumed that it was relatively efficient.

71 R. Pieper, *La Real Hacienda bajo Fernando VII*, provides the best analysis of Spain's tax system in the decades 1760–1790.

72 H. S. Klein, "La economía de la Nueva España," 592.

73 This view is found in A. Humboldt, *Ensayo politico*, p. 545.

74 Most studies that have examined the tax regime in prerevolutionary France emphasize the importance of the perception of tax injustice and argue that it was a motive for discontent with the government. See, for example, David R. Weir, "Les crises économiques et les origines de la révolution française," *Annales, Economies, Sociétés, Civilisations*, 4 (1991), 917–947; Alain Guéry, "Les finances de la monarchie française sous l'Ancien Régime," *Annales, Economies, Sociétés, Civilisations*, 33, 2 (March–April 1978), 216–239; P. Mathias and P. O'Brien, "Taxation in Britain and France," 601–650.

75 Particularly the English and Anglo-American cases: see the discussion in H. Root, *The Fountain of Privilege*, Chapter 8 and, more recently, D. Stasavage, *Public Debt*, passim.

for some type of legal concession. For example, tribute were only collected from Indian communities, in return for which they had been granted a series of legal and territorial concessions from the sixteenth century.[76] So too, the mining tax (*diezmo minero*) applied only to silver producers as a concession for the right to exploit the viceroyalty's rich mines, which in principle belonged to the Spanish crown, according to regalist tradition. Similarly, from 1783 certain taxes collected by the Mexico City Mining Tribunal also reflected a corporative character.[77] Other examples of this interchange of taxes for privileges are found in the case of the merchants: the collection of the *avería* tax by the Mexico City Merchant Guild, for example, was a contribution with a specific purpose; it was used to support the mercantile *Tribunal del Consulado*, an organization that ratified the exclusive jurisdiction of the great merchants of the capital over all commercial disputes as well as their oligopolistic control over a great number of commercial transactions in the viceroyalty.[78] Finally, it can also be argued that the taxes paid by the Church were conceived as instruments that guaranteed the traditional legal autonomy of ecclesiastical institutions.

All this suggests that the functioning of the New Spain's tax system was not equivalent to that of parliamentary regimes, such as those of the Anglo-American colonies.[79] The Spanish American colonies – which paid a far greater level of taxes than their northern neighbors – were obliged to adhere to the rules of an absolutist government that severely limited political autonomy and excluded all possibility of legislatures in the different viceroyalties. Taxes in colonial Spanish America were key elements in the functioning of a complex hierarchy of traditional corporations and social groups that operated within an equally complex judicial structure with secular roots. And it is precisely for this reason that we use the term "colonial fiscal constitution," suggesting that despite the harshness of the regime, over the long run there appears to have existed a certain consensus in New

76 Key concessions were guarantees to communal land and the protection of General Tribunal of the Indians. See W. Borah, *El Juzgado General de Indios*.

77 See Walter Howe, *The Mining Guild of New Spain and Its Tribunal General, 1770–1821* (Cambridge, Mass.: Harvard University Press, 1949).

78 See detailed discussion on the attributes of the Mexico City Guild in Guillermina del Valle, "El Consulado de Comerciantes de la Ciudad de México y las finanzas novohispanas, 1592–1827," Ph.D. thesis, El Colegio de México, 1997, and on the Veracruz Merchant Guild in Matilde Souto Mantecón "El Consulado de Comercio de Veracruz, 1796–1821," Ph.D. thesis, El Colegio de México, 1996.

79 In a classic study, George Beer emphasized that the English colonies in North America "were expected to provide the funds for their own local, public affairs and to a great extent with this object in view large powers of self-government were granted to them. . . . Under these conditions each colony, whether in the Antilles or on the continent had developed a vigorous political life of its own, in which the popular branch of the local legislature, through its control of the purse, had become the most important factor": G. Beer, *British Colonial Policy*, pp. 146–147.

Spain with regard to the legitimacy and functionality of the colonial tax system.

Such an implicit political/fiscal agreement would, perhaps, help to explain how it was possible that the numerous reforms of the fiscal system, including the multiplication of taxes at the end of the eighteenth century, did not produce generalized rebellions in New Spain. But it does not fully explain the extraordinary degree of compliance with the Spanish crown that demanded ever greater contributions in the last decades of that century with relatively scant local recompense.[80] For it should be recalled that almost half of all taxes paid in New Spain were not spent within the viceroyalty but rather were exported abroad (as a kind of tax surplus) to support empire and metropolis.

Fiscal Benefits of Empire for the Metropolitan Treasury

Although our analysis has so far concentrated on the fiscal burden that the inhabitants of New Spain were obliged to cover during the last half century of the colonial era, it is also important to underline, what we may term, the *fiscal benefits* derived by the metropolitan government from the colonial tax system. The overseas remittances of precious metals and coin on account of the royal treasuries of colonial Mexico and the rest of Spanish America represented a "unilateral" contribution of New Spain to the empire.[81] During each successive decade, a huge volume of royal silver left the viceroyalty with a remarkably low degree of recompense.[82] Of all the income received from the *Indies* by the General Treasury at Madrid, the viceroyalty of New Spain alone contributed with more than 60 percent in the period 1780–1810 as we have seen in the first chapter of this book. (See Figure 1.3) These transfers clearly represented *costs* for the colony but even more clearly *benefits* for the metropolis.

Following a secular tradition, the Spanish crown expected local taxes to cover local expenses (administrative and military), but also pressured the high-income treasuries of New Spain and Peru to remit significant amounts of silver coin to other colonies and to the metropolis itself. The sums remitted were extremely large. (See the Appendix, Tables 1.1 and 1.2) According to various authors, in the last fifteen years of the eighteenth century, approximately 20 percent of total income registered by the General Treasury of

80 Although it may be anachronistic to say that the crown provided few "public goods," it is well known that the colonial administration invested very little in education, health, or other social services, which were assumed basically by local institutions and the church.

81 See J. Coatsworth, "Obstacles to Economic Growth in Nineteenth Century Mexico," *American Historical Review*, 83, 1 (1978), 80–100.

82 John Coatsworth, *Orígenes del atraso*, pp. 108–109, presented the first estimates of this drainage and of possible effects on the colonial economy.

Madrid can be attributed to American silver shipments.[83] Historians Barbier and Klein have argued: "When the related receipts from the Cádiz royal treasury are added in, American-related funds may have accounted for one-fifth of total Madrid Treasury revenues in this period, making the Indies the largest ultimate source of Madrid income."[84] Their estimates are based on the sum of remittances of tax silver from the Americas plus revenues obtained from trade taxes at Cádiz-derived Spanish American trade.[85] But the Klein/Barbier figures are probably too low, since recent research has demonstrated that much of the tobacco monopoly's income in Spain was also derived from colonial inputs.[86]

Most of these transfers sent to Spain were covered with *ordinary tax revenues* obtained from the colonial treasuries of Spanish America. However, from the 1790s the enormous increase in the demands of imperial finance led to the ratification of a long list of loans and donations which were raised from Crown's subjects abroad. This new colonial debt policy was directly related to increases in military and financial expenditure by the Spanish government as a result of new wars, first against revolutionary France (1793–1795) and then the naval wars against Britain (1796–1801 and 1805–1808) which impelled a formidable increase in the debts of the monarchy.

Once again – and as in the case of the tax regime – silver from New Spain was the linchpin to much of the new financial policy. An example of the importance of American remittances to cover imperial debts can be found in the case of the *foreign loans* taken by the Spanish government in Amsterdam from the 1780s. All such loan contracts specified payment with Mexican silver. (See Appendix III.3.) Hence, as soon as news was had of ships arriving to Cádiz from Veracruz, Dutch bankers immediately pressed for the shipment of the precious metals to Holland to cover the debt service.[87] The importance of Mexican silver for the Spanish *internal debt* was equally marked. For the majority of authors who have dealt with *vales reales* (a new kind of public

83 J. Cuenca, *Ingresos netos del Estado español*; J. P. Merino, "La Hacienda de Carlos IV," 139–181; Leandro Prados de la Escosura, *De imperio a nación: crecimiento y atraso económico en España, 1780–1936* (Madrid: Alianza, 1988).

84 J. Barbier and H. Klein, *Revolutionary Wars*, p. 328. It should be underlined that the series of "Indias" income registered as going to the Madrid Treasury by J. Barbier and H. Klein, *Revolutionary Wars*, pp. 323 and 338, must be contrasted with other series, including the aforementioned data collected by J. Cuenca, *Ingresos netos del Estado español* and J. P. Merino, "La Hacienda de Carlos IV."

85 On this subject, also see Leandro Prados de la Escosura, "La pérdida del imperio y sus consecuencias económicas," in L. Prados de la Escosura and S. Amaral, eds., *La independencia americana: sus consecuencias económicas* (Madrid: Alianza Universidad, 1993), pp. 253–300.

86 C. Marichal, "Beneficios y costes fiscales," p. 480.

87 On this question, see the excellent studies by Marten G. Buist, *At Spes Non Fracta, Hope and Company, 1770–1815: Merchant Bankers and Diplomats at Work* (The Hague, the Netherlands: Martinus Nijhoff, 1975) and James C. Riley, *International Government Finance and the Amsterdam Capital Market, 1740–1815* (Cambridge, U.K.: Cambridge University Press, 1980).

bond that began to be issued in 1781), the receipt of American silver was the determining factor in the quotation of the market values of *vales reales*. These bonds became the favorite instrument of extraordinary finance in the later years of the reign of Carlos III as well as of the administration of Carlos IV.[88] News of the arrival of important shipments of silver to Cádiz would spur a sharp rise in the value of the *vales*, while news of suspension of shipments from Spanish America would provoke an equally abrupt fall in prices. What is less known is that much of the silver shipped was raised by a combination of forced donations and voluntary loans applied in the colonies, but with greatest vigor and frequency in the viceroyalty of New Spain. It is to this subject that we now turn.

88 The most detailed analysis of these operations is found in Pedro Tedde's monumental *Historia del Banco de San Carlos* (Madrid: Banco de España/Alianza, 1987) and in his essay "Política financiera y política comercial," 139–217.

3

Imperial Wars and Loans from New Spain, 1780–1800

> I have resolved that once only, and in character of a Donation, one peso be contributed to Me by each free man, including Indians, and other castes that make up the People; and two pesos from Spaniards and Nobles, making up the many distinguished Subjects found in the Indies. . . .
>
> Carlos III (August 17, 1780)

During the last third of the eighteenth century, the geopolitical and military strategy adopted by the Bourbon regime to strengthen the Spanish empire was based on an aggressive fiscal campaign in both the metropolis and the Spanish American colonies. Despite success in increasing tax income, a succession of wars pushed expenditures beyond the rise in revenues: these included a new war against Great Britain (1779–1783), the even more costly war against the French Convention (1793–1795), and then two naval wars with Britain (1796–1801 and 1805–1808). As a result, the Spanish monarchy eventually found itself obliged to recur to debt, although this was a recourse that royal officials at Madrid had long avoided.[1]

For the greater part of the eighteenth century, the Bourbon regime in Spain had used taxes to finance rising defense expenditures and wars, in contrast with its imperial rivals, Britain and France, which issued huge amounts of debt as a result of the pronounced expansion in military expenditures and particularly of naval forces. Inevitably, the relative weight of debt service tended to rise: in Great Britain debt service absorbed more than 40 percent of state income in the 1780s, whereas in France, the figure reached 50 percent in 1788.[2] In eighteenth-century Britain such high charges were met without great difficulty as the issue of debt allowed for what is now termed *tax-smoothing*, principally because the depth of capital markets facilitated the

1 Bourbon functionaries were bent on avoiding the Hapsburg legacy of excess indebtedness. An excellent account of Hapsburg debt policies is found in C. Álvarez Nogal, *El crédito de la monarquía hispánica*.

2 On debt service in Britain in the eighteenth century, see J. Brewer, *The sinews of power*, p. 117 and in France, A. Guéry, "Les finances de la monarchie française sous l'Ancien Régime," *Annales, Economies, Sociétés, Civilisations*, 33, 2 (March–April 1978), 231.

placement of government securities at low interest rates; these low rates, in turn, were possible because of a consistent rise in revenues and the regularity of debt service.[3] In France, on the other hand, much of the debt contracted after 1770 proved to be extremely expensive due to deficient financial policies and the difficulties faced by the administrations of both Louis XV and Louis XVI in raising new taxes. In fact, the combined fiscal and debt crisis would contribute decisively to the outbreak of the French Revolution in 1789.[4]

Surprisingly, during the greater part of the reign of the Spanish monarch Charles III (1759–1788), debts and debt service remained low since tax collection proved sufficient to meet expenditures in the metropolis, while fiscal reforms in Spanish America covered the costs of burgeoning imperial defense. But from the early 1780s, the rise in war expenses finally forced the cabinet at Madrid to seek loans and *donativos* (extraordinary contributions) both at home and in the colonies. The Spanish government began by adopting a new and more modern debt policy from 1781 that was reflected in the issue on a large scale of a new kind of public bond (*vales reales*) sold in Spain but not in the Americas.[5] However, these measures were insufficient to cover swelling military expenses in the Americas as a result of a succession of wars with Great Britain, which included numerous conflicts in the greater Caribbean. As a result, a new financial strategy was put in place in the colonies, but one which combined archaic and modern elements.

The greatest increase of *colonial debts* in Spanish America was registered in New Spain. There, in the last two decades of the century, the Crown collected four universal donations (forced contributions), three non-interest-bearing loans (known as "suplementos"), and *nine* interest-bearing loans (see Table 3.1). Altogether, between 1781 and 1800 more than seventeen million silver pesos were collected through loans and four million pesos from donations in the viceroyalty.[6] Nonetheless, the financial contributions

3 The financial strategies of the British government reflected the capacity of what is today known as *tax smoothing*: it spreads out the cost of expenditures in an efficient manner with low-interest debt, thereby avoiding fiscal crises. For the theoretical explanation, see Robert J. Barro, "Government Spending, Interest Rates, Prices and Budget Deficits in the United Kingdom," *Journal of Monetary Economics*, 20 (September 1987), 221–248.

4 Two excellent studies are Eugene N. White, "Was There a Solution to the Ancien Regime's Financial Dilemma?" *The Journal of Economic History*, 49, 3, (1989), 545–568 and Francois R. Velde and David R. Weir, "The Financial Market and Government Debt Policy in France, 1746–1793," *Journal of Economic History*, 52, 1, (1992), 1–39.

5 On the new Spanish debt policies, see Pedro Tedde, *El Banco de San Carlos, 1782–1829* (Madrid: Alianza-Banco de España, 1988), Chapter 2 and M. Artola, *La hacienda del antiguo regimen*, pp. 369–404.

6 For details see Appendix III.2, with lists and details of all loans and donations of New Spain between 1780 and 1810. Between 1782 and 1793 a little more than three million pesos were supplements – short-term loans – without interest.

from Mexico were not the only ones granted to Spain to prosecute costly wars. A number of short- and long-term loans began to be raised in Cuba, Guatemala, New Granada, Peru, Chile, and other Spanish American territories, although, generally, these were of smaller amounts and came later than the Mexican loans.[7] It was after the turn of the century that the Spanish colonies in South America began to make major contributions to the Crown as witnessed in the case of the viceroyalty of Peru, where miners, merchants, landed aristocrats, and various institutions including the secular and regular orders of the church contributed some six million pesos in the shape of war loans between 1804 and 1815.[8]

Whether in Mexico or Peru, the royal loans required the explicit collaboration of colonial elites that held large reserves of capital, basically in the shape of silver pesos. In New Spain most loans were contracted through the services of the Mexico City Merchant Guild (*Consulado de Comercio*) and the Mining Tribunal (*Tribunal de Minería*), although in both cases these privileged corporations were assisted by the Catholic Church, which also played a major role in the financial advances to the Crown. The large amounts of capital mobilized for the loans were testimony to the great wealth of the colonial Mexican plutocrats (merchants, silver miners, and landowners) who rivaled the wealthiest Europeans in the late eighteenth century. The royal administration at Madrid was acutely aware of the importance of private finance in the colonial realms, particularly at times of war when the Crown needed all the financial support it could obtain.

The key role of powerful, local intermediaries suggests the importance of taking into account the operation and special character of *colonial credit markets* – a fact underplayed in most of the historical literature on eighteenth-century Spanish America.[9] Nonetheless, it would be a mistake

7 On loans for the Crown from colonial Peru, see the study by Alfonso W. Quiroz, *Deudas olvidadas: instrumentos de crédito en la economía colonial peruana, 1750–1820* (Lima: Pontificia Universidad Católica del Perú, 1993), pp. 140–149 which should be complemented with Timothy Anna, *The Fall of the Royal Government in Peru* (Lincoln: University of Nebraska Press, 1978), pp. 11–14. Some loans from the merchants of Havana are registered in Julio Le Riverend, *Historia económica de Cuba* (Havana: Instituto Cubano del Libro, 1974), pp. 134–135 and in Johanna Von Graffenstein, "México y el Caribe durante los años de la emancipación, 1779–1808," Ph.D. thesis, Universidad Nacional Autónoma de México, 1994, p. 103 as well as extended comments in R. de la Sagra, *Historia económico-política y estadística*, pp. 240–265. For donations and loans from the Captaincy-General of Guatemala, see references in Ralph Lee Woodward, *Central America, A Nation Divided* (Oxford, Oxford University Press, 1985), p. 70; for New Granada, see J. L. Phelan, *The People and the King*, pp. 28–29; and for Chile, see references in Sergio Villabos, "Opposition to Imperial Taxation," in Robin Humphreys and John Lynch, eds., *The Origins of the Latin American Revolutions, 1808–1826* (New York: Alfred Knopf, 1965), pp. 135–136.

8 A. W. Quiroz, *Deudas olvidadas*, pp. 140–149.

9 For several studies on the colonial credit system in the second half of the eighteenth century in Mexico, see Leonor Ludlow and Jorge Silva, eds., *Los negocios y las ganancias: de la Colonia al México moderno*

to describe the financial activity of the period simply in terms of modern markets. In the absolutist regime the Crown had recourse to a peculiar combination of old and new financial instruments: royal functionaries turned to the powerful privileged corporations for loans, but they also had recourse to more coercive methods of obtaining funds from popular sectors.

In this chapter we review the principal financial operations adopted by the colonial administration of New Spain between 1780 and 1800 to assist in imperial defense and to help cover deficits of the metropolitan treasury in its successive wars with Britain or France. We emphasize the inherent contradictions in financial policy which combined the very different principles of coercion and collaboration.[10] This speaks to some of the archaic characteristics of colonial financial relations but also to the slow emergence of what may be considered more modern financial markets in Bourbon Mexico.

Royal Donations and Loans in the Colonies: Between the Archaic and the Modern

Colonial debts are a subject that has been largely neglected in the colonial history of Mexico as well as in most of the rest of Spanish America. Our survey of the financial instruments used by the Crown to obtain extraordinary resources from New Spain to cover war expenses focuses on their diversity. The review of the financial tools adopted by the colonial government also reveals their contradictory nature: some were clearly archaic, while others had modern characteristics. This is not strange, because the late eighteenth century was a time of financial innovations in the north Atlantic world, the impact of which was also felt in the Spanish-speaking realms.[11] As Larry Neal has demonstrated in a seminal book, this was the age of the rise of

(México: Instituto de Investigaciones "Dr. José María Luis Mora,"/UNAM, 1993); Pilar Martínez López-Cano, ed., *Iglesia, estado y economía, siglos xvi al xix* (México: UNAM, 1995); and Gisela von Wobeser *El crédito eclesiástico en la Nueva España: siglo XVIII* (Mexico: UNAM, 1994).

10 Actually, this combination of contradictory principles is typical of the majority of governments identified as absolutist regimes, while consensus is normally linked to parliamentary regimes. See discussion of these issues in R. Bonney, ed., *Economic Systems and State Finance* (Oxford: Oxford University Press/The European Science Foundation, 1995), pp. 423–431 and Hilton. L. Root, *Construction de l'Etat moderne en Europe: La France et l'Angleterre* (Paris: PUF, 1994), Chapters 8 and 9.

11 The origins of modern financial instruments are the object of a historiographical debate. See James C. Riley, *International Government Finance and the Amsterdam Capital Market, 1740–1815* (Cambridge, U.K.: Cambridge University Press, 1980) and Larry Neal, *The Rise of Financial Capitalism: International Capital Markets in the Age of Reason* (Cambridge, U.K.: Cambridge University Press, 1990). Also see the penetrating analysis in Marie Therese Boyer-Xambeau, et al., "A la recherche d'un âge d'or des marchés financiers: intégration et efficence au xviiie siècle," *Cahiers d'Économie Politique*, 21, (1992), 33–65.

modern capital markets in England and Holland.[12] But changes were also taking place in France and other Catholic monarchies, although at a slower pace.[13]

In the case of Spain and Spanish America, archaic and modern financial institutions coexisted. Among the former were donations (*donativos*) to be paid by every head of household in the viceroyalty. The *donativos* had a medieval origin but had been applied systematically from the sixteenth to the eighteenth century in Spain.[14] They were first applied in the Americas at the end of the sixteenth century during a series of international wars.[15] It is symptomatic of the archaic nature of donations that they could only be compulsory. Similar to taxes, the universal donations examined here (decreed in 1781, 1793, 1795, and 1798) were secular, financial instruments which obligated the population as a whole to contribute funds to the monarchy. Their collection depended not only on a systematic effort on the part of royal tax officials but also on launching religious/patriotic campaigns to obtain funds from all sectors of colonial society, ranging from the poorest inhabitants to the most opulent individuals of New Spain.[16]

Another somewhat antiquated form of extraordinary finance was the collection of non-interest-bearing loans that were requested repeatedly from the great merchants and landowners of New Spain. These credit instruments had some coercive characteristics insofar as the monarchy brought pressure to bear on colonial privileged corporations to collaborate in great emergencies.[17] But it is also clear that providing advances to the Crown was a way for rich lenders to accumulate political capital: according to a detailed study by Doris Ladd, more than a dozen wealthy miners and merchants in New Spain received titles of nobility in exchange for their generous contributions to the Crown.[18] Moreover, it should be noted that not all donations nor interest-free loans had military purposes since some were also used to

12 Larry Neal, *The Rise of Financial Capitalism.*

13 Marc Potter and Jean Laurent Rosenthal, "Politics and Public Finance in France," 577–612.

14 An example of the continuity of these exactions in Spain can be found in the case of the city of Cádiz, where not less than twenty-six *donativos* were collected between 1555 and 1763. See J. Canga Arguelles, *Diccionario de Hacienda*, vol. 1, p. 164.

15 On the first loans (*donativos graciosos*) applied in the New Spain – beginning in 1599 – there can be found documentation in Archivo General de la Nación (AGN), in the branch of documents titled *Archivo Histórico de Hacienda*, vol. 1292.

16 See Appendix III.1 for a complete list of conditions and amounts of donations to the Crown implemented in New Spain between 1780 and 1810.

17 Forced loans, known at times as *secuestros*, had been frequently applied against the Indies traders from the middle of the sixteenth century onward: for lists see M. E. Martín Acosta, *El dinero Americano*, pp. 198–199.

18 Doris Ladd, *The Mexican Nobility at Independence, 1780–1826* (Austin: University of Texas Press, 1976).

cover expenses on the occasion of natural catastrophes such as profound agrarian crises, famines, and/or disease, phenomena common enough in the *ancien regime* in Spanish America as in Europe.[19]

In contrast to the more archaic financial instruments mentioned, the long list of interest-bearing loans issued in Mexico from the early 1780s reveals features that reflect a certain degree of modernization in the management of colonial public finance, as is witnessed by new aspects of financial policy and practice imported from across the Atlantic.[20] (See Table 3.1 and for greater detail Appendix III.2 on all loans issued between 1780 and 1810.) That the colonial administration in Mexico should turn to local, wealthy investors for this new kind of loan suggests that there existed a colonial financial market, albeit of a rather special kind. One of the principal intermediaries in the operation of this market was the powerful Merchant Guild of the City of Mexico, which operated much as an investment bank, taking large-scale deposits which were placed in the interest-bearing loans to the Crown; the holders of these funds could later redeem them by selling the loan paper to other wealthy investors.[21] Whether this can be considered a secondary market is a question that awaits future research.

One of the reasons for success in attracting investors in interest-bearing loans was the increased efficiency of the Bourbon tax administration that assured regular debt service, particularly as it was effected in silver pesos. The increasingly sophisticated management of public credit in Bourbon Mexico is illustrated by the negotiation of loans issued in from the years 1782–1784 and later – on a larger scale – during the decade 1790–1800. The colonial administration experimented with various types of interest, repayment terms, financial premiums, and fiscal guarantees that speak to the increasing complexity of local financial policy and markets. But before analyzing the donations and loan operations in some detail, it is relevant to ask why metropolitan and colonial authorities found it necessary to resort to a policy of extraordinary funding?

19 An excellent analysis of the measures adopted to ease the 1785/1786 crisis can be found in the introductory essay by Rodolfo Pastor, in Enrique Florescano and Rodolfo Pastor *La crisis agrícola de 1785–86. Selección documental*, vol. 1 (Mexico: Archivo General de la Nación, 1981), pp. 29–63.

20 Among the financial innovations in the viceroyalty was the creation of the Banco de Avío de la Minería (1784) as well as the introduction of royal interest-bearing loans (with the backing of the tobacco monopoly) for the viceregal government. See W. Howe, *Mining Guild* and Guillermina del Valle Pavón, "El Consulado de Comerciantes de la Ciudad de México y las finanzas novohispanas, 1592–1827," Ph.D. thesis, El Colegio de México, 1997. The most detailed study of the process of financial modernization in the Spain of Charles III is Pedro Tedde, *El Banco de San Carlos*.

21 Detailed information on the sales and transfer of loan papers can be found in G. Valle Pavón, "Consulado de Comerciantes," pp. 180–194.

Table 3.1. *Principal Loans Raised in New Spain by the Royal Treasury, 1782–1802*[a]

Years	Amount (in Pesos)	Interest Rate (%)	Fiscal Guarantees	Financial Agent
1781–1784	1,655,415	Non-interest-bearing loan		Real Hacienda
1782	1,000,000	5	Averia tax	Consulado de Comercio
1782	1,000,000	5	Mexico City mint	Tribunal de Minería
1783	523,376	4	Tobacco and *alcabalas* monopoly	Real Hacienda
1786	150,000	5		Consulado de Comercio
1790	100,000	5		Tribunal de Minería
1792–1794	1,559,000	Non-interest-bearing loan		Real hacienda
1793	1,000,000	5	Increase on averia tax	Tribunal de Minería
1793	1,100,000	5	Mexico City mint	Consulado de Comercio
1794	1,000,000	5		Tribunal de Minería
1794	1,000,000	5		Consulado de Comercio
1795–1802	7,172,264	5	Tobacco monopoly	Tribunal de Minería and Consulado
1798	496,366	Non-interest-bearing loan		Real Hacienda
1798	500,000	5	Mexico City mint	Tribunal de Minería

Note: See Appendix III.2.

[a] The explicit purpose of all these loans was to assist in the Spanish monarchy with its wars.

Origins of the Policy of Indebtedness in the Viceroyalty, 1779–1783

It is an axiom of political economy that when taxes cover total government expenditure, no deficits exist and, consequently, no debt results. In this regard, we have already alluded to the fact that during the greater part of the eighteenth century neither the metropolitan government in Spain nor the colonial administrations suffered from important deficits.[22] This broke with the legacy of the Habpsburg dynasty in the seventeenth century which had accumulated a series of enormous debts that had "suffocated" the Crown. During the first three quarters of the eighteenth century, the Bourbon dynasty avoided debt like the plague but from the early 1780s,

22 P. Tedde, "Política financiera y política comercial," pp. 139–217.

treasury officials resolved to take a new tack. Pedro Tedde has demonstrated that during the war with Great Britain (1779–1783) the increase of army and navy expenses led to a short-term explosion of deficits in the metropolitan treasury. These were covered – as we have already indicated – by the introduction of a new debt instrument of the Spanish government known as *vales reales* (royal bonds or promissory notes); their service being assured by a new financial institution, the Bank of San Carlos, founded in 1782.[23] After the war, financial authorities were able to reduce deficits with increased taxes and, at the same time, to gradually retire some of the public debt.

In the Spanish American colonies, particularly in the greater Caribbean, military and naval expenditures, traditionally, were not met by loans, but by increasing the remittance of tax surpluses from Mexico to Havana. Nonetheless, from the early 1780s, wartime financial requirements also increased so dramatically that royal officials finally turned to the issue of loans. A case study of the donations and loans promoted by the colonial administration in Mexico can prove an excellent way to explore the complexity of colonial fiscal and financial policies in the late eighteenth century and, perhaps, facilitate comparative studies with other colonial regimes.

Colonial debts began to be contracted on a large scale during the administration of a new viceroy, Martín de Mayorga (1779–1783), who was initially reluctant to use extraordinary finance to cover either increasing defense or administrative costs. Such a position accurately reflected the contemporary attitudes of royal officials in the Americas, who preferred to rely on taxes. Mayorga was a high-ranking military officer of considerable experience when he was named the viceroy of New Spain in 1779, the same year when war was declared against Great Britian. He was charged by Charles III with strengthening the army of New Spain and ensuring the financing of the garrisons and colonial administrations in the greater Spanish Caribbean. At the same he was instructed to continue – when possible – with the deliveries of silver and gold to Cádiz.[24] In order to secure these major objectives, the Crown insisted that he apply a forced loan in the viceroyalty.[25]

23 P. Tedde, *El Banco de San Carlos*.

24 In late 1779, Gálvez ordered Mayorga to send funds to the Spanish settlements in Cuba, Puerto Rico, Trinidad, and Louisiana to neutralize the vessels of the British Navy and to prepare for the reconquest of Florida, ceded to England in 1763. In less than two years, Mayorga ordered the transfer of 15 million pesos from Veracruz to Cuba, together with provisions and munitions worth almost 1.5 million pesos. At the same time, he ordered the embarkation of one of the best Mexican infantry corps, the Crown Regiment (*Regimiento de la Corona*), destined for Havana to which he added a corps of 1,600 marines to be incorporated into the crew of the Spanish squadron; see J. A. Lewis, "New Spain during the American Revolution" and C. Marichal and M. Souto, "Silver and Situados," 606–610.

25 The royal instruction for the American donation was published in August 1780, but Mayorga did not want to apply it immediately.

In spite of the many demands by metropolitan authorities, Mayorga did not apply donations (forced contributions) nor did he contract loans during the initial stages of the war with Britain, but rather preferred to exploit to the maximum the traditional fiscal instruments at his disposal by increasing tax rates. In this he followed in the footsteps of his predecessor, Viceroy Antonio María Bucareli (1771–1779), who had devoted much attention to improving piscal receipts.[26] Mayorga began by imposing higher rates in 1779 on the sales taxes known as *alcabalas* and on *pulques* (the principal alcoholic beverage of the popular classes in Mexico). He also attempted to reduce administrative expenditures to compensate for the extraordinary increase in the defense budget.[27] Even so, the tax monies raised and/or saved after two years did not suffice to cover the huge demands of the military garrisons in the Caribbean and the naval expeditions against the southern flank of North America.

How and where could the viceroy find additional resources? An enormous portion of regular tax revenues was already committed to sustain the Caribbean treasuries, while the rest was absorbed by military expenses within the viceroyalty and by regular remittances to the treasury at Madrid. Rigidity characterized many of these disbursements since a number of fiscal branches in colonial Mexico had been assigned the task of paying quite specific expenditures. For example, the surplus income of the postal service of New Spain was sent annually to Havana to cover naval outlays at this strategic port.[28] Similarly, a part of the profits obtained from the sales of the mercury monopoly was remitted to Cuba to assist the tobacco monopoly finance the purchase of tobacco leaf from local planters on the island.[29] In addition, most of the surplus income of the Mexican mint (*la Casa de Moneda*) and certain taxes on officeholders (*vacantes y medias anatas*) were

26 In fact, Bucareli retired the greater part of the colonial government's term and floating debt and regularized payments to garrisons (*situados*) in the Caribbean: Bernard E. Bobb, *The ViceRegency of Antonio María Bucareli in New Spain, 1771–1779* (Austin: University of Texas Press, 1962), pp. 222–227.

27 Consistent with this effort, the viceroy's salary was reduced by half (30,000 in place of 60,000 pesos). More serious and cruel were reductions in the daily subsistence payments to convicts and other forced labor that undertook public works: the administrator in charge of the treasury Pedro de Cosio reduced each prisoner's supplies from two to one *real* per day, eliminating among other things the only "luxury" they had, the half *real* to buy tobacco and drink: J. A. Lewis, "New Spain during the American Revolution," pp. 172–173 and 175.

28 Heladio Galeana, "La renta de correos como monopolio estatal en la Nueva España, 1766–1821," Master's thesis, Universidad Autónoma Metropolitana-Iztapalapa, Mexico, 1998, Table 1.

29 Antonia Herrera Heredia, *La renta del azogue en Nueva España, 1709–1751*, (Sevilla: Escuela de Estudios Hispanoamericanos, 1978), pp. 156–158 and 261, notes that in the first half of the eighteenth century, half of the fiscal receipts from the sale of mercury in Mexico were used for this purpose.

habitually sent to the Cuba Treasury while the remainder went to Spain.[30] Furthermore, the most productive of all fiscal branches, the Mexican tobacco monopoly, had the obligation to send the greater part of its net income to the metropolis.

Owing to the extraordinary demands generated by the war with Britain and the insufficiency of the funds sent from New Spain to colonial garrisons in the Caribbean, Mayorga decided to adopt a heterodox measure. He proceeded to send accumulated surpluses from the tobacco monopoly to cover war expenses in Cuba – a measure that contravened traditional regulations, stipulating that such monies would be destined exclusively for the Iberian peninsula. In fact, the viceroy ordered that the huge sum of twelve million pesos from New Spain's tobacco monopoly be sent to Cuba between 1780 and 1783, but even this did not prove sufficient to cover all costs required by the naval and land forces.[31]

After the first and impressive effort to finance the enormous expenditures of the ongoing military-naval expeditions in the greater Caribbean, 1780–1781, Mayorga's resistance to loans and donations began to crack. The Spanish campaign to reconquer Florida as well as the reinforcement of positions in Louisiana, led by general Bernardo Gálvez (nephew of the minister of Indies), required additional finance. In March 1781, the viceroy finally decided to employ the royal authorization which he had received from Charles III to collect a large donation (*donativo gracioso*) from the Mexican population.

The "Gracious Donation" of 1781–1784: Compulsion as a Financial Instrument of War

When Viceroy Mayorga gave orders in 1781 for the collection in Mexico of the "universal donation" (originally decreed in August 1780 by Charles III) he was acting on the basis of many precedents in the history of Spain and

30 It is difficult to determine exactly what proportion of the *Casa de Moneda's* funds went to the metropolis and what to Cuba. Victor Soria has reconstructed the *situado* series and remarks: "Between 1777 and 1780, the consignment of funds to the Crown by the *Casa de Moneda* reached an average of 623.512 pesos . . . between 1781 and 1785, 952,000 pesos . . . in the quinquenium 1786–1790, 1,139,165 pesos, increasing in the following quinquenium to 1,440,000 . . . later declining (1795–99) to 1,160,000. The shipment of funds reached their highest annual average in 1801–1805 with 1,502,670 pesos." Victor Soria, *La Casa de Moneda bajo la administración borbónica, 1733–1821* (Mexico: Universidad Autónoma Metropolitana, 1994), p. 141.

31 J. A. Lewis "New Spain during the American Revolution," p. 219. Much of the money went to the important naval force under the command of Admiral Cacigal that operated throughout the Caribbean during these years, attacking the English garrisons in the Bahamas, Jamaica, Honduras, and Florida. At the same time, the military expedition, led by General Bernardo de Galvez, was charged with taking possession of the fort at Pensacola and to reinforce the Spanish positions in New Orleans and above, along the Mississippi river.

the Americas. What were the chief characteristics of this type of exaction? According to Miguel Artola's well-documented study on Spanish royal finances in the *ancien regime*, donations (*donativos*) were first collected in Spain by Phillip II during the late sixteenth century, but became more frequent during the reign of Philip IV in the first half of the seventeenth century.[32]

A number of these donations were collected in the colonies during the Hapsburg reign, especially from corporations such as the merchant guilds of Lima and Mexico and the church, occasionally being complemented by requests for non-interest-bearing loans (*suplementos*). The donations implied outright gifts while the *suplementos* were, in principle, to be returned to the gracious lenders. The first donation requested from the merchant guilds in Spanish America had taken place in 1624. This was followed by more demands during the 1630s, the era of military and financial campaigns, known as the *Unión de Armas*, when Spain engaged in wars with virtually all its numerous European rivals. The all-powerful prime minister, the Duke of Olivares, sought loan after loan and demanded that the colonies, in particular Peru, dispatch more and more silver shipments.[33]

Not surprisingly, after the Peace of Westphalia (1648), the requests of the Crown for money from the great merchants of Peru and New Spain diminished. This may be attributed to the decline in military activity and to the effects of Spanish economic and political decadence in the second half of the century, but in the Americas the drop in loans was also related to the growing rivalries between powerful, colonial corporations – a fact that made raising money difficult for royal officials. For instance, during the second half of the seventeenth century, conflicts between the Merchant Guild of Mexico City (*Consulado de Comerciantes*) and the municipal council (*cabildo*) of the capital limited the options open to royal financial authorities. In fact, the viceregal government in Mexico was not able not to extract new donations from the powerful and wealthy merchant guild until awarding it the lease to administer Mexico City's sales tax in the 1690s.[34] From this period, and throughout the eighteenth century, the requests for special contributions from the wealthiest merchants of New Spain were renewed once and again; for example in 1704, a donation to help finance the war with Algeria; another in 1744 during the conflict with Italy; and still another

32 Among the more important *donativos* under Philip IV were those of 1624, 1632, and 1635. During the War of Spanish Succession, 1702–1715, an additional number were requested, as again during the wars at the end of the eighteenth century. See M. Artola, *La hacienda del antiguo régimen*, pp. 108, 157, 321, 325, and 327.

33 Detailed information on these loans can be found in C. Álvarez Nogal, *El crédito de la monarquía hispánica*, passim.

34 The history of the tax farming activities of the Mexico City Merchant Guild can be found in G. Valle Pavón, "Consulado de Comerciantes," Chapter 2.

in the 1770s under Viceroy Bucarelli to strengthen imperial defenses. The same formula was applied with greater rigor during the war with Great Britain (1779–1783) and in decades following.[35]

But apart from the special financial contributions requested of the privileged corporations and wealthy men of the viceroyalty, it is also important to focus attention on the *universal donations* (*donativos universales*) that were explicitly compulsory and had to be paid in varying quotas by every head of family of all sectors of the colonial population, including the Indian communities.[36] Forced contributions had long been requested from all the popular classes and especially from the thousands of Indian towns in New Spain – a practice which began at the end of the sixteenth century, as confirmed by the donations imposed on those towns (*pueblos de indios*) in 1599, 1621, 1624, and 1678. On the other hand, for later periods the archival information is scarcer with regard to this type of exaction, which leads one to believe that during the early Bourbon period, such expedients may have been less frequent.[37] But from 1781 onward (and for over thirty years) the forcible contributions were repeatedly applied to assist the Crown with its imperial wars.

The majority of the universal donations were officially defined as "gracious," implying that no refund would be forthcoming. Furthermore, the royal instructions made explicit that no exemptions would be contemplated. As a result, donations from the Indian towns became a type of double taxation, being added to the annual tribute paid by all family heads in these communities. The coercive character can be observed in the archival documentation on donations in the years 1781–1784. The review of the long lists of contributors highlights their universality, extending to the entire urban and rural population of colonial Mexico.

When Viceroy Mayorga issued orders for the collection of the *universal donation* of 1781, he expected that the funds could be amassed relatively quickly. The first reports were encouraging; nevertheless, it should be noted

35 On the 1622 loan see José F. de la Peña, *Oligarquía y propiedad en Nueva España, 1550–1624* (Mexico: Fondo de Cultura Económica, 1983), pp. 257–260. According to G. Valle Pavón, "Consulado de Comerciantes," Chapter 1, between 1700 and 1750, each time the contract for collection of the *alcabalas* was signed with the guild, it would make some loan or donation to the government. A long list of loans, supplements, and donations made by the Mexico merchant guild can be found in AGN, *Archivo Histórico de Hacienda*, vol. 640, exp. 36, fs. 226–227, dated June 26, 1806. On the 1704 and 1744 donations, see AGN, *Archivo Histórico de Hacienda*, vol. 223, exp. 1, fs. 1–69 and exp. 5.2, fs. 258–376.

36 During the seventeenth century, more donations were applied to Peru than the New Spain, while in the eighteenth century this trend was inverted. For information, consult Manuel Ayala, *Diccionario de gobierno y legislación de Indias*, vol. IV (Madrid: Quinto Centenario, 1988), passim.

37 Natalia Silva Prada, "Contribución de la población indígena novohispana al erario real: el donativo gracioso de 1781," unpublished paper, El Colegio de México, 1995, p. 5.

that during the first months of the campaign (in March and April), most of the monies were collected in the capital of the viceroyalty and surrounding towns. To demonstrate their zeal for the cause of monarchy, the employees of royal offices in Mexico City hastened to deliver amounts of some importance. The bureaucrats of the *Real Tribunal de Cuentas*, for example, donated 938 pesos while the regent and judges (*oidores*) of the *Real Audiencia* gave 1,500 pesos. Pedro Cosío, quartermaster-general of the army and secretary of the Viceregal Chamber (*Cámara del Virreinato*), "gave for himself and the dependents of the said office, the sum of one thousand pesos."[38] Contributions were also paid in by the employees of the mint (*Casa de Moneda*) and the post office and the chief clerks of the mercury monopoly (*Oficina de Azogues*) and the office for collection of Indian tribute (*Reales Tributos*).

The tobacco monopoly and its employees proved to be among the greatest contributors. The almost 8,000 workers at the Royal Tobacco Factory in Mexico City provided 10,000 pesos (paying on the basis of 1 or 2 pesos per capita), while the monopoly's officers in regional districts (*intendencias*) supplied equivalent amounts, and sometimes more.[39] For example, the director of the offices of the tobacco monopoly in the city of Puebla (*Renta de Tabacos de Puebla*) sent 10,246 pesos while his counterpart in Valladolid transferred 29,819 pesos. In both cases the sums represented not merely the donations of the bureaucrats but also money collected from tobacco sales in numerous villages in these jurisdictions.[40]

The royal administration also pressed the Catholic Church to contribute to the donation.[41] One report from Mexico City indicated that among the religious leaders "of this court," the heads of various monastic orders had offered substantial amounts; a certain Friar Manuel de Cristo, head of the provincial order of the Carmelites, had delivered a thousand pesos while the head of the order of Our Lady of Charity (*Nuestra Señora de la Merced*) had donated 500 pesos, including 29 pesos that had been contributed by "the servant boys of this convent." Notwithstanding these contributions,

38 A list of these contributions can be found in AGN, *Donativos y Préstamos*, vol. 17, fs. 136–167.

39 One should take into account that there were 7,000 workers in the factory: S. Deans-Smith, *Bureaucrats, Planters and Workers*, p. 176.

40 This was also the case with the head of the tobacco administration agent in the city of Cordoba, who delivered 43,267 pesos collected from the employees as well as money collected "by the various Justices of the district that have charged local residents." AGN, *Donativos y Préstamos*, vol. 17, f. 159.

41 However, it should be noted that in the first months of the donation, an important effort was made to obtain funds from landowners/nobles and some merchants and miners. For example the Count of Rabago donated 10,000 pesos and 1,200 loads (*cargas*) of wheat (with a value of 14,955 pesos) and 1,000 horses; the Count of Santa María de Guadalupe del Peñasco, 2,000 pesos; the Marquis of Selva Nevada, 900 pesos; and the Countess of San Mateo Valparaíso, 2,000 pesos, among many others. See the complete lists in C. Rodríguez Venegas, "La sociedad novohispana," Annex. 2.

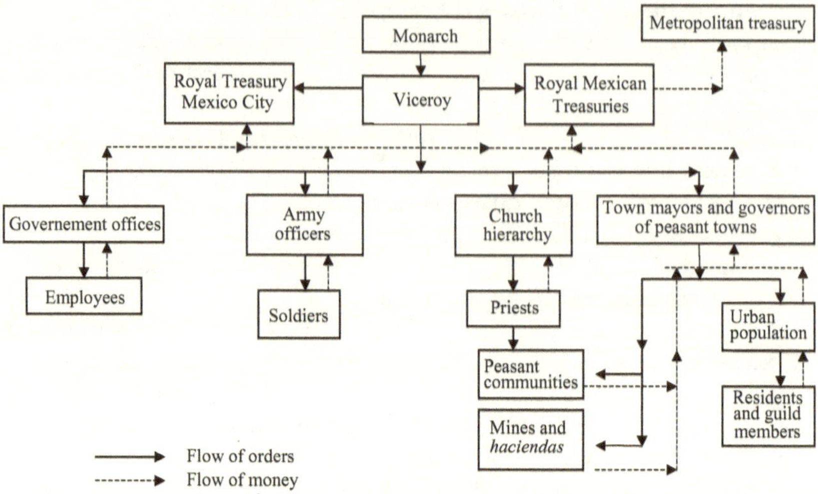

Figure 3.1. Typical universal donation in New Spain (late colonial period).
Source: Drawn by Carlos Marichal.

the clergy's greatest assistance to the donation was helping in the campaign to collect funds in several thousand peasant villages and in hundreds of estates – the length and breadth of the viceroyalty. An analysis of the extensive lists of donors shows that the bulk of the funds came from the popular classes: peasants, miners, artisans, and even slaves![42] During two long years, agents of the civil bureaucracy and the clergy called on the villages and urban neighborhoods, demanding a peso payment from each Indian and two pesos from each *Spaniard*, which presumably referred to both persons of European origin and *mestizos*.[43] (See Figure 3.1.)

As the collection of the universal donation proceeded into many rural regions, it became clear that time worked against the demands of the viceroy for speed in gathering coin from a vast and highly differentiated population. The estimated four months' period for collection was quite insufficient, given the vast and mountainous terrain of the viceroyalty, to which

42 In the case of laborers and slaves from the *haciendas*, it was the responsibility of the landowners to deliver the donation. The respective correspondence with detailed lists of contributions are found in AGN, *Donativos y Préstamos*, vols. 1–33, passim. For comments see Carlos Marichal, "La historiografía económica reciente sobre el México borbónico: los estudios del comercio y las finanzas virreinales, 1760–1820," *Boletín del Instituto de Historia Argentina y Americana Dr. E. Ravignani* (Buenos Aires), tercera serie, 2 (1990), 161–180.

43 In practice it is difficult to determine the royal treasury's definition of "Spanish" exactly, for, in practice, it not only refers to propertied classes but includes relatively poor whites (Spanish and mixed (*criollo*)) and mixed (*mestizos*) with specialized jobs particularly in ranches (*haciendas*) and mines.

were added bureaucratic slowness and, not infrequently, the difficulty of extracting money from peasant communities living in conditions of extreme poverty. As a result, the deliveries of monies dragged out and were only completed after three years. (See Appendix III.1.)

The first information of rural receipts collected for the royal donation is to be found in a report dated May 1781 from the Hacienda of San Nicolas Coatepeque, in the jurisdiction of Texcoco, close to the capital. There, each senior worker paid two pesos, including the steward, the maize grower, the foreman, schoolmaster, blacksmith, the financier (*el aviador*), and muleteer; the sum of one peso was taken from the monthly wage of the more modest workers such as shepherds, bricklayers, and laborers (almost all of whom were designated Indians in the official lists). The amounts paid were not insignificant, as they represented on average the equivalent of between one and two weeks' salary of each individual contributor.

The collection in the Indian peasant towns required the collaboration of the local authorities, including the clergy and the Indian governors.[44] In the late eighteenth century, there were more than 4,000 Indian towns and villages (*repúblicas de indios*) in the viceroyalty, most of which were obliged to participate in the donation. For example, in August 1781 the commissioner sent to collect in the peasant town of Tlocotepec in Veracruz reported that he had been accompanied by the parish priest to a meeting with the governor and mayors of the Indian community to explain the conditions "by which the Indians should contribute to His Majesty with a peso each for the royal donation."[45]

This universality of the donation is corroborated in a study by Natalia Silva Prada which demonstrates that the donation was collected by the local governors, clergy magistrates, and mayors, relying on the lists of family heads which were normally used to collect the annual tribute tax:

> The first step in the principal Indian towns was to meet on holidays in the "tecpan" or community houses where the royal request was communicated to the representatives of the nearby villages. The royal officials also visited work locations such as the wool manufactories (*obrajes*) in which numerous indentured Indian peasants labored. In the Indian towns, the local governors would name two official mayors (*alcaldes*) to collect the corresponding amounts in their neighborhood . . . , listing the names of each individual donor in a book. The verification of the tax collection, that is, the control stayed in the hands of the magistrates and clergy.[46]

44 See the excellent detailed study by Dorothy Tanck, *Pueblos de indios y educación en el México Colonial, 1770–1810* (México: El Colegio de México, 1998), Chapter 4.

45 AGN, *Donativos y Préstamos*, vol. 21, f. 74.

46 N. Silva Prada, "Contribución de la población indígena," p. 15.

In the more remote villages of the viceroyalty, the collection was hindered not only by distance but also by the extreme poverty of many peasant villages. In September 1784, three years after the campaign had first begun, the lieutenant of the senior mayor (*alcalde mayor*) of Xiliapam (in the northern territory of Sonora) issued a report on his visit to the *Pames* Indians and his negotiations with the local governor. The native population of this region was in such penury that most Indian peasants were not able to pay a peso apiece, and the royal functionary had to content himself with extracting only four *reales* per neighbor. The official added that while a good number of the inhabitants delivered their donation, others were unable to do so, "not because they are lazy . . . but they reply that they find themselves too insolvent. . . . "[47]

Success in obtaining funds from each village depended on the type of community or social group from whom the contribution was requested. In some regions, the officials used a caste classification that reflected the hierarchies and different socioethnic characteristics of colonial society. In Zimatlán, for example, the donation was levied on family heads based on various categories: those described as Spanish descendants (*españoles*) paid two pesos per head of family while mulattos and other mixed racial groups (*mestizos and castizos*), as well as Indian peasants, paid one peso. The Zimatlán donation lists reveal that Spaniards and *mestizos* (a total of 207) were concentrated in four towns, mulattos were workers in four rural estates (*haciendas*) and sugar mills (*trapiches*), while the 3,840 Indians were distributed among a broad spectrum of forty-six villages.

The methods used to convince the local population of the donation's importance were varied. Although it may be supposed that a sentiment of loyalty to the King may have prevailed, it is evident that the officials' zeal counted for a great deal in extracting funds, in many cases prompted by the ambition to be promoted up the bureaucratic-political ladder. When there was difficulty or resistance to collection, royal officials often appropriated the accumulated funds in the respective, community treasury (*caja de comunidad*). In others, the local mayors threatened Indian peasants with severe punishment. Silva Prada notes that in the jurisdiction of Maravitío, two Indian towns accused the mayor of transgressing the spirit of the royal instruction by demanding donations from "maids, widows, and old people, menacing the rest with threats and diverse apparatus for execution."[48]

In summary, the universal donation of 1781 was a compulsory fiscal requirement that all the king's subjects in colonial Mexico were obliged to pay. Donations, however, were not the only extraordinary financial

47 AGN, *Donativos y Préstamos*, vol. 21, exp. 20, f. 300.

48 N. Silva Prada, "Contribución de la población indígena," p. 10, who cites AGN, *Donativos y Préstamos*, vol. 24, fs. 252–255.

instrument adopted by New Spain in this period. Almost simultaneously, Viceroy Mayorga instructed high-level treasury officials to launch a campaign to obtain loans from the most affluent individuals and the most opulent corporations in New Spain: the Mexico City Merchant Guild, the Mining Tribunal, and the Catholic Church.

The 1781–1783 War Loans: The Financial Contribution of New Spain's Elite

While the donation for the war against England (1779–1783) provided the Crown with some 800,000 pesos, this sum was substantially less than the loans collected from wealthy members of New Spain between 1781 and 1783.[49] (See Table 3.1 and, for more details on loans, see Appendix III.2.) Requests for loans were not new. It was customary for the viceroys to ask for monies from the privileged corporations of New Spain at times of war. For example, in 1706 (during the War of the Spanish Succession), approximately one hundred members of the powerful Merchant Guild of the City of Mexico (*Consulado de Comerciantes de Mexico*) contributed a total of 903,000 pesos to finance metropolitan armies.[50] In 1727 the Mexican merchants again assisted the monarchy, collecting a million pesos for the war that the Spanish crown prosecuted against the English in the Mediterranean.[51] And in 1742, during another naval conflict with Britain, the viceroy, the Count of Fuenclara, asked for a loan from the Merchant Guild of Mexico City and a donation from the Catholic Church with the objective of financing the Spanish naval squadron operating in the Caribbean Sea.[52]

The loyalty to the Crown of the richest individuals of the viceroyalty was reconfirmed in 1778 when Viceroy Bucareli requested help for a naval rearmament campaign. On that occasion, the viceroy received a remarkably large loan from the Count of Regla, the richest miner in colonial Mexico, to finance the construction of two great warships at the Cuban arsenals, each with eighty cannon: the ships, appropriately enough, were named *Conde de*

49 Information on the loans borrowed from the Merchant Guild of Mexico City (*Consulado de comerciantes de la ciudad de México*) in the seventeenth and eighteenth century can be found in the doctoral thesis by G. Valle Pavón, "Consulado de Comerciantes."

50 AGN, *Archivo Histórico de Hacienda*, vol. 213, exp. 9; see the correspondence in vol. 223, exp. 3, fs. 39–69.

51 G. Valle Pavón, "Consulado de Comerciantes," pp. 117–121.

52 AGN, *Archivo Histórico de Hacienda*, vol. 213, exp. 5. The 1742 loan is an example of the enormous wealth of the leading silver merchants in Mexico: one million two hundred thousand pesos were collected, although the greatest contribution came from the leading silver merchant in the viceroyalty at the time, Francisco de Valdivielso, who personally lent the huge sum of 840,000 pesos to the king, possibly the greatest individual loan recorded in colonial history. For details see María Vargas-Lobsinger, "El ascenso social y económico de los inmigrantes españoles: el caso de Francisco Valdivielso (1683–1743)," *Historia Mexicana*, xxxv, 4 [140] (1986), p. 615.

Regla and *Mexicano* and cost 450,000 pesos to build.[53] (According to one much-used index, this would be equivalent to almost 200 million dollars in 2005,[54] a third of the cost of construction of a navy frigate today.[55])

To obtain loans, the royal authorities habitually used a combination of economic, political, and social incentives. Requests by the monarch for financial assistance were doubtless interpreted in a political way by his most affluent subjects: it was understood that the privileges enjoyed by the New Spain plutocrats – be they landowners, mine owners, merchants – depended upon good relations with the government. Financial advances to the royal treasury in emergency situations might reinforce these privileges and open doors to new business or favors. But, at the same time, it was also deemed proper that the Crown officials offer inducements that could reinforce the social prestige of the donors: granting noble titles in exchange for loans became an increasingly common practice in the second half of the eighteenth century. In fact, during this period, thirteen titles were granted to great merchants of New Spain in exchange for war loans – a phenomenon that illustrates the persistence of old regime values in these financial transactions.[56]

While retaining some traditional elements, the debt policies adopted from the 1780s were of greater complexity and modernity than in previous decades. This is confirmed by the diversity of creditors and by the types of guarantees offered by financial officials. Study of the privileged corporations of Bourbon Mexico suggests that important innovations in public sector debt management can be observed in the role of financial intermediaries, the Mexico City Merchant Guild and Mining Tribunal, both of which effectively began to operate as bankers to the colonial state. Some parallels can be suggested with the Bank of San Carlos established in Madrid in 1782 and charged with the issue and sale of the new instruments of public debt, *vales reales*, in financial markets in Spain. These novel securities served as commercial and investment paper, but also

53 B. Bobb, *ViceRegency of Antonio María Bucareli*, p. 114. Regla also donated 300,000 pesos to found the important institution the *Monte de Piedad* in Mexico City: Edith Couturier, "The Philanthropic Activities of Pedro Romero de Terreros, First Count of Regla, 1753–1781," *The Americas*, xxxii, 1 (1975), 13–30.

54 This calculation is based on the EH Net (http://eh.net/hmit/compare) complete index of the money wage rates paid for common or unskilled labor from 1774 to the present; three sources are used: a series published by Paul David and Peter Solar in 1977, the work of Robert Margo published in 2000, and various publications of the Bureau of Labor Statistics (BLS).

55 In 2005, according to U.S. Navy budget procurement reports, building an aircraft carrier cost approximately 5 billion dollars, a missile guided destroyer 2 billion dollars, and a frigate some 600 million dollars. Ronald O'Rourke, CRS Report for Congress, "Navy Ship Acquisition: Options for Lower-Cost Ship Designs: Issues for Congress, Updated June 23, 2005," published on CSR Web.

56 On the subject of noble titles granted in the eighteenth century, see the excellent study by D. Ladd, *The Mexican Nobility*, Chapters 1 and 2.

became a kind of paper currency in the metropolis, although circulation was mainly limited to the wealthier merchants and businessmen. In Mexico and the other colonies, such relatively modern securities did not yet circulate in significant quantities; rather, public loans were issued by offering a notarized certificate to creditors, guaranteeing interest payments and amortization with a lien on royal tax branches.[57]

Although a capital market for public financial claims had scarcely emerged in the viceroyalty, it developed with considerable rapidity in the 1780s.[58] The increasing supply of private capital is illustrated with clarity in a report prepared in 1782 by a religious official in charge of corporate ecclesiastical investments:

> Because of the abundance of pesos, originating in the mining bonanza, and other causes, each day has brought more loan repayments (*redenciones de gravámenes*) . . . and because the religious communities and foundations have more than enough money, they can meet the demands of the many who ask for loans. . . .[59]

As this document suggests, the viceroy of New Spain, Mayorga, was able to take advantage of a favorable financial situation to obtain funds for the Crown, although, initially, he resorted to a traditional resource, a non-interest-bearing loan (*suplemento*). This consisted of an advance of funds (without interest) to the government from a number of especially affluent individuals, to be repaid by the royal treasury in a term of no more than two years. To obtain this short-term credit, in March 1781, the viceroy ordered Pedro de Cosío – then quartermaster of the army and superintendent of the royal treasury of New Spain, and a respected member of one of the oldest mercantile dynasties of the viceroyalty – to organize a meeting at the government palace with the members of the merchant guild to ask for subscriptions to a loan of up to a million and a half pesos, but without any promise to pay interest.[60]

57 For the 1782–1783 loans, the creditors received *escrituras de imposición* on depósitos *irregulares* (an investment term) in government debt through *Tribunal del Consulado* or *Tribunal de Minería*. Later in the 1790s the terms of these documents were modified on account of new loans, utilizing on occasion the term certificates (*certificados*) or coupon (*cédulas*), but it would not be until 1798 that the term share (*acción*) appeared as synonym for what we know today as a government bond.

58 Guillermina del Valle Pavón "Las corporaciones religiosas en los empréstitos negociados por el Consulado de México a fines del siglo xviii," in P. Martínez López-Cano, ed., *Iglesia, estado y economía*, pp. 231–232, notes that it was not until the 1780s that the Mexico City capital market acquired dynamism.

59 The document was written by a financial official from the *Real Fisco de la Inquisición*. It is cited in Gisela von Wobeser, "La inquisición como institución crediticia en el siglo XVIII," *Historia Mexicana*, xxxix, 4 [156] (1990), p. 865.

60 On Cosío, see Vicente Rodriguez García, *El fiscal de Real Hacienda en Nueva España, Ramón de Posada y Soto, 1781–1793* (Oviedo: Universidad de Oviedo, 1985), pp. 72–77.

Mayorga informed the Crown that he expected to collect the monies quickly owing to the suspension of trading activities during the war: "for it is neither here nor there to the merchants whether they keep their treasure in their own houses or place it for the king's urgent requirements. . . ."[61] Intendant Cosío informed Mayorga that the meeting had been a success and that the majority of the merchants had agreed to make important contributions. He reported that four rich individuals had approached him, promising very considerable sums: Antonio Bassoco, merchant and a senior official of the merchant guild offered to deliver 100,000 pesos for war expenses; the Count of Rabago, a great landowner, engaged to provide 1,000 horses and 2,000 wagon loads of wheat for the troops as well as 102,000 silver pesos in cash; Pedro Antonio de Alles, a wealthy wholesaler, promised 100,000 pesos; and Servando Gómez de la Cortina, later named Count of Cortina for his services to the Crown, offered 50,000 pesos in gold and silver as well as 500 wagon loads of wheat from one of his *haciendas*.[62] Another nine individuals provided amounts between 40,000 and 50,000 pesos, while others gave lesser sums.

These contributions bespeak the enormous wealth of the Mexican mercantile and landowning plutocracy, not to speak of the wealthiest mining families. For comparative purposes it should be noted that a case study of Antonio Bassoco places his fortune circa 1800 at around 2.5 million pesos (dollars).[63] This was superior to practically any individual merchant banker in Europe at the time except, possibly, the Rothschilds. In the United States at the time there were not yet any millionaires while in late colonial Mexico "there were at least 18 families . . . that were reputed to be millionaires."[64] While it is possible to attempt formal conversions to modern purchasing power, we believe that what is important is to underline the extreme concentration of wealth in late colonial Mexico.[65]

Meetings of the wealthiest traders in the intendancy of Veracruz were held a few weeks later in the city of Xalapa de la Feria to raise additional funds

61 AGN, *Consulado*, box 306, exp. 7, f. 7.

62 Ibid., f. 10. Bassoco and Alles also received noble titles in later years. For information on fortunes of these Mexican merchant bankers, see D. Ladd, *The Mexican Nobility*.

63 D. Ladd, *The Mexican Nobility*, p. 36: this author provides much information on the greatest landed, mercantile and mining fortunes in New Spain at the end of the colonial period. It should be recalled that one silver peso was equal to one dollar from 1780 to 1850.

64 D. Ladd, *The Mexican Nobility*, p. 25.

65 Bassoco's fortune in 1800 would have been equivalent to 628 million dollars of 2005 according to the EH Net (http://eh.net/hmit/compare) index of the money wage rates paid for common or unskilled labor from 1774 to the present. Another possible calculation of relative wealth is the following: Bassoco would have earned at least 5% annually on his fortune, providing him with an income of 125,000 pesos, that is to say the equivalent of the joint income of at least 2,000 urban workers in Mexico in 1800.

for the Crown loan. The meetings were presided over by the governor of the port and various authorities from the royal treasury.[66] The contributions from Veracruz were less substantial than those of their colleagues in the capital, but this was not surprising since the great Mexico City merchants continued to dominate commerce in the viceroyalty. In any case, the monies collected among the three groups of affluent merchants and entrepreneurs amounted to slightly more than the sum of a million and half pesos. (See Appendix III.2.)

A year later, in August 1782, as the war in the Caribbean continued unabated, the viceroy decided to solicit two more loans through corporate intermediaries, but now offered to pay an annual interest rate of 5 percent. First, he urged the Mexico City Merchant Guild to obtain subscriptions for a loan of one million pesos, in exchange for which he authorized an increase in the *avería*, a tax that allowed the mercantile corporation to recoup the debt service.[67] The guild would therefore not have to use its own funds but could act as a financial intermediary, collecting monies in the colonial capital market. A detailed study of Guillermina del Valle identifies the leading investors, including seven wealthy merchant bankers of the city of Mexico, nine landowners, and nine ecclesiastical corporations.[68] (See Figure 3.2.)

Mayorga then approached the country's principal silver miners and requested that they assume responsibility for completing another one-million-peso loan. The miners replied that they expected a series of concessions in exchange for this subscription and further recalled that they had recently made loans (300,000 pesos for the construction of the docks at Coatzacoalcos and 100,000 pesos as a donation to the Prince of Asturias). They also argued that they did not desire that the Mining Tribunal be regarded as a bank with unlimited funds. Mayorga agreed with their petition to freeze the price of mercury sold by the Crown and authorized the Tribunal to charge four grams of silver on each silver mark produced by the Mexico City mint in order to guarantee a part of the interest payments on the loan by the miners' association.[69] In the final event, the miners did not have to subscribe to more than a fraction of the credit, since a diverse group of rich landowners, merchants, rentiers, and ecclesiastical

66 AGN, *Donativos y Préstamos*, vol. 21, exp. 5, fs. 110–119.

67 Mayorga wrote to Galvez on July 6,1782, explaining that in exchange for the loan, the *Consulado* would charge an additional four to six per thousand that they collected on the port tax known as *avería*, but added that "they will cease to charge this sum when the million peso loans is paid off. . . ." "AGN, *Correspondencia de virreyes*, vol. 131, exp. 1691, fs. 48–49.

68 G. Valle Pavón, "Consulado de Comerciantes," Chapter 3, Table III.2.

69 For details on the mine owners' loans, see the classic study by W. Howe, *Mining Guild*, pp. 84–85, 96, 118–119, 372, and 376–379.

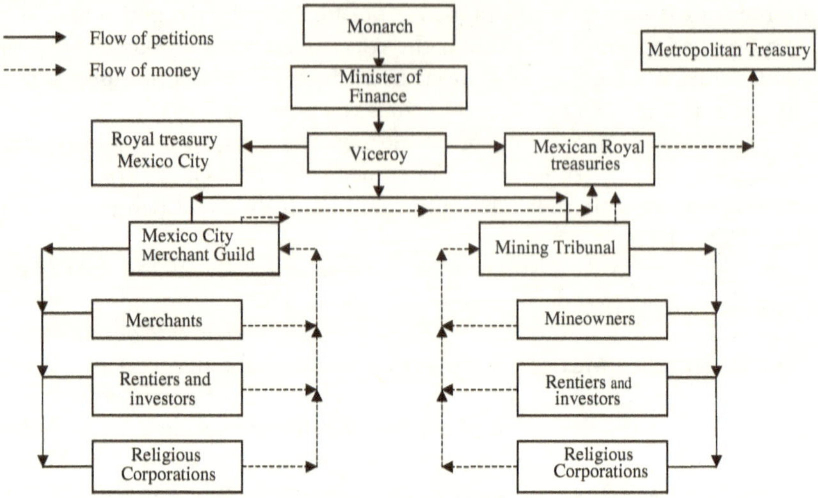

Figure 3.2. Administration of loans for the Crown by the Mexico City Merchant Guild and Mining Tribunal.
Source: Drawn by Carlos Marichal.

institutions underwrote the rest.[70] Nonetheless, the officials of the Mining Tribunal were obliged to guarantee the entire debt service of the loan and spent a substantial amount of their capital reserves for this purpose, rather than extending credits to the mining industry.[71] As Walter Howe points out: "The crown's requirements left no funds available to finance the mines so, in consequence, this important objective for the *Tribunal* could not be met after 1786. . . ."[72]

To finance the war against Great Britain, Mayorga managed to collect a grand total of over five million pesos in donations, advances, and loans: 840,000 pesos from the donation between 1781 and 1784; 1,655,00 pesos (without interest) as a *suplemento* from the wealthy merchants in 1781; two million pesos from interest-bearing loans from the Merchant Guild and Mining Tribunal in 1782; and half a million pesos for a loan guaranteed by a mortgage on the tobacco monopoly in 1783.[73]

70 The complete list of the investors (who provided 890,000 pesos) is in the *Archivo de Minería*, vol. 63, fs. 145–146. This archive is located in the Palacio de Minería in Mexico City. The Mining Tribunal (*Tribunal de Minería*), itself, was obliged to provide 110,000 pesos to complete the million-peso loan.

71 Eduardo Flores Clair, "Las deudas del Tribunal de Minería, 1777–1823" (Mexico, Instituto Nacional de Antropología e Historia, 1996) provides information on the principal creditors of the *Fondo Dotal* as well as the loans granted.

72 W. Howe, *Mining Guild*, p. 382.

73 There are small discrepancies with regard to the total, depending on the document consulted. For example, according to a document to be found by María Elena López Godínez, "Monografía de los

Information about these credits confirms that a considerable amount of capital in specie was available in New Spain, especially among the wealthiest merchants. There are various explanations for the fact that colonial capital markets should have been flush with cash at this time. On the one hand, as Mayorga noted in his correspondence with minister Galvéz, the abrupt decline of external trade during the war had forced the great merchants to reduce the amount of capital engaged in transatlantic commerce. Trade with Cádiz normally absorbed a considerable part of the silver pesos available in the viceroyalty, but now money reserves were abundant. Secondly, as a result of the silver mining boom, both miners and merchants in New Spain enjoyed extraordinary liquidity.[74]

To lend funds to the royal treasury could be an attractive proposition for investors, because debt service was guaranteed with the relatively abundant tax resources available to the colonial administration. Indeed, the fiscal opulence of the tobacco monopoly was one of the important factors that inspired investors' confidence since it served as guarantor for annual interest payments during and after the war. In this regard, public credit policy functioned in a rational and systematic way: lenders – including merchants, mine owners, landowners, *rentiers*, and colonial corporations – received regular interest payments and succeeded in having a substantial part of their capital returned.[75] On the other hand, the Crown was not averse to oblige the tobacco monopoly itself to make huge direct contributions to the royal treasury for a total of twelve million pesos between 1780 and 1783.[76] This was not welcome news for the long-term financial solvency of the colonial administration.

donativos y préstamos en Nueva España, 1780–1815," B.A. thesis, Universidad del Claustro de Sor Juana, Mexico, 1993, p. 145–148, the total amount of the donation, 1783–1784, in the New Spain was 887,809 pesos, including more than 100,000 pesos sent from Manila. The document, however, is somewhat late, dated 1793, and is to be found in AGN, *Donativos y Préstamos*, vol. 28, exp. 8, fs. 105–362.

74 Pedro Pérez Herrero notes: "An indirect indicator of the liquidity of Mexico City merchants during the second half of the eighteenth century . . . is shown by the loans and interest-free loans made by the *Consulado* to the monarch for the purpose of defraying the Crown's war costs. In an environment, where the general trend was an increasing scarcity of silver currency, these traders collected enormous amounts of specie. . . . "; Pedro Pérez Herrero, "Los beneficiarios del reformismo borbónico: metrópoli versus élites novohispanas," *Historia Mexicana*, xii, 2 [162] (1991), 235–236.

75 There is abundant but disperse documentation on debt service payments by the Merchant Guild of Mexico City in the many volumes of the *Consulado* branch in the national archive (*Archivo General de la Nación*). The issue is discussed in some detail in G. Valle Pavón, "Consulado de Comerciantes," Chapter 4, who notes, nevertheless, that after 1800 the regularity of debt service left much to be desired.

76 S. Deans-Smith, *Bureaucrats, Planters and Workers*, p. 64, cites a report of the controller-general of the Mexican Treasury in 1788, noting that in the same year the central treasury owed the tobacco monopoly fourteen million pesos; however, in 1799, according to a later report the debt had been reduced to a little more than seven million pesos.

The War Loans of 1793 and 1795

After the signing of the Versailles peace treaty in 1783, and for almost a decade, the Spanish royal authorities suspended loans and donations in the colonies. During this peaceful interlude tax receipts remained high. The fiscal transfers from Mexico to the Madrid Treasury averaged three million pesos a year, while substantial tax remittances continued to be sent to the Spanish Caribbean and the Philippines.[77] The solvency of the Spanish government and of its richest colony seemed assured, but this was actually a mirage.

A series of external pressures soon undermined crown finance as a result of increasing diplomatic and military tensions between Spain and France. The Spanish monarch Charles IV (1789–1808) was incensed by the measures taken by the French revolutionary assembly that had proclaimed France a republic in September 1792 and later condemned his cousin, the king of France, Louis XVI to execution in January 1793. Already in September 1792 – and in anticipation of future war – Charles IV had requested a six- to eight-million-peso loan from his American subjects. On receipt of this petition, the new viceroy of Mexico, the Count of Revillagigedo, informed the finance minister at Madrid, Diego de Gardoqui, that he would begin to collect new loans in New Spain but advised him that more than thirty million pesos had already been remitted from the viceroyalty to the metropolis and the Caribbean garrisons since he had assumed his position in 1789.

However, after the outbreak of war with France in March 1793, the Spanish government found itself in acute need of money for the payment of troops and to cover debts of the royal treasury. The confrontation between the French revolutionary troops and the army of the Spanish monarch lasted almost two and a half years, provoking a huge increase in the military expenditures of the metropolitan treasuries. Initially the bulk of these commitments were covered by taxes and bond issues in Spain itself, but the sustained increase in the costs of war provoked steeply rising deficits and grave problems in covering expenses in hard cash. Soldiers and creditors sought payments in silver while hard currency was becoming increasingly scarce in Spain. The situation worsened with the French conflict, reducing the possibilities of the royal treasury in securing hard currency within the peninsula. An extract from a secret report of the Bank of San Carlos confirmed the capital flight from Spain from mid-1793:

77 Between 1785 and 1789, the amounts remitted from New Spain (basically tobacco surpluses) were substantial; 11,754,996 pesos between 1785 and 1789, according to F. Fonseca and C. de Urrutia, *Historia general*, Appendix, Table 3.

Lack of confidence has removed much silver from circulation that now hides in idleness; the withdrawal, from the kingdom, for commerce and contraband . . . continues to be perhaps equal to the quantity of silver imports from the Indies: the entrance of the Spanish armies in French territory cannot but provide an outlet for incalculable amounts; and lastly the nature of the war itself opens infinite channels and directions for the money of the nation to run and escape.[78]

The initial success of the Spanish troops was followed by defeats, obliging the Crown to seek urgent financial help from affluent sectors in the metropolis. This domestic campaign, however, had limited success as is demonstrated by the fact that the only significant merchant groups in Spain to advance funds in 1793 were the Indies merchants trading from Cádiz who delivered a million silver pesos in exchange for tax concessions. Evidently, many Spanish wealthy feared the new offensives by the French revolutionary armies and did not discount the possibility of a capitulation by the monarchy.

The scarcity of funds (particularly of silver coin) in the metropolis forced finance minister, Diego de Gardoqui, to instruct American viceroys to send to Spain as much treasure as possible. According to Miguel Artola, almost 30 percent of the 3,000 million *reales* collected between 1792 and 1796 as extraordinary income for the metropolitan treasury came from America. The huge sum of colonial silver remitted approached 42 million silver pesos, with the greatest contribution coming from New Spain: it made up mostly of tax monies, but also of loans and donations.[79]

The first application in Mexico for new war loans came in January 1793. Viceroy Revillagigedo appealed to merchants, mine owners, estate owners, senior officials, and clergy to support the Crown in its war preparations.[80] In scarcely six months, an amount equivalent to the earlier loans of 1781–1782 was gathered (see Table 3.1). But since royal authorities initially did not offer interest payments, they encountered considerable difficulty in convincing wealthy members of colonial society to collaborate. The correspondence with merchants and landowners is illustrative as much for their show of loyalty as for their misgivings about the loan itself.

78 "Informe de la Junta de Directores del Banco de San Carlos sobre los medios para evitar las péridida s de los Vales Reales," November 1, 1794, Archivo Histórico del Banco de España (AHBE), *Banco de San Carlos*, leg. 708.

79 According to Artola's estimates, the extraordinary income received between 1792 and 1796 consisted of a 5% in tax increases, 20% in advances and various donations, 47% from the issuance of *vales reales* and foreign credit, and 28% in funds sent from America: M. Artola, *La hacienda del antiguo régimen*, pp. 404–405.

80 G. Valle Pavón, "Consulado de Comerciantes," pp. 219–220.

Some of the most opulent entrepreneurs of New Spain did not hesitate to show their support for the Crown and offered substantial sums: for example, the Count of Cortina gave 50,000 pesos; Francisco Pérez de Sorranez, a lieutenant-colonel of the militia and rich merchant, gave another 50,000 pesos; Antonio Bassoco provided 50,000 pesos; the partners of the merchant firm of Iraeta 40,000 pesos; and the wealthy trader Tomas de Acha 25,000 pesos.[81] However, other wealthy men refused to make similar sacrifices, alluding in general to business difficulties. The merchant Francisco Bazo Ibañez argued in a letter to the viceroy that his mercantile firm had no liquidity:

> so deplorable is the activity and decline of trade, it has forced me to invest a part of my liquid wealth in an estate, another in interest-bearing investments, and the remainder in goods and other effects that cannot be easily liquidated....[82]

The viceroy answered by urging him to make a donation equivalent to the subscription he had made to a loan in 1782 (when Ibanez had contributed 29,000 pesos to the Crown), arguing brusquely that since then his merchant house "had not experienced decay."

Somewhat different were the arguments of the rich merchant and mine owner Gaspar Martin Vicario who informed Revillagigedo that in the three previous years he had lost 105,000 pesos in various badly conceived mining investments, adding that:

> The rest of my wealth consists of goods that I have in my warehouse and in a store; in the current state of commercial conditions these cannot be sold, at least without being subject to a considerable loss.[83]

That a significant number of merchants and miners should have refused to contribute to the royal purse was due to many factors. The most frequent cause cited was decline in commercial activity, although a review of the trade trends suggests that the years 1792–1793 were not especially prejudicial to New Spain's trade. On the other hand, it is true that as a result of the recent ratification of the free trade decree in New Spain (1789), the merchants of Mexico City were exposed to greater competition from the Veracruz merchants, who were already mobilizing to organize their own merchant guild.[84] Moreover, many of the most affluent merchants claimed that that

81 For the list of subscribers up to June 28, 1793, see AGN, *Donativos y Préstamos*, vol. 1, exp. 80–88, fs. 317–324. One has to take care in comparing the promise to pay with actual investment. In practice the ecclesiastical corporations supplied the greatest amounts.

82 AGN, *Donativos y Préstamos*, vol. 1, exp. 33, fs. 88–89.

83 The correspondence with these merchants is to be found in AGN, *Donativos y Préstamos*, vol. 1, exp. 4, f. 8 and exp. 33, fs. 88–89.

84 G. Valle Pavón, "Consulado de Comerciantes," Chapter 4, states that from the establishment of free trade in New Spain, 1789, the Mexico City merchants faced competition from those of Veracruz,

they lacked cash because they had so much of their capital committed to the purchase of goods in Europe or to transactions with Peru and other colonies in America. The wealthy entrepreneur Isidro Icaza, for example, deplored that he could not make a contribution owing to large commitments that he had in "regular commercial activities that continue with Peru via Acapulco that require remittances in advance. . . . "[85]

Another argument used by the great property owners was to call attention to the large amounts they had invested in cattle, wheat, and sugar properties, details of which can be found in the correspondence between the royal officials and such rich landowners as Juan de Oteyza, the Marquis de Inguanzo, or the Count of Medina y Torres.[86] For his part, Gabriel de Yermo, merchant and landowner, later to become an important political figure, wrote to the viceroy that the considerable expenses incurred on his estates in Cuernavaca and on a new sugar mill, which he had just bought, made it impossible for him to make significant contributions to the government. He also pointed out that the greater part of his liquid capital was tied up in business related to sugar exports and to the import of European cloth that he had ordered from his agents in Cádiz and Santander.[87]

The correspondence with the wealthiest individuals reflects the heterogeneity of their fortunes. This appears to confirm the arguments of historian Perez Herrero with regard to the diversification of investments by the great merchant houses of New Spain, particularly from the 1780s, having placed much capital in mines, estates, and urban real estate, as well as in trade.[88] For the leading merchants it was necessary to adopt strategies to protect fortunes during periods of abrupt changes in the economy of the viceroyalty,

Havana, and other parts of the Spanish empire, reducing the hoarding of silver and obliging them to put it into circulation. This reinforces the arguments of Pedro Pérez Herrero, *Plata y libranzas: la circulación mercantil en el México borbónico* (Mexico: El Colegio de México, 1988), Chapters 9 and 10. There he argues on the greater circulation of bills of exchange (in place of silver) to finance commerce within the viceroyalty.

85 Icaza wrote the viceroy that his firm's prosperity would depend on maintaining the "continuous movement" of his capital and that he did not dispose silver pesos for royal loans. Similarly, his colleague, the merchant Juan Dosamentes, insisted that the great bulk of his goods had been consigned "internally . . . in this capital and in the port of Veracruz." AGN, *Donativos y Préstamos*, vol. 1, exp. 3, f. 7 and exp. 29, f. 75.

86 Medina y Torres pleaded poverty, telling the viceroy that from 1786 his many estates (*haciendas*) were doing badly and that in the previous year he had to spend 80,000 pesos in corn to feed his laborers (*sirvientes*) – permanent laborers in the core of the *hacienda* – as a result of which he had to find new mortgages for his lands. AGN, *Donativos y Préstamos*, vol. 1, exp. 12.

87 The viceroy was disappointed with Yermo's reply and told him he would have to tell the king about his unwillingness to contribute. AGN, *Donativos y Préstamos*, vol. 1, exp. 38, f. 101.

88 P. Pérez Herrero, *Plata y libranzas*, Chapter 9, argues that mining investment was one of the mechanisms adopted by Guild merchants to maintain their monopoly of silver circulation in spite of the Crown's attempts to limit their control over this key facet of the colonial economy.

caused by international wars, sharp trade fluctuations, and the Bourbon regime's administrative and fiscal reforms.

But the reluctance of a considerable number of the wealthy to contribute to the first loan requested by Viceroy Revillagigedo was also due to the fact that this transaction carried no interest payments. The refusals indicate that a good number of the capitalists of New Spain were not disposed to risk their funds without a reasonable return. In fact, in the majority of the subsequent loan operations, the colonial administration was forced to offer interest payments and more secure fiscal guarantees, together with a series of special concessions, including the granting of titles of nobility to some of the greatest creditors.[89]

The new methods of raising loans suggest a growing complexity in the way that financial markets functioned in the viceroyalty. Illustrative of the financial innovations were the attempts by Viceroy Revillagigedo in 1793 to convince the powerful Mining Tribunal and Merchant Guild of Mexico City to act as intermediaries for a new million-peso loan. The viceroy asked these privileged corporations to act as financial intermediaries (much like merchant banks) and charged them with seeking individual investors interested in placing their capital in government loans. Nevertheless, their functions were more complex, since they were also commissioned to cover future debt service, using specific fiscal resources for the payment of future interest. This reflected one way in which the public and the private intertwined in the colonial *ancien regime*.[90] The negotiations with the merchants of the Mexico City were laborious. As Guillermina del Valle has pointed out:

> On March 8, 1793 one day after the French Assembly formally declared war on Spain . . . the *Consulado* notified Revillagigedo that they had only been able to raise 527,000 pesos with great difficulty. Various individuals and corporations had advanced 309,200 pesos, plus the 218,000 pesos already delivered by the Royal Tribunal (*Audiencia*). . . .[91]

Later, the authorities in Madrid informed Revillagigedo that they required additional amounts and urged him not only to mortgage the branches of the royal treasury but also to appropriate the "capital of pious

89 The granting of titles of nobility to merchants such as Antonio Bassoco or Pedro Antonio de Alles is described in D. Ladd, *The Mexican Nobility*. Other rewards included appointments as militia officials.

90 The basic model for placing capital had been successfully tried since 1782–1783. Now each Tribunal was offered a tax resource to guarantee the service of new debts: five per thousand of the *avería* tax to be collected by the *Consulado* and 1% of minting taxes by the *Tribunal de Minería*. The most detailed research about this type of colonial financial intermediary is G. Valle Pavón, "Consulado de Comerciantes," Chapters 3 and 4. For some comparisons with Peru, see A. W. Quiroz, *Deudas olvidadas*, pp. 142–149.

91 G. Valle Pavón, "Consulado de Comerciantes," p. 229.

works, entailed estates, chaplaincies, Indian community funds ... " as well as "loans from wealthy subjects, under the just premise that it benefits them." However, the viceroy answered the Minister of Finance, Diego de Gardoqui, that the viceroyalty's resources were strained to the utmost.[92]

The marquis of Branciforte, who became viceroy in July 1794, had somewhat better luck than his predecessor – quickly completing successful negotiations with the Mining Tribunal and the Merchant Guild for two loans of one million pesos.[93] Initially, the wealthy miners resisted Branciforte's request, pointing out that the royal treasury had not returned the greater part of the old loan of 1782. But finally, they agreed to give money under the condition of being able to collect additional receipts from the Mexico City mint and with the royal promise that there would no further increases in the price of powder, which was as essential as mercury for mining.[94] The Mining Tribunal met the financial requests of the viceroy but, as Flores Clair points out, this drastically reduced the credit available to mining firms and reflected the Crown's "crowding out" of private investment.[95]

The difficulties in negotiating new loans with the most affluent privileged corps of New Spain in 1793 and 1794 do not imply that funds in local financial markets or fiscal branches were exhausted. It is important to note that the greatest financial operation of this era (the so-called tobacco loan) produced more than 7 million pesos for the treasury between 1795 and 1802. This loan had been authorized in 1795 by the Spanish minister of finance for the huge sum of 15 million pesos (300 million *reales*) to be raised among all investors in New Spain, offering to mortgage the revenues of the tobacco monopoly as a guarantee for interest payments.[96] This loan was to be placed among subscribers by both the influential Mexico City Merchant Guild and the Mining Tribunal. As financial intermediaries, each body was expected to raise three and a half million pesos from individual investors. In exchange for their monies, the subscribers would receive certificates (a kind of bond) which were guaranteed with "written pledges based on the

92 Revillagigedo relied on the reports of the officials, Luis Gutierrez and Juan de Axandoy, June 28, 1793, indicating that they had now collected 3,559,000 pesos of the supplement from wealthy men and each one of the loans from the *Consulado de Comercio* and the *Tribunal de Mineria*. AGN, *Donativos y Préstamos*, vol. 1, exp. 88, f. 319.

93 The fact that Branciforte was the brother-in-law of Manuel de Godoy, the favorite of Charles IV, probably was important for the success of these transactions: G. Valle Pavón, "Consulado de Comerciantes," Chapter 4.

94 W. Howe, *Mining Guild*, pp. 376–378.

95 E. Flores Clair, "Las deudas del Tribunal," 33.

96 The figure of 15 millions was a maximum. In practice more than 7 million pesos were collected from New Spain between 1795 and 1802. The measure was similar to those adopted in the metropolis where royal income had been mortgaged with the purpose of offering the security of specific tax branches to their debtors. See M. Artola, *La hacienda del antiguo régimen*, pp. 388–420.

mortgage of tobacco income" (*escrituras de caución con hipoteca de la renta del tabaco*), which showed the amount and date of the delivery of the funds to the offices of royal treasury.[97] (See details in Appendix III.2.)

The merchant guild and the Mining Tribunal were charged with supervising interest payments and authorized to collect the required 5 percent annual interest from funds obtained by the tobacco monopoly – a function which they punctually fulfilled for a number of years.[98] In the first quarter of 1798, for example, the guild presented a list of payments made to ninety-four creditors. Among the largest lenders were the Marquis de Apartado, rich mine owner who had placed 200,000 pesos in this loan; various chaplaincies from Guadalajara which invested 344,000 pesos; the merchant Antonio Bassoco, 160,000 pesos; and the Countess of San Mateo Valparaíso, 113,000 pesos. These were substantial amounts for the period and speak of truly colossal fortunes – equivalent or superior to the wealthiest merchants and bankers of eighteenth-century Spain.[99] (According to a much-used contemporary index, it is possible to calculate that the personal fortune of the Marquis de Apartado worth 4 million pesos in 1800 would have been equivalent to more than a billion dollars of the year 2005. His loan of 200,000 pesos to the Crown would have been equivalent to more than 80 million dollars of the year 2005.[100])

Apart from wealthy individuals, a good proportion of the other investors were religious institutions: chaplaincies, convents, ecclesiastical councils, bishoprics, congregations, colleges, and religious seminaries. In addition, many Indian peasant villages and towns were pressed to release funds from

97 Documentation on the tobacco loan is to be found in various sources; for example, see, AGN, *Consulado*, vol. 312, exp. 8, leg. 4; *Donativos y Préstamos*, vol. 33, exp. 5, fs. 130–137.

98 There are some parallels between the financial measures adopted in 1795 in the colony and the metropolis since in both cases help was requested from trading institutions to collect and administer the Crown loans. An example is the issue of *vales reales* with a value of 240 millions in Spain in 1795 with the help of the powerful commercial association *Cinco Gremios Mayores* who provided advances to the government and presumably were responsible for the placement of the majority of the bonds. The information published regarding this credit operation is incomplete. See M. Artola, *La hacienda del antiguo régimen*, pp. 404, 412, and 416.

99 Certainly, the total capital of the great Mexican trading houses was greater than the principal banks in Madrid; for example, in 1808 it is estimated that Bassoco's fortune was greater than 3.5 million pesos (70 million *reales*) while the capital of Madrid's most powerful banker Alvaro Benito scarcely amounted to 18 million *reales*. Compare data in Pedro Tedde "Comerciantes y banqueros madrileños al final del Antiguo Régimen," *Historia económica y pensamiento social: Estudios en Homenaje a Diego Mateo del Peral* (Madrid: Alianza,1983), p. 311 with data on the fortunes of Mexican merchant bankers in D. Ladd, *The Mexican Nobility*, passim.

100 The data on Apartado's fortune is from D. Ladd, *The Mexican Nobility*, pp. 33–34. The subsequent calculation is based on the EH Net (http://eh.net/hmit/compare) complete index of the money wage rates paid for common or unskilled labor from 1774 to the present; three sources are used: a series published by Paul David and Peter Solar in 1977, the work of Robert Margo published in 2000, and various publications of the BLS.

their community treasuries for the same purpose. The merchant guild and miner's association complied with the task of paying interest to individuals and creditor institutions during several years.[101] From the point of view of the government, the tobacco loan was a success, collecting an annual average of around a million pesos per year between 1795 and 1801.

The Universal and Compulsory Donations of 1793–1795

Although loans with interest constituted an important and efficient financial instrument to collect funds for the royal treasury, both viceroys, Revillagigedo and later Branciforte, also resorted to the well-tried instrument of the donation. These forced contributions had the advantage of not requiring the money to be returned to donors and, as such, permitted the exercise of traditional, compulsory measures as applied to both affluent and popular classes. In 1793, Revillagigedo began the collection of a new donation from the entire population of New Spain. He successfully raised 460,000 pesos from merchants and proprietors and various religious institutions in a little less than eight months, followed by an additional fund-raising campaign which was applied in hundreds of peasant villages.[102] Two years later in 1795, the new viceroy Branciforte returned to the charge.[103] The collection of the new donation was more rigorous than in previous years, extending not only to the towns but also to most landed estates, mines, guilds, and religious foundations in the viceroyalty.

In Mexico City, for example, the donation of the year 1795 was requested of the artisans' guilds, which contributed a total of 5,267 pesos: among the participants were the guilds of coachbuilders, wax chandlers, confectioners, silk spinners, master tailors, shoemakers, blacksmiths, hat makers, and dyers. Each guild member contributed, with a sum of approximately 2 pesos per head[104]; and the same applied to the cotton dealers, saddlers, boiler makers, and potters. Even the comics, dancers, and musicians of the Royal Coliseum Theatre participated, offering the receipts of various performances to this end.[105]

101 For a partial list of the creditors to whom interest was paid by the Consulado, see AGN, *Consulado*, vol. 312, exp. 8, leg. 4.

102 For the amounts collected from the wealthy in 1793, see AGN, *Donativos y Préstamos*, vol. 28, exp. 7, f. 94. Information on rural donations is more dispersed, but see AGN, *Donativos y Préstamos*, vol. 26, fs. 338–341.

103 Branciforte's request to collect the donation was published on two occasions, May 13 and June 24, 1795; AGN, *Donativos y Préstamos*, vol. 30, f. 50.

104 Some carpenters gave as much as twenty pesos and some silk spinners up to thirteen pesos but the average was nearer two pesos per head. See the complete membership lists for each association and the quantities supplied in AGN, *Donativos y Préstamos*, vol. 13, fs. 13–188.

105 Primary school teachers also gave small amounts. AGN, *Donativos y Préstamos*, vol. 13, f. 326.

At the same time, senior fiscal bureaucrats circulated instructions to the Mexico City Council officials to collect small sums from each neighborhood resident. Again the contributions varied according to social position; in the *Plazuela de las Vizcainas* a prosperous contributor offered twenty-five silver pesos while other poor residents, could not give more than two *granos* (the equivalent of two pennies). Appropriately enough, in Rat Street (*Calle de las Ratas*) the average donation was between one and four *granos* while in the *Callejón de Dolores* the contribution ranged between one and twenty-nine *granos*.[106]

Although the amounts obtained in the cities were substantial, the total volume of funds extracted from towns and peasant communities was more considerable. The administrator of the General Court of Indians (*Juzgado General de Indios*) boasted of the monies collected from the Indians who lived in the capital's suburbs:

> The Indians of the *Parcialidades* de San Juan and Santiago in this capital, their towns and neighborhoods... whose communal properties are administered under my direction for the General Court of Indians (*Juzgado General de Naturales*)... donate 10,000 pesos.[107]

The majority of these sums came from community funds, which were normally used to pay primary school teachers as well as the expenses of certain festivities.[108]

The amounts contributed by the workers in mines and estates were also substantial. In Guanajuato, for example, workers from seventeen mines gave (or were forced to give) 4,396 pesos, while those of twenty-six landed estates supplied almost 2,000 pesos and city workers contributed 1,840 pesos.[109] In most cases, the bureaucrats sent complete lists of contributors, with job, family, and given names; in Guanajuato one-third of the amount collected came from the great mine of La Valenciana, whose administrator included a complete list of more than 2,000 workers: the more specialized laborers (mostly Spanish or *mestizo*) contributed 1–2 pesos per capita, the mulattos 1 peso apiece, and the Indians 4 *reales* per head.[110]

106 A silver peso was worth eight *reales* and each *real* twelve *granos*. (One silver peso was equal to one silver dollar: therefore one real was worth the equivalent of twelve cents and one *grano* was worth one penny; for data on the contributions in the different neighborhoods of the capital, see AGN, *Donativos y Préstamos*, vol. 13, fs. 274–283.

107 AGN, *Donativos y Préstamos*, vol. 13, f. 348.

108 The compulsory character of these contributions from community funds is analyzed in D. Tanck, *Pueblos de Indios*, pp. 495–499.

109 AGN, *Donativos y Préstamos*, vol. 30, f. 53.

110 The total collected for the donation in Guanajuato was 7,770 pesos of which 2,390 came from La Valenciana. The priest, however, told the governor (*intendente*) Riaño that the mine was failing. AGN, *Donativos y Préstamos*, vol. 30, fs. 50–54.

The monies collected were sent from the regional treasuries to Veracruz and thence to Spain in various ships that also carried other income belonging to the Crown.[111] In March 1796, after a year and eight months as viceroy of New Spain, the marquis of Branciforte sent a general report to the Madrid government, boasting that he had authorized the remittance of the huge sum of twenty-six million pesos in a very short time; fifteen million pesos in silver had been sent directly to Spain in the warships *Conquistador*, *Santiago la España*, *San Pedro Alcántara*, *Santiago la América*, and *Europa*; another nine million pesos were sent via merchant fleets that had transshipped the funds in Havana to royal ships of the line; finally, two million pesos had been remitted to the Philippines to pay for royal garrisons in Manila.[112]

The Donation and Loans of 1798 for the Naval War against Britain

Despite the enormous transfers of silver sent from New Spain, the metropolitan treasury continued to suffer large deficits. The situation worsened markedly when naval war with England began at the end of 1796. Customs revenues in Spain – a primary tax revenue in the metropolis – declined abruptly as a result of the drop in transatlantic trade, as all Spanish shipping was persecuted mercilessly by the British Navy. In 1796, government expenditures were covered with a loan contracted with merchants in Madrid and Cádiz for 100 million *reales* and with several American silver consignments that had escaped the British warships.[113] On the other hand, in 1797 the rising deficits and the scarcity of hard currency in Spain spurred renewed speculation in *vales reales* – the main form of public debt – provoking a strong decline in their value, and making new issues increasingly costly.[114]

In November 1797, in the midst of the growing crisis, the distinguished bureaucrat and military officer Francisco de Saavedra was named minister

111 On May 29, 1795, a little after assuming his position as Viceroy, Branciforte reported to the king that he had ordered that work in the Mexico City mint (*Casa de Moneda*) should be continued on festive days and Sundays, with night shifts: the result was a production of the impressive sum of three million pesos in less than a month, all with the objective of speeding up deliveries to Spain. AGN, *Correspondencia de Virreyes*, 1 serie, vol. 180, exp. 361, fs. 240–241.

112 AGN, *Correspondencia de Virreyes*, 1a serie, vol. 183, exp. 637, fs. 122–124.

113 The attempt to obtain funds through credits from Spanish merchants was a complete failure. The Cádiz and Madrid merchant guilds, for example, offered an advance of fifteen million *reales* each, but under conditions unacceptable to the Ministry of Finance. On financial policy at the beginning of the war, see José Patricio Merino, "La Hacienda de Carlos IV," *Hacienda Pública Española*, 69 (1981), 139–181.

114 For a theoretical analysis of the origins and mechanisms of the speculation (*agio*) with royal promissory notes, see the interesting document of the Banco de San Carlos, entitled "Report of the Bank Regarding the Reduction of the Loss of Notes and the Circulation of Bank Documents," November 1, 1794. Archivo Histórico del Banco de España, (AHBE), *Banco de San Carlos*, leg. 708.

of finance, and he immediately began a revision of the overall state of the monarchy's revenues. In early 1798, he presented a plan of extraordinary measures to avoid the bankruptcy of the government. Historians have praised his proposals to reform and modernize royal finance, but it is worth noting that the major planks of Saavedra's proposals were limited to the well-worn policy of exacting wealth from America to compensate for declining metropolitan tax income.[115] In fact, the first measure proposed by the minister was to authorize a patriotic loan in Spain and the Indies. The second was to transfer America's wealth in warships, but ensuring the British Navy did not intercept them. Saavedra wrote:

> More or less everywhere in the different parts of (Spanish) America it is possible to collect considerable capital, but New Spain in particular offers great resources . . . It is necessary, then, to immediately send instructions for the collection of funds in America. . . .[116]

Saavedra's proposal to launch a royal loan in metropolis and colonies (denominated *préstamo patriótico*) was partially successful, but there were problems in transferring the monies from the colonies due to the ongoing naval war with Great Britain. The decree requesting a loan and a donation for the war was signed in May 1798 although it was not until October of the same year that the donation actually began to be collected in Mexico. According to a recent study, approximately 60 percent of the total amount collected for this loan between 1798 and 1800 came from America, most from New Spain.[117] Senior civil bureaucrats, high-level church officials, and affluent merchants and miners were the first to show their support for the monarch. Viceroy Azanza contributed 50,000 pesos of his own salary, the bishop of Vallodolid sent 50,000 pesos, and the bishop of Puebla delivered 20,000 pesos. As always, the wealthy merchants contributed large sums, but other wealthy groups outside Mexico City also contributed, as is testified by the contribution of the recently formed Merchant Guild of Veracruz (*Consulado de Comercio de Veracruz*), which sent 100,000 pesos as a loan.[118] The list of contributors was published in the principal newspaper of the viceroyalty, the *Gazeta de México*.[119]

115 See the favorable comments on Saavedra's policy in J. P. Merino, "Hacienda de Carlos IV" 159–161.

116 See the *Memoria* of Saavedra in J. Canga Arguelles (1833–34), vol. 2, 183–186.

117 J. P. Merino, "Hacienda de Carlos IV," p. 176.

118 See Matilde Souto Mantecón, "El Consulado de comercio de Veracruz, 1796–1821," Ph.D. thesis, El Colegio de México, 1996, that explains in detail the relationship between the loans granted to the Crown and the agreement to establish the *Consulado de Veracruz* from 1796.

119 Among the Mexico City merchants, the first to make contributions was, as always, Antonio Bassoco with 25,000 pesos for the loan and 10,000 pesos as a donation. Among the miners, the marquis of Apartado (descendant of a great silver mining fortune) promised 40,000 pesos for the loan and

To ensure the greatest possible collection, the viceroy sent letters to many different bodies, requesting the donation: ecclesiastical councils, the provincials of different religious orders, the merchant guilds, the Mining Tribunal, the town councils, the courts, the governors (*intendentes*), the militia commanders, public officials, and regional mining associations (*diputaciones territoriales de minería*). From the published lists, it can be observed that not only wealthy subjects but virtually all members of colonial society contributed to this donation. In the capital, both rich and poor residents were urged by district officials to contribute, and agents were sent house to house to collect the monies from each family.

Again, as in 1795, the artisan guilds all made contributions, including bakers, tanners, dyers, tailors, cobblers, saddlers, coachbuilders, silk spinners, cotton weavers, needlewomen, and carpenters among others.[120] The military and militia of the viceroyalty gave larger amounts to this credit than previously. The Standing Infantry Regiment (*Regimiento de Infantería Fija*) under the command of a future Viceroy, Pedro Garibay, contributed 2,361 pesos; the Urban Regiment of Mexico City 7,125 pesos; the Provincial Cavalry of Querétaro 5,000 pesos; the Regiment of Provincial Dragoons of Puebla 4,324 pesos; the Standing Infantry Regiment of Puebla (*Regimiento de Infantería Fijo de Puebla*) 10,289 pesos; and so on, throughout the whole New Spain.[121] In general, individual officers contributed amounts between 20 and 100 pesos, the noncommissioned officers between 5 and 20 pesos, and soldiers between 1 and 4 pesos. The militia also made important contributions. On August 3, 1799, for example, the *Gazeta de México* recorded donations from the Merida White Militia Battalion (*Batallón de Milicias Blancos de Mérida*) as well as from the Division of Free Coloreds (*División de Pardos*) and three regiments of Urban militia, including Urban Blacks (*Negros Urbanos*) and Urban Free Coloreds (*Pardos Urbanos*).

Numerous merchants and mine owners offered donations to strengthen and supply the militias in the hope that the viceroy would name them officers in these bodies, since these positions carried high social prestige. For example, Ignacio Obregón, "legitimate son of the Count of Valencia," one of the richest miners in Mexico, gave 7,200 pesos "to kit out and arm three companies of cavalry from his native province of León."[122] At the

10,000 pesos as a donation. See lists published in the *Gazeta de México*, from October 1798 onward, with particularly rich material in the final volumes of 1799.

120 For a complete list of contributions from the capital city guilds, see AGN, *Donativos y Préstamos*, vol. 18, fs. 222–223.

121 Information about individual and institutional contributions are to be found in supplements of the *Gazeta de México* from November 1798 until September 1799. Abundant information can also be found in AGN, *Donativos y Préstamos*, vols. 2, 14–16.

122 Christon Archer, *El ejército en el México borbónico, 1760–1810* (Mexico: Fondo de Cultura Económica, 1983), p. 268.

same time he offered a war contribution of 1,500 pesos through the Mining Tribunal; in recompense, Viceroy Branciforte named him captain of a militia company.

Local merchants were the principal contributors to the militia. The trader Juan Ibañez Celorvera, from the city of Oaxaca, sent a letter that spoke of the measures adopted by the governor (*intendente*) to collect the donation;

> He met with all the merchants so that each one, for his part, might contribute with a quantity proportional to his means; now proposing a gracious donation, or (alternatively) a loan.... I offered two hundred pesos, the same amount I had provided previously ... having, in addition, contributed last year three thousand, eight hundred pesos for the uniforms and armaments for a company of the battalion of the militia (*Compañía del Batallón de Milicias*) of this city, of which a son of mine is captain....[123]

Neither did the great and medium estate owners fall behind; the marchioness of San Francisco donated 10,000 pesos, the marquis of Inguanzo another 10,000 pesos, the merchant and owner of sugar plantations, Gabriel de Yermo, 20,000 pesos. On the other hand, one of the richest proprietors in the country, the marquis of Jaral de Berrio wrote to the viceroy, telling him that he would only be able to contribute 6,000 pesos as "I suffered a severe drought this year, with the loss of more than ninety thousand head of sheep and goats as well as a large number of cattle of my properties."[124]

At the same time, the royal administrators increased their pressure on those least able to pay: the estate laborers and the inhabitants of the Indian peasant communities. For example, on a large estate in Apan (a famous *pulque* zone), the overseer contributed ten pesos while the laborers were obliged to make lesser contributions; twelve individuals paid four *reales* per head and fifty-five sent two *reales* per head.[125] The official responsible for receiving donations in the town of Guaxuapa in the Intendencia de Oaxaca commented on some of the difficulties in collecting funds from the most miserable population:

> There have been collections among the very poorest people, who were unable to sign their name, some giving a half *real*, others one *real*, the total collected here being scarcely eight pesos, seven *reales*.[126]

From early 1799, the local governors (*intendentes*) and their representatives began to collect silver accumulated in the Indian town treasuries. As

123 AGN, *Donativos y Préstamos*, vol. 16, f. 22.

124 AGN, *Donativos y Préstamos*, vol. 16, fs. 1–2.

125 *Gazeta de México*, IX, 84 (September 1799), supplement.

126 For the complete list of contributions from each inhabitant of Guaxuapa, see AGN, *Donativos y Préstamos*, vol. 15, fs. 86–88.

of March of the same year, the *Gazeta de Mexico* began to publish notices of these contributions. For example, the newspaper reported: "the communal funds of the indigenous republics" (*las Repúblicas de Naturales*) from Xiquilpan donated 13,709 pesos; from Apacingan 11,924 pesos; from Xicayan 7,4551 pesos; from Zitaquaro 4,235 pesos; from Orizava 4,390 pesos; and from Huetamo 12,811 pesos.[127]

That the government had decided to take funds from the Indian towns was indicative that the royal treasury of New Spain had begun to hit rock bottom. The community funds were not only the principal source for the payment of the tribute tax, but also a cushion that assured survival in periods of subsistence crisis. The treasury officials were aware of this since the 1782–1784 donation, when the extraction of community funds had caused serious problems: as historian Dorothy Tanck has demonstrated, these measures left a large number of poor populations unprotected at the time of the severe agrarian crisis and the famines of 1785–1786.[128]

Nevertheless the treasury officials proved impenitent and continued to clean out the community funds during the 1790s. In his famous *Political Essay on New Spain*, Alexander Humboldt expressed his indignation at the arbitrary behavior of the royal functionaries:

> The *intendentes* were accustomed to regard community funds as if they had no considered purpose. The *Intendente* of Valladolid sent around 40,000 pesos to Madrid that probably had taken some 12 years (for the local Indian communities) to save up, telling the king that it was a free and patriotic donation from the Indians of Michoacán to him as a contribution to continue the war against England.[129]

Conclusions

As this chapter has demonstrated, the chain of successive loans and donations taken from 1780 until 1798 weighed ever more heavily on colonial finance and society. Indeed, on both sides of the Atlantic, the rise in royal debts bespoke the lurking dangers of potential bankruptcy. This was so because in the Spanish realms, financial markets were not especially deep and in the case of colonial Mexico, depended altogether too much on the productivity of the silver mines. But in the 1780s and early 1790s, the Mexican silver boom was in full swing and the Crown found little difficulty in obtaining extraordinary funding.

127 *Gazeta de México*, IX, 32 (March 18, 1799).

128 D. Tanck, *Pueblos de Indios*, Chapter 4.

129 A. Humboldt, *Ensayo político*, pp. 70–71. [The original work was published in Paris in two editions in 1807 and 1810–1811. The first complete, Spanish translation is from 1822, which is actually the basis for the 1991 edition cited; the latter has excellent notes by Juan Ortega y Medina.]

The success of the royal authorities in carrying out their campaigns of emergency finance can be attributed mainly to the contributions of the affluent sectors of colonial society, reflecting their commitment to sustain a royal administration that guaranteed the status quo. It is more difficult to evaluate the attitude of the popular sectors as a result of the royal treasury's repeated campaigns to collect forced donations. It may be presumed that the incidence of these contributions on their well-being and consumption level were considerable, but this must be left to future research. In any case, the financial campaigns contributed to the indebtedness of the colonial government, mortgaged diverse various tax branches, squeezed the credit system, and contributed to a growing scarcity of specie in the colonial economy.

The accumulation of donations and loans confirm the progressive extension of the metropolitan financial crisis to the Americas. The crisis would reach its apogee with the extension of the Royal Consolidation (*Real Consolidación*) to New Spain at the end of 1804 which, in essence, constituted another type of forced loan, but on a larger scale, as we will see in the next chapter, and with much graver consequences. This step severely affected both the Catholic Church and the multitude of debtors that had borrowed ecclesiastical funds and would eventually be one of the detonators of the colonial regime's political and financial crisis.

4

The Royal Church and the Finances of the Viceroyalty

> The wheels on which runs the weighty Monarchy [...] are the sectors of agriculture, mining and trade. [...] The entire metallic currency of the kingdom is distributed among them and incorporated into the Pious Foundations. This is the blood that runs through the veins of the political body of the kingdom and keeps it alive. Thus, if for any reason the blood were to be drained from that body, its ruin would be inescapable.
>
> Municipal Council of Mexico City (1805)[1]

By 1800 the government of the viceroyalty in New Spain had already amassed a voluminous debt that had been contracted essentially to pay for war expenses of monarchy and empire. This debt was in good measure the result of loans collected among Mexican elites, merchants, miners, landowners, and *rentiers*, but the royal administration had also garnered much financial support from the church, which constituted a multifaceted array of institutions with an unparalleled ideological and economic influence on colonial society. Indeed, a close analysis of revenues collected by the viceregal administration from 1780 to 1800 reveals that the Catholic Church was perhaps the most important individual supplier of funds to the colonial treasury and hence to the monarchy for its war efforts. These included transfers to the state of substantial portions of tithes, donations, and direct loans from cathedral chapters, monasteries, convents, bishoprics, and pious foundations throughout the viceroyalty.

The financial collaboration between ecclesiastical institutions and the royal administration reflected the fact that in Spanish America – as well as in Spain – the *state* was not merely a *civil* power but a dual entity, based

1 A copy of the document titled *Representación* against the *Consolidación de Vales Reales* sent by the Municipal Council of Mexico City to Viceroy Iturrigaray is found in Masae Sugawara, *La deuda pública de España y la economía novohispana* (Mexico: Instituto Nacional de Antropología e Historia, 1976), pp. 27–35 (Colección Científica, 28).

on a secular alliance between the Crown and church.[2] What is more, the bonds between them were so strong in fiscal and financial areas – and in many other domains – that it is entirely proper to speak of a *Royal Church*, as William Callahan has suggestively argued.[3] This alliance – we contend – was crucial for the survival of the Spanish empire in the Americas at the end of the eighteenth century since the collaboration of the church was essential both to raise funds for the many wars in which the crown engaged as well as to assure popular support for these costly endeavors.

It is well known, of course, that the relationship between the two bodies (civil and ecclesiastic) was asymmetric, since in terms of worldly powers the monarchy was prevalent and could implement statist policies – such as the expulsion of the Jesuits in 1767. As many authors have stressed, the regalism of the Bourbons entailed a clear division between the government and the church in their respective rule over temporary and spiritual domains. Even so, it is worthwhile emphasizing that the church was still extremely influential in ideological terms among all social classes. This explains, in turn, why royal officials were repeatedly obliged to seek the active collaboration of hierarchy and clergy of the Catholic Church in New Spain in the monarchy's grand financial campaigns to raise money for the successive wars against the principal European rivals of Spain.

The Catholic Church agreed to the royal demands for war finance, but by the end of the eighteenth century the pressure by the monarchy to extract resources from religious corporations surpassed all historical precedent. In New Spain the fiscal campaigns involved increasing transfers to the royal treasuries of monies collected by various ecclesiastical branches – tithes, papal bulls, *vacantes*, and *medias anatas*.[4] In addition, revenues from special branches such as the *Temporalidades* – which managed the old Jesuit properties – were remitted to Spain. And, increasingly, the government in both metropolis and colonies called for ecclesiastical subsidies and a series of loans and donations from religious institutions.[5] Financial contributions

2 David Brading, *Una iglesia asediada: el obispado de Michoacán, 1749–1810* (Mexico: Fondo de Cultura Económica, 1994), p. 19: "In fact, in some areas of the empire the Church was the State and its ministers acted as judges and representatives of the monarchy."

3 William Callahan, *Church, Politics and Society in Spain, 1750–1874* (Cambridge, Mass.: Harvard University Press, 1984), especially pp. 2–5.

4 These were percentages to be paid to the royal treasury of salaries of newly appointed ecclesiastical functionaries.

5 Perhaps the most important study on this issue is D. Brading, *Una iglesia asediada*, pp. 195–282. According to the author (p. 210): "In the last decades of the Spanish government, the cathedral chapters of New Spain overtly confronted the crown, when ministers and officers tried to invade their jurisdiction and levy on their incomes. Attempting to take control of tithes collection from *jueces hacedores*; charging an ecclesiastic subsidy on every religious income, and disentailing church properties were some striking examples of the bureaucratic assault."

reached a peak in the years 1805–1808 as a result of the establishment in New Spain of offices of the Consolidation Fund (*Consolidación de Vales Reales*), a sinking fund for the amortization of public debt. In 1798 the officials of this fund had begun to collect a great income in Spain by affecting various fiscal branches but also by the transfer of church properties to the state, in exchange for royal bonds. The new strategy, put into practice in November of 1804, was to extend the same policies to Spanish America and finance royal debt by the disentailment of assets and properties belonging to convents, religious foundations, and charitable works. This inevitably implied a massive capital transfer from religious institutions to the royal treasury.[6]

While the Catholic Church resented the wrenching demands of the monarchy of Charles IV, the exigencies of war prevailed. Despite the imperative nature of the demands by the Crown, religious authorities in New Spain did not refuse to take part but rather became key actors in campaigns to collect donations and loans to pay for military expenses of the monarchy. Indeed, if we ask why inhabitants of the viceroyalty provided so much money – and so systematically – to the royal treasury between 1780 and 1810, it would appear that the reason was not simply coercion – which indeed existed – but also the desire of broad sectors of the population to cooperate with authorities and the monarchy. But one might justifiably ask whether it was likely that the loans were a sign of marked devotion by the inhabitants of colonial Mexico toward the Spanish sovereign? The answer is not self-evident, for the question of loyalties and identities in colonial society was complex. In this respect, it is worthwhile keeping in mind that the inhabitants of the Spanish empire in America had *mixed loyalties* and, almost certainly, the strongest were not toward the monarch but to the corporations they belonged to and, particularly, to the Catholic Church.

In the case of the campaigns to raise emergency funds, the fiscal rigor of the monarchy was therefore tempered by the spiritual persuasion of the church. When priests, bishops, and other ecclesiastical authorities asked the members of the flock to cooperate in donations or loans for the monarchy, the reaction of the faithful poor generally was linked to social and

6 Despite their importance, ecclesiastical loans and donations have been less studied than the *Consolidación*, on which there is a broad literature. See, for example, Masae Sugawara, "Los antecedentes coloniales de la deuda pública en México. España: los Vales Reales, orígenes y desarrollo de 1784 a 1804," *Boletín del Archivo General de la Nación*, 2a serie, 8, 1–2 (1967), 129–402; M. Sugawara, *La deuda pública*; Romeo Flores Caballero, "La Consolidación de Vales Reales en la economía, la sociedad y la política novohispanas," *Historia Mexicana*, xvii, 3 [71] (1969), 334–378; Asunción Lavrin, "The Execution of the Laws of Consolidación in New Spain: Economic Aims and Results," *Hispanic American Historical Review*, 53, 1 (1973), 27–49; Margaret Chowning, "The Consolidación de Vales Reales in the Bishopric of Michoacan," *Hispanic American Historical Review*, 3, 69 (1989), 451–478; and Carlos Marichal, "La Iglesia y la Corona: la bancarrota del gobierno de Carlos IV y la consolidación de Vales Reales en la Nueva España," in Pilar Martínez López-Cano, ed., *Iglesia, estado y economía*, pp. 241–262.

religious concerns and not to political or administrative duties.[7] On the other hand, among the wealthy and professional classes, financial participation was undoubtedly linked to considerations regarding the maintenance of the *status quo* in both an individual and a collective way. This complexity obliges us to reconsider the true nature of the *state* in the old regime and how the different sectors of colonial society perceived it.

This chapter explores the complex network of fiscal and financial ties that linked an increasingly subordinated colonial church to the royal treasury. We will explore, first, the historical mechanisms for transferring a portion of tithes and other ecclesiastical contributions to the royal coffers. Secondly, we will present an overview of loans supported by Mexican religious personnel and institutions to help finance the wars of the monarchy. Finally, we conclude by reviewing how and why the royal authorities implemented the most important and extortionate measure to appropriate church revenues and property in the years 1804–1808: these included the disentailment of capital, land, and buildings under religious control in order to provide money for the royal debt office, known as the *Consolidación de vales reales* in Spain. It should be stressed that funds collected in New Spain by the Crown on this account reflected the fact that the Mexican church was then the richest in the American hemisphere, although it was rapidly impoverished by these measures.[8]

Ecclesiastical Revenues and the Royal Treasury in New Spain

A recent and important literature has analyzed the role of ecclesiastical finance in Mexico during the eighteenth century, underscoring the importance of the church in the colonial economy and, particularly, in the functioning of its complex, credit system.[9] These studies demonstrate the

7 A study that stresses this problematic aspect of the relationship between church and government is Oscar Mazín, *Entre dos majestades. El obispo y la iglesia de Michoacán ante las reformas borbónicas, 1758–1772* (Zamora, Mich.: El Colegio de Michoacán, 1987).

8 It is hard to make an accurate appraisal of the wealth of the church in the Americas, but there are revealing data in documents presented by D. Brading, *Una iglesia asediada*, Appendix 1: according to this source, the income of the church in New Spain was roughly equivalent to 40% of the total revenues of the Spanish American church as a whole.

9 The most significant overview on ecclesiastical credit for the private sector in New Spain toward the end of the colonial regime is G. von Wobeser, *El crédito eclesiástico en Nueva España* and the most comprehensive regional quantitative analysis is Francisco Cervantes, "El crédito eclesiástico en Puebla, 1800–1856," Ph.D. thesis, El Colegio de México, 1993. Other relevant works are Arnold Bauer, "The Church in the Economy of Spanish America. Censos and Depósitos in the 18th and 19th Centuries," *Hispanic American Historical Review*, 63, 4 (1983), 707–733; Linda Greenow, *Credit and Socioeconomic Change in Colonial Mexico: Loans and Mortgages in Guadalajara, 1720–1820* (Boulder, Colo.: Westview, 1983); Asunción Lavrin, "El capital eclesiástico y las elites sociales en Nueva España a fines del siglo XVIII," in Enrique Florescano, ed., *Orígenes y desarrollo de la burguesía en América Latina,*

significant role of a varied number of religious institutions in providing working and investment capital and loans to landowners, merchants, and miners in all regions of New Spain. On the other hand, the contribution of the church to the fiscal and financial machinery of the royal administration in Bourbon Mexico and to the military campaigns of the Spanish crown has attracted less attention.[10] In the pages following, we contend that an analysis of the complex and varied contributions of the church to the royal treasury is extremely useful to understand how this influential, privileged corporation shared power with the government in the colonial regime.

One feature that clearly illustrates this symbiosis is the well-known existence of a *double taxation system* by government and church, for – just as in any other Catholic society of the time – the Spanish American church had its own fiscal system which ran parallel to the civil fiscal structure.[11] In Spain, France, Italy, and Portugal, tithes had long constituted the main source of annual income for both the ecclesiastical hierarchy and parish priests, although great revenues were also obtained from renting urban and rural properties. Generally speaking, these funds served to finance the church and, in principle, could not be claimed by the Crown. However, in the case of Spanish America, the situation was different because a share of funds collected by the church had to be *transferred* to the royal coffers. This was a practice that dated back to the sixteenth century, but it was reinforced

1700–1955 (Mexico: Nueva Imagen, 1985), pp. 33–72; Tomás Calvo, *Guadalajara y su región en el siglo XVII: población y economía* (Guadalajara: CEMCA/Ayuntamiento de Guadalajara, 1992), Chapter XI; María Isabel Sánchez Maldonado, *Diezmos y crédito eclesiástico: el diezmatorio de Acámbaro, 1724–1771* (Zamora, Mich.: El Colegio de Michoacán, 1994); and essays in Pilar Martínez López-Cano, ed., *Iglesia, estado y economía*. See additional bibliography in C. Marichal, "La historiografía económica reciente," 161–180.

10 Some aspects of the ecclesiastical role in royal finances are *explicitly* discussed in G. Valle Pavón "Las corporaciones religiosas en los empréstitos negociados por el Consulado de México a fines del siglo xviii," in Pilar Martínez López-Cano, ed., *Iglesia, estado y economía*, pp. 225–240 and Carlos Marichal, "La Iglesia y la crisis financiera del virreinato, 1780–1808; apuntes sobre un tema viejo y nuevo," in *Relaciones. Estudios de Historia y Sociedad*, 10, 40 (1989), 103–130. Data on financial relations between the church and the civil government are also found in D. Brading, *Una iglesia asediada*, passim. The basic documents on the *Consolidación de Vales Reales* are presented by M. Sugawara, *La deuda pública* and M. Sugawara, "Antecedentes coloniales." A. Lavrin, "Execution of the Laws," offers an insightful analysis.

11 Literature on the ecclesiastical fiscal system is copious but scattered, with few comparative studies. For an overview on tithe administration in the Spain of the eighteenth century, see Gonzalo Anes, *Las crisis agrarias en la España moderna, El antiguo régimen: los Borbones* (Madrid: Alianza/Alfaguara, 1975). For the case of France in the sixteenth and seventeenth centuries, see the dissertation by Claud Michaud, "Les Receveurs Généraux du Clergé de France aux XVIe et XVIe siècles," Ph.D. thesis, Université de París I, 1987. For New Spain, see Fredrick Schwaller, *Origins of Church Wealth in Mexico. Eclesiastical Revenues and Church Finances, 1523–1600* (Albuquerque: University of New Mexico Press, 1985); Arístides Medina Rubio, *La iglesia y la producción agrícola en Puebla, 1540–1795* (Mexico: El Colegio de México, 1979); and essays in Arnold Bauer, ed., *La iglesia en la economía de América Latina, siglos xvi al xix* (Mexico: Instituto Nacional de Antropología e Historia, 1986).

in the last quarter of the eighteenth century as a result of Bourbon reforms and the increasing expenses resulting from interimperial wars.

The *fiscal* system of the Spanish American church was based on a complex set of revenues which included collection of *tithes*, sale of *papal bulls*, a percentage of earnings of chaplaincies and religious foundations, as well as *parish income* charged by priests for masses and other liturgical services such as baptisms, marriages, and last rites.[12] For the royal treasuries in Mexico, the appropriation of a percentage of tithes collected by the church was customary, in particular through the fiscal department known as *novenos reales*. This fiscal branch was based on the transfer from the ecclesiastical coffers to government treasuries of a ninth (11 percent) of tithes collected by the clergy in the viceroyalty.[13] Originally – in the sixteenth century – the object of *novenos* was to finance the construction of cathedrals in America, but later they began to be channeled directly to the royal administration. (See Figure 4.1.) As recent research suggests, control and accounting of tithe collection was considerably improved in the eighteenth century by more professional ecclesiastical administrators. As a result, royal functionaries everywhere began to take special notice of the increasing weight of the tithe contributions.[14]

Broad sectors of colonial society had to pay tithes, which were levied on the agricultural/livestock production of every *hacienda* and ranch, but also, on occasions, on the agricultural commodities produced by Indian populations.[15] An evaluation of the impact of these ecclesiastical taxes on

12 For abundant information, see D. Brading, *La iglesia asediada*, passim.

13 This figure of 11% was equivalent to what the church called *two novenos*, based on a royal general decree issued in 1541 and still in force in the eighteenth century. Borah describes that "according to this regulation, half the total tithe collection should be divided into two equal parts, one for the bishop and the other for the cathedral chapter. The other half should be divided into nine equal parts, two of which were set aside for the king and should be collected and spent to his satisfaction. . . . " Woodrow Borah, "La recolección de diezmos en el obispado de Oaxaca," in A. Bauer, ed., *La iglesia en la economía*, p. 6. For similar studies on other regions of the Bourbonic Mexico, see M. I. Sánchez Maldonado, *Diezmos y crédito eclesiástico*, p. 34 and Michael P. Costeloe, "La administración, recolección y distribución de los diezmos en el arzobispado de México, 1800–1860," in A. Bauer, *La iglesia en la economía*, p. 121.

14 Bourbon government's capacity to secure greater and steadier shares of tithes was dependent on the increasing control that the clergy itself managed to implement in tithe collection, while leasing to individual persons was eradicated as a secular practice. According to Costeloe: "The church expanded the system of direct collection, whereas leased areas were increasingly reduced until the annulment of the last one in 1782." M. P. Costeloe, "La administración, recolección y distribución," p. 102.

15 According to Borah: "in general terms, Indians were still paying tithes only on '*cosas de Castilla*,' although the list had expanded from wheat, silk, and animals, in the sixteenth century, to include every plant and animal from the Old World. Both Indians and Spaniards were forced to pay a 10 percent tithe on salt [. . .] they paid 5 percent on sugar [. . .] 4 percent on honey." Small and big cattle were levied differently for Indians and Spaniards. Woodrow Borah, "La recolección de diezmos," p. 88.

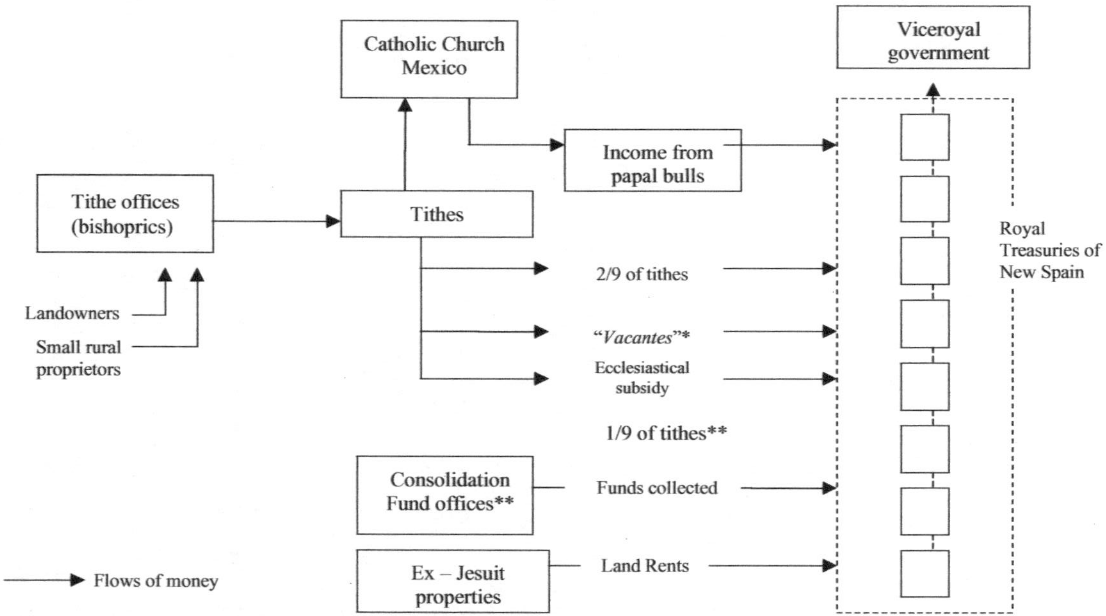

Figure 4.1. Transfers of Church Revenues to Royal Treasuries in New Spain (circa 1806).
* Vacantes were vacant religious positions.
Source: drawn by Carlos Marichal.

Table 4.1. *Royal Treasury Income Derived from Religious Fiscal Branches, Mexico*[a], *1785–1799 (Annual Averages in Thousand Pesos)*

Years	Papal Bulls	2/9ths of Tithes	Other Ecclesiastical Income[b]	Total
1785–1789	266	233	209	708
1792	224	207	212	643
1795–1799	302	222	163	687

[a] We have not included the ecclesiastical subsidies nor the fiscal branch known as *Temporalidades* because of imprecision in sources.

[b] This complementary income was from the categories of *vacantes*, *mesadas*, and *media anatas*, which were transferred to the royal treasuries.

Sources: For data of 1785–1789, Fabian de Fonseca and Carlos de Urrutia, *Historia general de la Real Hacienda*, vol. 3 (Mexico: Vicente G. Torres, 1845–1853), p. xxxix. For data of 1792, Archivo General de Indias (AGI), Audiencia de México, 2358. For data of 1795–1799, Biblioteca Nacional (Mexico), ms. 1282.

each social group would require a fiscal sociology of tithes – a challenging task that researchers should nonetheless consider worth undertaking in the future.[16] Only then shall the increasing pressure of a *double taxation* system on New Spain's society be fully understood.

By the end of the eighteenth century, certain operative aspects of the double taxation system revealed the increasing economic subordination of the ecclesiastical system to the civil system, which included not only the transfer of *novenos* to government's treasuries, but also revenues from other sources, such as *bulas*, *medias anatas*, *mesadas*, and *vacantes mayores y menores*.[17] According to the overall fiscal statistics for New Spain, the *reales novenos* yielded the royal treasury an annual average income of 178,111 pesos in 1785–1789, 179,227 pesos in 1792, and 192,833 pesos in the years between 1795 and 1799.[18] (See Table 4.1.) These figures represented the sum total of tithes revenues transferred to the state by the archdiocese

16 There are several studies on tithe collection in different Mexican regions in the eighteenth century, including A. Medina Rubio, *La iglesia y la producción agrícola*; Claude Morin, *Michoacán en la Nueva España del siglo XVIII: crecimiento y desigualdad en una economía colonial* (Mexico: Fondo de Cultura Económica, 1979). However, only M. I. Sánchez Maldonado, *Diezmos y crédito eclesiástico*, applies a detailed sociological approach to analysis of the functioning of the complex ecclesiastical machinery.

17 One must be careful in considering each type of branch and tax: a useful source is F. Fonseca and C. Urrutia, *Historia General*, a veritable dictionary of colonial state finance. For example, in addition to novenos there was a similar but separate fiscal category called "ecclesiastical tithes" (*diezmos eclesiásticos*); the purpose was to assist poor bishoprics and missions: funds from this branch began to be directly transferred to the royal treasury toward the end of the eighteenth century. F. Fonseca and C. Urrutia, *Historia General*, vol. 1, p. xxxiii.

18 Sources for *noveno* income are cited in Table 4.1. I am grateful to Guillermina del Valle Pavón for help in finding these documents.

of Mexico and the dioceses of Puebla, Valladolid, Guadalajara, and Oaxaca: they constituted almost 20 percent of the nearly two million pesos collected in tithes by the church in New Spain during those years for which there are relatively reliable estimates.[19]

As imperial war expenses increased, the royal authorities decided to restructure the branch of *novenos* in 1798 in order for the Crown to obtain an even higher proportion of tithes. The decree of November 28, 1804 requested the church to pay the government an additional ninth part of tithe revenues in order to contribute to cover rising government debt service in the metropolis.[20] As a result of this new measure, the income of the Mexico City Treasury increased by almost 500,000 pesos annually in 1804–1808 – a fact which indicates that almost 25 percent of tithe revenues collected in all the dioceses of New Spain were being transferred to the Crown.[21]

But royal officers were also attentive to other ecclesiastical income that might relieve the increasingly severe financial crisis of the monarchy. The income from the *sale* of papal bulls (indulgences), the transfer to the state of salaries of vacant positions in the religious hierarchy, the rental income from old Jesuit properties now administered by a state foundation, as well as a number of additional ecclesiastical contributions were carefully monitored by the royal treasury. Among the most significant were the *bulas de la santa cruzada* (papal bulls) that the faithful acquired (by means of stipulated donations to the church) in exchange for indulgences: the latter were religious documents that purportedly remitted punishments due on certain sins, for example, by reduction of the years he or she would pass in purgatory after death.[22]

According to ancient norms, the money earned from the papal bulls was to be devoted to "fighting the unfaithful and preserving the faith." Not

19 The annual net total of tithes in New Spain fluctuated between 1,600,000 and 2,000,000 pesos during 1785–1810, according to calculations by D. Brading, *Una iglesia asediada*, p. 242, and Juan Carlos Garavaglia and Juan Carlos Grosso, "De Veracruz a Durango: un análisis regional de la Nueva España borbónica," *Siglo XIX*, 2, 4 (1987), 52. Stanley Stein indicates that in the 1780–1790 decade the tithe annual average collection was 1,835,382 pesos: "Prelude to Upheaval in Spain and New Spain, 1800–1808: Trust Funds, Spanish Finance and Colonial Silver," in R. Garner and W. Taylor, eds., *Iberian Colonies, New World Societies*, p. 191.

20 This additional *noveno* was levied on the *totality* of collected tithes. See AGN, *Diezmos*, vol. 21, pp. 274–280.

21 These estimates are based on the *novenos* collected since 1804, representing 22% of all tithes, to which other minor branches must be added. R. Garner and S. E. Stefanou, *Economic Growth and Change*, pp. 47–53 present the most exhaustive discussion of tithe dynamics in the viceroyalty: they estimate that tithes produced a total average of 1,570,000 pesos per year in the period 1770–1790 and almost 2,000,000 pesos annually in 1790–1800.

22 The complex organization of this branch and the methods used for their predication and sale, including solemn processions, are described in detail in AGN, *Bulas de Santa Cruzada*, especially vol. 23, file 8 and vol. 25, file 19, pp. 417–426.

surprisingly, the Crown felt justified in promoting them on an increased scale to pay for wars against protestant Britain or, alternatively, against revolutionary France in the last years of the eighteenth century. The revenues from the placement of indulgences increased for several years, the annual average total rising from 240,000 pesos in 1780–1784 to 300,000 pesos in 1795–1799 – although reliable data for the whole period is scarce.[23] Though the acquisition of indulgences was in principle voluntary, in practice they were administered as almost any other religious or civil tax. More than once, the head of administration of papal bulls (known grandiloquently as the general commissioner and apostolic judge of the Holy Crusade) instructed bishops in New Spain that priests should make a census of "people likely to buy the papal bulls."[24] Thus, the church, like the Crown, resorted not only to persuasion but also to coercive mechanisms for extracting money from the pious, whether rich or poor.

As could be expected, impositions triggered frequent protests and even rejection among the peasantry. In 1792, for example, Viceroy Revillagigedo ordered that Indian towns not be exempted from the sale of indulgences despite their likely opposition to the measures. The task, however, was not always easy, as revealed by the letters of the priest of municipality of Teoloyuca, where the placement of indulgences had fallen off "due to the exploitation that natives from this town have endured, being forced to work in the mines of the Count of Regla."[25] Regardless of harsh punishments, the desired outcomes were not always forthcoming. For example, in 1791, in the town of Xochimilco, near Mexico City, the local priest recommended imprisonment for a number of natives who were in arrears on payments of indulgences which, evidently, they had acquired without enthusiasm. The priest accused the villagers of being "poorly educated and exemplars of inebriation," although this was not an obstacle for him to extract more than 2,000 pesos from the community that same year on account of the sales of papal bulls.[26]

Since the tax administration of the viceroyalty became increasingly dependent upon these and other ecclesiastical branches of revenue (and considering that it would be impossible to pay off arrears), in 1800 the new Viceroy Berenguer supported the top functionaries of the colonial treasury of Mexico when they asked Madrid to include the ecclesiastical contributions

23 Income on sales of indulgences amounted to 180,000 and 200,000 pesos per year in 1765–1780, reaching 250,000 pesos in 1780–1790, according to F. Fonseca and C. Urrutia, *Historia General*, vol. 1, p. xx.

24 C. Morin, *Michoacán en la Nueva España*, p. 41.

25 AGN, *Bulas de Santa Cruzada*, vol. 14, file 19, pp. 340–341.

26 AGN, *Bulas de Santa Cruzada*, vol. 14, file 19, pp. 324–325. The priest in question explained to royal treasury officers that the best method for selling bulls to the natives was through a credit system, with partial payments. AGN, *Bulas de Santa Cruzada*, vol. 14, pp. 326–341 and vol. 15, pp. 324–330.

in the *common branches* of the treasury. This would help to settle debts of the royal treasury to the church by means of a simple accounting measure, and simultaneously facilitate the use of the annual revenues of those same branches to cover a part of ordinary expenditures. The Minister of Finance Miguel Soler answered that he was in agreement but emphasized that all surplus obtained from sale of indulgences should be directly dispatched to the peninsula. This, however, proved impossible, since – according to treasury officials of New Spain – those ecclesiastical branches were essential to balance the accounts of the royal treasuries in Mexico. The official correspondence reflected the numerous tensions between metropolitan and colonial representatives – and revealed important underlying disagreements with regard to the operation of the empire's fiscal machinery.[27]

In 1802 the Council of the Indies decided to implement a new policy aimed at reorganizing the sale of papal indulgences in New Spain and Peru and requiring the remittance of a third part of revenues to the Royal Consolidation Fund (*Caja de Consolidación*) in Madrid. The Council instructed the local delegates of the *Caja* to record full listings of the money reserves accumulated in the administration of indulgences in each intendancy in New Spain and ordered them to take the third part of the cash out of the regional treasuries and send it on to the peninsula. The functionaries were ordered to keep a close watch on:

> the monies yielded (to be kept) in a three-keyed coffer, without laying a hand on them for any reason until they are transferred to the treasury officers at authorized ports and then embarked on ships heading to any of the authorized ports in Spain, where they shall be put at the order and will of the Council, and thus, of the *Comisión de Vales Reales*. . . . [28]

The officers of the viceregal treasury also worked hard to extract resources from other special fiscal branches which included, for example, the salaries of vacant positions in the religious hierarchy that were customarily transferred to the state treasuries and sent to Spain. These branches were known as *vacantes mayores y menores*, *medias anatas*, and *mesadas*, each of which had its own administration and treasury where surpluses were amassed.[29] Traditionally, the government had authorized that such sums be channeled

27 See the interesting letter from Viceroy Iturrigaray, dated February 26, 1803 in which he comments on the disputes between Soler and royal treasury officers, concerning the use of funds from ecclesiastical sectors; see AGN, *Correspondencia de Virreyes, 1a series*, vol. 214, file 330, pp. 201–203.

28 This quotation is from AGN, *Bulas y Santa Cruzada*, vol. 25, p. 420. The Council developed a detailed outline, itemizing the amount of each bull that would be used for that purpose.

29 Some of the various minor religious incomes collected in New Spain in 1810 were the branches of *Santos Lugares de Jerusalén*, the royal chapel (*capilla real*), the pension of His Majesty's chaplain, and the pension of the bishop of Louisiana, among others. AGN, *Caja Matriz*, "Libro Común de la Tesorería de Ejército y Real Hacienda de 1810." For a more complete list, including those branches collected in previous decades see H. Klein, "La economía de la Nueva España," pp. 601–609.

to the spiritual, educational, or charitable goals for which they had originally been established. However, by the end of the eighteenth century the government decided to amend that policy. In the first place, supervision of the collection of each religious "tax" was made more rigorous, and secondly, the royal functionaries began to systematically use the surplus funds to cover deficits in other branches of the government treasuries.[30]

The branch known as *vacantes mayores y menores* was a source of revenues indirectly derived from tithes, since it consisted of transfers to the government by the Catholic Church of salaries corresponding to *vacancies* in bishoprics, abbeys, and minor ecclesiastical positions such as the *racioneros* and *medios racioneros*. So long as the church kept those positions unfilled, it was obliged to provide the royal treasury with the corresponding share of salaries that these religious officers would have earned – as salary – in their dioceses. The vacant positions yielded average revenues to Mexican royal treasuries between 110,000 and 150,000 pesos per year in the period 1780–1800, while from 1800 to 1808 the amounts transferred to the royal administration were even higher.[31] Additional transfers were obtained from those church fiscal branches, known as *medias anatas* and *mesadas*: newly appointed prelates were required to render half of their incomes to the treasury during their first year in office, amounting to a not insignificant, annual sum of close to 60,000 pesos in the last decades of the eighteenth century, all of which was to be remitted to the metropolitan royal treasury.[32]

From 1790 onward the Crown also demanded that bishops in New Spain pay *ecclesiastical subsidies* traditionally collected in the metropolis, but not in the colonies.[33] In practice, these cotributions constituted a fiscal branch that had been on the colonial books for decades, but had not been

30 The Crown did not begin extracting money from the "ramos particulares" until the 1790s. Both Klein and TePaske agree that a study of these branches is extremely difficult without a thorough review of the *libros manuales* (detailed financial accounting records) of New Spain's royal treasury, many of which are to be found in the Archivo de Indias in Sevilla. H. Klein, "La economía de la Nueva España," p. 590 and J. J. TePaske and J. and M. L. Hernández Palomo, *La Real Hacienda*, Introduction. The Archivo General de la Nación in Mexico City contains a large number of still unclassified *libros manuales*.

31 According to F. Fonseca and C. Urrutia, *Historia General*, vol. 2, p. XXX the annual average levy corresponding to *vacantes mayores y menores* amounted to 137,818 pesos in 1785–1789. In 1792 the amount increased to 154,006 pesos, while the annual average for 1795–1799 was 112,733 pesos: data in tables in Archivo General de Indias (AGI), *Audiencia de México*, 2358 and Biblioteca Nacional (Mexico), ms. 1282. I am grateful to Guillermina del Valle Pavón for copies of these documents.

32 See the previous note for sources on revenues resulting from *medias anatas*. Other ecclesiastical branches that were to be sent to Spain from 1798 onward were the *indulto cuadrigesimal*, the *subsidios eclesiásticos*, the increase of the *Bulas de Santa Cruzada*, and the *noveno decimal*. AGN, *Caja Matriz*, "Libro Común de la Tesorería."

33 For data regarding the religious subsidy in Spain during the last decades of the eighteenth century, see M. Artola, *La hacienda del antiguo régimen*, pp. 366–367.

put into practice. David Brading points out that in 1783 the minister of the Indies José de Gálvez ordered every viceroy, governor, and bishop in the American empire to pay off all arrears of the ecclesiastical subsidy. The measure, however, was not actually implemented until the 1790s when the demands of war made it imperative.[34]

By May 1794 viceroy Revillagigedo could report to Madrid that he had already collected 382,299 out of the 573,741 pesos in arrears of the (ecclesiastical) subsidy. Encouraged by the success of this measure, the ministers obtained new subsidies, in 1795 and again in 1799, each totaling one million and a half pesos.[35]

Apart from collecting subsidies, the Crown required religious authorities to render detailed reports on overall church revenues which provided evidence of a significant concentration of wealth in the bishoprics of Mexico, Puebla, and Michoacán: these three dioceses yielded 75 percent of total church income and 68 percent of the ecclesiastical subsidy collected in the entire viceroyalty in the year 1799.[36]

To complete our picture of fiscal contributions collected by the viceregal government from ecclesiastical sources, we should mention a series of funds that were separately managed by the royal treasury. These included the branch of *Temporalidades* that administered the old properties of the Jesuit order which had been violently ejected from the viceroyalty in 1767. Jesuit assets mainly consisted of colleges and churches in urban areas and *haciendas* and ranches in rural regions. According to a contemporary source, the branch of *Temporalidades* was in charge of the administration of forty *haciendas* in Mexico's archbishopric and fifty-three *haciendas* and ranches in the diocese of Puebla.[37] Since the royal treasury account books lack many details, it is hard to make an accurate estimation of total revenues from *Temporalidades*, most of which were sent to the peninsula to support military and financial expenses of the monarchy. During the 1779–1783 wars against Britain, for example, three different studies mention that viceroy Mayorga took out loans for the Crown amounting to 2.7 million pesos from the revenues collected through the *Temporalidades* branch, with the promise of paying them off as soon as possible with an annual interest rate of 5 percent.[38]

34 D. Brading, *Una iglesia asediada*, pp. 244–245.

35 D. Brading, *Una iglesia asediada*, p. 245.

36 Estimates based on D. Brading, *Una iglesia asediada*, Appendix, Table 1.

37 F. Fonseca and C. Urrutia, *Historia General*, vol. 5, p. 227.

38 J. Lewis, "New Spain during American Revolution," p. 217, mentions that profits from sales and leasing of properties of *Temporalidades* were traditionally sent to the metropolis, but between 1779 and 1782 (date of the loan) they were kept in royal coffers in Mexico. F. Fonseca and C. Urrutia, *Historia General*, vol. 1, p. xx present data, as well as José Antonio Calderón Quijano, *Los virreyes de la Nueva España durante el reinado de Carlos III*, vol. 2 (Sevilla: Escuela de Estudios Hispanoamericanos, 1968), p. 160.

In later years, the remittance of surplus funds derived from the former properties of the Jesuits was renewed: 300,000 pesos produced by *Temporalidades* were sent from New Spain to the peninsula in 1790, and 400,000 pesos in 1792.[39] After the onset of the war against the French Convention in 1793, the share of this branch in loans to the Crown acquired additional importance.[40] Metropolitan authorities encouraged the sale of the old Jesuit properties to obtain more hard cash – a measure which anticipated the subsequent policy of disentailment of religious properties adopted by the Crown at the turn of the century.[41] The clearest evidence of the Spanish government's objective of resorting to revenues from *Temporalidades* to redress the monarchy's financial crisis was the royal decree issued in 1798, ordering "any remaining fund from *Temporalidades* in Spain, the Indies, and Philippine Islands to be added into the royal treasury for the service of *vales reales*." The ordinance also stressed that while funds were mainly meant to relieve the government's domestic debt, in case of emergency a share could be used for "the monarchy's urgent needs," presumably of military nature.[42]

Church Donations and Loans to Finance the Wars of the Spanish Crown, 1780–1804

While the Spanish crown lost no time in forcing the church to increase tax transfers to pay for wars, it also began pressing for a series of loans and donations from religious institutions throughout Spanish America. According to practice established in New Spain since the seventeenth century, fiscal authorities commonly solicited the aid of church officials in the collection of donations, especially in wartime.[43] Parish priests were particularly effective agents for this purpose as they were ideally placed to collect small donations

39 F. Fonseca and C. Urrutia, *Historia General*, vol. 5, p. 192.

40 The *Tribunal de Minería* received considerable sums from *Temporalidades* to complete its loans to the Crown. W. Howe, *Mining Guild*, pp. 84–85, 118–119, and 372–382.

41 Detailed studies on the sale of these *haciendas* are lacking, though it must be stressed that there is much unexplored documentation in the section of *Temporalidades* at the Archivo General de la Nación which could serve for future analysis. Based on a preliminary review, we can suggest that the sales of old Jesuit properties tended to increase toward the end of the century, accounting for an increase of remittances to the metropolis. See AGN, *Temporalidades*, vols. 4, 5, 93, 114, 117, 130, 136, 151, 161, 171.

42 See the "Real Cédula sobre el destino de los fondos y bienes de Temporalidades a remitirse para la amortización de vales reales, dada en San Lorenzo a 2 de noviembre de 1798." AGN, *Reales Cédulas Originales*, vol. 171, exp. 163, pp. 204–205.

43 This was quite typical of Catholic societies in this period. In France, from the sixteenth century it was standard practice for the clergy to provide a substantial donation to the monarchy every five years and special contributions in times of war: Michel Bottin, *Histoire des Finances publiques* (Paris: Economica, 1997), p. 16.

in the several thousand peasant towns and villages of the viceroyalty.[44] A study by the historian Thomas Calvo on a donation requested from the Catholic Church in New Spain at the time of the War of Spanish Succession at the beginning of the eighteenth century highlights the importance of this financial collaboration: the colonial authorities reported in the year 1709 that the clergy had helped to garner the very considerable amount of a million silver pesos sent to Spain.[45] Additional examples of church contributions were the 1743 Mexican donation (to finance Spanish troops in Italy) and that of 1777 granted by the Archbishops of Mexico and Valladolid (Michoacán) providing 160,000 pesos to help the naval rearmament program championed by Viceroy Bucareli.[46]

In the case of the donation decreed by Charles III in August 1780 to pay expenses for the war against Britain, Viceroy Mayorga made special appeals to the archbishop of Mexico as well as to chapters of the main churches, convents, religious colleges, and other ecclesiastical institutions. The upper level prelates instructed parish priests to gather the residents of their urban and rural parishes and persuade them of the benefits of the war contribution.[47] Funds directly donated by cathedral chapters and other religious institutions amounted to barely 4.7 percent of the total donation,[48] but parish priests – in contrast – played a very active role in mobilizing Indian peasants to comply with the Crown: the latter provided some 400,000 pesos, approximately half of all monies collected for this purpose in the viceroyalty.[49]

Numerous religious organizations made substantial and direct subscriptions to the 1782 loans that were managed by the Mexico City Merchant Guild and the Mining Tribunal, bearing good fiscal guarantees since they

44 "Donations were collected with the help of religious personnel in 1624, 1636, 1647, 1696, 1703, 1710, 1723, 1765 and 1780, just to mention some cases." Quotation from A. Lavrin, "Los conventos de monjas en la Nueva España," in A. Bauer, *La iglesia en la economía*, p. 195. For a more detailed review of the Mexican church support for the donation of 1703, see Tomás Calvo "Los ingresos eclesiásticos en la diócesis de Guadalajara en 1708," in P. Martínez López-Cano, ed., *Iglesia, estado y economía*, pp. 47–59.

45 For a review of the Mexican church support for the donation of 1709, see Tomás Calvo "Los ingresos eclesiásticos en la diócesis," pp. 47–59.

46 AGN, *Archivo Histórico de Hacienda*, vol. 223, exp. 5, fs. 252–257 and B. Bobb, *ViceRegency of Antonio María Bucareli*, pp. 112–114.

47 See, for example, the letter, dated March 1781, from the archbishop of Mexico City to the viceroy, reporting that "instructions have been given to every member of the diocese concerning the donation. . . . " AGN, *Donativos y Préstamos*, vol. 10, file 30, pp. 263–270.

48 For exact figures, see C. Rodríguez Venegas, "La sociedad novohispana," Table 2, p. 107.

49 C. Rodríguez Venegas, "La sociedad novohispana," Chapter 4 offers detailed tables on the sums collected for the 1781–1783 donation, showing that half of the funds were private contributions (among which there where very few clerics) and the other half came from peasant villages.

yielded an annual interest rate of 5 percent.[50] The principal ecclesiastical investments came from convents that provided a total of 147,000 pesos, plus 200,000 pesos from the financial branch of the Inquisition (*Real Fisco de la Inquisición*).[51] Other individual investors also participated actively in the loan, alongside the religious institutions.[52] Additional evidence of the relevance of ecclesiastical contributions can be found in the case of the 1783 interest-bearing loan, the service of which was guaranteed by a mortgage on the tobacco monopoly: of a total sum of 523,000 pesos lent to the government, almost 462,000 pesos (88 percent) – a huge sum – came from ecclesiastical institutions in Guadalajara, including the cathedral chapter, the local foundation for charitable works (*juzgado de obras pías*) and various religious organizations. (According to one modern index that sum would be equivalent to almost 200 million dollars of 2005.)[53]

In the case of the 1793 loan the Catholic Church mobilized its followers with extraordinary rapidity, following Charles IV's appeal to gather funds to finance preparation of an imminent war against France. The Spanish authorities greatly feared the radical turn of the national assembly in Paris – still dominated by the Girondists – which had carried out the prosecution and execution of King Louis XVI (January 21, 1793). Actually, war preparations had begun from mid-November 1792, when the young military officer and lover of the queen Manuel de Godoy was named prime minister of the Spanish Cabinet. Godoy initiated secret negotiations with British authorities to explore the possibility of coordinating actions between the Royal Navy and the Spanish naval forces in order to constrain French trade. But it was not until March that the war actually broke out when French troops made incursions into northern Spain. To their surprise, the Spanish Army was prepared and fought off the invading troops. The Spanish troops

50 See the suggestive and thorough discussion by G. Valle Pavón, "Consulado de Comerciantes," Chapter 3, on the role of ecclesiastical institutions in loans negotiated by the merchant guild in 1782 and 1793.

51 G. von Wobeser, "La inquisición como institución crediticia," pp. 865–866 includes a study of this operation and concludes that the from this moment the church became more amenable to loans to the royal treasury even though they did not carry real estate guarantees: G. Valle Pavón, "Las corporaciones religiosas," in P. Martínez López-Cano, *Iglesia, estado y economía*, pp. 232–234. For additional references on ecclesiastical loans administered by the *Consulado de comerciantes*, see Pedro Pérez Herrero, *Catálogo del ramo de Consulados*, vol. II (Mexico: Archivo General de la Nación, 1982), p. 540.

52 AGN, *Minería*, vol. 63, fs. 145–146 includes the complete list of suscribers. In addition to the investment by the Inquisition, we should mention the large loan of 110,000 pesos lent by the presbyter Juan Francisco Castañiza, member of a noble family from New Spain and rector of the San Idelfonso university seminary.

53 For data on the loan, see J. A. Calderón Quijano, V*irreyes de la Nueva España*, vol. 2, p. 147. The subsequent calculation is based on the EH Net (http://eh.net/hmit/compare) complete index of the money wage rates paid for common or unskilled labor from 1774 to the present.

later advanced into the Rousillon on May 18, 1793, where they won a major engagement. As the historian Blanning argues:

> From that point, the fortunes of war became more mixed . . . but when peace was signed at Basle on 22 July 1795 the Spaniards were still able to negotiate the most favourable peace achieved by any opponent of France in the 1790s.[54]

Before the start of the conflict, royal authorities turned to the colonial church in Mexico to assist in the financing of a major naval campaign against France. Subsequently, as war broke in the Iberian peninsula, colonial functionaries joined ecclesiastical authorities in New Spain in an ideological attack upon the French National Convention – increasingly dominated by the Jacobins – which was denounced not only as antimonarchical but also as atheistic. In barely four months (January–April 1793), the sum of 1,559,000 pesos was collected for the Crown through an interest-free loan raised among affluent corporations and individuals in colonial Mexico, with ecclesiastical institutions leading the pack.[55] Contributions gathered by Mexico City's archbishop included 60,000 pesos from the cathedral dean and chapter; 100,000 pesos from the Foundation of Pious Works (*Juzgado de Obras Piás y Capellanías*); and 320,000 pesos from a religious institution devoted to the administration of legacies of deceased individuals (*Juzgado de Bienes Difuntos*). Another huge donation was the 300,000 pesos awarded by the cathedral dean and chapter of Guadalajara. In the case of the city of Puebla, after considerable bargaining, the cathedral chapter agreed to donate funds totalling 50,000 pesos: 21,000 from tithes and 29,000 pesos from alms be collected among the faithful.[56] Simultaneously, several religious institutions in the intendancy of Valladolid sent 70,000 pesos and the College of San Luis Gonzaga from the silver-rich city of Zacatecas remitted an additional 80,000 pesos.[57]

But ecclesiastical contributions were not limited to interest-free loans. Indeed convents, confraternities, and pious works and foundations generally attempted to assure a reasonable return on their assets. For example, in the case of the 1793–1794 war loan for two million pesos (which paid annual interest at the rate of 5 percent), dozens of religious and private institutions made substantial investments.[58] In contrast, in the case of the interest-free

54 T. C. W. Blanning, *The Origins of the French Revolutionary Wars* (New York: Longmans, 1991).

55 Figures based on 1793 donation lists and tables included in various files in AGN, *Donativos y Préstamos*, vol. 1, such as file 80, fs. 317–318 and vol. 32, fs. 272–276.

56 AGN, *Donativos y Préstamos*, vol. 1, file 55, fs.173–174 and vol. 32, fs. 272–276.

57 The *Juzgado de Obras Pías* of Valladolid sent 40,000 pesos and the cathedral dean and chapter of that city donated 30,000 pesos.

58 The Mining Tribunal reported on February 3, 1793, that it had collected 300,000 pesos from the expropriated Jesuit properties of San Pedro and San Pablo and 24,000 pesos from the Hospice of San Nicolás. AGN, *Donativos y Préstamos*, vol. 28, f. 20. W. Howe, *Mining Guild*, p. 382, mentions

loan negotiated by the merchant guild in 1793 (amounting to one million pesos), most money came from private contributions, and only 16 percent of the funds were provided by convents, confraternities, and charitable works.[59]

The relevance of subscriptions by religious entities was stressed by the Mexico City Mining Tribunal in a letter to the Crown:

> With regard to the said donations and loans that the general revolution in Europe has made necessary, this Tribunal, as well as the merchant guild and the authorities of this kingdom's towns and villages, have found the religious foundations to be the primary source for garnering funds, taking their capital at interest to put them at the Crown's feet as everyone has done in such times of emergency. . . .[60]

A few years later, a new donation – that of 1798 to finance a new naval war against Great Britain – also required the collaboration of the colonial church. Its analysis sheds light on the way religious convents involved themselves in the financial campaigns for the monarchy. Meetings directed by the heads of religious orders were held in order to mobilize loyalty to the monarch, appealing to the religious to pray and donate cash. A vivid example is provided by the report of José Joaquín Oyarzabal, provincial minister and supervisor of the nuns of Santa Clara, of Mexico City who urged that a meeting be held among "the most illustrious and experienced prelates that are at present in this City . . . " to take cognizance of the great dangers faced by the Crown and church as a result of naval war with Britain. He also requested every nun to pray against the English enemy. Oyarzabal added: "This is with reference to the Spiritual; and concerning the Temporal [. . .] each Community is asked to play its part [in the donation]. . . . "[61]

The Convent of Santa Clara did, in fact, make a substantial *temporal* contribution (40,000 pesos) which was slightly higher than that of other convents in the capital. Contributions of various regional bishoprics were also considerable – Valladolid (50,000 pesos), Puebla (20,000 pesos), and Guadalajara (40,000 pesos) – but, in contrast, the bishop of Oaxaca notified his colleagues that he could only send 6,000 pesos, arguing that the poverty of his diocese made it impossible to collect larger sums.[62]

that the amount of 2.5 millions that the Mining Tribunal the subscribers to loans for the Crown in 1793–1794 had included almost one hundred investors, including a large number of religious institutions with cash to spare. The Archivo de Minería, at the Palacio de Minería in Mexico City, contains abundant materials for research on this subject.

59 For a detailed list of ecclesiastic contributions to the loan negotiated by the consulate, see G. Valle Pavón, "Las corporaciones religiosas," pp. 236–238.

60 See the text of the 1805 representation in M. Sugawara, *La deuda pública*, p. 40.

61 AGN, *Donativos y Préstamos*, vol. 16, fs. 169–170.

62 The records of personal and institutional contributions to both the 1798 donation and loan can be found in lists published by the *Gazeta de México*, from October 1798 to September 1799. There is

In the last decade of the eighteenth century, the most substantial ecclesiastical contributions went to the tobacco loan, subscription of which began in 1795. This loan was issued to finance the war against the French Convention (1793–1795) but was later extended to help pay for the naval war with England (1796–1802). The success of this financial operation was predicated on the fact that the loan carried the guarantee of the largest and most secure all fiscal revenues in the viceroyalty: the tobacco monopoly. A number of ecclesiastical institutions in Guadalajara invested large amounts, including the Convent of Santa Gracia (49,800 pesos), the Convent of Santa Monica (54,000 pesos), and the Foundation of Pious Works of that diocese with the enormous sum of 453,000 pesos. The *Archicofradía del Santísimo Sacramento* in Mexico City invested 250,000 pesos at the 5 percent rate offered, while the Third Order of San Francisco contributed 105,000 pesos. Various religious colleges subtracted money from their reserves for the same purpose: the Royal College of Indians of Our Lady of Guadalupe bestowed 100,000 pesos and the *Colegio de Niñas Educandas* of San Luis Potosi invested 69,000 pesos from their funds.[63]

In short, the amounts lent by diverse ecclesiastical institutions to the royal treasury were considerable. Nonetheless, as historian Guillemina del Valle has stressed, the contribution of religious institutions of New Spain to the diverse loans cannot be explained simply in terms of their loyalty to the monarch. Equally important was the awareness of church financial managers of the profitability of investing funds in government securities with an interest rate of 5 percent. It may be argued that such loans were less risky than lending money to landowners whose properties were often already heavily burdened with debts.[64] Moreover, given the profitability of this type of investment, and the guarantees offered by the state, most religious agencies did not demand short-term liquidation of their debts but held on to the government paper.[65]

That the church and other privileged corporations of New Spain should have participated enthusiastically to help raise loan after loan in the 1790s suggests that there was not yet a major financial crisis in colonial Mexico. On

also much additional information in AGN, *Donativos y Préstamos*, vols. 2, 15, 16, 18, 19, 20, 25, 27, and 28.

63 For more data on ecclesiastical contributions to the tobacco loan, see AGN, *Consulado*, vol. 312, file 8, dossier 4 and A. Lavrin, "El capital eclesiástico," pp. 52–55.

64 G. Valle Pavón, "Las corporaciones religiosas," explains, for example, that the treasury of the Inquisition in New Spain had been forbidden by high authorities in the metropolis to enter into loans with no mortgage guarantee. But after the 1782 loan for the Crown, it was allowed to make that kind of investment.

65 For details, see Guillermina del Valle Pavón, "El apoyo financiero del Consulado de Comerciants a las guerras españolas del siglo XVIII," in Pilar Martínez and Guillermina del Valle, eds., *El crédito en Nueva España*, pp. 131–150.

the other hand, in the metropolis, both fiscal and financial crises had already become severe as was evinced by the financial reform adopted in 1798 under the name of the *Consolidación de Vales Reales* (Consolidation Fund for Public Debt). This measure actually implied the disentailment of ecclesiastical properties on a huge scale in order to cover the rapidly mounting deficits of the Spanish monarchy. Despite the promise of revenues to be obtained with this initiative, the Spanish crown was about to embark upon a dangerous course which threatened to undermine its secular alliance with the Catholic Church. The new financial strategy, however, was not extended to Spanish America until the year 1804, when the government of Charles IV resolved to do so, confiding that, once again, the colonies would save the metropolis.

The Consolidation Fund as Second Royal Treasury

The urgency felt by the Spanish authorities to adopt a series of major financial reforms was the result of the growing deficits of the metropolitan government. From the onset of the war with the French Convention (1793–1795) the senior administrators of the Spanish Treasury had begun to perceive the increasing incapacity of the Madrid Treasury to cover the enormous expenditures created by military conflict. We have already noted that the solutions adopted by the Madrid Cabinet to finance the war included introducing several new taxes, the issue of large quantities of domestic public debt (*vales reales*), and the negotiation of foreign loans in Holland. But, for the first time in the century, the debt burden became a major problem for the Bourbon administration.

From the 1780s, the Bank of San Carlos had been the agency responsible for paying interest on domestic debt paper as well as on the external bonds issued in Amsterdam. From the mid-1790s, however, the bank directors recognized the difficulty of the bank in fulfilling this function as a result of the growing scarcity of its own resources as well as of those of the Ministry of Finance itself. They therefore sought new ways of overcoming the growing difficulties involved in sustaining royal credit. In 1794 the managers of the bank issued a number of reports in which they claimed that speculation in public debt paper was impossible to control, criticizing the speculators who mercilessly worked the Spanish financial markets.[66] The fall in the value of debt securities made it more and more difficult to obtain loans for the monarchy, a fact that obliged it to consider various options for reform.

66 See, for example, the long, interesting document in AHBE, *Archivo del Banco de San Carlos*, leg. 708, doc. 5, entitled "Real Orden para que el Banco informe en razón de los medios para evitar la pérdida de los Vales Reales."

Several reform proposals advocated adoption of the British model of public debt management, while others appealed to the quite different financial experiments that had been applied by the French revolutionary government. The British example of managing the debt with a sinking fund was particularly attractive for the senior financial authorities in Madrid, since they believed that by adopting a similar mechanism they might be able to cover the debt service and liquidate a portion of the principal of Spain's internal debt. The same officials pressed to obtain royal permission for assignment of different tax branches to this end, but eventually they were forced to recognize that in order to obtain sufficient capital for the future sinking fund, it might be necessary to adopt radical policies for the disentailment (*desamortización*) of ecclesiastical properties, such as those applied from 1791 in neighboring France.[67]

During the ephemeral peace of 1795–1796, which lasted only fourteen months, the financial reform proposals were suspended. The resumption of remittances of American silver to Spain contributed to the recovery of the market value of the public debts securities and there was a brief financial respite. Nonetheless, the outbreak of naval war with England in December of 1796 soon provoked a new bear market: news of the disastrous naval defeat of Cape Saint Vincent (1797) caused a precipitous fall in the price of bonds of the Spanish internal debt. (See Figure 4.2.) The markets reflected the fact that the metropolis' latent financial crisis was now out in the open. Expenditures continued to rise while taxes declined, particularly customs revenues which were hard hit by the naval war and by the subsequent suspension of transatlantic trade. Customs revenues – the single most important tax branch in Spain – dropped by 75 percent in 1797 and stayed depressed for five long years. Also hard hit were the remittances of silver that came as fiscal surpluses from the American colonies: in the years 1790–1796 the metropolitan treasuries had received an average of more than 7 million pesos per year from the colonies in remitted tax revenues, but after 1797 these dropped to 2.3 million pesos.[68] (See the Appendix, Table 1.2.) The result of the abrupt drop in revenues was a fiscal and financial catastrophe. The Ministry of Finance could no longer cover all its military disbursements, and the

67 Admiration for the British model of public debt management is evident from the reports (*Memorias*) of eighteenth-century, Spanish finance ministers. See the summaries of the *Memorias* in J. Canga Arguelles, *Diccionario de Hacienda*, vol. 2, pp. 125–191. Given the ostensibly conservative character of Charles IV's administration, financial officers avoided making explicit reference to the financial experiments carried out during the French Revolution in the years 1790–1794, including disentailment and the issuance of *assignats*. A detailed analysis of the French reforms is to be found in the monumental study of François Crouzet, *La grande inflation: la monnaie en France de Louis XVI à Napoléon* (Paris: Fayard, 1993).

68 For annual data, see tables in José Patricio Merino, *Las cuentas de la Administración central española, 1750–1820* (Madrid: Instituto de Estudios Fiscales, 1987).

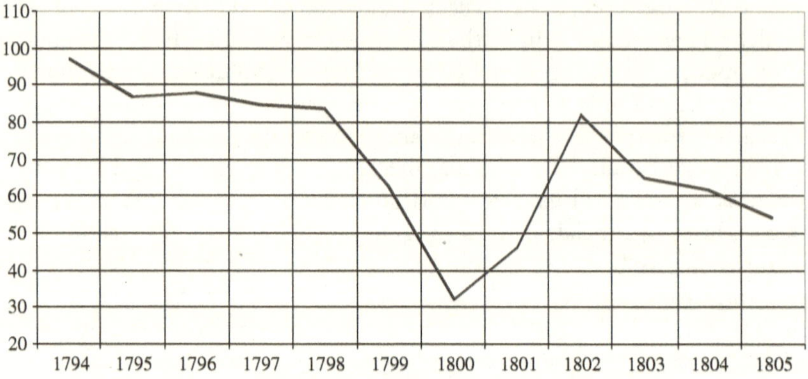

Figure 4.2. Annual market prices of *vales reales* in the years 1794–1808 in Spain. *Source:* Pedro Tedde, *El Banco de San Carlos (1782–1829)*, Madrid: Banco de España, Alianza, 1988, p. 234.

Bank of San Carlos was unable to adequately service both the foreign debt held in Holland and the domestic debt, particularly the famous *vales reales*.

New fiscal and financial instruments were now desperately needed to permit the Spanish government to obtain additional resources and alleviate growing deficits. There now appeared to be no alternative but to carry out a radical reform, which included both debt restructuring and a campaign to forcibly obtain much capital from the Catholic Church, the oldest ally of the Crown. The reform began by assigning additional powers to the government's Sinking Fund, known as *Caja de Amortización de Vales Reales*, which was instructed to take charge not only of internal and external debt service payments but also of a broad range of military and financial requirements.[69] The establishment of the Consolidation Fund (*Consolidación de Vales Reales*) in 1798 represented a further step that implied a series of fundamental changes in the monarchy's financial administration. Among other things, the measure heralded recognition of the inefficacy of the Bank of San Carlos as the government's international financial agent, being replaced, in part, by the fund.[70]

69 Already by 1798, the Sinking Fund (*Caja de Amortización de vales reales*) was responsible for the greater part of operations related to the Spanish government's public debt management, but from then on its functions were redefined and expanded to be converted into the Royal Consolidation Fund (*Real Caja de Consolidación*). For details, consult the excellent report, prepared in 1808 by the director of the Manuel Sixto Espinosa fund (*caja Manuel Sixto Espinosa*) at the request of the Napoleonic government, entitled "Resumen histórico de la Real Caxa de Consolidación." [Historical Account of the Royal Consolidation Fund] *Archives Nationales* (París), *AF IV*, 1608 B-2.

70 On the operational failures of the Banco de San Carlos, see the penetrating analysis by M. Artola, *La hacienda del antiguo régimen*, pp. 423–428. On the expanded functions of the Real Giro (Royal

The most important functions assumed by the Consolidation Fund involved the management of the internal and external public debt. To cover domestic debt service (in particular the interest payments on *vales reales*), the decrees of April 6 and 8, 1799, established that the treasury of the fund would receive revenues from at least ten important taxes.[71] On the other hand, to amortize the *vales* (actually a form of public bond), an additional set of funds was designated, the most important being the monies to be derived from sale of properties of a broad range of ecclesiastical foundations known as *Obras Pías y Capellanías*. Other resources were added to the treasury of the Consolidation Fund, including the sales of a set of estates belonging to the Crown but not deemed indispensable for the royal family; the product of the auctions of the old Jesuit properties that had been expropriated by the state many years before (*Temporalidades*) in Spain and America; and the sale of some properties of the aristocratic Military Orders (*Ordenes Militares*).

With this regular and extraordinary income, the Consolidation Fund acquired a singular financial importance. As Richard Herr points out:

> Although the final results (of the Consolidation) could not be predicted at the beginning, the long term impact was to create a second state treasury charged with the national debt, with its own income and funds that came to be known as the Consolidation Fund (*Fondo* or *Caja de Consolidación*).[72]

Apart from covering the debt service, the treasury department of the Consolidation Fund was responsible for covering the expenses of several government military departments. For example, from 1798 onward, it became responsible for the greater part of supplies to the navy and some army provisions.

As director of the Consolidation Fund, Manuel Sixto Espinosa soon became the second most powerful man in the financial machinery of imperial Spain, although he acted in close coordination with the Minister of Finance, Miguel Cayetano Soler. Given rising financial demands and declining fiscal receipts in the metropolis, Manuel Espinosa began to acquire a pronounced interest in New Spain's financial resources, particularly as they came in the form of silver pesos. The extension of the Consolidation Fund to Spanish America was ratified in late 1804, six years later than in the metropolis.

Remittance Office) after 1802, see "Reglamento e instrucción del Real Giro de Tesorería Mayor, Madrid (1802)," in AHBE, *Archivo del Banco de San Carlos*, leg. 708.

71 See the list of revenues assigned to the *Caja de Amortización* in Pedro Tedde "Crisis del Estado y deuda pública a comienzos del siglo XIX," *Hacienda Pública Española* (1987), pp. 188. See text of the decree in M. Sugawara, *La deuda pública*, 1976, p. 305.

72 The quote is from the essay by Richard Herr, "Hacia el derrumbe del antiguo régimen: crisis fiscal y desamortización bajo Carlos IV," *Moneda y Crédito*, 118 (1971), 50. This pioneering research was later expanded into the major study by the same author in his work titled *Rural Change and Royal Finances in Spain at the End of the Old Regime* (Berkeley: University of California Press, 1989).

The Consolidation Fund and the Appropriation of Church Assets in New Spain, 1804–1808

The tardy implementation of the Consolidation in the colonies was probably due to the fact that treasury officials in Madrid knew that the American church possessed fewer properties (in the form of urban and rural real estate) than in Spain. In contrast, it was well known that religious institutions in Mexico and other colonies did have considerable amounts of capital, most of which was administered by religious foundations to which wealthy persons had left monies in legacy. These funds were usually lent to different groups of landlords, miners, and merchants, shaping the essential foundation of the long-term credit system of the colonial economy. But touching those assets was potentially dangerous, as it risked provoking the opposition of many private debtors and of the Catholic Church itself.[73]

Despite the clear danger of alienating both the colonial wealthy and the church, the imperial authorities decided in 1804 to act with severity and firmness in the final campaign to drain as large a volume of funds as possible from religious institutions in New Spain and the other American colonies. By extending the Consolidation to the whole of the Spanish empire on November 24, 1804, the Madrid Cabinet sent the unequivocal message that it considered that the time had come for the church to transfer the larger part of its liquid assets to the state. This was, however, not strictly speaking an expropriation since the religious institutions were to receive public bonds (paying 3 percent interest) in exchange for delivering their outstanding money capital.[74] Moreover, as the royal edict indicated, not all ecclesiastical assets were to be affected:

> Properties belonging to churches and religious communities will not be included in alienation whenever they constitute funds whose yield constitutes the support and sustenance of its members....[75]

But the new policy did force many religious institutions and foundations to call in outstanding credits and hand them over to the government by means of a rigorous campaign that affected a considerable number of the most influential merchants, miners, and landowners of the viceroyalty who had taken loans from the religious institutions. The illustrious nineteenth

73 Numerous testimonies of these fears were expressed in protests: see D. Brading, *Una iglesia asediada*, pp. 248–250.

74 Still in 1813, for example, religious corporations owned 47% of Mexico City's houses, "not including religious buildings: convents, churches, parishes, teaching establishments, and welfare institutions that covered a considerable share of the urban area." Dolores Morales, "La distribución de la propiedad en la ciudad de México entre 1813 y 1848," *Historias*, 12 (1986), 81.

75 See the text of the edict in M. Sugawara, *La deuda pública*, pp. 13–26.

century historian Lucas Alamán recognized the serious injury that the recall of credits caused to the private economy of the viceroyalty:

> The affluence of the clergy (in New Spain) did not consist so much in their properties – which were many, especially in the most important cities, such as Mexico, Puebla, and so on –, but of interest-bearing loans applied to particulars. Furthermore, the business resulting from the imposition and redemption of those funds made each *juzgado de obras pías y capellanías* (pious works) a sort of bank.... [76]

Alaman's account, however, should be qualified, since – in each region of the viceroyalty – the respective *juzgado de obras pías y capellanías* was not actually a bank but rather a sophisticated institution created by the Catholic Church to supervise the financial legacies made by thousands of individuals and families to religious foundations. The *juzgados* in each diocese of Mexico received and managed funds donated for the maintenance of charitable organizations, religious colleges, and hospitals or for the performance of certain services, most frequently to pay chaplains to offer prayers and masses for the dead on a regular schedule, often during decades. Generally speaking, the officers in charge of these legacies lent most of the available monies to property owners at a 4 or 5 percent annual interest rate. The total sum of capital managed in this way is not known with precision, although according to well-informed contemporaries in late, colonial Mexico, it may have amounted to perhaps as much as forty to fifty million pesos.[77] These funds were pillars of the old-regime credit system in the Spanish American colonies and they constituted precisely the monies with which crown expected to amortize or "consolidate" the growing stock of public debt held in the shape of securities known as *vales reales*.[78]

The new decrees, thus, did affect not only the church but virtually all property owners, landowners, merchants, and miners, who had borrowed money from religious foundations. The royal decrees also represented a serious blow for numerous foundations, schools, hospitals, and persons that received the benefits of funds bequeathed to pious works or chaplaincies.[79] According to the exhaustive study by historian Gisela von Wobeser, the Consolidation affected the capital assets of four classes of religious

76 Lucas Alamán, *Historia de México*, 5 vols. (Mexico: Fondo de Cultura Económica/Instituto Cultural Helénico, 1985) [facsímile of the first edition of 1849–1852], p. 66.

77 Abad y Queipo, who was for many years in charge of the *Juzgado de Obras Pías* at the bishopric of Michoacán, provided similar estimates as did almost all the written protests by diverse corporations of New Spain: among the contemporary estimates of capital available for loans, see M. Sugawara, *La deuda pública*, pp. 29, 36, and 48.

78 For an insightful review of this problem, see the introductory essay in A. Bauer, *La iglesia en la economía*.

79 M. Chowning, "The Consolidación de Vales Reales," p. 472, claims that the *Consolidación* had a more direct impact on the wealthy elite of the Michoacán region.

organizations, all of which were expected to transfer at least a part of their assets to the monarchy.[80] In the first place, the decrees struck the core institutions of the church: cathedrals, parishes, sanctuaries, monasteries, and convents. In the second place, they hit a great number of charitable socially beneficent entities, such as religious schools, hospitals, orphanages, asylums, and poor houses. In the third place, they affected associations that were not necessarily ecclesiastical, such as fraternities and brotherhoods. Finally, the extraordinary measures allowed the state to take funds from a vast number of religious foundations and chaplaincies. Not surprisingly, the implementation of this extraordinary financial measure spurred a large number of complaints, known as *representaciones*, demanding the annulment of the decrees.[81]

Despite mounting complaints, Viceroy José de Iturrigaray complied with the peremptory orders of the Minister of Treasury, Soler, to act promptly to begin collection of funds and remittance to the peninsula. The Council of the Indies and the *Junta Suprema de Consolidación* (Supreme Council of the Consolidation Fund) in Spain ordered the viceroy to proceed with the establishment of a supervisory board (*Junta Superior de Consolidación de Vales Reales*) in Mexico City, to be composed of the viceroy, the archbishop, the regents, and the fiscal of the leading colonial court (*Audiencia*) as well as two officials appointed by the Crown, General Deputy Antonio José Arangoiz and bookkeeper Diego Madolell.[82] The latter took several months to arrive from Spain, so the archbishop begged the viceroy to provisionally suspend the process of disentailment of church assets. But Iturrigaray peremptorily refused to do so and ordered the creation of subordinate *juntas* in every intendancy aimed at carrying out a preliminary record of existing funds or properties to be eventually incorporated into the Consolidation Fund.[83] (See Figure 4.3.)

From the fall of 1805, the regional *juntas* began collecting the required funds, obliging debtors to reimburse the loans they had taken from local,

80 Gisela von Wobeser, *Dominación colonial: la Consolidación de vales reales, 1804–1812* (México: UNAM, 2003).

81 M. Sugawara, *La deuda pública*, includes a splendid selection of *representaciones* against the *Consolidación* in New Spain.

82 For a very clear depiction of the organization of the *Junta*, see L. A. Jáuregui, "La anatomía del fisco colonial," Chart 14, p. 235. As to the appointment of officials for the *Consolidación* in New Spain, see the letters to Iturrigaray from the Count of Montarco, president of the Council of the Indies, and from Antonio Porcel, secretary of Charles IV, in AGN, *Reales Cédulas Originales*, vol. 195, file 30, fs. 61–63 and file 114, fs. 243–246.

83 The basic rules for keeping the books of collected funds are contained in the exhaustive "Real instrucción que S. M. se ha servido aprobar para el cumplimiento del Real Decreto de enagenación de bienes pertenecientes a Obras Pías en los Dominios de América y en las Islas Filipinas," in M. Sugawara, *La deuda pública*, pp. 13–26, which transcribes the document in AGN, *Reales Cédulas Originales*, vol. 192, file 143, fs. 149–161. Also see the regulations signed by Manuel Sixto Espinosa, director of the *Caja de Consolidación* in Madrid, dated January 21, 1805. AGN, *Consolidación*, vol. 1, file 5, fs. 84–85.

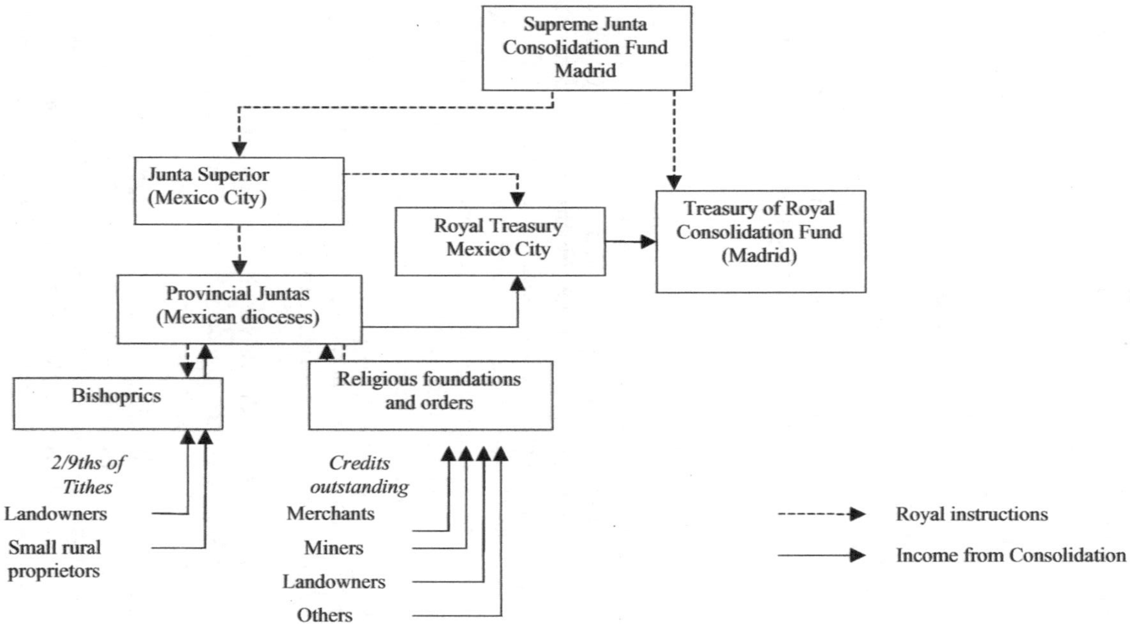

Figure 4.3. Income of the Royal Consolidation Fund, Mexico, 1805–1808.
Source: drawn by Carlos Marichal

religious foundations and pious works. In other cases the real estate of charitable institutions was auctioned off with the same purpose.[84] Among the individuals most affected by the abolition of the traditional credit system, were many large landlords who had been assiduous clients of credits offered by religious foundations. For example, the Marquis of Aguayo, an extremely affluent livestock breeder, was pressed to restore 462,000 pesos to his creditors (and thence to the Consolidation Fund), a huge amount for that time, although he apparently was successful in reducing this sum to 43,000 pesos. Gabriel de Yermo, owner of numerous sugar *haciendas*, was instructed to return loans amounting to 131,000 pesos, although he later negotiated a first payment of 15,000 pesos to be followed by successive installments over various years.[85] Similarly, the Count of Santiago Calimaya, owner of a huge *hacienda* in the Toluca valley, was ordered to reimburse 51,300 pesos. Not surprisingly, the leading landowners – headed by the Marquis of Aguayo – reacted to fiscal pressures and sent a formal petition that enraged the viceroy.[86]

The wealthier miner owners also protested against the Consolidation. A fair number had arrears on money lent to them by pious works, convents, and confraternities. The Count of La Valenciana, owner of the most productive silver mines in Guanajuato, was asked to repay 57,000 pesos, and so were the enormously wealthy Count of Regla (70,000 pesos), the Count of Rul (83,348 pesos), and several members of the affluent Fagoaga mining family (115,937 pesos).[87] The *Junta de Consolidación* also requested the Mining Tribunal to pay off half a million pesos it owed to several religious foundations, instructing it to deposit the money in the royal treasury. However, the miners answered that they had already advanced funds to the Crown as donations in 1793 and 1798 and, therefore, did not feel obligated by this new claim. For that reason and with the intention of protecting its members, the miners sent a protest (*representación*) to the viceroy, declaring that the new fiscal policy entailed a threat of bankruptcy to silver miners, in general:

> Mine owners do not possess by themselves enough capital [...] nor can they otherwise obtain it, since there are no moneychangers, banks, or public funds in this kingdom from which to obtain monies... and the only recourse they had

84 Often, when authorities required ecclesiastic properties to be sold in auction, complaints and fights arose. See, for example, the fiery protests by the cathedral chapter of Mexico City in AGN, *Consolidación*, vol. 6, files 1 and 2. In the same volume, fs. 340–344, the nuns of the Convent of Santo Domingo in Querétaro claimed they would not auction some urban properties since these were vital for their survival.

85 For actual payments realized, see G. von Wobeser, *Dominación colonial*, p. 189–192.

86 See the text of the letter in M. Sugawara, *La deuda pública*, pp. 88–92. Also see commentaries in D. Ladd, *Mexican Nobility*, p. 102.

87 D. Ladd, *Mexican Nobility*, pp. 100–101.

in the past were the religious foundations, the coffers of convents, those of the confraternities, in sum, the Pious Works . . . [88]

But pressures by the officers of the Consolidation Fund did not only affect the leading landlords, merchants, and mine owners: less affluent sectors were also forced to pay their outstanding debts to the Crown officials.[89] In the intendancy of Valladolid, for example, 537 property owners signed a protest written by the distinguished cleric Manuel Abad y Queipo, censuring land concentration in the hands of the major *hacendados*, and the meat-trade monopoly in Mexico City controlled by "four rich cattle raisers of that court."[90] But, above all, these regional property owners demanded the annulment of the Consolidation since it seriously injured regional agriculture by undermining the local credit system.

Information on repayment of outstanding loans by property owners of the intendacy of Valladolid (Michoacán) is not complete, but enough is known to make a preliminary estimate. According to a recent study by Margaret Chowning, it would appear that while the larger landlords and merchants repaid part of their loans relatively quickly, medium-size farmers and ranchers did not. In many cases, they were allowed to repay in low installments in ten- or twelve-year terms (known as a *composición* to their debts). Chowning claims, therefore, that the economic impact of the Consolidation in Michoacán was not acute, although she suggests that in political terms it was a cause of discontent among the elite and medium-size owner sectors.[91] Nonetheless, her views are at odds with other historical studies.

The recent and exhaustive analysis of the Consolidation in New Spain, published by Gisela von Wobeser indicates that in the intendancy of Valladolid alone, total payments between 1805 and 1808 reached the colossal figure of almost one million pesos.[92] Cathedral chapters in the bishopric were required to deliver to the Consolidation some 25,000 pesos in cash, religious schools approximately 65,000 pesos, chaplaincies 330,000 pesos, parishes over 80,000 pesos, and convents 269,000 pesos. In some cases, the money was taken from the operating funds of these institutions. But

88 M. Sugawara, *La deuda pública*, p. 37.

89 For a detailed review of contributors to the *Consolidación* in the intendancy of Oaxaca, see Brian Hamnett, *Politics and Trade in Southern Mexico, 1750–1821* (Cambridge, U.K.: Cambridge University Press, 1971), pp. 110–111 and Appendix 9.

90 M. Sugawara, *La deuda pública*, pp. 66–67.

91 M. Chowning argues that the economic impact of the *Consolidación* in Michoacán was a decline in the short-term credit, but that prices or real estate transactions did not drop: M Chowning, "The Consolidación de Vales Reales," 460–478.

92 Calculated on the basis of lists published in the appendix from G. von Wobeser, *Dominación colonial*, pp. 265–449.

in most cases it came from loans which had been quickly reimbursed by debtors, fearful of losing their properties since the rapacious royal functionaries threatened with auctioning off houses, ranches, and *haciendas* of those who did not liquidate their debts to religious institutions. The Indian peasants communities also felt the brunt of the campaign: in the intendancy of Valladolid, close to 60,000 pesos were collected from the communal funds of the peasant towns and villages in the years 1807 and 1808. In this sense, it can be suggested that the Consolidation represented the deathblow to a great number of communal funds of peasant towns which were forced to hand over two-thirds of their reserves to the royal treasuries.[93]

An especially significant testimony that confirms the extractive nature of the Consolidation was that of Bishop Abad y Queipo, former director of the *Juzgado de Obras Píás* (administration of pious works) in the city of Valladolid, who presented a document that contained the protests by medium and small ranchers and farmers from Michoacán against the Crown.[94] The historian David Brading has reviewed the texts of Abad y Queipo in a recent monograph on eighteenth-century Michoacán and argues that the bishop was undoubtedly right about the negative impact of this policy for the debtors and the clergy.[95] Moreover, in other regions of the viceroyalty, numerous disagreements were also voiced against the *Consolidación*, such as the protests presented by the *hacendados* of Tepeaca's wheat region (in the intendancy of Puebla), who deplored the forced collection of funds. The careful quantitative review by historian Francisco Cervantes of the impact of such measures on the economy of Puebla indicates that the claims were not rhetoric; he demonstrates that the result of the *Consolidación* was a drastic reduction of agricultural credit in Puebla during and after this period.[96]

As Gisela von Wobeser has argued in her detailed study of the Consolidation Fund in Mexico, disentailment had a negative impact on the complex system of reciprocities which underlay the colonial credit system. One of the principal reasons was that the Consolidation in New Spain concentrated

93 This was the resolution of the *Junta Superior de Consolidación* approved on June 25, 1806. On long-term consequences of this resolution, see A. Lavrin, "Execution of the Laws," pp. 41–42.

94 Several documents written by Abad y Queipo are contained in José María L. Mora, *Crédito Público* (Mexico: UNAM, 1986) [facsimile of the first edition, París, 1837]. See the superb portrait of Abad y Queipo, the bishop in D. Brading, *Una iglesia asediada*, pp. 254–282.

95 The recent survey by Iván Franco, "La Intendencia de Valladolid de Michoacán, 1787–1809. El proceso de formación del poder civil en una región de la Nueva España," Master's thesis, El Colegio de Michoacán, Zamora, Mich., 1995, Chapter 7, also stresses the negative impact of the *Consolidación* on Michoacán's economy and society.

96 See F. Cervantes, "El crédito eclesiástico en Puebla," and by the same author "La iglesia y la crisis del crédito colonial en Puebla, 1800–1814," in Leonor Ludlow and Carlos Marichal, eds., *Banca y poder en México, 1800–1925* (Mexico: Grijalbo, 1986), pp. 51–74.

on appropriating the capital managed by religious foundations (88 percent of total collections) whereas it raised little money by sale of mortgaged properties.[97] By forcing property owners to return a great number of loans outstanding, the Crown not only weakened a vast mass of debtors, but it also wiped out most of the capital reserves of the great number of religious institutions and foundations that had provided the bulk of credit in the viceroyalty for more than two centuries.[98] The result was doubly severe: by weakening the credit markets and the organizations that supported it, the Crown contributed to destroy a secular tradition of donations and legacies that was essential to the social welfare of Mexican society; at the same time, the disentailment of capital assets of the church gravely weakened the entire financial system of the colonial, old regime economy.

Contemporary testimonies confirm this view. The Mexico City Merchant Guild and the Mining Tribunal, as well as other privileged corporations and groups of property owners, stressed the negative impact of the Consolidation because of the devastating impact on the credit system.[99] The many written protests (*representaciones*) they sent to the viceroy are one of the most revealing evidences of the intensifying political and economic tensions within the viceroyalty, shortly before the outbreak of insurgency in 1810.

The Importance of New Spain's Consolidation: Some Imperial Comparisons

According to the most reliable estimations, the process of *Consolidación* in New Spain yielded *in toto* 10,321,800 pesos to the Crown (see Table 4.2).[100] A regional analysis reveals that the diocese of Mexico was the salient contributor, followed by those of Puebla, Michoacán, Guadalajara, and Oaxaca; this appeared to correspond to the relative wealth level of each bishopric (see Table 4.2).[101] Since many of the wealthiest men and women of the viceroyalty then lived in the capital city and since it was there that the

97 G. von Wobeser, *Dominación colonial*, p. 242, documents that real estate auctions only produced 12% of the ten million pesos collected in New Spain by the Consolidation Fund.

98 This symbiotic relationship between ecclesiastic financial institutions and the landlord class is one of the main arguments of the detailed research monograph by M. I. Sánchez Maldonado, *Diezmos y crédito eclesiástico*.

99 These texts are included in M. Sugawara, *La deuda pública*.

100 There are some divergences on total sums collected via the *Consolidación*, but the most reliable figures appear to be those in A. Lavrin, "Execution of the Laws," quoted in Table 4.2. Compare with Brian Hamnett, "The Appropriation of Mexican Church Wealth by the Spanish Bourbon Government: The Consolidación de Vales Reales, 1805–1809," *Journal of Latin American Studies*, 1, 2 (1969), 100–110 and R. F. Caballero, "La Consolidación de Vales Reales," pp. 362–364.

101 There are exhaustive lists with geographical and chronological distribution of collected funds in G. von Wobeser, *Dominación colonial*, appendixes, pp. 265–449.

Table 4.2. *Revenues of the Royal Treasury from the Royal Consolidation Fund in New Spain, 1805–1809 (in Pesos)*

Bishoprics	1805	1806	1807	1808	1809
México	785,826	2,273,982	1,522,028	671,433	–
Puebla	142,094	548,420	1,006,053	460,517	–
Michoacán	6,483	243,610	461,106	253,578	–
Guadalajara	125,385	269,028	345,155	150,365	1,027
Oaxaca	30,300	244,559	149,429	98,482	24,851
Mérida	–	11,450	72,896	69,177	26,284
Durango	3,910	35,082	42,588	53,701	–
Monterrey	–	–	–	21,781	40,748
Arizpe	–	–	–	39,068	3,974
TOTALS	1,093,998	3,626,131	3,599,855	1,818,102	98,727

Source: Based on Asunción Lavrin, "The Execution of the Laws of Consolidación in New Spain: Economic Aims and Results," *Hispanic American Historical Review*, 53, 1 (1973), Tables 4.1 and 4.2, 35 and 45.

largest number of religious institutions was found, it is not surprising that the diocese of Mexico collected the highest volume of funds.[102]

However, we must bear in mind that sums collected do not reflect the total assets managed by religious foundations and institutions in each region, but speak only of the capital value of redeemed loans that had been sent to royal treasuries.

The Mexican contribution to this great debt operation for the Crown was the most important in Spanish America. The ten million pesos collected in New Spain through the *Consolidación* corresponded to almost two-thirds of the sum total funds collected by the same means in all the Spanish American colonies. In the rest of the American viceroyalties and general captaincies, only 5,100,000 pesos were collected, with the main contributors being the general captaincy of Guatemala and the viceroyalty of Peru (see Table 4.3).[103]

The divergence in the collected sums in various colonies did not correspond precisely to ecclesiastic wealth distribution in the Americas, but rather would appear to suggest that the *Consolidation* was more severely implemented in New Spain.[104] Several factors requiring further research

102 D. Ladd, *Mexican Nobility*, Chapter 5, pp. 89–104.

103 Reinhard Liehr, "Statsverschuldung und privatkredit: die consolidación de vales reales in Hispanoamerika," *Ibero-Amerikanishes Archiv*, N. F. Jg. 6, 2 (1980), 150–183 is still the only comprehensive study on the *Consolidación* in the Americas, as a whole.

104 According to D. Brading, *Una iglesia asediada*, Appendix 1, revenues of the Mexican church equalled 40% of total revenues of the Catholic Church in all of Spanish America. However, New Spain's contribution to the total collection for the *Consolidación* in the Americas represented roughly 67%.

Table 4.3. *Revenues Collected through the Royal Consolidation Fund in Spanish America and the Philippines, 1805–1810 (in Pesos)*

Provinces	Total Revenues	Overhead	Transfers to Europe
Viceroyalty of New Spain	10,321,800	923,700	9,398,000
Viceroyalty of Peru	1,487,093	136,222	1,350,970
Viceroyalty of New Granada	447,779	n. i.	n. i.
Viceroyalty of Río de la Plata	366,573	26,191	n. i.
General captaincy of Guatemala	1,561,673	134,988	1,422,685
General captaincy of Cuba[a]	350,000	n. i.	308,409
General captaincy of Caracas[a]	350,000	n. i.	n. i.
General captaincy of Chile	164,063	n. i.	164,063
General captaincy of Philippines	353,059	27,265	325,794
SUBTOTAL	15,402,040		12,969,921

Note: n.i., no information available.

[a] Income of Cuba and Caracas are estimates.

Source: Reinhard Liehr, "Statsverschuldung und privatkredit: die consolidación de vales reales in Hispanoamerika," *Ibero-Amerikanishes Archiv*, N. F. Jg. 6, 2 (1980), table on p. 20.

could account for this fact. Uneven external fiscal pressures on colonies could explain it, revealing more stringent demands by the Spanish crown as regards to New Spain viceroyalty's contributions. Also, an alternative explanation could be an improved efficiency in the organization of Mexico's religious foundations, or else there was more liquidity among debtors of pious works in this viceroyalty than in other regions of the Americas.

Some comparisons with the outcome of the Consolidation Fund in Spain between 1798 and 1808 can be illustrative as well. In terms of contributing to the solvency of the royal treasury, the *Consolidación* may be regarded as a success for the government of Charles IV. It allowed for the collection of a huge amount of money, in both the metropolis and the colonies: approximately 1,300 million *reales vellón* were raised through the auction and sale of ecclesiastic properties in the peninsula over a period of ten years, while a lesser but not insignificant amount of 300 million *reales* (almost 15.4 million pesos) was collected in three years in the Americas.[105] This represented a huge transfer of wealth from church to the state. It temporarily staved off

105 The classic study on the *Consolidación* in Spain is R. Herr, "Hacia el derrumbe del antiguo régimen," 37–100 and his monumental *Rural Change and Royal Finances in Spain*. Herr suggests that the auction within Spain of properties belonging to the church or to religious foundations generated 1,600 million *reales vellón* (81.5 million *pesos fuertes*); nonetheless, Herr's nominal figures must be analyzed critically, since the Spanish government accepted not only cash but also (highly depreciated) *vales reales* in exchange for the properties auctioned. Manuel Espinosa, director of the *Consolidación*, estimated that 850 million *reales* worth were received in *vales*. See the report prepared in 1808 by

the bankruptcy of the monarchy but, at the same time, it signalled impending royal insolvency and the marked weakening of the greatest secular ally of the monarchy, the *Royal Church*.

The Consolidation Fund reflected the paradox of a monarchy which still depended on religious institutions but which, at the same time, siphoned off their wealth to pay off international war costs. This strategy, moreover, was not adopted by a revolutionary government (as in neighboring France) but by a reactionary, absolutist administration, headed by a not particularly enlightened despot, Charles IV of Spain. In sum, the adoption of these policies signalled the imminent crisis of the ancient regime in both the metropolis and the colonies.

An overview of church financial contributions in New Spain indicates the dimensions of the sacrifice made on behalf of the Crown and its wars. Apart from the sizeable amounts collected via the Consolidation in the viceroyalty between 1805 and 1808, we must also consider the already huge donations to the viceregal government provided in previous decades by Mexican ecclesiastical institutions in the form of taxes, donations, loans, and subsidies. A rough estimation of these contributions suggests that the church in New Spain handed over to the Crown treasuries a total of close to 35 million pesos (700 million *reales*) between 1780 and 1808, a truly huge sum for that era.[106] The loans and donations were used explicitly to help finance the wars of the monarchy. But an unanswered question refers to the final destiny of the funds collected through the Consolidation Fund: officially, those monies were transferred to the Spanish royal treasury to pay off domestic debt (in *vales reales*). In practice, however, the funds remitted from New Spain between 1805 and 1809 served to meet a more diverse series of financial obligations, including payments of provisions for the Spanish Navy and Army, the service of foreign loans subscribed by the Crown in Holland, as well as a series of subsidies to be paid to Napoleon as a result of a secret treaty signed with Charles IV in late 1803.

Since some of these commitments were secret, both Finance Minister Soler and the Director of the Consolidation Fund Espinosa did not dare to inform anyone of the details except Viceroy Iturrigaray and his staff.

Manuel Sixto Espinosa at the request of the Napoleonic government, entitled "Resumen histórico de la Real Caxa de Consolidación," *Archives Nationales* (Paris), *AF IV*, 1608 B-2, p. 14.

106 We estimate that revenues from ecclesiastical tax branches transferred to the Crown treasuries (listed in Table 4.1) produced at least 12 million pesos between 1780 and 1800. We add 7 million pesos for the years 1800–1808, which includes the same branches as well as the new *noveno decimal* and proceeds from additional sales of indulgences. To this must be added at least 5 million pesos in donations and loans from the church for the Crown Wars during 1780–1808, as well as 2 million pesos in "subsidios ecclesiastícos," plus 10 million pesos in funds taken for the *Consolidación*. Fom the 36 million pesos total, we subtract 1 million pesos that can be ascribed to Indian communal funds, which gives us a figure of approximately 35 million pesos.

Thus, except for the viceroy and a small circle of utterly reliable officers, neither church authorities nor others affected by the Consolidation Fund apparently knew that much of the money collected was not to go to the metropolitan coffers of the Spanish monarchy, but rather to the treasury of the Napoleonic empire! This clandestine transaction reflected the increasing complexity of the international finances of the Spanish monarchy at its most critical juncture.

5

Napoleon and Mexican Silver, 1805–1808

Prime Minister Pitt agreed to collaborate in my operations. England promised to supply four frigates to carry the *piastres* (silver pesos) from the New World on behalf of Charles IV but in practice for Napoleon.

Gabriel Julien Ouvrard, *Mémoires* (1826)[1]

After the Peace of Amiens, signed between Great Britain and France in March 1802, Atlantic commerce received a welcome respite from several years of exhausting maritime warfare.[2] The pent-up demand for manufactured goods in all of Spanish America impelled a tremendous wave of activity in transatlantic shipping. European imports were paid for with large, accumulated stocks of silver in Mexico, Peru, and Chile or exchanged for local exports such as tobacco and sugar from Cuba, cacao from Venezuela, hides from the River Plate. Most of this trade continued to be handled by Spanish shippers from Cádiz and a few other metropolitan ports, since the old imperial trade monopoly basically remained in place. The importance of this peaceful interlude should not be underestimated, particularly because of the high volume of silver remittances that began to arrive in Cádiz following the cessation of hostilities. Indeed, 1802–1804 marked the peak of American silver transfers in *three centuries* of colonial history. More than 100 million pesos of silver and gold were dispatched from Spanish American ports to the metropolis in less than two and a half years.[3]

1 Gabriel Julien Ouvrard, *Mémoires*, vol. I (Paris, 1826–1828), p. 110.

2 The conclusion of the First Naval War (1796–1801) with England inaugurated a surge in transatlantic commerce. The intensity of naval and commercial movements was especially notable in the port of Veracruz. More than 400 ships entered and departed in 1803, demonstrating the continued dynamism of New Spain's economy. See statistics in Javier Ortiz de la Tabla, *Comercio exterior de Veracruz, 1778–1821: crisis de dependencia* (Sevilla: Escuela de Estudio Hispano-Americanos, 1978).

3 In his monumental study on silver and gold remittances from Spanish and Portuguese America in the colonial era, Michel Morineau provides the figure of 114 million pesos: M. Morineau, *Incroyables Gazettes*, p. 454. S. Stein, "Crisis metropolitana, comercio atlántico y descapitalización colonial: España y Nueva España, 1804–1808," in *Academia Nacional de Historia, Congreso bicentenerario de Simón*

Of the total sum of silver and gold sent, an important portion (forty million pesos) was delivered on account of the Spanish government, helping to prop up the monarchy's finances. Colonial tax remittances and loans helped cover deficits and boosted the market value of debt securities in Spain which had tumbled during the naval war with Great Britain, especially in the years 1798–1801. As on so many occasions, the colonies rescued the mother country. This was demonstrated with startling clarity in the Madrid Treasury accounts of 1802–1804, since remittances sent from the royal treasuries in America contributed more than 30 percent of the regular revenue of Spain's national treasury.[4] Initially, the Spanish government took advantage of the renewed flow of funds to pay off short-term debt arising from military and particularly naval requirements that had pushed overall expenditures upward. At the same time, service on the debt of the most important domestic public bonds (*vales reales*) was guaranteed, and as a result, the quotations on the Spanish debt increased notably. (See Figure 4.2) But by the end of 1803, hopes of attaining fiscal equilibrium were dashed again as a result of new and huge, external financial demands forced upon the Spanish crown by the French government, avid to obtain silver.

In October 1803, Napoleon Bonaparte obliged Charles IV to sign a secret agreement known as the Subsidy Treaty (*Tratado de Subsidios*) which exempted the Spanish government from participating in new French military land campaigns in exchange for large annual specie payments. The treaty committed the Spanish monarchy to deliver an annual payment of 192 million *reales* to the French Treasury (some 10 million silver pesos or dollars). To avoid wiping out the reserves of specie in the Madrid coffers, the royal authorities turned to consignments of Mexican silver to guarantee most of these payments.[5] Inevitably, however, this measure would aggravate the already prolonged financial crisis that afflicted the Spanish Treasury. On the one hand, it implied a loss of autonomy over government fiscal policy that now became subject to Napoleon's imperative requirements for funds.

Bolivar, vol. iv (Caracas: Academia Nacional de Historia, 1985), p. 204, reproduces a contemporary British estimate, noting that between October 1801 and August 1804, 113 million pesos were sent from Spanish America to Spain.

4 M. Morineau, *Incroyables Gazettes*, p. 454, estimates that 40% of all remittances were for royal finance, which coincides with C. Marichal, *Bancarrota*, p. 173. For additional details on gold and silver exports, see Javier Cuenca, "Statistics of Spain's Colonial Trade, 1792–1820: Consular Duties, Cargo Inventories and Balance of Trade," *Hispanic American Historical Review*, 61, 3 (1981), 381–428. On consignments to the royal treasury between 1763 and 1810, see C. Marichal, "Beneficios y Costes Fiscales", 480–482.

5 The classic study on these operations is André Fugier, *Napoleón et l'Espagne, 1799–1808*, 2 vols. (Paris: F. Alcan, 1930), Chapters 1 and 2. It is useful to compare this data with information in Marten G. Buist, *At Spes Non Fracta: Hope and Company, 1770–1815: Merchant Bankers and Diplomats at Work* (The Hague, Holland: Martinus Nijhoff, 1974), Chapters 9–12.

On the other, it tied the tax and financial machinery of the Spanish crown to the French Treasury in ways that would have grave consequences.[6]

The treaty reinforced the Spanish crown's chronic habit of mortgaging its most valuable colonial fiscal assets to pay for its enormous financial and military commitments generated by direct or indirect participation in international wars. The payment of the subsidy to France was formally assigned to the treasuries of New Spain, beginning in 1805 with the issuance of bills of exchange delivered to the powerful, French merchant banker Gabriel Julian Ouvrard who operated in his dual capacity as war contractor and navy supplier as well as agent of the Napoleonic treasury. These drafts, signed by Manuel Espinosa, director of the Consolidation Fund (*Caja de Consolidación*), were payable only at the royal treasuries of Mexico.

But why was it necessary to resort again to the colonial treasuries? The explanation is found in the growing difficulties facing the authorities in charge of the Consolidation Fund in the metropolis, which as we have argued had already become a kind of secondary treasury of the Crown. This financial agency had two main sources of income in Spain: the revenues derived from the disentailment of religious properties and receipts from a broad but rather motley array of taxes. Nonetheless, the administrators of the Fund soon found that these receipts were no longer sufficient to cover the totality of the obligations they were obliged to pay, which had multiplied extraordinarily as they now included not only covering most of the internal and external debt service but also covering a substantial part of the costs of the navy, as well as substantial supplies for Spanish land forces.[7] As a result, they found it more expedient to assure payments to France by diverting a part of the official silver shipped from Mexico.

Both the Spanish and the French governments hoped that the Mexican funds would be sent as soon as possible from Veracruz in Spanish warships to Europe. However, the outbreak of the naval war with England in December 1804 made this extremely difficult, and after the catastrophic defeat of the French–Spanish fleet at the battle of Trafalgar (October 1805), communications and commerce between Spain and its American colonies were interrupted due to the control of the British Navy over the Atlantic and adjacent seas. Yet despite the war, not all trade was suspended. A vigorous *neutral commerce* soon developed, as many traders and shippers from nonbelligerent countries plied manufactures to be sold in New Spain and the

6 The policy of requiring forced subsidies from allies was common practice of Napoleon's financial strategy, as shown in the study of John H. Sherwig, *Guineas and Gunpowder. British Foreign Aid in the Wars with France, 1793–1815* (Cambridge, MA: Harvard University Press, 1969).

7 According to one historian, "the Caja de Consolidación in Madrid probably was bankrupt by 1805": Jose Patricio Merino, "1805: La crisis financiera internacional y deuda española," in M. Artola and L. M. Bilabo, eds., *Estudios de Hacienda: de Ensenada a Mon* (Madrid: Instituto de Estudios Fiscales, 1984), p. 396.

other colonies, in exchange for large quantities of silver and primary goods dispatched to Europe between 1805 and 1808.[8] The secret to this trade was the issue of licenses to neutral shipping by the Spanish and British governments since both desired the maintenance of transatlantic exchange in the midst of international conflict.

For the Spanish crown the attractions of neutral commerce were manifest: it allowed the mercantile and financial operations of the already tottering imperial state to continue, including the shipment to Europe of the monies collected in Mexico by the Consolidation Fund. For the British government as well, neutral trade was a priority, for, as historian François Crouzet has demonstrated, trade with Spanish America became indispensable to English export industries, especially in the years of the Napoleonic blockade of trade with continental Europe (1806–1813).[9] More surprising was the fact that the British authorities should have authorized the transfer of Spanish royal funds (10.5 million silver pesos) from Mexico to Europe in the first years of the blockade, when it was at war with both Spain and France. A second and equally astonishing fact was that the final disbursements were not made to the metropolitan Spanish government but to Napoleon's treasury.

To transfer the Mexican silver across the Atlantic would involve collaboration between some of the most prominent and adventurous Spanish, French, Dutch, English, and North American merchant bankers and traders of the age. They were engaged in an extraordinary, secret compact in the years 1805–1808 to carry the treasure from Veracruz in neutral ships and in several British warships to Europe.[10] The leading figures in this grandiose, clandestine operation included the Napoleonic banker, Gabriel Ouvrard, the banking houses of Hope & Company of Amsterdam, and Baring Brothers of

8 On neutral trade, see John Lynch, "British Policy and Spanish America, 1783–1808," *Journal of Latin American Studies*, 1, 1 (1969), 1–30; J. Barbier, "Peninsular Finance and Colonial Trade," 21–37 and "Venezuelan Libranzas, 1788–1807: From Economic Nostrum to Fiscal Imperative," *The Americas*, 37, 4 (1981), 457–479.

9 François, Crouzet, *L'Economie Britannique et le Blocus Continental (1806–1813)*, vol. 1 (Paris: Presses Universitaires de France, 1958), pp. 179–191.

10 A group of historians (Dutch, North American, Spanish, and French) have reconstructed part of the complicated history of the transfer of Mexican silver to Europe in this naval war period in the Caribbean and the Atlantic. The following studies are fundamental: A. Fugier, *Napoleón et l'Espagne*, who undertook the first explorations of the subject by revising French and Spanish archives; Stuart Bruchey, *R. Oliver, Merchant of Baltimore, 1783–1819* (Baltimore: The Johns Hopkins Press, 1956); and S. Stein, "Un raudal de oro y plata que corría sin cesar de España a Francia: Spanish Mercantile Policy and Trade with France under Charles III," paper presented in the *International Congress "Carlos III y la Ilustración"*, Madrid (1988), 80 pp.; M. G. Buist, *At Spes Non Fracta*; and Guadalupe Jiménez Codinach, *La Gran Bretaña y la independencia de México, 1808–1821* (Mexico: Fondo de Cultura Económica, 1991) chapters 4 and 5 which have much material from British archives. Also of importance is John Alexander Jackson, "The Mexican Silver Schemes: Finance and Profiteering in the Napoleonic Era, 1796–1811," Ph.D. thesis, University of North Carolina, 1980, based on primary sources to be found in the AGN, Mexico.

London.[11] But equally fundamental was the collaboration of royal officials and merchant firms in Mexico who facilitated the transatlantic expeditions.

This chapter analyzes three key issues with the purpose of clarifying the complex mechanisms used to send the huge quantities of Mexican pesos across the Atlantic in the midst of major, military conflict between Britain, Spain, and France. First, attention is directed to the financial demands of Napoleon and why he required silver. Secondly, we review the implementation of the Subsidy Treaty and in particular the agreements negotiated between Madrid officials in charge of the Consolidation Fund and the extraordinary alliance of European bankers and merchants already mentioned. Lastly, attention is devoted to the analysis of the singular methods used by the bankers, Hope and Baring, and their local agents to extract various millions of pesos from the port of Veracruz during the years 1805–1808. The analysis of these transactions (complicated because of their secret nature) illustrates the ways in which a network of private banking and trading houses contributed to the maintenance of transatlantic financial and commercial flows at a time of total war between the European powers.

The Consequences of the Subsidy Treaty (1803) with Napoleon and the Negotiations with the Banker, Gabriel Julian de Ouvrard

The reasons why Napoleon should have become so interested in silver shipments from Spanish America were directly linked to the recommencement of hostilities between France and Great Britain in May 1803. The new military plans of Bonaparte required extraordinary financing. Most costly was his projected invasion of England, which he had been planning for some time and implied great naval and army expenses.[12] The First Consul ordered a vast and secretive program of shipbuilding in various French ports in the summer of 1803 and, at the same time, began concentrating thousands of troops in northern France with the intention of having his great army cross the Channel on more than a thousand ships and barges. Nonetheless, given the marked superiority of the British Navy – the *wooden walls* of Britain – Napoleon had to assure that his amphibious force was large and powerful enough to have a possibility of success in the projected crossing. Naval forces were concentrated at the port of Boulogne, and three army camps were set up at Bruges, St. Omer, and Montreuil.[13] At the same time,

11 For detailed information on the participation of these houses in this operation, see S. Bruchey, *R. Oliver, Merchant of Baltimore*; M. G. Buist, *At Spes Non Fracta*; and J. A. Jackson, "The Mexican Silver Schemes."

12 An excellent source continues to be the classic work by Alfred T. Mahan, *The Influence of Seapower upon the French Revolution and Empire, 1793–1812*, vol. 2 (London: Sampson Low, Marston, 1892), pp. 111–139.

13 Alan Schom, *Trafalgar: Countdown to Battle, 1803–1805* (New York: Oxford, 1990), pp. 122–126.

French navy arsenals were ordered to build hundreds of ships and barges. All this required enormous resources in the shape of supplies, food, materials for shipbuilding, and military equipment. As expenses mounted, Napoleon forced his principal war contractors to advance increasing amounts of money to cover these necessities, but he was also obliged to mortgage tax revenues to them. Eventually, it became clear that the French Treasury would not be able to cover the bulging expenditures.

There were two main reasons why the Napoleonic regime had difficulties in financing its war plans. The first was that the postrevolutionary administrations had considerable difficulty in raising new taxes. French society looked askance at traditional, fiscal resources which were identified with the old regime, in particular sales taxes which had been the first target of the populace in 1789 since they affected practically all food staples. By 1805 the principal revenues of the French government were direct taxes, mainly on rural and urban real estate.[14] A successful set of innovations had included establishment of more precise cadastres and increased centralization of tax administration. Customs duties, on the other hand, were a relatively small item in the Napoleonic budgets – a fact that may be attributed to the success of the British naval blockades in reducing the maritime trade of France.

A second difficulty confronting the French financial officers was the growing lack of confidence of investors in public debt policies. After the default of 1797 on two-thirds of public debt, the government could no longer obtain long-term loans.[15] Bonaparte relied on short-term advances by syndicates of financiers and tax collectors ("receveurs generaux"), but they charged high interest rates, averaging 15 percent annually, which contrasted with the much lower costs of public debt in England.[16] This put the French war administration at a marked disadvantage vis-a-vis the British government that was able to finance rapidly increasing military expenditures partly through increasing taxes and in part through issuing debt which was absorbed without difficulty by the broad and deep financial markets of England.[17]

Napoleon was inevitably obliged to devise new forms of war finance. The most obvious was emergency finance, by which his troops were ordered to live off the land. His armies also exploited the old fiscal regimes in conquered

14 *Archives Nationales* (France) *AF IV*, vol. 1082, "Etats relatifs a la fin de l'an neuf: Trésors publics," doc. 2, in particular annex titled "Dépenses et Recettes, 1806."

15 F. Crouzet, *La grande inflation*, pp. 466–471.

16 See the correspondence of the French Minister of Finance, Barbé-Marbois, with Napoleon, providing him with details of current interest rates and of banker groups dealing with the French government. *Archives Nationales* (Paris), *AF IV*, vol. 1082, "Etats relatifs a la fin de l'an neuf: Trésors publics" doc. 5.

17 Patrick O'Brien, "Public Finance in the Wars with France, 1793–1815," in H. T. Dickinson, ed., *Britain and the French Revolution, 1789–1815* (New York: St. Martin's Press, 1989), pp. 165–187.

territories to the utmost and proceeded to extract forced loans and provisions from local economic elites and from the church in the occupied Catholic states. Napoleon further obliged his subordinate allies to provide monies in the way of subsidies. In contrast to Great Britain, which based much of its military strategy on the European continent by *providing* subsidies to its allies, Napoleon *demanded* considerable financial assistance, including annual subsidies paid to the French Treasury by the kingdoms of Holland, Piedmont, Naples, and Spain, as well as by the duchies of Parma and Modena and the Papal states.[18]

In the case of Spain, collaboration with France between 1796 and 1801 had come mainly in the form of putting most of the Spanish Navy at the disposal of its powerful neighbor, including a large number of its warships stationed at the port of Brest, which the Madrid government was obliged to supply with provisions and salaries. But Napoleon wanted more, and in 1800 he demanded that the Spanish authorities hand over the vast territory of Louisiana, which he later proceeded to sell to the U.S. government for 80 million francs to fund his military campaigns. Subsequently, as we have already indicated, Napoleon forced the Spanish monarch, Charles IV, to sign the Subsidy Treaty in October 1803, insisting that the previous Treaty of San Ildefonso of 1796 (by which Spain had agreed to furnish military assistance to France) was still in force. The First Consul claimed payment of a monthly subsidy of 16 million *reales* (1.6 million silver pesos or dollars) from the Spanish government, retroactive to March 1803.[19] However, it was not until the beginning of 1804 that the French authorities made their demands felt with all severity. Furious, Napoleon insisted that Spain was in arrears and owed him 160 million *reales* for the subsidies which corresponded to ten months of the year 1803, arguing that the Spanish government's agents at Paris had delivered only a small amount.[20]

The recently crowned Emperor, however, was not the only one interested in receiving funds. The urgency of accomplishing the transfer of Spanish silver was also of the greatest concern to the powerful *Compagnie des Négociants Réunis*, a leading syndicate of moneylenders and military suppliers to the Napoleonic administration, that wished to receive reimbursement for their multiple advances to the French government and military

18 The classic study on British subsidies is J. H. Sherwig, *Guineas and Gunpowder*. An important source on Napoleonic finance is Louis Bergeron, *Banquiers, négociants et manufacturiers parisiens: du directoire á l'Empire* (Paris: Ecole des Hautes Etudes en Sciences Sociales/Mouton, 1978).

19 The Subsidy Treaty was signed on October 19, 1803 but Napoleon demanded the subsidy be paid retroactively from March of the same year.

20 The story is told in André Fugier, "Un financier diplomate: José Martínez de Hervas, chargé d'affaires d'Espagne à París, 1803–04," *Revue des Études Napoleoniennes* 23 (1924), 92–97; additional observations can be found in J. A. Jackson, "The Mexican Silver Schemes," p. 54.

forces.[21] At this point the most important of Napoleon's naval contractors, Gabriel Julien Ouvrard, proposed to the French Minister of Finance, François Barbé-Marbois, the possibility of opening informal negotiations with the Spanish government to devise a method of extracting the silver subsidy from colonial Mexico.

Ouvrard and his financial associates of the *Compagnie des Négociants Réunis* wanted to liquidate the payments owed to them by the Spanish Treasury for having made large advances of money and supplies to the Spanish Navy, in particular to the arsenal and squadron at the port of El Ferrol and to warships stationed at Brest.[22] The French merchant banker worked out an ambitious plan of financial reforms to be proposed to the Madrid Cabinet for increasing the monarchy's extraordinary resources. This included a project to negotiate a new loan in Holland and, at the same time, a singular scheme to obtain funds from Spanish America by extending the scope of the Consolidation Fund to the colonies.

Ouvrard hoped to convert himself into the architect of this complex financial strategy, but to do so he needed to ratify a series of new contracts with the Spanish crown. To facilitate his negotiations with the Spanish government, the banker agreed to make an advance on behalf of a part of the Spanish subsidy owed to the French Treasury; in exchange, he received authorization from the Minister of Finance, Barbé-Marbois, in Paris to negotiate a set of private contracts with Charles IV in Madrid. These accords would allow the effective implementation of the Subsidy Treaty by creating the necessary instruments to obtain the silver remittances from Mexico and other Spanish American possessions.[23]

With this purpose firmly in mind, Ouvrard embarked on a journey to Madrid in September 1804, where he remained for three months,

21 This company, managed by the naval contractors, Ouvrard, Vanlerberghe, and Désprez, played an important financial role for the Napoleonic government, advancing funds and discounting huge amounts of commercial paper with the Ministry of Finance. This complex fiscal and financial history, between 1802 and 1806, is summarized in Maurice Payard, *Le financier, G. J. Ouvrard (1770–1846)*, (Paris: Académie Nationale de Reims, 1958) and Arthur Lévy, *Un grand profiteur de guerre sous la Révolution, l'Empire et la Restauration: G. J. Ouvrard* (Paris, 1929). A more complete view can be found in the correspondence of the French Ministers of Finance with Napoleon, especially ANF, *AF IV*, vols. 1082 and 1087.

22 Ouvrard held a considerable number of bills of exchange drawn on Mexico for debts of the Spanish Navy, which he had not been able to collect. With this aim, he had sent his brother, Francois (partner of the Bordeaux merchant house), at the end of 1802 on a trip to Mexico (via the United States). An interesting description of his trip and his impressions of Veracruz, Xalapa, and Mexico City in 1802 is found in *Archives Nationales* (Paris), *AF IV*, vol. 1211.

23 The terms of this contract had been established in prior negotiations between José Martínez Hérvas (banker and representative of the Spanish government in Paris) and Talleyrand, French Minister of External Affairs. See the essay by A. Fugier, "Un financier diplomate," 81–97, and the references in the more important work of the same author, A. Fugier, *Napoleón et l'Espagne*, vol. I, pp. 266–275.

negotiating financial schemes with the Prime Minister Manuel Godoy, the Finance Minister Miguel Cayetano Soler, and the Director of the Consolidation Fund, Manuel Sixto Espinosa.[24] According to his memoirs, Ouvrard breakfasted frequently with Godoy. On more than one occasion, the Spanish prime minister invited Queen María Luisa to accompany them at morning chocolate, allowing the *Prince of Peace* (Godoy's new title) to show the French banker who was the true master in Spain.[25] Ouvrard liberally showered the Spanish prime minister with presents and encouraged him to think about achieving the domination of Portugal (even including the Portuguese crown) with Napoleon's help. Gratified, Godoy adopted the banker as his confident and very soon agreed to his ambitious proposals for financial reform that depended, in great measure, on substantial remittances of American silver.[26]

Ouvrard's first agreement was embodied as a royal warrant to negotiate a new Spanish loan in Holland with service payments guaranteed by bills of exchange for eight million pesos to be drawn on the royal treasuries of Mexico. The Dutch loan would help cover the Consolidated Fund's debts to the French Treasury, especially the arrears in the subsidy payments.[27] To guarantee the possibility of obtaining additional funds in Mexico, Ouvrard helped convince the Spanish authorities to press forward with their plan to extend the Consolidation Fund (and ecclesiastical disentailment) to the Americas. Charles IV signed the royal decree on November 28, 1804, but the royal order that specified how funds should be collected in the colonies was ratified only on December 26.[28] The silver to be sent from New Spain would serve various purposes: payment of the service on Dutch loans, liquidation of advances made by Ouvrard to the Spanish Navy, the requirements of the Subsidy Treaty signed with Napoleon, and a series of military expenses of the Spanish crown. (See Figure 5.1.)

24 Ouvrard, one of the outstanding bankers of the revolutionary and Napoleonic regime, wrote his own recollections: see G. J. Ouvrard, *Mémoires*, 3 vols. (Paris), 1826–1828. There are also several biographies: A. Lévy, *Un grand profiteur de guerre*; M. Payard, *Le financier*; Otto Wolf, *Ouvrard, Speculator of Genius, 1770–1846* (New York: Barrie and Rockliff, 1962); and references in L. Bergeron, *Banquiers, négociants et manufacturiers*, pp. 156–165.

25 Recounted in his *Mémoires*, vol. I, pp. 92–93.

26 For the details of these complicated negotiations, see A. Fugier, *Napoleón et l'Espagne*, vol. I, Chapters 2 and 3 and vol. II, pp. 54–60; also see M. G. Buist, *At Spes Non Fracta*, Chapters 9 and 10.

27 This ten-million florin loan was finally issued in Amsterdam in November 1805 by the house of Hope against the guarantee of bills of exchange for Mexico, sent by Ouvrard, valued at 8,484,375 pesos. Prolonged and complex negotiations eventually brought delivery of the bills of exchange to Hope to be settled in Veracruz, the purpose being to use part of the funds to pay some of Ouvrard's debts with the French Treasury. For details of these operations, consult M. G. Buist, *At Spes Non Fracta*, Chapters 10 and 11 and J. A. Jackson, "The Mexican Silver Schemes," Chapter 3.

28 Spanish financial officials had considered this possibility, but Ouvrard's visit speeded up the arrangements. For the texts of the decree and the order, see AGN, *Reales Cédulas Originales*, vol. 192, exp. 142, f. 348 and exp. 143, fs. 349–360.

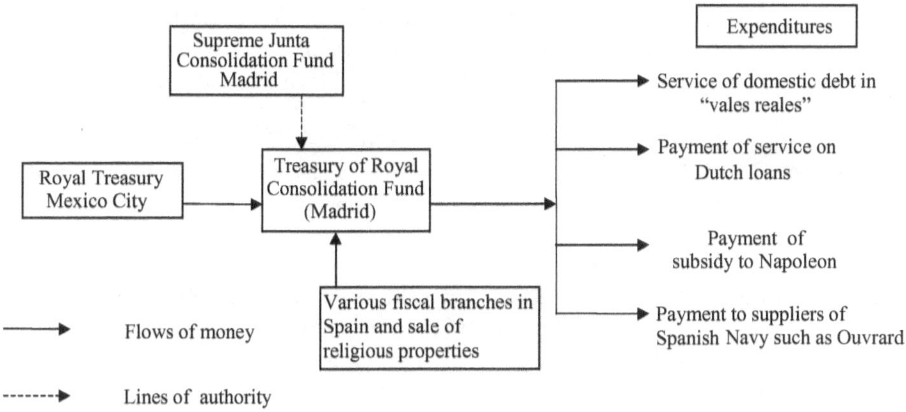

Figure 5.1. Royal Consolidation Fund: Flow of Funds, Mexico to Spain, 1805–1808.
Source: drawn by Carlos Marichal.

While the Spanish authorities proved willing to approve measures aimed at complying with the exigencies of Napoleon and Ouvrard, they also asked for a series of urgent concessions. In particular, they asked the French banker and war contractor to help alleviate the grave agrarian crisis that had devastated various provinces of Spain: from mid-1803 onward a series of bad harvests had provoked starvation, pestilence, and epidemics, causing large segments of the population to suffer.[29] To reduce the impact of the crisis on the most affected regions, the Spanish finance minister asked Ouvrard to import grain from France.[30] The French banker responded quickly, negotiating a large number of shipments of wheat to Spain. The immediate result was a steep decline in wheat prices, forcing hoarders to begin selling their abundant reserves.[31] Scarcity was suddenly converted into abundance of supply, and the ravages suffered by the most needy Spaniards tended to diminish.

The culmination of the set of agreements between the Madrid government and Ouvrard was a broad-ranging contract, ratified by Manuel Sixto

29 On the agrarian crisis consult, see the classic study of G. Anes, *Crisis agrarias en la España moderna*.

30 Ouvrard – who had been in charge of supplying allied French and Spanish fleets since 1798 – handled large quantities of cereals because of these contracts. The agreement to import French grain to Spain was signed by Ouvrard on November 26, 1804. In his *Mémoires* (1826), vol. I, pp. 104–106, Ouvrard pictured himself as a philanthropist who was able to arrange the delivery of two-million quintiles of grain by obtaining permissions from British Navy to allow this trade. Nevertheless, according to Wolf, this was an attractive business in which Napoleon also took part, obtaining large profits: O. Wolf, *Ouvrard, Speculator of Genius*, pp. 107–108.

31 According to A. Fugier, *Napoleón et l'Espagne*, Chapter 2, Ouvrard finally imported a little more than 100,000 quintiles of wheat to the peninsula. However, Fugier also suggests that the banker Martínez-Hervas, the French representative in Paris, was the real author of idea to import grains and that he received financial help from the banking house of Gardoqui of Madrid.

Espinosa, the director of the Consolidation Fund, providing the Parisian merchant banker with numerous drafts to be settled in silver at the royal treasuries in Mexico.[32] As the historian José P. Merino has argued:

> Soler, the minister of finance and Espinosa, director of the Fund, appeared to have discovered with Ouvrard the key to the network of credit they were desperately trying to broaden. The idea would be to integrate America directly into the Spanish and European financial circuits.[33]

Simultaneously, and as part of this pact, a private contract was signed between the Consolidation Fund and Ouvrard to jointly participate in trade with Spanish America. The banker was given a large number of permits authorizing the import of merchandise into Veracruz and the export of silver and produce from that port in ships flying neutral flags. These extraordinary trade concessions would, in principle, allow Ouvrard to control a considerable part of the port's trade. As we shall see, the trading concessions were later transferred to other merchant bankers but, in any case, they prompted a surge in Veracruz's "neutral commerce" between 1805 and 1808.[34]

On his return to the French capital, Ouvrard used some of the drafts from the Consolidation Fund to pay off many of his creditors, who included a good number of the most important French merchant bankers. However, the success of these transactions depended on the likelihood of the bills of exchange being cashed in silver at Mexico and shipped to Europe – a difficult if not impossible task for French and Spanish ships, given the dominant control of the Atlantic by the British Navy. There was no alternative but to negotiate a parallel and complementary agreement with neutral merchants authorized to pass through the British maritime blockade. With this idea, Ouvrard set out for Amsterdam at the end of 1805, to call on the house of Hope & Company, one of the leading Dutch financial firms which, coincidentally, had excellent relations with the politically influential British merchant bank of Baring Brothers.

The Agreements with the Firms of Hope and Baring to Transfer Mexican Silver

According to contemporary accounts, when Ouvrard made his visit to Amsterdam to the house of Hope in May 1805, the partners of the prestigious

32 M. G. Buist, *At Spes Non Fracta*, pp. 306–308.

33 J. P. Merino, "1805: La crisis financiera internacional," pp. 390–391.

34 The classic study on Veracruz's neutral trade is that of S. Bruchey, *R. Oliver, Merchant of Baltimore*. Additional information is to be found in J. A. Jackson, "The Mexican Silver Schemes," Chapters 4–8.

banking firm were initially mistrustful.[35] Ouvrard explained with enthusiasm the set of astounding transatlantic financial and trading transactions to be realized in Mexico. Although there were clearly great risks involved in such complex business operations at a time of international war, the Dutch merchant bankers carefully considered the possible losses lest they let slip this singular business opportunity.[36] The head of the firm Pierre Labouchère soon agreed to negotiate with the French banker and signed various contracts.

To begin with, the house of Hope promised to explore the possibility of opening a new and large loan for the Spanish crown on the Amsterdam stock market; in exchange for taking charge of the issue of the Spanish bonds, Hope & Company would receive bills payable by the Consolidation Fund to be drawn against Mexican royal treasuries, as guarantee of debt service payments. In the second place, the Dutch firm proposed to hire a group of young and adventurous traders, led by the merchant banker David Parish, to take charge of the trade with Mexico. They were to organize various fleets of neutral vessels that would be provided with royal licenses to transport European merchandise (mainly textiles) to Veracruz for sale to local merchants. As commercial agents of the Hopes, they were also authorized to cash the drafts issued by the Consolidation Fund on the royal treasuries of Mexico and to transport the silver pesos on U.S. (neutral) merchant ships to Europe. The Hope bankers demanded stiff commissions, but Ouvrard had little choice but to accept. Probably no other continental, financial firm would have been able to launch this complicated and delicate mission with much chance of success.[37]

That the directors of Hope were willing to enter into such a singular business venture reflected not only their audaciousness but above all their confidence in their capacity to manage complex financial and trade transactions. But it was also a fruit of long experience with the finances of the Spanish crown.[38] Already in 1782, the Hopes had been charged by the Spanish government with the placement of an external loan on the Amsterdam bourse in order to help finance war against England. A decade later, in 1792, the house of Hope again issued a new Spanish loan worth six million florins on Dutch financial markets, negotiating a contract with a Madrid banker, Juan Ignacio Gardoqui, who was brother of the minister of

35 The negotiations with the financial house of Hope of Amsterdam are described in considerable detail by M. G. Buist, *At Spes Non Fracta*, Chapter 9.

36 In his *Mémoires* (1826), vol. I, p. 113, Ouvrard underlined the surprise of the Hope partners at this extraordinary proposal.

37 Details about the commissions are included in M. G. Buist, *At Spes Non Fracta*, Chapters 9 and 10.

38 A Dutch loan had been negotiated between Hope and the well-known Spanish banker Cabarrús in 1782, when the latter was exploring the creation of the Banco de San Carlos. M. G. Buist, *At Spes Non Fracta*, Chapter 9 and P. Tedde, *Banco de San Carlos*, Chapter 2.

finance of the Spanish government. Subsequently, between 1799 and 1801, the Hopes had collaborated with the Croese bank of Amsterdam to issue another three foreign loans for Charles IV's administration.[39] (For details of the Dutch loans arranged for Spain, see Appendix III.3.)

The Hopes' relations with the Spanish Treasury, therefore, were close. They had a marked interest in ensuring a regular flow of funds from Spain to cover payments on the many loans that had been issued and sold in the Amsterdam financial market. But, above all, their objective was to directly control a part of the lucrative business of American silver remittances. All Spanish foreign loan contracts signed between 1791 and 1801 invariably stipulated that funds from the royal treasuries of Mexico would serve as guarantor of payment. The same procedure was adopted in the negotiations that took place between Ouvrard and Hope in preparation of the new Spanish loan of 1805. The transactions were guaranteed with ten bills of exchange issued by the Consolidation Fund (for a total of 8,484,375 pesos), payable by the royal treasuries in Mexico.[40]

According to the ever-modest Ouvrard, the pact negotiated with the Hope banking firm promised to become "one of the greatest commercial and political operations ever conceived."[41] Nevertheless, there were substantial obstacles to this complicated transatlantic transaction. The most serious was the probable opposition of the British government to the transfer of Mexican treasure to Europe, particularly if destined to end up in the coffers of their principal enemy, Bonaparte. For other banking firms, this would have been a difficulty almost beyond repair, but not for Hope & Company. They had long maintained close relations with one of the most important banking houses of London, Baring Brothers, and this critical alliance would eventually facilitate key negotiations with the British Cabinet.[42]

Baring Brothers, like Hope, had special reasons for being interested in the Mexican silver shipments. To begin with, the scion of the firm Alexander Baring was a director of the Bank of England, which was actively engaged in assisting the government with the acquisition of silver coin, essential to the payment of military subsidies to Britain's wartime allies on the European continent. In the second place, Sir Francis Baring, the head of the banking firm, was director of the East India Company (the largest private company in England), which required a constant supply of silver to sustain purchases

39 For details see M. G. Buist, *At Spes Non Fracta*, pp. 281–285.

40 M. G. Buist, *At Spes Non Fracta*, p. 284.

41 G. J. Ouvrard, *Mémoires*, p. 135.

42 The trading relations between both banking houses were strengthened by matrimonial alliances: Pierre Labouchère, director of Hope, was married to the daughter of Sir Francis Baring. For details about personal and financial relations between both firms, see M. G. Buist, *At Spes Non Fracta*, pp. 40–61.

of tea, cotton textiles, and silk in India and China.[43] During the Napoleonic wars, particularly from 1804 the naval conflicts had created severe problems for the Eastern trade. As historian Javier Cuenca has demonstrated in a detailed study of the role of India in the British balance of payments in these years, in the years 1803–1805, 4.2 million pounds of bullion "sent to India by the (East India) Company directors was diverted by (Secretary) Wellesley for war purposes."[44] As a result the Barings had already fixed their attention on the possibility of obtaining silver from New Spain. The question was how to do so, and the business proposition made by the Hopes appeared to offer a singular opportunity, despite its complexity.

To put the transatlantic financial transaction in practice posed a formidable challenge but there were, in fact, recent precedents. Both merchant firms of Hope and Baring had collaborated in the transatlantic financial operations derived from the Louisiana Purchase in 1803, by which the Napoleonic administration received fifteen million dollars in bonds of the U.S. government.[45] The payment of this sum involved the sale of the bonds in Amsterdam and the subsequent transfer of funds to Paris, demonstrating the firms' capacity – acting in consort – to resolve financial and commercial obstacles during a time of war. Moreover, the merchant banker Ouvrard had also been involved in these business deals, as he was charged by the French Navy with using a part of the Louisiana funds to buy large quantities of Russian timber which was transported to France by Dutch merchants and shippers.[46]

In early 1805, when the directors of the Hope firm communicated to the London bankers the proposal to transport large quantities of silver from New Spain, Baring Brothers confirmed their wish to participate in this grand transatlantic enterprise but warned of the need to obtain the agreement of the British authorities to these unorthodox operations.[47] The

43 See observations about situation of the East India Company by two contemporary witnesses: G. J. Ouvrard, *Mémoires*, vol. I, pp. 109–110, and Vincent Nolte, *Fifty Years in Both Hemispheres: Reminiscences of the Life of a Former Merchant* (London , 1854), p. 77. Also useful are references in J. A. Jackson, "The Mexican Silver Schemes," pp. 64–66 and G. Jiménez Codinach, *Gran Bretaña y la independencia de México*, pp. 206–208.

44 J. Cuenca, "India's Contribution to the British balance of payments, 1757–1812," p. 8.

45 The reference is to delivery of fifteen million dollars, 1803–1804, from the United States to Napoleon's treasury for the sale of territory of Louisiana. On the participation of Hope and Baring in this operation, see G. Labouchère, "L'Annexion de la Louisiane aux États-Unis et les maisons Hope et Baring," *Revue d'Histoire Diplomatique*, 30, 3 (1916), 423–455 and J. A. Jackson, "The Mexican Silver Schemes," pp. 19–22 and 37–43.

46 M. G. Buist, *At Spes Non Fracta*, pp. 60–61, points out that Hope had been in charge of payments to the French Treasury for the Louisiana sale in 1803, which were used for the purchase of a large quantity of naval materials in Russia on behalf of Ouvrard, principal supplier to the French Navy.

47 For correspondence between Pierre Labouchère and Sir Francis Baring, see S. Bruchey, *R. Oliver, Merchant of Baltimore*, pp. 274–275.

negotiations proved to be complex on account of the distrust of Prime Minister William Pitt as well as the opposition of the admirals of the British Navy to participate in operations which might aid the enemy.[48] According to one study, "Pitt initially opposed the importation of large sums of pesos into England because four fifths of these shipments were destined for the Caja de Consolidación and hence the French treasury."[49] But eventually, the arguments of Barings helped convince the British Cabinet that approval for the transfer of silver from New Spain would be of enormous utility to replenish the metallic reserves of the Bank of England as well as to provide the government with hard currency, needed to continue with its policies of providing military subsidies to allies on the European continent.

Of special importance was the pressure generated by the financial demands of Britain's allies on the continent. The Anglo-Russian Treaty signed in April 1805 "called for a British subsidy to Russia of 1,250,000 pounds sterling for each 100,000 soldiers that Czar Alexander raised for the war."[50] Confirmation of Pitt's approval of the Mexican silver scheme can be found in his correspondence at the end of 1805 with William Huskisson, of the British Treasury.[51] At the same time, the admirals of the British Navy were eventually brought around by Pitt who explained the urgency of obtaining silver from Spanish America for the war effort: in addition, the admirals were promised they would personally receive 1–2 percent of the silver transported (fairly standard practice at the time). The treasure was to be extracted from Mexico in two distinct ways.[52] The first procedure, authorized by the British government, was to grant neutral ships' licenses to enter and exit from Veracruz and to cash the bills drawn upon the Consolidation Fund that were carried by the ships' captains, hired by the firms of Baring and Hope and their agents.[53] The second more unorthodox proposal was to send English warships directly to Veracruz and there load the treasure on board.

48 G. Jiménez Codinach, *Gran Bretaña y la independencia de México*, p. 211, citing Pitt's personal archive, notes that in the negotiations between Ouvrard, Hope, and Baring: "Pitt was only willing to participate under certain conditions. . . ." However, by December 1805 – a little before he died – the prime minister had given his approval.

49 J. A. Jackson, "The Mexican Silver Schemes," p. 202.

50 J. A. Jackson, "The Mexican Silver Schemes," p. 206.

51 The key references from the British archives can be found in G. Jímenez Cudinach, *La Gran Bretaña y la independencia de México*, pp. 211–212 and 220–221.

52 M. G. Buist, *At Spes Non Fracta*, pp. 326 and J. A. Jackson, "The Mexican Silver Schemes," pp. 65–67 and 203–206.

53 The British Board of Trade itself recommended a licensing policy for neutral trade in June 1805 in order to assure benefits for English commerce: S. Stein, "Crisis metropolitana," pp. 163–164.

The 1805 Financial Crisis in Paris and the Bankruptcy of Ouvrard

After receiving news of approval by the British Cabinet, Ouvrard moved to put the grandiose transatlantic operation into practice, but, unexpectedly, the outbreak of a financial crisis in Paris (between August and October 1805) crippled his plans. The crisis had several causes, but one of the most decisive was the difficulty in cashing the hundreds of Spanish Treasury drafts that Ouvrard had put into circulation in French financial markets from early 1805, and which had been accepted by an important number of private bankers in Paris and provincial cities, confident of the solvency of the Spanish Consolidation Fund.[54] Ouvrard and his partner Vanlerberghe tried to sustain confidence in the letters of credit, but the firm had inadequate liquidity and was weakened by the huge amount of debt accumulated as the result of provisioning the French and Spanish fleets; neither the Paris nor the Madrid authorities were disposed to pay Ouvrard on his advances because of their respective fiscal crises.[55]

The most important factors that undermined French financial markets from June 1805 onward can be quickly summarized. The first was a set of acute difficulties faced by French bankers and the *Banque de France* as a result of capital flight and monetary depreciation. By August 21, the official bank's metallic reserves had fallen to 3,900,000 francs, having had to extend numerous subsidies for the French army in Italy.[56] When the reserves fell to scarcely a million francs at the beginning of September, the bank regent and financier Médard Desprez tried desperately to save the situation by bringing precious metals to Paris from Madrid, Milan, Strasbourg, and even London. This was little more than a palliative, although it saved the bank.[57]

A second contributory factor to the deepening French financial crisis was the bankruptcy of the firm of Ouvrard and Vanlerberghe in October 1805. The French Finance Minister, Barbé-Marbois, was later to attribute this failure to what he termed the bankruptcy of the Spanish Consolidation Fund, arguing that its inability to pay the numerous bills of exchange in Ouvrard's power and those of the bankers connected with his operations

54 The extensive correspondence of the French Minister of Finance, Barbé-Marbois, with Napoleon in 1805 is found in ANF (Paris), *AF IV*, vol. 1082: it reveals that apart from Ouvrard, a large number of important Parisian bankers were also committed to these negotiations, such as, Michel, Bastide, Recamier, Fulchiron, Désprez, and others, including the Spanish banker Martínez Hervas, the representative of the Banco de San Carlos in París. See additional comments in J. P. Merino, "1805: La crisis financiera internacional," passim.

55 J. A. Jackson, "The Mexican Silver Schemes," pp. 73–75, describes these financial operations.

56 The correspondence of the Minister Barbé-Marbois with Napoleon about the crisis is particularly enlightening. See ANF (Paris), *AF IV*, vol. 1082, in particular the letters of August 20, 21, and 31.

57 ANF (Paris), *AF IV*, vol. 1082, letter of September 28.

had led to the financial debacle.[58] Some twenty of the most important Paris bankers went under, including the important houses of Recamier, Bérard, Borgstrom, Delon, Enfantin, and Bastide, together with eight banking firms in Marseilles.[59]

A third factor, unmentioned in the French minister of finance's correspondence, but which exercised a powerful influence on the last phase of the banking and financial crisis, was the defeat of the combined French and Spanish navies at the battle of Trafalgar (October 21, 1805). The news of this naval disaster could not but have a depressing effect on the already buffeted financial markets, although they recovered on news of the great victory of Napoleon and the French army at Austerlitz (December 2, 1805).

After his triumph at Austerlitz, Bonaparte intervened to resolve the financial crisis in Paris. He decided to force the partners of the *Compagnie des Négociants Réunis* to settle their multiple debts with the French government. On his return to Paris, in January 1806, he demanded the resignation of the Finance Minister, Barbé-Marbois, who was replaced by François Mollien, director of the French public debt office. The new minister renegotiated the outstanding debts with Ouvrard and the Consolidation Fund's representative in Paris, Eugenio Izquierdo.[60] The total value of the Mexican bills of exchange held by Ouvrard amounted to approximately 20 million pesos, to which were added the bills to be cashed in Madrid at the offices of the Consolidation Fund for 32.5 million francs (6 million pesos). Following Ouvrard's bankruptcy and the delivery of his assets to the French Treasury at the beginning of 1806, Minister Mollien and the financial agent of Godoy in Paris, Eugenio Izquerdo, came to an agreement to use the proceeds of the Spanish loan issued in Holland, plus Ouvrard's drafts on Mexico, to liquidate the pending debt of the Consolidation Fund with the French Treasury, which now amounted to perhaps 60 million francs. The agreement stipulated that the Fund would send instructions to the viceroy of New Spain to pay drafts up to a value of 10 million pesos. At the same time, from May 1806, the Consolidation Fund in Madrid would agree to pay 3 million

58 ANF (Paris), *AF IV*, vol. 1082, the letter of October 11 to Napoleon, where Barbé-Marbois commented on: "l'espèce de Banqueroute faite para la Caisse de Consolidation," although it could be supposed that this was linked to the fall in the price of bills of exchange from 63 at the beginning of the month to 51 by the end of October. Annexed to this letter to the Emperor – then in campaign in Austria – Barbé-Marbois included a copy of the message from the French ambassador in Madrid who backed Ouvrard's efforts (then in the Spanish capital) to obtain funds for France, achieving an agreement from the Spanish Treasury to send 50,000 silver pesos to France per week via Bayonne. On the prices of the *vales reales*, see P. Tedde, "Crisis del Estado y deuda pública," Table 3.

59 ANF (Paris), *AF IV*, vol. 1082, letter of Barbé-Marbois to Napoleon, October 20, 1805.

60 The correspondence with Napoleon and the final report of Barbé-Marbois from August 1805 to January 1806 are of exceptional interest. See these documents in ANF (Paris), *AF IV*, vol. 1082.

francs monthly to French Treasury agents until the total amortization of the bills of exchange (24 million francs), in the hands of various bank creditors of Ouvrard and the *Compagnie des Négociants Reunís*.[61]

In spite of the collapse of Ouvrard's firm, this did not disrupt the plans of Hope and Baring (now in progress) but simply changed part of the equation. Hope was now responsible for delivering the funds from the New Spain silver operation directly to the French Treasury, replacing Ouvrard, who was at the point of being imprisoned on Napoleon's orders.[62] To carry out the plan to bring Mexican silver to Europe, Hope had prepared with care. In mid 1805, the merchant house had sent three agents to the United States and to Mexico, and from early 1806, the dispatch of the silver commenced from Veracruz by way of neutral commerce and more directly by using English warships. But the Hopes also counted on the collaboration of the Spanish Consolidation Fund and the top royal officials in Mexico.

The Viceroy, the Hope/Parish Consortium, and the Dispatch of Silver from Veracruz

While the extraordinary Mexican silver scheme required complex financial and political negotiations in Europe, it also required the acquiescence of the viceroy of New Spain and the small circle of his closest advisers. The correspondence of Viceroy Iturrigaray in 1805 shows that, from the first, he was informed that multiple drafts had been extended to merchants who were involved in the provisioning of the Spanish Navy as well as other pressing financial commitments of the Consolidation Fund, including the payment of the subsidy to Napoleon and the service of foreign loans of the Spanish crown.

That Iturrigaray knew a substantial part of the funds requested were to be sent to Napoleon is revealed in a letter of June 1805 to the Finance Minister Soler. In it he acknowledged the royal instructions and reported

61 The remaining bills of exchange for 10 million pesos and 8.5 millions of francs in the hands of the French Treasury were returned to the Consolidation Fund: M. G. Buist, *At Spes Non Fracta*, pp. 306–308. There is an interesting document about these transactions in AHN (Madrid), *Ministerio de Hacienda, Serie General*, leg. 5848, "Index of Documents and Correspondence Referring to the Dutch Credits and the Debt with France (1805–1808)," although various pertinent documents have apparently disappeared. The correspondence in ANF (Paris), *AF IV*, vols. 1082 and 1608 is important as it throws light on the redemption of the Fund's bills of exchange by other French bankers such as Michel and Séguin.

62 It can be estimated that Hope had around ten million pesos in bills of exchange in their power (previously sent by Ouvrard) with the obligation to transfer to the French Treasury at 75% of their face value, discounting expenditures and commissions for the delivery and transport of the strong pesos (*pesos fuertes*) from Mexico to Amsterdam; M. G. Buist, *At Spes Non Fracta*, pp. 306–309.

that he had ordered the local commissioner of the Consolidation Fund in Mexico to:

> ... authorize the extraction of all drafts (to be paid in silver) belonging to the *French treasury*, entirely at liberty and without any constraint in Spanish or neutral embarkations and allow them to be trans-shipped to any vessel of war, even if it be an enemy warship.[63]

The viceroy was, evidently, referring to the fact that he had received instructions indicating that British warships would also be authorized to transport the funds of the Consolidation to Europe.

An additional set of bills sent by the Consolidation Fund to Mexico was intended to help cover the interest payments due on the Spanish external debt service since neither the Bank of San Carlos nor the Royal Remittance Office in Madrid (*Real Giro*) had the necessary hard currency for this purpose. A significant portion of the silver consignments from New Spain was intended to cover the service of the Dutch loans taken by the monarchy, although it should be recognized that there was nothing new in these circumstances. In the 1790s, the Spanish exchequer had contracted various loans in Amsterdam; in each case the Dutch bankers had demanded Mexican silver as security for the international credits being negotiated. (See Appendix III.3.) Proof that the top officials of the viceroyalty were also aware of these arrangements is to be found in the letter of July 16, 1805, in which the Finance Minister Soler wrote to the Viceroy Iturrigaray, ordering the payment of royal bills to the amount of 500,000 pesos, stating that:

> ... for the punctual payment of capital and interest on the loans of the Crown taken in Holland ... it has been required that the Royal Consolidation Fund (*Real Caja de Consolidación de Vales*) hand over at once 21 million 930 thousand *reales*... so it has pleased the king to ask me to expedite ... five bills of exchange drawn on the royal treasuries of Mexico.[64]

The Madrid officers in charge of the Consolidation Fund also sent an additional eighty drafts to Iturrigaray with the ostensible object of obtaining the silver with which to cover the debt service of some of the older loans issued and managed by the banking firm of Weduwe E. Croese and Company of Amsterdam.[65] The fact that the Dutch claimed these guarantees

63 AGN, *Correspondencia de Virreyes*, 1a serie, vol. 233, exp. 1326, fs. 244–245. For additional details, see AGN, *Reales Cédulas Originales*, vol. 197, exp. 257, f. 362, and vol. 198, exp. 130, f. 196.

64 AGN, *Reales Cédulas Originales*, vol. 196, exp. 85, f. 111. See also the file 185 in the same volume and in which are included other orders about the royal fund of Mexico for 1,200,000 pesos to cover advances to the Royal Remittance Office (*Real Giro*) for the service of the Spanish external debt.

65 AGN, *Reales Cédulas Originales*, vol. 196, exp. 11, fs. 13–14. It should be noted, however, that a year and half later, instructions were sent to the viceroy not to pay these bills of exchange as their payment was now covered by a new credit negotiated with the banking house of Hope and Company.

was indicative of the contrast between the straitened circumstance of the metropolitan treasuries and those of the viceroyalty of New Spain, which continued to project an image of prosperity and wealth.

For the top Spanish financial officials in Madrid – faced by an increasingly severe fiscal crisis in the metropolis – the image of apparently inexhaustible resources (in the shape of silver coin) in the richest colony encouraged them to send bill after bill for payment by the government of Mexico. The functionaries later calculated that they had obtained approximately 20 million pesos (400 million *reales*) between 1804 and 1808, although a substantial part of these funds never arrived to Spain but were paid out in Holland to the Crown bankers and/or to French Treasury officials, anxious to obtain the funds specified in the Subsidy Treaty signed between the Spanish government and Napoleon.[66]

The commissioners of the Consolidation issued many of the drafts on the royal treasury at Veracruz, since this port was the point at which the colonial administration concentrated most of the silver that was to be remitted abroad. The initial transfers of Mexican silver on account of the Consolidation Fund began to take place from August 1805; the collection of funds in Mexico is detailed in lists (recently published by historian Gisela von Wobeser) that are found in the Spanish archives.[67] The documents of the governing council of the Consolidation Fund in Mexico City (*Junta Suprema Gubernativa de Consolidación*), which began sessions in early 1805, permit a fairly precise reconstruction of the flow of bills of exchange. A review of the correspondence between the Spanish financial authorities and the viceroy in Mexico shows that among the first expenditures covered by the offices in Mexico of the Consolidation Fund were those related to the Navy. On January 27, 1805, the finance minister in Madrid, Soler, signed and sent instructions to Viceroy Iturrigaray to pay a series of drafts signed by Espinosa, head of the Royal Consolidation Fund, to the tune of 319,000 pesos. These bills were intended to cover advances for the acquisition of armaments for the Spanish arsenals of Cartagena and El Ferrol. In February, Soler sent another five bills of exchange for 500,000 pesos payable by the Mexican treasuries for the same purpose.[68]

66 A singular document entitled "Razón de las cantidades que se han librado sobre las Cajas Reales de América desde el 2 de agosto de 1804 hasta 8 de febrero de 1808", AGI, *Ultramar*, 833, cited in J. Antonio Calderón Quijano, *Los virreyes de la Nueva España durante el reinado de Carlos III*, 2 vols. (Sevilla: Escuela de Estudios Hispano-Americanos, 1968), pp. 242–243, records that the bills of exchange submitted for payment by the Consolidation Commission (*Caja de Consolidación*) amounted to the extraordinary sum of 20 million pesos from New Spain alone.

67 G. von Wobeser, *Dominación colonial*, p. 198 and Appendixes 1–5, 265–449.

68 AGN, *Reales Cédulas Originales*, vol. 195, exp. 47, f. 87 and exp. 54, f. 96.

These drafts were sent on warships which took several months to arrive to Veracruz, and thus it was not until April 23, 1805, that the viceroy sent the first notification to Madrid that he had received the bills.[69] Iturrigaray notified Soler that he had received four orders dated December 24 and 28, 1804 "relating to the shipments to Veracruz under neutral flag of bills for remittance of the funds of the Pious Works."[70] Two weeks later, the viceroy informed the minister of finance in Madrid that he had received an additional eleven bills of exchange worth 1,150,000 pesos from the Consolidation Fund and that he had handed these funds over to the Militia Colonel Lorenzo Angulo de Guardamino, responsible for transporting the silver pesos to Veracruz and loading them on the ships that were to set out for Spain. Iturrigaray later broadened the authorization so that these same bills of exchange could be paid directly to the merchant firms in charge of transporting the silver to the port of Veracruz. There, a large number of neutral vessels began to arrive from the summer of 1805.[71]

In September 1805, one month before the battle of Trafalgar, the director of the Consolidation Fund sent an additional four bills of exchange to Mexico to cover naval expenditures in Cádiz.[72] However, the subsequent defeat of the Spanish Navy made it increasingly difficult to maintain regular lines of communication with the colonies. During the rest of 1805 and 1806, the officers of the Fund in Madrid continued sending new packets of drafts to the viceroy in Mexico, despite the increased obstacles to shipping silver from New Spain as the British Navy was lying in wait for each transatlantic transfer.[73]

69 The first letter from Iturrigaray to the Minister Soler, indicating he had received the decrees regarding the establishment of the Consolidation Fund in the New Spain and four orders "relating to the expeditions to Veracruz under a neutral flag" is dated April 23, 1805, AGN, *Correspondencia de Virreyes*, 1a serie, vol. 224, leg. 740, f. 104; see also in the same volume, the letters concerning this subject in fs. 127, 174, 214, 215, 274, 288, 289.

70 The new nine-tenths (*noveno decimal*) charged by the Royal Exchequer was intended to swell the coffers of the Consolidation Fund: AGN, *Correspondencia de Virreyes, 1a serie*, vol. 224, exp. 740, f. 104.

71 Already in November 1804, Iturrigaray had delivered 500,000 pesos to Guardamino for the payment of the Consolidation Fund's bills of exchange. Of this amount, 150,000 pesos were sent to Havana, but there is no information about the rest. It remains a mystery exactly how Guardamino sent the remaining 1,500,000 pesos that he received between November 1804 and May 7, 1805. For some details, see AGN, *Correspondencia de Virreyes*, 1a serie, vol. 219, exp. 653, f. 282 and vol. 224, exp. 766, f. 127 and *Marina*, vol. 217, exps. 50 and 78.

72 These amounted to almost one million pesos. AGN, *Reales Cédulas Originales*, vol. 196, exp. 95, f. 123; exp. 141, f. 179; exp. 158, f. 198; and exp. 163, f. 204.

73 The bills of exchange sent almost monthly were to cover payments for armaments, provisions, copper sheets, and other essential articles for the Spanish Navy. See references AGN, *Reales Cédulas Originales*, vol. 195, exps. 47, 54, and 126; vol. 196, exps. 95, 141, 158, 163, and 194; vol. 197, exps. 62, 251, 252, and 253.

On January 27, 1806, the viceroy received another bulky package of bills of exchange sent by Espinosa and endorsed to the agents of the Hope/Baring consortium.[74] The value of the thirty-four drafts was the enormous sum of 5,586,000 pesos, to be paid to the local employee of the Consolidation Fund, Colonel Guardamino, who, in turn, was to transport the treasure from Mexico City to Veracruz and deliver it to the merchant Gabriel Villanueva, agent of the Hope/Baring syndicate, responsible for their shipment to Europe.[75] In a letter dated March 7, 1806, the military governor of Veracruz informed the viceroy of the arrival of "the American ship *Aspacia* out from New York.... in which has come Gabriel Villanueva."[76] Soon after disembarking, Villanueva set off for the capital to present his letters and credentials to Iturrigaray. The viceroy offered his support for the mission and provided him with a large amount of silver accumulated by the Consolidation Fund in exchange for an undisclosed number of bills of exchange. Nevertheless on his return to Veracruz, Villanueva found to his dismay that the port officials refused to allow him to load the silver on the *Aspacia* and prevented its departure to the United States.

Villanueva wrote to the viceroy, asking him to extend his orders to ensure the cooperation of both the Military Governor Pedro Alonso and the head of the city government of Veracruz, Pedro Telmo Landero. He wrote: "The transfer to Europe of the considerable amounts in my power will depend in great part on the favorable sale of the cargos and the swift return of the neutral ships."[77] The viceroy did not hesitate to comply and ordered the Veracruz officials to permit the entrance and exit of the neutral ships consigned to Villanueva. From then on, no greater difficulties arose with the presentation and payment of the bills of exchange from the Fund, nor with the dispatch of close to ten million pesos in the vessels chartered by the Hope/Baring consortium between 1806 and 1808.[78]

74 For details on the bills of exchange sent to Villanueva, see AGN, *Correspondencia de Virreyes*, 1a serie, vol. 229, exp. 932, f. 53; exp. 933, f. 54; exp. 934, f. 55; exp. 935, f. 56; exp. 936, f. 57; exp. 937, f. 58; exp. 938, f. 59; and exp. 952, f. 77.

75 The French-Basque trader Armand de Lestapis (alias Gabriel Villanueva) had been employed by Hope for some time, carrying correspondence from the firm to their agents in Spain, so it is evident that he was well trained for his mission. Nevertheless in Veracruz, he depended on his partners, the traders Pedro de Echeverría and Francisco Septien, who received 6.5% of all profits from the joint operations. For details on Villanueva, see M. G. Buist, *At Spes Non Fracta*, pp. 295–297 and J. A. Jackson, "The Mexican Silver Schemes," pp. 68 and 129–130.

76 AGN, *Marina*, vol. 233, f. 1.

77 AGN, *Marina*, vol. 233, fs. 2–3.

78 It is not easy to estimate the precise value of the silver sent by this consortium or by the rival Gordon/Murphy group between 1806 and 1808, as in most cases the documentation of neutral shipping (which is to be found dispersed in the volumes of the naval branch of the General National Archive (*Archivo General de la Nación*) does not ascribe a value to the produce exported nor

While the greater part of Mexican silver left in neutral vessels, the single greatest shipment was carried – somewhat surprisingly – in a British war frigate. The shipment was valued at more than three million silver pesos and loaded on to the British frigate *Diana* that had arrived at Veracruz toward the end of August 1806, carrying on board the young banker Charles Baring.[79] The English financier brought both instructions and bills of exchange to be paid to the Hope/Baring account. The viceroy did not hesitate to order delivery of the huge amount of 3,829,835 pesos, "resulting from the said bills of exchange (*libranzas*)" to be loaded onto the *Diana*.[80]

This was the largest individual silver delivery to the Hope/Baring conglomerate. It was, however, not the only one; smaller amounts of silver were shipped out from Veracruz, on some seventy neutral merchant vessels between 1806 and 1808 sent from different North American ports by the various agents of the British/Dutch merchant bankers. This neutral trade has been largely ignored in Mexican historiography but was of great financial significance for the viceroyalty, and it is therefore worth describing in some detail.[81]

The Mercantile Operations of the Hope/Baring Consortium in Veracruz, 1805–1808

The most complex part of the Mexican silver operation, coordinated by the Hope/Baring conglomerate, was organizing the arrivals and departures of the neutral ships at the viceroyalty's principal port between 1805 and 1808. This triangular commerce between Mexico, the United States, and Europe is of special interest because it revealed important changes in New Spain's external trade. Further, it set a precedent for the liberalization of trade that would later gain strength during the wars of independence.

As already noted, at the end of 1805, the bankers Hope and Baring had sent three agents to the United States where they began to hire neutral vessels to sail for Veracruz and to cash the royal drafts (on the Consolidation

to the value of the precious metals. The calculations are based on overall estimates in S. Bruchey, *R. Oliver, Merchant of Baltimore*, M. G. Buist, *At Spes Non Fracta* and J. A. Jackson, "The Mexican Silver Schemes."

79 J. A. Jackson, "The Mexican Silver Schemes," pp. 209–213, describes the voyage of *Diana* and of Charles Baring in some detail. The Diana's cargo was insured for 658,600 pounds sterling, the largest risk covered by Lloyd's insurance company in this era: G. J. Cudinach, *La Gran Bretaña y la independencia de México*, p. 211.

80 The relevant documents are to be found in AGN, *Correspondencia de virreyes*, vol. 233, exp. 1326, fs. 244–245.

81 The study that records these operations in greatest detail is S. Bruchey, *R. Oliver, Merchant of Baltimore*; a later very helpful work is J. A. Jackson, "The Mexican Silver Schemes"; G. Jiménez Codinach, *Gran Bretaña y la independencia de México*, pp. 210–215 also has some materials on these transactions.

Fund) as well as to carry on a brisk import/export trade with licenses authorizing North American ships to enter and leave the chief Mexican port. David Parish, an Anglo-German trader, was responsible for the supervision and leadership of the whole enterprise. After an apprenticeship in his father's Hamburg merchant house (correspondent to both Hopes of Amsterdam and Barings of London), the young speculator had opened a house in Antwerp and committed himself to a risky but lucrative commercial business in the midst of the Napoleonic wars.[82]

Parish's acceptance of Hope's offer to run the Mexican silver operation using neutral shipping was the most audacious of his adventures. In December 1805, he traveled to the United States, having chosen Philadelphia as headquarters for the consortium's operations. The other two agents selected by Hope were also young traders; Vincent Nolte was sent to New Orleans, a port near to Veracruz which offered excellent possibilities for the dispatch of commercial shipments.[83] The third agent Gabriel Villanueva was charged with establishing an office in Veracruz and implementing what was, perhaps, the most delicate part of the business as he had to negotiate the settlement of the bills of exchange with the viceroy and, at the same time, make arrangements with Veracruz merchants for the sale of the cargos sent by Parish and Nolte from the United States. (See Figure 5.2.)

The work of this adventurous trading trio required considerable coordination. The first part of their business consisted in organizing the dispatch of numerous cargos (authorized by the licenses already mentioned) from the United States to Veracruz, where the imported goods would be sold to local merchants. In exchange, they hoped to receive payment in silver coins and some commodities, sugar, dyes, cocoa, vanilla, cotton, etcetera, to be exported in the same neutral vessels. The profit from these commercial transactions went beyond that expected on the settlement of the royal drafts, which in themselves promised extremely lucrative commissions.[84]

82 Parish made huge profits from speculating on various imported raw materials whose price fluctuated wildly on account of the war. Some of his business was associated with Talleyrand, Napoleon's minister of Foreign Affairs, who supplied secret information about his government's political-military strategy in exchange for a share in Parish's commercial speculations. On Parish's dealings with Talleyrand and the house of Hope, see V. Nolte, *Fifty Years in Both Hemispheres*, pp. 80–82 and P. G. Walters, "The American Career of David Parish," *The Journal of Economic History*, 4, 2 (1944). The classic, but little known, study of the house of Parish in Hamburg is that of Richard Ehrenberg, *Das Haus Parish in Hamburg* (Jena: G. Fischer, 1925.)

83 For an autobiographical account with abundant information about this fantastic mercantile adventure, see the work of V. Nolte, *Fifty Years in Both Hemispheres*.

84 With each shipment sent from Veracruz in the hired neutral vessels, Villanueva would include quantities of silver that fluctuated between 50,000 and 100,000 pesos, the result of cashing in bills of exchange of the Consolidation account.

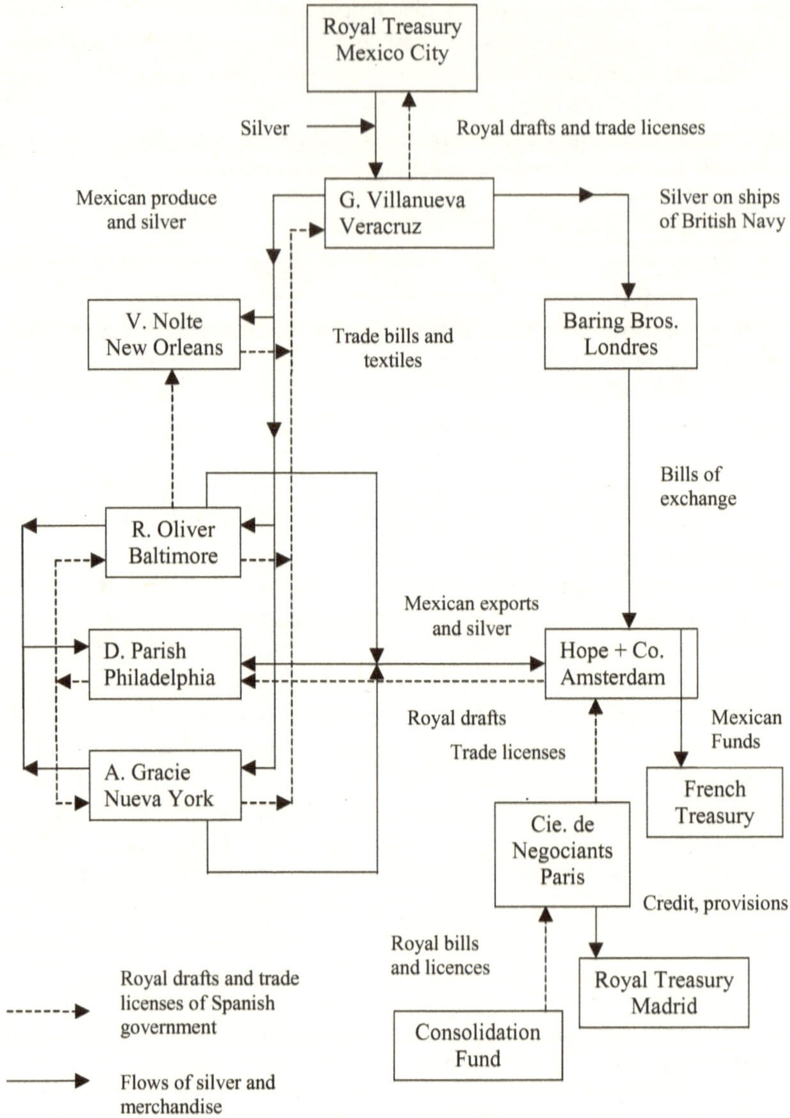

Figure 5.2. Operations of the Hope/Baring Consortium with Mexico, 1805–1808.
Source: Drawn by Carlos Marichal

On his arrival at Philadelphia in January 1806, David Parish apparently did not have a clear idea which naval and mercantile houses would be used for the proposed trade. However, in less than two weeks he had made agreements with the influential firms of John Craig of Philadelphia and Robert

Oliver of Baltimore. John Craig became a key figure in the transactions owing to his ample range of personal contacts; on the one hand, he was the father-in-law of Francisco Sarmiento, Spanish citizen, then resident in the United States, and the official envoy there of Manuel Sixto Espinosa, director of the Fund (*Caja de Consolidación de Vales Reales*); on the other, he was brother-in-law of Robert Oliver, owner of one of the most important trading houses in Baltimore, a port renowned for the number and speed of its sailing ships.[85]

The link with Oliver was of great importance. This house was to be in charge of sending at least thirty-eight expeditions to Veracruz between 1806 and 1808.[86] The choice by Parish of this particular firm was probably based on its ample experience in Caribbean commerce, having specialized from 1790 in coffee and sugar exports from Haiti, Santo Domingo, San Croix, Martinique, Cuba, and Trinidad. Moreover, the house of Oliver's principal European correspondents was none other than Hope in Holland and Baring Brothers in England.[87] Their participation in the Veracruz business fitted perfectly with the consortium's plans.

While Parish was negotiating the contracts with Oliver and other firms such as Archibald Gracie of New York, Vincente Nolte concentrated on establishing relations with New Orleans' most prominent mercantile houses, including the well-known house of Amory and Callender.[88] Between mid-1805 and the end of 1806, approximately twenty ships left from New Orleans for Veracruz on Nolte's account and a similar number in the following two years.[89] All the expeditions sailing to Mexico from New York, Baltimore, and New Orleans had Gabriel Villanueva as their consignee, who was now settled in the port of Veracruz. There, he faced the critical issue of choosing which local trade houses would be the most appropriate to take charge of the unloading, storage, and sale of the merchandise.

Villanueva soon reached agreement with the Veracruz firms of Pedro Miguel de Echeverría and Francisco Luis de Septien. Working together, they were to look after the dozens of merchant ships sent by the Hope/Baring

85 The classic work that describes these operations is S. Bruchey, *R. Oliver, Merchant of Baltimore*, who used the papers from the house of Oliver. On Craig's commercial career, see J. A. Jackson, "The Mexican Silver Schemes," p. 107.

86 Official documentation regarding the permissions obtained by the house of Oliver by and for other North American houses can be found in AGN, *Reales Cédulas Originales*, vols. 195–197; see in particular, the files 31–72 in vol. 196.

87 S. Bruchey, *R. Oliver, Merchant of Baltimore*, Chapters 4 and 5.

88 Nolte's autobiography, *Fifty Years in Both Hemispheres*, is the indispensable source.

89 For a list of arrivals at Veracruz of neutral shipping convoys between September 1805 and September 1806, see AGN, *Marina*, vol. 229, fs. 9–14. The neutral shipping arrivals in 1807–1808 are dispersed among documents in *Marina*, vols. 223–226, 233, and 234; however, there are gaps in these registries, making it premature to attempt a definitive calculation.

conglomerate.[90] Echeverría was one of the most experienced merchants in neutral commerce, having participated in this activity between 1797 and 1800: the proprietor of a Veracruz trading house that specialized in the import of manufacturing goods from Europe as well as in the export of silver and cochineal (the most expensive dye in the world), Echeverrría was also prominent in the newly founded Veracruz Merchant Guild (*Consulado de Comercio de Veracruz*), acting as a board member from 1798 and also as mayor (*alcalde ordinario*) of the port from January 1805.[91] In the latter year he was named special commissioner of the Fund (*Caja de Consolidación de Vales Reales*), presumably to facilitate the financial operations as well as those of neutral trade.[92] Echeverría's close collaborator in many of these transactions was Francisco Septien, member of a distinguished Guanajuato mining family who had founded a small but dynamic merchant house in Veracruz.[93] The many tasks of Echeverría and Septien – closely coordinated with Villanueva – included unloading the ships, paying taxes, storing the merchandise in Veracruz and Xalapa, and proceeding to their sale. At the same time as they were concentrating on these commercial activities, Echeverría and Septien spent much time in organizing the parallel activity of transport of the Consolidation Fund's silver assets from Mexico City to the port, collaborating closely with the merchant, Lorenzo Angulo de Guardamino, who had been named special agent of the Fund in charge of the transport of the precious metals to Veracruz.

Echeverría and his colleague Septien managed the sale of a great quantity of imported merchandise in Mexico between 1805 and 1808. Commercial houses such as Robert Oliver of Baltimore, which supplied the greater part of the neutral ships, depended on information sent by the Veracruz merchants about local markets and the products in greatest demand. Initially, the value of the commodities sent by Oliver did not amount to more than 500,000 or 600,000 *reales* per ship, but after a time, average cargos reached 2 or 3 million *reales* (100,000–150,000 silver pesos or dollars). The business was so lucrative that Oliver bought various ships for these transactions (almost

90 The repository with the richest information about the expeditions for which Echeverría was responsible and documentation used for the payment of the Fund's bills of exchange is in AGN, *Marina*, in particular, vol. 218, fs. 57–78; vol. 238, passim; and vol. 222, fs. 19–22. Also see J. A. Jackson, "The Mexican Silver Schemes," p. 129, on the arrangements between Villanueva and Echeverría.

91 On Echeverría's participation in the cochineal trade from 1790, see B. Hamnett, *Politics and Trade in Southern Mexico*, pp. 178–180. On the posts he held, see *Gazeta de México*, ix, 19, 14 (December 1798) and xii, 26, 8 (January 1805).

92 See AGN, *Marina*, vol. 206, f. 57 (1806), a letter in which the secretary of the viceroy registered: "Pedro Miguel de Echeverría, commissioner for loading the treasure of the Consolidation Fund (*Caxa de Consolidación*) on to the neutral vessels."

93 According to the genealogical table in D. Brading, *Mineros y comerciantes*, p. 463, Francisco Luis probably was the son of Francisco Septien y Arce, a Guanajuato miner and merchant.

all consigned to Echeverría or Septien). They were given names that alluded to speed of navigation: among them were *Dash* (which made two voyages to Veracruz), *Matchless* (four voyages), *Fox* (eight), *Meteor* (seven), *Messenger* (three), *Rapid* (four), and six other ships that made between two and four voyages each.[94]

The merchandise sent by Oliver from Baltimore, by Nolte from New Orleans, and by Archibald Gracie from New York consisted principally of textiles. The increase in commercial activity is highlighted by trade statistics. In 1805 the value of foreign textiles imported by Veracruz was scarcely one million pesos; in 1806 it amounted to three million pesos; and by 1807 it reached the extraordinary sum of ten million pesos. Ninety percent of these shipments were carried on neutral ships.[95] The cloth with the greatest demand in New Spain was cotton (six million pesos in 1809), followed by linen and hemp, silk, and finally, wool.[96]

The neutral trade was not limited exclusively to textile imports. For example, the *Aspacia* that arrived from New York in March 1806, with Villanueva on board, brought a relatively small cargo composed of sherry, Valencia brandy, cotton, and linen cloth (from England, Holland, France, and Germany), as well as silk and cotton stockings (from Valencia and Lyon).[97] Another example of the type of shipments is given by the cargo list of the *Messenger* sent by Robert Oliver to Veracruz with a total value of 1,200,000 *reales*, the bulk made up of textiles but including small quantities of paper, furniture, crockery, cod, and cheese. The textiles sent were varied: *bretañas*, *mahones* from China, English cotton stocking, white *morselinas*, white jerkins, white English corduroy, narrow chintz, and foreign cashmere, among others.[98] An examination of the different bills of lading does not permit a certain knowledge of the origins of all imports, but it can be surmised that English textiles led, being followed by those of German and French origin. In contrast, manufactures of Spanish origin – including Catalan cloth – were rarely included in these shipments. But this neutral

94 For detailed information on shipments sent to Oliver in Veracruz, see S. Bruchey, *R. Oliver, Merchant of Baltimore*, passim. This data can be compared with the registries and correspondence on ships that entered and departed Veracruz: AGN, *Marina*, vols. 223–226 and 233–236.

95 According to Smith's careful calculations, "Shipping in the Port of Veracruz," Table 5, p. 13, a total of 119 North American ships arrived in Veracruz between 1805 and 1808, 43 from New Orleans, 56 from Baltimore, 13 from New York, and 7 from Philadelphia.

96 For a detailed analysis of these imports, see Javier Cuenca, "Comercio y hacienda en la caída del imperio español, 1776–1826," in Josep Fontana, ed., *La economía española al final del antiguo Régimen, vol. 3 Comercio y colonias* (Madrid: Alianza y Banco de España, 1982), p. 440, who uses the annual statistics of the *Balanzas del Consulado de Veracruz*.

97 The total shipment was worth 351,000 *reales*: AGN, *Marina*, vol. 223, fs. 61–66.

98 A broad list of contemporary textile terms is to be found in the appendixes of Inés Herrera Canales, *El comercio exterior de México, 1821–1857* (Mexico: El Colegio de México, 1977).

commerce did not only facilitate imports. Acting on behalf of Parish, Oliver, and Nolte, Echeverría and Septien also purchased large amounts of local merchandise and exported it to the United States and Europe – cochineal from Oaxaca, indigo from Guatemala, cotton, sugar, sarsaparilla, and vanilla from Veracruz.

To summarize, the participation of Echeverría and Septien was absolutely essential for the success of the numerous Hope/Baring shipments to Mexico – perhaps even more than that of the foreign traders and agents. This can be shown, for example, from the correspondence between Echeverría and various senior government viceregal officials, including the Viceroy Iturrigaray, the military governor of Veracruz, Pedro Alonso, the acting mayor, Pedro Telmo Landero, the top official royal treasury in Mexico City, Javier de Borbón, and others. The letters refer to various issues, including payment of the bills of exchange of the Consolidation Fund, permissions to disembark neutral ships arriving on Villanueva's consignment, and tax payments on imports.[99] Quite clearly, the success of the neutral trade operations run by Hope/Baring in Mexico depended to a large degree on the viceroy's consent and his orders to key officials to facilitate the transactions. As a result the merchants engaged did not face significant obstacles neither for the import of a huge volume of textiles nor for the export of vast quantities of silver and a lesser amount of primary products from the viceroyalty.

Indeed, it should be noted that in spite of the protests of a considerable number of Mexico City and Veracruz merchants who felt marginalized by neutral trade, the viceroy insisted that absolute priority should be given to these transactions. On September 4, 1806, Iturrigaray wrote to Landero, one of the top royal officials at Veracruz, stressing the urgency of moving the cargos "that are arriving in the said neutral ships" from the port of Veracruz to the upland town of Xalapa for their sale. According to the viceroy, this step would avoid the spread of disease and fever – especially the black vomit/yellow fever (*vómito negro*) – that had caused so many deaths in the port of Veracruz in earlier years. He also added that the military commander of Xalapa ought to provide all possible help to the merchants transporting goods from the neutral vessels, indicating that he should "scrupulously take care and look after those that provide the mule trains for the neutrals with preference over those living in that city...."[100]

The profits gained by the merchant houses and foreign agents responsible for these transactions were extraordinary. This is a subject discussed in detail by various monographs on the trading houses of Oliver and Hope. According to historian Robert Bruchey, Oliver's profits approached $775,000 between 1806 and 1808. In his memoirs, Vincent Nolte, one of the chief participants

99 AGN, *Marina*, vols. 206, 218, 223–226, 229, 233–234, passim.

100 The full text of Iturrigaray's instructions to Landero is in AGN, *Marina*, vol. 226, fs. 97–102.

in the consortium, indicated that the bankers Hope and Baring had quite probably reaped one million pesos (dollars) apiece.[101] The exact amount of Echeverría and Septien's profits is not known, although it is known that by 1808 they had accumulated formidable trading fortunes. Given their crucial role as direct agents, they were the principal beneficiaries of this business in Veracruz, although it should not be forgotten that other local and Mexico City merchants were also involved in many of these extremely lucrative transactions.[102]

Neutral trade offered a powerful stimulus to New Spain's imports and exports in the critical period 1805–1808, but even more important was the role it played in facilitating the export of silver from the royal treasuries of Mexico, required by the Consolidation Fund for the fulfillment of its international commitments in the midst of war. As has been seen, a substantial part of these funds passed through the United States or through England and Holland, but a large portion finally ended up in the Napoleonic treasury.[103] Nonetheless, the shipments organized by the banking firms of Hope and Baring and their partners were not the only ones authorized by the Spanish royal officials. In parallel, various dozens of ships arrived to Veracruz from Europe and Jamaica, under the control of another powerful trading conglomerate, which is the subject of the following chapter.

101 According to S. Bruchey, *R. Oliver, Merchant of Baltimore*, pp. 326–332, Oliver's profits were as much as $775,000. V. Nolte, *Fifty Years in Both Hemispheres*, states that the bankers Hope and Baring made equivalent amounts, pp. 110 and ss. Additional information about David Parish's profits and those of other traders involved is to be found in J. A. Jackson, "The Mexican Silver Schemes," Chapter 10. To research this issue in-depth would not only help clarify Parish's business affairs but also those of Villanueva and the Veracruz merchants, Echeverría and Septien. It would require research into Parish's abundant personal correspondence located in the New York Historical Society archives, used in part by J. A. Jackson, "The Mexican Silver Schemes" and by S. Stein, "Crisis metropolitana."

102 Government officials also made money with these secret operations, which could be for relatively substantial amounts, although it is not easy to locate reliable documentation. Some information might be found in the legal papers of the court case against Iturrigaray that took place years later. It was claimed that the viceroy had received commissions for at least 72,000 pesos from the Fund's bills of exchange. Lucas Alamán, *Historia de México*, vol. 1, Appendix, docs. 11–13, includes transcriptions of various documents relating to this court case.

103 J. A. Jackson, "The Mexican Silver Schemes," pp. 271–273, notes that between 1806 and 1808, 12.5 millions of silver pesos were exported by the Parish'/Baring/Hope consortium. However, he does not make mention of the 3.8 million silver pesos sent on the warship *Diana* in 1807 on Baring and Hope's account, already discussed. According to J. A. Jackson, "The Mexican Silver Schemes," p. 286, of these amounts, only 6 million pesos were actually paid in to the French Treasury.

6

Between Spain and America: The Royal Treasury and the Gordon & Murphy Consortium, 1806–1808

> We have seen with great pain and indignation the Royal licences granted through the Consolidation Fund (Caxa de Consolidación de Vales Reales) to various foreign trading houses from Europe and the United States . . . to send to this port as many vessels as they wish and to return with gold, silver and the products of this country . . . directly to Spain or to neutral ports.
>
> Merchant Guild of Veracruz (*Consulado de Veracruz*) (1809)[1]

For the administration of Charles IV, the transfers of American silver to Europe were fundamental not only to pay for wartime obligations such as the Subsidy Treaty signed with Napoleon but also to sustain the overall finances of the monarchy. To ensure a regular flow of bullion from the colonies, it was essential that the fiscal system in the Americas continue to produce and remit tax surpluses, despite the obstacles and interruptions caused by naval wars. This depended on both the ability of royal officials to collect resources in the colonies and the smooth functioning of the most important state monopolies, which required regular dispatches of vital materials from Spain to the colonies as well as return shipments of key commodities and silver from the Americas. In sum, an indispensable condition for the continuity of the empire lay in the sustained functioning of what was a complex, transatlantic fiscal machine.

There were two *strategic* monopoly branches in this vast fiscal system that maintained major commercial and financial activities across the Atlantic. The first was the great and extensive tobacco monopoly which operated throughout the Spanish empire and was composed of a great number of interrelated units. The tobacco monopoly was not only a money machine for the extensive network of imperial treasuries but, in practice, also a powerful *transatlantic enterprise*. During the last third of the eighteenth century, it became one of the most important sources of revenues for the

1 "Representación presentada por el Consulado de Veracruz a la Suprema Junta Central de España" (document dated March 1, 1809), AGN, *Consulado*, 252, exp. 5, f. 4.

entire royal administration. A second fiscal branch of strategic importance was the mercury monopoly that supplied silver mines throughout Spanish America. The mercury extracted principally from the Almadén mines in southern Spain was shipped to the colonies from Cádiz in warships and merchant vessels on a regular basis, but during naval blockades the drop in exports could throttle the enormously important silver production in the American colonies.[2] By the end of the eighteenth century, tobacco and mining together supplied at least half of the total net income of the treasuries of the viceroyalty of New Spain and a similar proportion in the case of the viceroyalties of Peru and New Granada.[3] As a result, continuance of the wide range of transatlantic transfers of both monopolies was vital to the financial solvency of the empire and of the monarchy itself.

From the late 1790s, successive naval wars with Britain threatened to interrupt the transatlantic operations of the well-oiled fiscal machinery of the Spanish empire. The suspension of mercury shipments threatened with undermining silver mining in Spanish America, the effects of which would be potentially devastating for both public and private economies. Moreover, the possible breakdown of the tobacco monopoly – a leading source of revenues for the royal administration in Spain, New Spain, Cuba, and New Granada – also presented a grave menace to the imperial economy. These potential dangers became a reality after the decisive defeat of the combined Spanish and French naval forces at the battle of Trafalgar (October 1805).

To ensure that royal trade with the royal monopolies in New Spain could continue despite naval defeats, the minister of finance at Madrid arranged a series of private supply contracts in 1806 with various international merchant houses – among which the Anglo-Spanish commercial house of Gordon & Murphy was outstanding. The contracts made these merchants responsible for official shipments to Mexico and, at the same time, provided them with permits for exports of bullion from Veracruz, to be sent to Europe and the Spanish General Treasury.[4] In contrast to

2 The fundamental source is Rafael Dobado Gonzalez, "El trabajo en las minas de Almadén, 1750–1855," Ph.D. thesis, Universidad Complutense de Madrid, 2 vols., 1989.

3 For comparative information on Peru, see H. Klein, *The American Finances*, Chapter 2 and on New Granada, J. Jaramillo, A. Meisel, and M. Urrutia, "Continuities and Discontinuities in the Fiscal and Monetary Institutions of New Granada, 1783–1850," pp. 414–452. Between 1795 and 1799 tobacco and mining taxes provided 57% of fiscal income in New Spain: see Table 2.1.

4 On Gordon & Murphy's operations with New Spain in these years, see the pathbreaking work of Guadalupe Jímenez Cudinach, "An Atlantic Silver Entrepot: Veracruz and the House of Gordon and Murphy," paper presented at Simposium *Atlantic ort Cities, 1650–1850*, Johns Hopkins University, 1986 and by the same author, *Gran Bretaña y la independencia de México*, Chapter 6, as well as references in Stanley Stein, "Crisis metropolitana" and John Alexander Jackson, "The Mexican Silver Schemes: Finance and Profiteering in the Napoleonic Era, 1796–1811," Ph.D. thesis, University of North Carolina, 1980, pp. 215–226.

the transactions of the Baring/Hope consortium (analyzed in the previous chapter), designed for payment of the Crown's international debts during the years 1805–1808, the activities of their commercial rivals, Gordon & Murphy, had the complementary but distinct aim of ensuring the continued operation of the *imperial fiscal system* of the Spanish state in the most adverse circumstances.

The mercantile agreements analyzed in the pages that follow are of interest because they show how the Spanish government avoided the interruption of the royal treasury's transatlantic lines of communication and commerce. Such a breach would have drastically reduced the flow of silver from the colonial treasuries and undermined the finances of an increasingly menaced monarchy. But before examining the complex business of the Gordon & Murphy conglomerate, we shall focus on the interdependence that traditionally existed between colony and metropolis with respect to the principal state monopolies of the Spanish crown.

The Import Dependence of the Colonial Fiscal Monopolies

The tobacco monopoly was one of the most lucrative of fiscal branches of the Spanish empire but relied on a set of important and varied transatlantic trade transactions that had to be carried out on a regular basis. The size and variety of these exchanges demonstrates that the Spanish tobacco monopoly was one of the most complex economic organizations in the Western world at the time.[5] From the 1760s until 1810, its operations included an interconnected set of fiscal administrations in metropolis and colonies, including a group of factories in Spain, Cuba, New Spain, New Granada, and Peru, as well as thousands of sales points in these and many other territories.[6] The Spanish tobacco monopoly also operated commercially in Buenos Aires, Chile, Guatemala, Puerto Rico, Santo Domingo, Venezuela, Louisiana, as well as in the Philippines. Historian Susan Deans-Smith affirms that at the end of the century, the tobacco factories in New Spain alone employed more than 13,000 workers, apart from several thousand commercial and administrative employees in the viceroyalty. To these should be added the 2,000 workers in the Havana factory, the 5,000 in the Seville tobacco factory, and fewer numbers in other parts of the empire. In fact, it is unlikely that there was any manufacturing enterprise in Europe, at this time, which had an equivalent number of employees. The only commercial enterprise that

5 S. Deans-Smith, *Bureaucrats, Planters and Workers*, p. 159. On the early history of the monopoly, see José Manuel Rodríguez Gordillo, *La creación del estanco del tabaco en España* (Seville: Fundación Altadis, 2002).

6 For a broad, comparative analysis, see L. Nater, "El tabaco y las finanzas del imperio español: Nueva España y la metrópoli, 1760–1810," Ph.D. thesis, El Colegio de México, 1998.

exceeded the size of the Spanish tobacco monopoly in the late eighteenth century was the British East India Company.[7]

The performance of this Spanish *imperial company* depended strategically on a series of trading and financial operations carried out between the royal treasuries of Spain, Mexico, and Cuba.[8] These included the shipment of large quantities of paper from Valencia, Malagá, and Cádiz to Veracruz since this commodity was an essential input for the manufacture of cigarettes at the tobacco monopoly's great factory in Mexico City and smaller manufacturing establishments in other cities. The annual consignments of tens of thousands of reams of paper sent from Spain were fundamental for the monopoly's smooth operation.[9] If supplies were not received, manufacture and packing would be disrupted, sales would fall, and there would be a reduction in the monopoly's large, annual financial surplus sent from New Spain to the tobacco administrations in both Cuba and Spain.[10] To guarantee the provision of paper for the great tobacco factories in Mexico, the Spanish government signed contracts with international trading firms that were to send dozens of ships from Europe to Veracruz in the years 1806–1810.

The productivity of the tobacco administration in Mexico influenced other units of the monopoly across the empire. The Cuban tobacco administration, for example, depended on regular fiscal transfers (known as the tobacco *situados*) from New Spain that financed a large proportion of costs associated with the annual tobacco harvest in the island. In the second half of the eighteenth century, New Spain yearly sent between 500,000 and 750,000 silver pesos to the officers of the tobacco monopoly in Havana so that they could acquire the tobacco leaf from local producers.[11] In turn, Cuban tobacco output was vital for the monopoly's metropolitan operations. Havana was already famous as the source of the best cigars and snuff in the world and it also provided much raw tobacco for manufacture in Spain. A great volume of tobacco leaf (*tobacco en rama*) was shipped annually from Havana to Cádiz: this was the essential raw material for the Spanish state tobacco factories, especially for the famous establishment at Seville that

7 "The Mexican monopoly played a pivotal role in the financing of an empire-wide tobacco monopoly." S. Deans-Smith, *Bureaucrats, Planters and Workers*, p. 61.

8 The tobacco monopoly also carried on trade between Louisiana and New Spain and between the different branches of the tobacco monopoly in South America. For references, see L. Nater, "El tabaco y las finanzas del imperio español," Chapter 5.

9 Most of the paper came from factories in Barcelona, Aragón, and Valencia, generally being sent to Málaga and Cádiz for transshipment to the Americas. For useful references on the paper trade, see S. Deans-Smith, *Bureaucrats, Planters and Workers*, pp. 101–105.

10 By regulation the net income from the tobacco monopoly in New Spain was sent to the metropolis and, in smaller proportion, to Cuba.

11 On the tobacco *situados* for Cuba, see C. Marichal and M. Souto, "Silver and Situados."

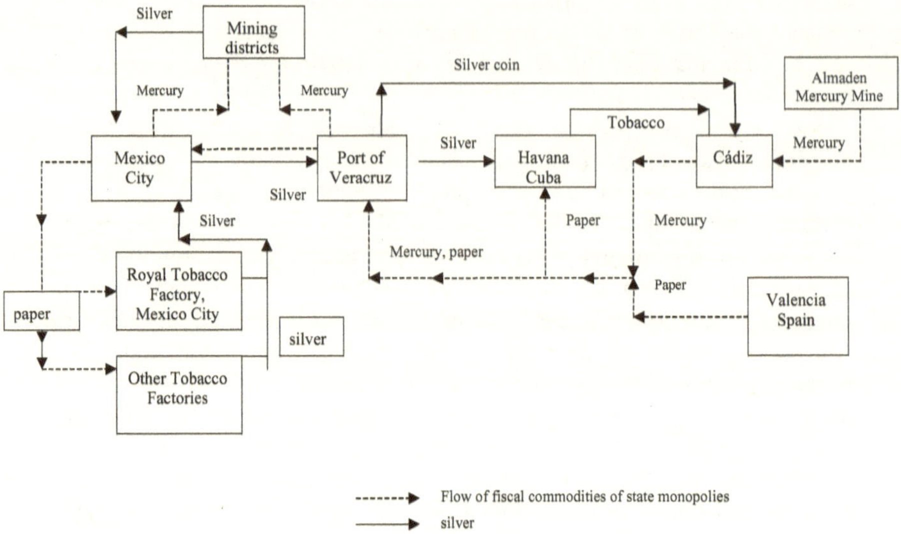

Figure 6.1. Flows of Fiscal Merchandise and Silver between the Royal Treasuries of Spain, Cuba, and Mexico, (circa 1790).
Source: Drawn by Carlos Marichal.

supplied the bulk of cigars, cigarettes, and snuff consumed throughout the peninsula. In effect, by remitting tobacco leaf, the Cuban tobacco monopoly provided a valuable subsidy *in kind* to one of the most important revenue sources of the metropolitan treasury at the end of the eighteenth century: tobacco produced close to 30 percent of total ordinary revenues of the royal tax administration in Spain.[12] The complexities of the transatlantic transfers are illustrated in Figure 6.1.

The importance of the tobacco monopoly for imperial revenues was exceeded only by silver mining, which, in turn, depended to a considerable degree on mercury (quicksilver) imports from Spain. The use of large quantities of mercury for silver amalgamation and refining in the colonial mining centers was not new, having begun in the mid-sixteenth century in Mexico. Although it was possible to process the silver minerals without mercury, the alternative procedures were time-consuming and inefficient,

12 C. Marichal, "Beneficios y costes fiscales" offers an estimate of the minimum figure, but it is necessary to undertake more detailed research on the monopoly's cost structure in Spain. On deliveries of tobacco leaf from Cuba to Spain, see the classic work of R. de la Sagra, *Historia económico-política y estadística*, pp. 240–265.

a phenomenon especially noticeable in the larger mines.[13] Indeed, the level of silver production in New Spain depended to a remarkable degree on the amounts of mercury shipments. Richard Garner has demonstrated the close relationship between the two during the eighteenth century: the annual increase in minting of silver in Mexico grew by 1.4 percent per annum, almost identical to the annual increase in mercury imports.[14]

The provision of a growing amount of supplies of quicksilver for the mining establishments in Spanish America was one of the objectives of the administrative reforms of the early Bourbons.[15] The supply of quicksilver had a fundamental importance for colonial exchequers and economies. An increase in the annual silver yield tended to increase the money supply and stimulate overall production and popular consumption, with a positive impact on fiscal resources, including direct taxes (on silver) as well as sales taxes and monopolies.[16] In the 1720s, Spain exported an annual average of little more than two hundred thousand pounds of mercury per year to the Americas, but by mid century, mercury exports to the colonies had tripled and by the end of the century reached two and a half million pounds per year.[17] These exports had a positive effect on silver mining, as is witnessed by the volume of minting in Mexico between 1780 and 1810, when silver coinage reached the highest levels in all colonial history.[18]

During periods of naval conflict the maintenance of a regular supply of mercury posed especially difficult challenges for the imperial administration. For almost three centuries, the Spanish government had organized regular remittances of mercury as a crown product that was carried in

13 An alternative smelting method (*plata de fuego*) had been developed in the second half of the seventeenth century (when deliveries of mercury from Almaden were scarce). However, this method required large amounts of charcoal, resulting in forest devastation around mining zones. In the eighteenth century, the mercury amalgamation method became dominant.

14 R. Garner and S. E. Stefanou, *Economic Growth and Change*, pp. 112 and 132.

15 The decline of mercury production at Almadén in the second half of the seventeenth century and its recovery after the reforms of 1708–1709 is reviewed in M. F. Lang, *El monopolio estatal del mercurio en el México colonial* (Mexico: Fondo de Cultura Económica, 1977), Chapter 4.

16 D. Brading, *Mineros y comerciantes*, p. 248, points out that the Fagoaga family, the wealthiest silver miners Guanajuato in the eighteenth century, insisted on the association between mining productivity and taxes, arguing that "fiscal branches such as tobacco and the sales tax (*alcabalas*) have benefited from the acquisitive power created by the payment of salaries to workers (in the mines)."

17 The figures are from Antonia Heredia Herrera, *La renta del azogue en Nueva España, 1709–1751* (Sevilla: Escuela de Estudios Hispanoamericanos, 1978), pp. 238–239 and R. Garner and S. E. Stefanou, *Economic Growth and Change*, p. 133.

18 The minting rate at the *Casa de Moneda de México* in the decade 1781–1790 increased from 19.2 million pesos per year to an average 23.2 million pesos per annum in 1791–1810, greater than that in any previous era in the colonial epoch. Víctor M. Soria, *La Casa de Moneda bajo la administración borbónica, 1733–1821* (Mexico: Universidad Autónoma Metropolitana, 1994), p. 69.

warships traveling from Seville and Cádiz to the Spanish American ports of Veracruz and Cartagena. Nevertheless, during the First Naval War with Britain (1796–1801) and, above all, during the Second Naval War (1804–1808) the supply of mercury for the American mines as well as the paper required by New Spain's tobacco monopoly required new carriers. Neither royal warships nor Spanish merchant vessels could cross the Atlantic without running the risk of being captured by the dominant British Navy.

To overcome these serious obstacles, the Madrid authorities decided to use neutral commerce to their advantage and to negotiate private trade agreements with merchant houses that could guarantee delivery of key supplies from Europe to the colonial administrations.[19] In the case of the tobacco and quicksilver monopolies, the Anglo-Spanish merchant firm of Gordon & Murphy received the most important contracts and hence was in a position to exercise a prominent role in the royal commerce and finance of New Spain. This private enterprise thus assumed the traditional functions of supplier of crown commodities, receiving, in return, the right to extract large volumes of silver, both on public and private account.

Gordon & Murphy's successful management of these operations was due, in good measure, to the fact that it already operated as an international trading conglomerate with a broad-ranging network of mercantile partners and correspondents in Malaga, Cádiz, Lisbon, London, Hamburg, Jamaica, New Orleans, Havana, and Veracruz. Also of critical importance were their excellent political contacts in Spain, New Spain, and England.[20] This is confirmed, on the one hand, by the fact that in the midst of wars, the Spanish crown assigned this merchant house responsibility for the transfer of official correspondence between the metropolis and the colonies and, in the second place, by their ability to obtain English government licenses allowing free passage to Spanish America and avoiding dangerous confrontations with the British Navy.

The fiscal and financial significance of these special mercantile contracts for the sustenance of the Spanish empire has been underestimated by the majority of historians that have analyzed neutral commerce between 1797–1799 and 1805–1808. It is traditionally argued that the main factor leading to authorization of neutral trade in Veracruz and other American ports was the desire of Spanish authorities to sustain private transatlantic trade in years when the French and Spanish navies were at a clear disadvantage to

19 The policy was not a complete novelty. In fact, from the early 1790s the Crown had looked for alternative mercury sources to those from Amaden by buying large amounts from mines in Saxony. According to D. Brading, *Mineros y comerciantes*, p. 320, already by 1793, sales of German mercury tripled those of Castilian mercury in New Spain.

20 The most detailed analysis is that of G. Jiménez Codinach, "An Atlantic Silver Entrepot," Chapter 6.

the British Navy: for example, as a result of the naval blockade imposed by British warships in 1797, imports to the port of Veracruz declined from a level of 6 million pesos in 1796 to barely 500,000 pesos the following year; exports declined even more abruptly from 7 million pesos to a meager 238,000 pesos in 1797.[21] However, by supporting neutral trade, metropolitan and colonial officials not only sought recovery of private trade but also sustained the important lines of communication and of commerce under the direct control of the Crown, which were essential to the operation of the fiscal system of the Spanish *imperial state*.

The First Naval War with England (1798–1802) and the Royal Licenses for Neutral Trade at Veracruz: The Role of the Murphy Trading Firm

Neutral trade formally began with the royal decree issued by Charles IV on November 18, 1797, authorizing the entrance and exit of ships from *neutral countries* at different Spanish American ports. This measure was adopted after the outbreak of war with England and the consequent blockade by the British Navy of Spain's communications with its colonies. After the defeat of the Spanish Navy at the great battle of San Vicente, off the coast of northern Spain, on February 14, 1797, the interruption of the Spanish transatlantic fleets and even shipping within the Caribbean virtually paralyzed the external trade of Spanish America as well as financial transactions essential to the empire's survival.

To renew trade flows and public and private silver remittances from the Indies, the Madrid Cabinet approved a new commercial policy which broke with the traditional monopoly of the Cádiz merchants and shippers over most Spanish American trade. Permits were granted to captains of ships from neutral countries – the United States, Portugal, Denmark, and several German states such as the city-state of Hamburg – to land and load merchandise at specific Spanish American ports.[22] In good measure, the success of this policy depended on the British Navy's agreement to the free movement of neutral shipping. Between 1797 and 1802, the British government's attitude was ambivalent since neutral trade was perceived to be not entirely in its interest, especially because of competition of the merchant marine of the United States. Nonetheless, British authorities did consider that more

21 See statistical tables in Balanzas de Comercio del Consulado de Veracruz in M. Lerdo de Tejada, *Comercio exterior de México desde la conquista hasta hoy* (Mexico: Rafael, 1853).

22 Important studies that deal with neutral commerce with New Spain in the years 1797–1800 and 1805–1808 are those of J. Ortiz de la Tabla, *Comercio exterior*; J. Cuenca, "Comercio y hacienda," in J. Fontana, ed., *La economía española*; J. Lynch, "British Policy and Spanish America"; J. Barbier "Peninsular Finance and Colonial Trade"; and M. Souto "Consulado de Veracruz."

open trade with Spanish America could have some positive results. As a result, the Foreign Office also began to supply permits to numerous vessels (of diverse nationalities) in the Caribbean to land and load cargos at various ports in the Gulf of Mexico and in the West Indies.[23] A report of 1801, for example, indicated that over one hundred, mainly Spanish, vessels left Port Cabello, in colonial Venezuela, with English licenses to carry cotton, coffee, mules, and other items for the British West Indies.[24]

Despite the fact that the English authorities recognized the possible benefits of neutral trade, they also feared that its legalization could favor their competitors (especially the North Americans) and reduce the profits of the British ships and merchant firms operating out of the Bahamas, Trinidad, and above all Jamaica, with its ample Caribbean-wide smuggling trade. Hence it was not strange that British frigates applied themselves to capturing many neutral ships sailing in the zone.[25] The risks were high, but U.S. shippers increased their activities in Caribbean using Spanish trading licenses.[26] According to a statistical analysis by economic historian Javier Cuenca, North American exports to Spanish America shot up from scarcely one million dollars in 1796 to close to ten million dollars annually, between 1798 and 1801, while imports grew even more rapidly.[27] The bulk of this trade was initially with Cuba and Venezuela, although it soon expanded to San Juan de Puerto Rico, Santo Domingo, Veracruz, and various other Spanish American ports. A study of Philadelphia trade confirms that the growth of commerce with Cuba was particularly notable: in 1793 only nine North American ships had arrived to Philadelphia from Havana, but after

23 Interestingly, Mahan explained this phenomenon in terms of the growing importance of neutral trade in Europe itself, beginning with the War of the French Convention (1793–1795) and increasing in later years as a result of maritime conflicts between France, Great Britain, and other powers. Alfred Mahan, *The Influence of Seapower upon the French Revolution and Empire, 1793–1812*, vol. 2 (London: Sampson Low, Marston, 1892), Chapter 17.

24 Dorothy Buerne Goebel, "British Trade to the Spanish Colonies, 1796–1823," *American Historical Review*, 43, 2 (1938), 292.

25 An important historical source on neutral trade in the Caribbean and the role of the British Navy is François Crouzet, *L'Economie Britannique et le Blocus Continental (1806–1813)*, vol. 1 (Paris: Presses Universitaires de France, 1958), pp. 178–185, but also see A. Mahan, *The Influence of Seapower*, pp. 218–252. The French corsairs were very active in this period, taking 580 merchant ships in the Antilles between 1797 and 1800. See the exhaustive analysis in Ulane Bonnel, *La France, les États Unis et la guerre de course, 1797–1815* (Paris: Nouvelles Editions Latines, 1961).

26 According to one estimate, a total of fifty-six neutral ships arrived in Veracruz between 1797 and 1799 of which forty-four were North American. See J. Ortiz de la Tabla, *Comercio exterior*, p. 327.

27 Javier Cuenca Esteban, "Statistics of Spain's Colonial Trade, 1792–1820: Consular Duties, Cargo Inventories and Balance of Trade," in *Hispanic American Historical Review*, 61, 3 (1981), 381–428.

the ratification of neutral trade in 1797, forty-eight ships arrived in that year, then fifty-eight ships in 1798, and ninety-eight in 1801.[28]

Historical research on trade in the port of Veracruz in this period has emphasized the high volume of neutral trade but neglected the commerce conducted by the Spanish crown to ensure supplies for the state monopolies of New Spain.[29] The members of the Veracruz Merchant Guild (*Consulado de Comercio de Veracruz*) were the principal beneficiaries of the new transactions, although clearly, some firms profited more than others.[30]

Among the most conspicuous participants in neutral trade in Veracruz in the years 1797–1799 were the associates of the merchant house of Thomas and Matthew Murphy, in alliance with their Spanish kin. This activity would constitute a key precedent for their later activities between 1806 and 1808. The history of this cosmopolitan family of Atlantic traders reveals the complexity of the economic, political, and family networks that were indispensable to the success of the largest commercial operations carried out in the midst of the maritime wars between Great Britain, France, and Spain in these tumultuous decades. The Murphy family was Irish Catholic and – like other compatriots – had originally settled in southern Spain at the beginning of the eighteenth century. The first Murphys to arrive in Andalusia opened trading houses in Malaga and Cádiz, specializing in the export of sherry to England.[31] Toward the end of the 1780s, the Malaga Shipping Company (*Compañía de Navieros de Málaga*), led by Juan Murphy, negotiated important contracts for the delivery of large quantities of paper and other essential products for the royal monopolies of New Spain.[32] In short, the links between this merchant company and the royal treasury had, for some time, constituted a solid source of this cosmopolitan firm's income. In the 1790s, Juan Murphy acquired several frigates and in 1802 opened a branch firm in London in conjunction with William Gordon, a nephew of James Duff, English merchant at Cádiz.[33] The London house eventually

28 Roy Nichols, "Trade Relations and the Establishment of the U.S. Consulates in Spanish America, 1779–1809," *Hispanic American Historical Review*, 13 (1933), 289–313.

29 An exception is J. Barbier, "Peninsular Finance and Colonial Trade," 25–31.

30 On the Merchant Guild of Veracruz, founded in 1796, and its members, see the excellent doctoral thesis, M. Souto, "Consulado de comercio."

31 Many of the Irish Catholic who emigrated to Andalusia became engaged in the production and export of sherry to England, the major market. Domecq, a well-known firm in this sector, was originally an off-shoot of Gordon & Murphy after the latter declared bankruptcy in 1822; G. Jiménez Codinach, *Gran Bretaña y la independencia de México*, p. 249.

32 S. Stein, "Crisis metropolitana," p. 201 contains details; also see S. Deans-Smith, *Bureaucrats, Planters and Workers*, p. 101.

33 S. Stein, "Crisis metropolitana," p. 201–202; according to Ramón Solís, *El Cádiz de las Cortes: la vida en la ciudad en los años de 1810 a 1813* (Madrid: Alianza, 1969), p. 127, Juan Murphy was the owner of six frigates in Cádiz in 1810.

became regarded as one of the most important in that great city because of the volume of their commercial operations. According to a report in 1811, Gordon & Murphy had more than 60 employees in their London house and 300 elsewhere, including various European countries and, of course, in Spain and Mexico.[34]

It is not known exactly when the brothers of Juan Murphy, Mateo, Lorenzo, and Thomas, emigrated to Veracruz, but they were among the most important merchants of that port in the 1790s. The Murphy brothers immediately became prominent members of the Veracruz Merchant Guild when founded in 1796. Their international links were more extensive than those of the majority of their colleagues at the leading Mexican port – a fact that reflected the importance that family networks had for international trade operations in the period.[35] Perhaps the most politically active member of the Veracruz branch of the family was Thomas Murphy, who had been a confidant of Viceroy Revillagigedo (1789–1794) and who also became friendly with Spanish Prime Minister, Manuel de Godoy, as a result of travels from Mexico to Madrid, presumably to strengthen the contacts necessary for his transatlantic business. Murphy's opportunism can be seen in his marriage to Manuela Alegria, daughter of one of the chief treasury officers at Veracruz. This was a key alliance as this connection made Thomas Murphy brother-in-law (*concuñado*) of the new Viceroy Azanza (1798–1800), who subsequently favored the Veracruz trader with much business that later helped the expansion of his firm.[36]

The concession in 1798 of two kinds of trading licenses promoted a considerable increase in the business of the Murphy's company at Veracruz. The permits allowed for the entrance of merchant ships into Veracruz, flying a neutral flag, bringing mainly textile cargos. As a result, the house of Murphy rapidly developed a strong network of partners and correspondents active in various ports, ranging "from Veracruz to Havana, New York, Boston, New Orleans, Salem, Lisbon, Cádiz, Malaga, London, Hamburg, Copenhagen and other European and American ports."[37]

Another kind of permits granted by the viceroy to Thomas Murphy were licenses to negotiate the recovery of consignments of mercury and paper that had been carried by Spanish ships but captured by the British

34 Profits for 1811 were estimated at £237,000. Few merchant houses in London rivaled them. See G. Jiménez Codinach, *Gran Bretaña y la independencia de México*, p. 257, n. 119.

35 Mateo Lorenzo Murphy was named an elector (*elector*) of the Veracruz Merchant Guild in January 1804, while Thomas Murphy was elected to the same guild in 1807. On the international partners of Gordon & Murphy, see G. Jiménez Codinach, "An Atlantic Silver Entrepot," pp. 14–16.

36 M. Souto, "Consulado de comercio," Chapter 6 describes the special contracts for the rescue of Spanish ships in Jamaica arranged by the Viceroy Asanza with the Murphy's house and the Cuban trader Pedro Juan de Erice.

37 J. Ortiz de la Tabla, *Comercio exterior*, p. 332

and retained at the port of Kingston, Jamaica.[38] These rescue operations were linked to the attempts by Spanish authorities to maintain the supply of crown commodities essential to the imperial, fiscal system. In these circumstances, it is not surprising that they should have turned to a trading house – that of Murphy – which had already been acting as one of the principal paper suppliers for the Mexico City tobacco factory for a number of years.[39] Murphy's profits increased on this trade as the price of paper increased from five pesos per ream before the war with Great Britain to between ten and twenty-six pesos per ream after the defeat of the Spanish fleet at Cape St. Vincent in 1797.[40] The historian Susan Deans-Smith confirms that the volume of traffic was considerable: according to the correspondence of Viceroy Marquina, the Mexico City and Queretero tobacco factories consumed 100,000 reams of paper per year in the mid- and late 1790s, with a value of close to three million silver pesos.[41] Unfortunately, there is less data on the annual amounts and value of mercury imports for this period – much also transported by ships of the Murphy family – but they were also considerable.[42]

Thomas Murphy's success in obtaining licenses for his naval expeditions to Jamaica to obtain mercury and paper were largely the result of his excellent political connections with senior government authorities in Spain, but equally important were the political contacts in England of the firm Gordon & Murphy of London, in which his brother Juan Murphy was a senior partner.[43] William Gordon, the head of Gordon & Murphy of London, was Member of Parliament at the time and well connected with the Board of Trade and the Admiralty. The London firm had traditionally

38 During the naval war, 1796–1802, various Spanish ships were captured by the British Navy in the Caribbean and taken to Jamaica where their cargos were auctioned off. Spanish officials used the expression *rescates* to refer to operations by which the royal treasury authorized the house of Murphy to send ships to Kingston to buy these cargos, which included mercury, paper, and other products sent from Spain. Some of these expeditions are mentioned in J. Ortiz de la Tabla, *Comercio exterior*, pp. 291–292 and 328–330; S. Stein, "Crisis metropolitana," p. 201; and M. Souto, "Consulado de comercio," Chapter 6.

39 Thomas Murphy not only benefited from the consignments (*rescates*) of paper from Jamaica to Veracruz, but was also able to obtain a license for his Havana agent, Francisco Santa Cruz, who imported paper from Kingston and then reexported a substantial part to Veracruz: J. Ortiz de la Tabla, *Comercio exterior*, p. 329.

40 S. Deans-Smith, *Bureaucrats, Planters and Workers*, p. 101.

41 S. Deans-Smith, *Bureaucrats, Planters and Workers*, pp. 101–103.

42 R. Garner and S. E. Stefanou, *Economic Growth and Change*, Chapter 4 offers some data but not a complete series.

43 It should be taken into account that ships traveling with Spanish licenses for neutral trade also required licenses from the British government to avoid being captured by British frigates of war that were constantly traversing the Caribbean seas. F. Crouzet, *L'Economie Britannique*, vol. 1, pp. 175–185 is the fundamental source on this issue.

worked with the house of Porro & Murphy (headed by Juan Murphy) of Cádiz and Malaga, importing the finest Spanish sherries, but by the end of the century they were participating more and more actively in different business ventures for the royal treasuries in Mexico and Caracas.[44]

The fact that the Murphys could use Jamaica as an *entrepôt* for much of their business in the Caribbean allowed them to dominate a significant part of New Spain's textile imports from England.[45] Such an activity was not free from danger as it bordered on contraband, exposing the traders to the possibility of being captured by Spanish or English ships of war and to long and vexatious litigation in the Veracruz or Kingston tribunals.[46] Moreover, it awakened the enormous hostility of their rivals in port city of Veracruz, who did not enjoy the same privileges.[47]

The Murphys, however, did not act alone during this first phase of neutral trade. Other Veracruz firms were also quite active. Pedro Echeverría, whom we have already met, played a prominent role in the neutral commerce between Mexico and the United States in the years 1797–1800, importing textiles and exporting considerable amounts of cochineal, sugar, dyes, and other raw materials.[48] In summary, prior experience in neutral trade operations explained much about the performance of these cosmopolitan and adventurous merchant firms in later years.

Even though a certain number of neutral vessels continued to arrive in the years 1800–1801 to Veracruz with trade licenses issued by the Spanish government, after 1802 this type of trade transaction was suspended across the empire. This was a consequence of the peace signed with England but was also the result of lobbying by the Cádiz Merchant Guild (*Consulado de Comercio de Cádiz*) that had systematically opposed the permissions granted to

44 S. Stein, "Crisis metropolitana," p. 202, notes "Thomas Murphy in Veracruz in 1799 advanced 430,000 pesos to buy sugar and cochineal for the Royal Remittance Office (*Real Giro*)..." and in 1803 its director Antonio Noriega "contracted with Juan Murphy for the transfer of 100,000 pesos annually for five years of bullion from Caracas to Cádiz."

45 Anthony Ignace Palyart and Guillermo Gregory were agents for the Murphys in Jamaica moving back and forth to Veracruz. AGN, *Correspondencia de Virreyes*, vol. 236, exp. 1446, f. 54 and G. Jiménez Codinach, "An Atlantic Silver Entrepot," p. 22. In New Orleans, the Murphy agent was Procopio Jacinto Pollock, who would also travel to New Spain's principal port. AGN, *Marina*, 226, fs. 97–102 and S. Bruchey, *R. Oliver, Merchant of Baltimore*, p. 270.

46 This type of dispute which involved the Murphy firm as well as Pedro Echeverría took place on arrival of the North American schooner "Tanner" from Hamburg to Veracruz in February 1800, just after the end of the first period of neutral trade. For details see AGN, *Correspondencia de Virreyes*, vol. 229, exp. 142, fs. 310–311.

47 See "Representación del Consulado de Veracruz a la Suprema Junta Central de España" (March 1, 1809), AGN, *Consulado*, 252, exp. 5, f. 4.

48 J. Ortiz de la Tabla, *Comercio exterior*, pp. 328–330. For information on other merchant houses in Veracruz as well as Havana, Tabasco, and Campeche that carried out trading operations in neutral ships as well as *rescates* in Jamaica, see M. Souto, "Consulado de comercio," Chapter 6.

foreign vessels since this undermined their traditional control of American trade.[49] In fact between 1802 and 1804, it appeared that normalcy had returned to transatlantic operations of the Spanish empire. The Spanish General Treasury received more than 30 million pesos in tax funds from Veracruz alone in these years. However, the return to the classic Spanish trade monopoly regime did not last long. In 1805, as a result of naval conflicts, the shipments of silver were abruptly suspended, and official reports noted that in that year only "the miserable amount of 404,313 pesos arrived in Cádiz."[50] Threatened by bankruptcy, the Madrid Cabinet was once again obliged to issue licenses for irregular trade with Spanish America.

The Royal Treasury and Its Financial and Trading Agreements with the Gordon & Murphy Consortium, 1806–1808

The outbreak of the new naval war with England in 1805 initiated a new phase of neutral trade, but in contrast to the years 1797–1800 – a time of considerable rivalry between the merchant houses engaged in neutral trade through Veracruz – the same business now became much more concentrated.[51] In fact it was largely monopolized by the two conglomerates already mentioned: the Hope/Baring consortium participated directly and indirectly in the dispatch to Veracruz (between 1805 and 1808) of approximately seventy ships from the United States while the Gordon & Murphy group sent thirty-eight ships from Europe and Jamaica between 1806 and 1808.[52] According to the Veracruz Merchant Guild's official figures, neutral trade was responsible for the bulk of the silver exported from Mexico in these years, amounting to more than twenty-five million pesos between 1805 and 1808.[53]

Why did these two trading conglomerates receive these extraordinary privileges simultaneously from the Spanish crown?[54] As we have already seen, the Madrid authorities had first granted royal drafts and trading

49 Regarding the Cádiz Merchant Guild's opposition to neutral trade, see J. Ortiz de la Tabla, *Comercio exterior*, Chapters 7 and 8.

50 G. Jiménez Codinach, *Gran Bretaña y la independencia de México*, p. 223.

51 The most complete information on participants in the Veracruz neutral trade is in J. A. Jackson, "Mexican Silver Schemes," Chapters 9 and 10.

52 G. Jiménez Codinach, "An Atlantic Silver Entrepot," p. 18, records thirty-eight ships arriving on the account of the Murphy's at Veracruz. Compare these figures with J. A. Jackson, "Mexican Silver Schemes," pp. 215–226.

53 For annual silver exports, see P. Pérez Herrero, *Plata y libranzas*, Table 3, p. 161.

54 In Gordon & Murphy's case, it is worthwhile noting their alliance with the important London banking firm of Reid, Irving & Company, specialists in the silver and gold trade as well as in cochineal, which linked them to trade with New Spain. It would be interesting to explore what kind of relationships Reid, Irving & Company might have had with the British government and Admiralty.

licenses for Mexico to Ouvrard and his associates of the house of Hope in December 1804. But it soon became clear that there were disadvantages in granting a virtual monopoly in such transactions. Although the highest financial authorities of the Spanish government had agreed to deliver the bulk of the several million pesos accumulated by the Consolidation Fund in Mexico to pay Napoleon's subsidy, the Crown was also interested in using funds from the royal treasuries of Mexico for other purposes of equally vital interest to the imperial state. At the end of 1805, Miguel Soler, the Spanish finance minister, and Manuel Espinosa, the director of the Consolidation Fund, Espinosa, began to issue royal drafts and additional licenses on colonial treasuries to other international merchants, in particular to the firm of Gordon & Murphy, which promised to fulfill essential fiscal and trading functions for the Crown.[55] Madrid immediately informed the viceroy of Mexico of these transactions.

Already from the beginning of 1805, the viceroy of New Spain, Iturrigaray, had begun to appeal for urgently required provisions, such as mercury and paper for the tobacco monopoly and the silver mines, respectively. Although a risky enterprise – given British hostility – ships began to be dispatched directly from Europe for this purpose, many of them hired by the Gordon & Murphy firm. These operations were quite different from those negotiated with the Hope/Baring consortium as is shown by the special contract signed in May 1806 between Gordon & Murphy, the Spanish General Treasury, and the Consolidation Fund. The first copy of this document reached the Mexican viceroy's hands only in the autumn of 1806. It specified that the purpose of the agreement with the private trading firm was to supply New Spain's royal treasuries with indispensable goods, such as mercury and paper, as well as official stamped paper and hundreds of boxes of playing cards and papal bulls (*indulgencias*), which were also state monopolies.[56]

The contract signed by the Spanish finance minister with the firm of Gordon & Murphy and its associates, Reid and Irving and Company, London

55 By royal command, August 9, 1805, permissions began to be granted to trade with Spanish America in neutral ships to a variety of firms, apart from Hope. These included both Gordon & Murphy and Joaquín Fernández da Silva, merchant of Oporto; Basilio Bayón, merchant of Santander, the merchants Guillermo Barrón and Mariano Malancó y Badía of Cádiz; the commercial companies of José Antonio Pereyra and Francisco María Montano of Lisbon; the Duke of Osuna, Spanish minister to Washington. Further, licenses were granted to the house of Atkinson and Zogle, Jamaica, to send boats with Swedish registrations to the Spanish American colonies. AGN, *Reales Cédulas Originales*, vol. 196, exp. 73, f. 85, exp. 156, f. 238, exp. 221, f. 286; vol. 197, exp. 157, f. 238; and vol. 198, exp. 4, f. 5, exp. 16, f. 21, exp. 21, f. 30, exp. 129, f. 195; and AGN, *Correspondencia de Virreyes*, vol. 229, exp. 1047, fs. 187–188 and vol. 233, exp. 1191, f. 83.

56 See the secret (*muy reservada*) letter from the Minister of Finance, Miguel Cayetano Soler, to Viceroy Iturrigaray, signed May 19, 1806, by which the Gordon & Murphy operations were authorized. AGN, *Reales Cédulas Originales*, vol. 197, exp. 30, fs. 37–42.

bankers, established that the foreign traders would have the right and obligation to:

> carry to the port of Veracruz mercury, paper for cigars and other effects of the Royal Treasury and return bearing fruits and other colonial items belonging to His Majesty (Charles IV) with the condition that the said merchant houses obtain permits or licences from the British Government such that the ships transporting these effects and fruits do not meet with the least obstacle in their outgoing and incoming passages....[57]

Additionally, it was established that a third of each fleet's cargo of merchandise from Veracruz would be reserved for the royal treasury while a quarter of the return cargo should be used for the remittance of bullion and "cocoa of Soconusco, cochineal, indigo dyes, and other commodities on the Consolidation Fund's account." In addition, Gordon & Murphy were to be responsible for maintaining a system of mail ships (*buques correos*) for the Spanish government, sending one mail ship per month from Lisbon but also specifying that "two or three other ships will carry the correspondence of the Royal Service and the Consolidation Fund, from the ports of Veracruz, Cartagena de Indias, and Havana to Jamaica, and that these merchant houses will receive them in London and will transfer them to the same Consolidation Fund."[58] (See Figure 6.2.)

Lastly, Gordon & Murphy were authorized to cash drafts for approximately ten million silver pesos from Veracruz to pay for the mercury, paper, and other articles purchased by them for the Spanish royal exchequer in the Americas. The historian Jiménez Codinach points out:

> Gordon & Murphy were at liberty to send pesos directly to London or via Jamaica in English ships. The traders were to deliver letters of exchange to the Spanish Consolidation Fund at the rate of £177 per 1,000 pesos so that the Spanish government (effectively) received 885 pesos.[59]

In exchange for carrying Mexican silver to Europe, the Consolidation Fund accepted a discount of almost 11 percent, which was profit for the traders, shippers, and bankers involved in the business.[60] The firm of Gordon & Murphy was in a splendid situation to coordinate these transactions – thanks

57 AGN, *Reales Cédulas Originales*, vol. 197. exp. 30, f. 37.

58 Ibid., fs. 41–42.

59 G. Jiménez Codinach, "An Atlantic Silver Entrepot," p. 341.

60 The captains of British warships that arrived to Veracruz to collect the silver received a percentage that oscillated between 1.5 and 2.0% of the total value of the treasure loaded. For a description of one of the negotiations with British captains, see G. Jiménez Codinach, *Gran Bretaña y la independencia de México*, pp. 139–141.

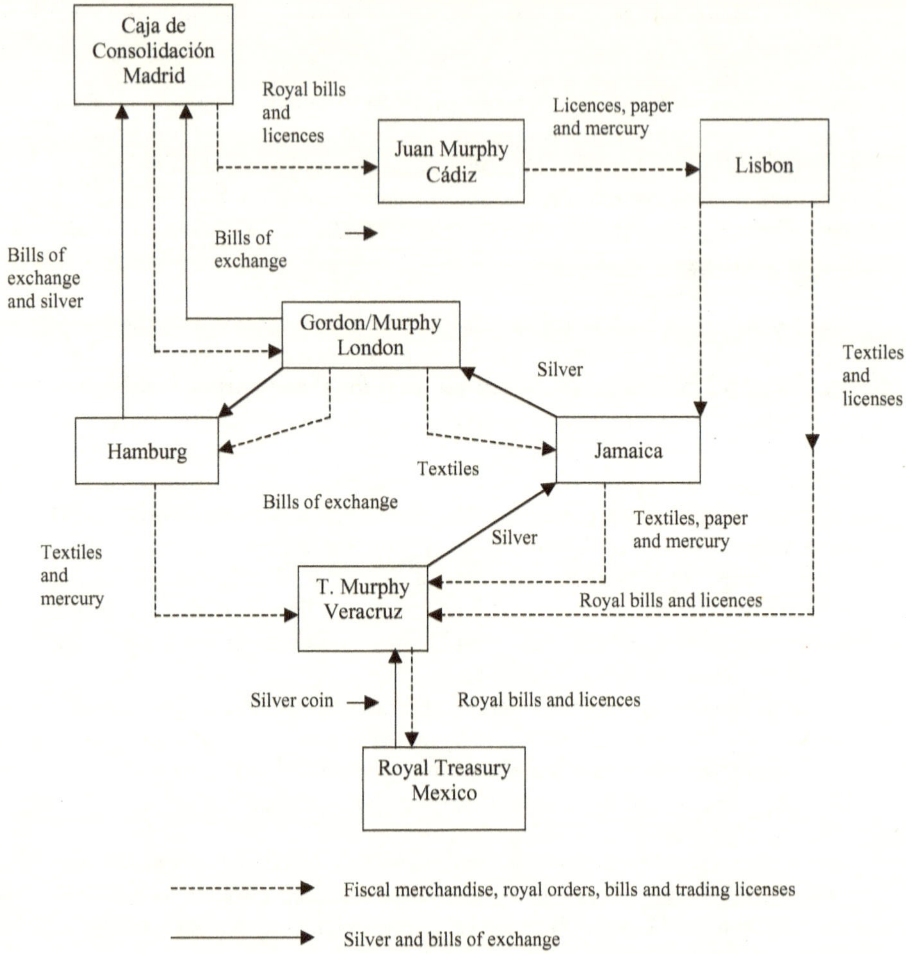

Figure 6.2. Transatlantic Operations of the Gordon Murphy Consortium, 1806–1808.
Source: Drawn by Carlos Marichal.

to their good relations with both the British government and the Spanish administration and also to the mobilization of their extensive network of mercantile agents in northern Europe, Spain, the Caribbean, and the port of Veracruz.[61]

61 For further details on Gordon & Murphy's network of international contacts, see Guadalupe Jiménez Codinach, "Veracruz, almacén de plata en el Atlántico. La Casa de Gordon y Murphy, 1805–1824," *Historia Mexicana*, xxxviii, 2 [150]; S. Stein, "Crisis metropolitana"; and F. Crouzet, *L'Economie Britannique*, vol. 1, pp. 175–185.

Gordon & Murphy's "Neutral" Expeditions to Veracruz during the Second Naval War with England, 1806–1808

A small number of neutral ships began to reach the principal port of New Spain from mid-1805, but it would not be until the following year that the expeditions arrived in large numbers. According to studies by historian Robert Smith, six neutral ships arrived at Veracruz from the United States in 1805, thirty-six in 1806, fifty in 1807, and twenty-seven in 1808.[62] At the same time, there arrived twenty ships to Veracruz chartered by Gordon & Murphy between 1806 and 1808, while eighteen additional ships were dispatched from Jamaica to their account. The ships dispatched from Europe (from Hamburg, Lisbon, Oporto, Cádiz, or Malaga) were few in number than those from the United States but they had considerably heavier tonnage than those arriving to the Mexican port from New York, Philadelphia, Baltimore, and New Orleans.[63] Indeed, between 1805 and 1808, probably no other Caribbean port witnessed such intense trading activity.

This mercantile dynamism can only be explained if one takes into account that both the Spanish and British governments shared interests in making transatlantic commerce and the transfer of silver from Mexico a wartime priority. Neutral shipping dominated not only imports but also exports. The latter included raw materials (cochineal, sugar, vanilla, and cotton) as well as enormous quantities of silver, in part on behalf of the Consolidation Fund and in part on the accounts of the Mexican royal treasuries. But, it can be emphasized once again that the main objective of the Spanish Finance Ministry in authorizing Gordon & Murphy to extract some ten million pesos of Mexican silver was to cover the purchase and dispatch of mercury, paper, and other items needed urgently by the royal administration in Mexico.

The most important item of merchandise sent was mercury (which came from quicksilver mines in Germany and from Almaden). The first mercury consignment from Germany was carried by the *Seculum*, a neutral ship that left Hamburg in March 1806, arriving at Veracruz at the beginning of May.[64] Other ships, hired by Thomas Murphy, with mercury cargos were the *Gosport* from Cádiz, which arrived to Veracruz on January 12, 1807; the

62 Robert S. Smith, "Shipping in the Port of Veracruz," 13, Table 5. The statistics from the Merchant Guild (*Consulado*) published by M. Lerdo de Tejada, *Comercio exterior de México*, do not include complete information about the origin of the neutral ships arriving from Europe.

63 See R. Smith, "Shipping in the Port of Veracruz" for general information about tonnage of vessels entering Veracruz. The majority of the North American schooners utilized by firms such as Oliver did not weigh over 150 tons; see S. Bruchey, *R. Oliver, Merchant of Baltimore*, p. 301. A review of documents in AGN, *Marina*, vols. 224–226, 233, 234, indicates that the neutral ships from Europe had a tonnage varying between 250 and 1,000 tons.

64 AGN, *Marina*, vol. 229, fs. 9–14.

Indiano from Lisbon, entering the same port on 12 March with 300,000 pounds of mercury; the *Statira*, also from Lisbon, which arrived on July 30, 1807, with 900 flasks of "iron with mercury"; the *Jupiter*, a North American vessel bringing 3,333 flasks of mercury from Cádiz; the Portuguese ship, *Nuestra Señora de la Concepción*, which left Cádiz with 200,000 pounds of mercury, arriving at New Spain on October 10, 1807, and various smaller craft that brought mercury and other merchandise from Europe to Jamaica and thence to Veracruz.[65]

Other items urgently requested by Viceroy Iturrigaray included paper bales for the great tobacco factories at Mexico City and Queretaro. The tobacco monopoly in New Spain obtained an annual gross income of some six million pesos per year from the sale of its products in the viceroyalty. Of this sum, almost half went to pay for the costs of the tobacco leaf itself, for paper supplies, and for the payment of salaries of approximately 10,000 workers in the two major Mexican cigar and cigarette factories. After discounting costs, in the mid-1780s and early 1790s, the monopoly could count on remitting almost four million pesos in net receipts to Spain. But during times of naval war – particularly from the late 1790s – costs increased notably as the prices of paper increased, a fact exacerbated by the Crown prohibition of the manufacture of paper in the viceroyalty. As a result, paper became one of the most important components of the cargos carried by Murphy's expeditions. For example, on October 6, 1806, the *Bella Elisa* docked in Veracruz (from Cádiz), with 1,336,000 pounds of paper. Another ship, the *Herald* that had sailed from Malaga, arrived on February 24, 1807, with 1,675 bales of paper, "for the cigars (cigarettes) of these factories." A few months later, on 24 April, the Danish vessel *Neutralidad* arrived in Veracruz from Barcelona with 2,317 bales of paper and 57 reams of white paper, both for the tobacco factory.[66]

Less important articles in terms of weight but of great interest to the treasury officials were stamped paper from Spain and the boxes of papal indulgences, which were to be sold throughout the viceroyalty and produced considerable fiscal income. For example, the *Bella Eliza* from Malaga brought boxes of *bulas* weighing 43,500 pounds as well as 421 boxes of official stamped paper (*papel sellado*) and 300 boxes of playing cards for the

65 Among the ships from Jamaica that brought between 150 and 200 quintiles of mercury were the *Tomás* (which arrived in Veracruz, April 26, 1807), the *Alcance* (May 16, 1807), and the *Correo Ordinario* (May 25, 1807). Information on mercury cargos is found in lists and licenses of ships entering Veracruz in AGN, *Marina*, vols. 229, 234–236 and AGN, *Reales Cédulas Originales*, vol. 199, exps. 27–29, 66–68, and 121–126.

66 On these and other Gordon & Murphy shipments, see AGN, *Marina*, vols. 233–236 and *Reales Cédulas Originales*, vol. 197, exp. 143, f. 218, exp. 144, f. 220, exp. 145, f. 222, exp. 214, f. 306, exp. 238, f. 340, exp. 283, f. 401; vol. 198, exp. 5, f. 7, exp. 6, f. 8, exp. 84, f. 111, exp. 85, f. 112, exp. 155, f. 224, exp. 156, f. 226, exp. 245, f. 371.

respective state monopolies.[67] These articles were necessary to ensure a high level of tax collection by various treasury departments and hence to sustain a constant flow of funds to the metropolis.

In toto, Gordon & Murphy organized the expedition of thirty-eight vessels to Veracruz between 1806 and 1808, thirteen from Spain (Cádiz, Malaga, Cartagena, and Barcelona), seven from neutral ports in Europe and the United States (Hamburg, Oporto, Lisbon, Baltimore, and New Orleans), and eighteen directly from Jamaica.[68] The ships were mainly North American, Danish, Portuguese, and German. In contrast to their Anglo-Dutch rivals of the Hope/Baring group, Gordon & Murphy's ships brought a larger proportion of Spanish goods, including hats from Galicia, Catalan cloth, Valencia silk, Catalan spirits and wine, and beer from Santander, among other articles. On the other hand, the packet ships sent from Jamaica brought predominantly English textiles.[69] The rivalry with Hope/Baring was intense, but over time the different merchant houses came to a tactical understanding to divide and control the markets of New Spain. Robert Oliver, Baltimore merchant and correspondent of Hope, wrote in the following terms to Gordon & Murphy of London in March 1807:

> You know, without doubt, the nature and extent of our operations in Veracruz as we know of yours in this port. Normally we send three or four ships to Veracruz each month, and knowing that up to date information is important for you – and that you must obtain it – we are disposed to allow our ships to take letters for you on the condition that you inform us of ships and departure dates that you plan from Europe to Veracruz, with a list of cargos. . . .[70]

Whether this understanding successfully divided the Veracruz market between the conglomerates is not known, but it is clear that the agents of each merchant group understood the dangers of saturating this profitable market with similar commodities.

67 This ship also brought 11,336 *tercios* of white paper: AGN, *Reales Cédulas Originales*, vol. 197, exp. 142, f. 217 and vol. 198, exp. 188, f. 295.

68 This information is from G. Jiménez Codinach, "An Atlantic Silver Entrepot," p. 18. The author adds that the total value of the cargos was greater than 9 million pesos, without clarifying her calculations. Compare the data with J. A. Jackson, "Mexican Silver Schemes," pp. 215–226.

69 The ship list of the schooner *Tomás*, sailing from Jamaica, chartered by Gordon & Murphy supplied a select list of Kingston merchant houses that habitually sent goods to Veracruz. Among the most important were Dicks, Orn, and Clark; other that sent textiles to the Murphys in Veracruz were the firms of Alexander, Miller, J. Bourke, Moffat, Hill and Longmore, Hatchwell and Retz, Sampson, Lucas, and Henry West and Co. AGN, *Marina*, vol. 236, f. 195. For a full list of the principal Jamaican traders and their declaration in favor of neutral trade, see *The Royal Gazette* (Kingston, Jamaica) February 23–March 2, 1805, "Postscript," p. 20, a copy of which is to be found in AGN, *Marina*, vol. 121, fs. 368–380.

70 S. Bruchey, *R. Oliver, Merchant of Baltimore*, p. 316.

The total value of the cargos carried by ships chartered by the Gordon & Murphy consortium between 1806 and 1808 is difficult to estimate because of the complicated accounts, although the value was considerable for the period and involved several million pesos.[71] The information is not complete because the merchandise brought by the neutral ships used simulated bills: the lading lists were deliberately falsified to deceive the British Navy. Even so, some ships contracted for Gordon & Murphy were confiscated by British frigates and their cargos were auctioned in Jamaica. It is surprising that a greater percentage of ships were not captured.

The Agreements with the British Government and Jamaica-to-Veracruz Mail Packets

We have previously summarized several reasons why the British government did not seriously impede neutral trade with Veracruz and approved the business transactions of consortia such as Hope/Baring and Gordon & Murphy, ensuring access to Mexico, the world's largest producer of silver. We have already suggested that there were powerful trading interests in Great Britain that insisted on the importance of a regular supply of precious metals from Spanish America to finance trade with India and China and that, equally important, the British government needed the Mexican silver to provide subsidies to its European allies fighting against Napoleon.[72] However, there were other benefits for the English economy, derived from the activities of the neutral merchant fleets of both consortia since a considerable part of the consignments sent to Veracruz were made up of English textiles. Historians have established that, in fact, the markets of Mexico and the rest of Spanish America became particularly important to English industry precisely as it began suffering as a result of Napoleon's continental blockade imposed in 1806.[73] More specifically, the historian François Crouzet, doyen of studies on the international aspects of the economy in the Napoleonic age, has argued that British textile exports to Spanish and Portuguese America avoided the closure of a great number of factories and helped maintain the dynamism of the industrial revolution in Britain, during the crisis years of 1806–1808. In his classic work on the Continental Blockade, Crouzet explained in detail the different kinds of neutral licenses

71 Our extensive revision of the Naval (*Marina*) records in the National Archive (*Archivo General de la Nación*) shows that the records of the Gordon & Murphy shipments are more dispersed and less complete that those of their rival, Hope/Baring, which makes it difficult to reconstruct the joint accounts of both fleets.

72 The best source on this subject is J. H. Sherwig, *Guineas and Gunpowder*.

73 See F. Crouzet, *L'Economie Britannique*, vol. 1, Chapters 4 and 5. Statistical estimates of Veracruz trade for this period are found in J. Cuenca, "Comercio y hacienda."

and the special ones granted to the Gordon & Murphy mercantile consortium.[74]

In 1806 as British trade began to seriously suffer from the Napoleonic blockade, the Privy Council in London extended a considerable number of licenses to allow trade between Veracruz and the principal ports of Jamaica, the Bahamas and Trinidad. Gordon & Murphy's previous experience in neutral trade explains why they should have obtain many of these permits, ensuring that, in principle, their vessels would not be captured by the British frigates of war crusading in the Caribbean and the Gulf of Mexico. More surprising is the fact that the British authorities should have allowed this firm to hire monthly mail ships (which were paid for by Madrid) to freely send the official correspondence of the Spanish crown between Lisbon, Jamaica, and Veracruz, under the supervision of the feared British frigates.[75] (See Table 6.1.)

The house of Gordon & Murphy acquired several sailing ships to fulfill this mail service under contract with the Spanish government. Every month, from the beginning of 1806 to mid-1808, the mail packets would leave Kingston, Jamaica, for Veracruz, carrying Spanish government correspondence. That this exchange between enemy ports should have taken place on such a regular basis seems extraordinary, considering that Spain was at war with Great Britain. Nonetheless, it is important to realize that there were influential trading interests involved on both sides. An example is provided by the *Memorial* of the Merchants of Kingston, Jamaica, presented in February 1805 to Vice Admiral John Thomas Duckworth, commander in chief of the British Navy fleet in the West Indies. In this text, more than eighty of the leading merchants of Kingston protested the capture by a British frigate of a Spanish vessel, significantly named *La Paz*, carrying considerable specie and merchandise. The merchants argued:

> It is scarcely necessary to inform you that the trade carried on between this Island and the Spanish Settlements is of the utmost advantage to the Colony and to the Empire at large, affording a most extensive market for British manufactures, in exchange for the precious metals and raw materials necessary for the manufactures of Great Britain.[76]

The British vice admiral in charge of naval forces at Kingston replied that he was aware of the importance of the "Spanish trade" and that the captain

74 F. Crouzet, *L'Economie Britannique*, vol. 1, pp. 179–182.

75 The viceroy followed closely the arrival of these ships that brought correspondence from the Spanish ministers. AGN, *Correspondencia de Virreyes*, vol. 233, exp. 1193, exp. 1200, f. 101, f. 85, exp. 1218 exp. 117, exp. 1227, f. 130, exp. 1258, exp. 165.

76 *The Royal Gazette* (Kingston, Jamaica) February 2–March 2 1805, "Postscript," p. 20, a copy of which is to be found in AGN, *Marina*, vol. 121, fs. 368–380.

Table 6.1. *Ships[a] Sent from Veracruz to Jamaica by the Gordon & Murphy Consortium, 1806–1808*

Name of Ship	Date of Departure	Value of Silver Carried	Value of Merchandise (in Silver Pesos)
Merrimack	July 7, 1806	128,284	234,084
Ordinario	January 1, 1807		28,655
Eliza y Ana	February 5, 1807	45,410	124,600
Ordinario	March 23, 1807	42,000	63,262
Ordinario	April 3, 1807	30,000	68,775
Extraordinario	April 24, 1807	30,000	51,270
Indiano	May 12, 1807		127,177
Alcance	May 26, 1807	200,000	97,800
Ordinario	May 28, 1807		93,371
Heraldo	August 16, 1807		203,747
Tomasito	August 22, 1807	9,000	104,400
Ordinario	October 20, 1807		113,946
Libertad	October 26, 1807	190,140	9,988
Extraordinario	October 31, 1807	200,000	126,945
Neutralidad	November 7, 1807	150,000	393,971
Rally	November 7, 1807		133,490
Manuela	November 22, 1807		72,757
Pepe	December 8, 1807	50,000	6,600
Statira	January 17, 1808	160,000	174,121
Volador	January 31, 1808		23,962
Princesa de Brasil	February 16, 1808		60,760
Pepe	February 17, 1808	300,000	45,600
Concepción	March 2, 1808	50,000	5,622
Júpiter	March 7, 1808	75,067	16,072
Voladora	March 29, 1808	300,000	
TOTAL VALUE (silver pesos)		1,959,901	2,380,976

[a] Ships that carried Spanish royal mail.

Source: John Alexander Jackson, "The Mexican Silver Schemes," (1980), Ph.D. thesis, University of North Carolina, 1980, p. 219.

responsible was new and had been unacquainted with the nature and importance of the neutral trade in the West Indies.

Similar uncertainty about the irregular commerce was also felt by royal officials in New Spain. The correspondence of Viceroy Iturrigaray reveals as much, but he had no alternative but to comply with the instructions from Madrid sent by royal functionaries, Soler and Espinosa. That the viceroy obeyed these orders without protest has been attributed by some historians to his obsequious character, but this view does not take into account the special circumstances of the war.[77] By reducing the danger of British attacks against the ships that entered and departed from the port of Veracruz, neutral trade actually offered many advantages to the royal administration since it facilitated the shipment of fiscal surpluses to the metropolis and also to the main Spanish colonies in the Caribbean, including Cuba, Santo Domingo, and Puerto Rico, which needed Mexican silver for payment of army, navy, and even civil administrations there.[78]

Before receiving the news of the new international agreements regarding neutral trade, the viceroy had prohibited all coastal trade in the Gulf of Mexico. But once it was confirmed that the British frigates were no longer persecuting the majority of licensed neutral ships, he renewed permits and authorized a series of convoys to carry funds from Mexico to different points in the Spanish Caribbean. According to a report by Ciriaco de Cevallos, military commander of Veracruz, 18 expeditions left port between January and September 1806 for Louisiana, Florida, Campeche, and Cuba, but unlike the previous war (when the British Navy had attacked many Spanish ships as well as those with a neutral flag), the expeditions sailed safely.[79] Indeed, as Cevallos emphasized, it was remarkable that between September 1805 and September 1806 – when there were 364 departures and arrivals at Veracruz, including 64 neutral vessels and 82 ships coming directly from Spain – none were seized.[80] The Veracruz military commander reported:

In fact, in spite of cruising near the shore by the (British) enemy by the frigates *Sourvaillante*, *Diana*, *Boston*, *Fortunate*, *Friquard*, and *Piqué*, as well as the brigantines *Viper* and *Port Mahon* and other fighting ships (English corsairs from Jamaica), not one Spanish craft has been captured in the Gulf of all the 200 departures from this port to the seas of Europe and islands of the *Barlovento* (Caribbean). This seems

77 Iturrigaray's venal character is mentioned in J. A. Calderón Quijano, *Virreyes de la Nueva España*, p. 240. Criticisms of his venality were common in Mexican historiography during the first half of the nineteenth century, as can be seen in the acid comments in Lucas Alamán, *Historia de México*, vol. 5, pp. 46–49.

78 The viceroy's correspondence concerning the dispatch of the different *situados* could provides material for an interesting study of New Spain and the defense of the empire. An important issue discussed is the French occupation of Santo Domingo, financed in part by funds from New Spain. Iturrigaray's references to the grave military and financial situation in the Caribbean are constant: AGN, *Correspondencia de Virreyes*, vols. 213–238.

79 Between 1796 and 1802, 186 Spanish ships were lost to the English frigates and corsairs, which represented a loss of about twenty-two million pesos: John Fisher, *Commercial Relations between Spain and Spanish America in the Era of Free Trade, 1778–1796* (Liverpool: University of Liverpool, Centre for Latin American Studies, 1985), p. 48. (Monograph Series, 13).

80 For the complete text of Cevallos' report to Iturrigaray, September 9, 1806, including a detailed list of all the ships that entered and departed Veracruz between September 1805 and September 1806, see AGN, *Marina*, vol. 229, fs. 9–21.

incredible, when in the previous war scarcely one in ten of the ships that left Veracruz for the peninsula arrived safely, but it is nonetheless true.[81]

The agreements on neutral trade between Spain and England explain the dynamism of trade in Veracruz in these critical years. However, the English were not passive actors. As Cevallos noted, the British Navy was supervising maritime activity in the Caribbean and the Gulf of Mexico with great care to assure that corsairs (especially French) did not interfere in a trade benefiting many Jamaica merchants as well as English trade and industry.

But even these circumstances of *armed neutrality* do not fully explain the surprising decision of Spain's financial officials to authorize various British Navy frigates to approach Veracruz between 1806 and 1807 and load vast quantities of silver belonging to the royal treasury and to the Consolidation Fund. The viceroy himself was surprised by these transactions, although he saw himself obliged to facilitate them.

British Warships and Silver Exports from Veracruz, 1806–1808

The first British warship to present itself at the port of Veracruz (during the naval war between Spain and England) was the *Resistance*, which arrived at the end of December 1806 to collect silver and commodities on Gordon & Murphy's account. On receiving news of the arrival of enemy vessel, Viceroy Iturrigaray authorized payment of the drafts and gave permission for the ship be loaded, but with mixed sentiments. In a letter to Finance Minister Soler, the viceroy underlined his discomfiture:

> I state . . . the most delicate question regarding the visit to Veracruz of the English war frigate, *Resistance*, that requested permission to enter the harbor in order to take on board the silver pesos . . . Not having agreed to this strange pretension . . . the transshipment was carried out at sea; it sailed at last with 3,100,000 pesos which amounted to the total of the royal drafts (issued by the Consolidation Fund) and set out for England with the official correspondence for the month, without having had more news of the voyage, apart from vague rumors that this ship has arrived in London."[82]

The viceroy later added that he had received news that on the way to England the same warship had captured a Spanish merchant vessel, the *Bella Elisa*, taking its cargo to London. Apparently the merchant ship belonged to one of the Gordon & Murphy expeditions, having sailed with special permissions from both the Spanish and British governments. To clarify

81 Ibid.

82 Letter from Iturrigaray to Soler, dated May 23, 1807, in AGN, *Correspondencia de Virreyes*, vol. 233, exp. 1231, f.136.

this situation, Anthony Palyart, an agent of the consortium, traveled from Veracruz to Jamaica, but his negotiations with British authorities were unsatisfactory. In May 1807, the same Palyart returned to Veracruz on the English warship *Thames*. The viceroy wrote to Soler:

In these circumstances, I have just witnessed the visit of the English war frigate named *Thames*, bringing the already mentioned agent (Palyart) in order to receive the 2 million pesos on board; a million and a quarter to be drawn upon the Royal treasuries of this Kingdom, four hundred thousand pesos upon the Guatemalan Consolidation Fund (*Caja de Consolidación de Vales de Guatemala*) and the remainder to be delivered by the Militia Colonel, Don Lorenzo Angulo de Guardamino, to whom the Royal Drafts have also been endorsed.[83]

On this occasion the viceroy was even more uncertain about authorizing the transshipment of the large sum of two million silver pesos to the British warship, as he recalled the bellicose conduct of its predecessor. He also feared that he might contradict a recent circular sent out by the Spanish naval authorities which declared all English property as legitimate prize, including those loaded on neutral ships. The viceroy informed the captain of the *Thames* that he could not deliver the bullion and, at the same time, wrote to Soler to find out if the contract with Gordon & Murphy had been cancelled.[84]

It would appear that the viceroy soon received contrary orders since the *Thames* returned to Veracruz at the end of August, and the transaction was completed. The military governor of the port ordered that the frigate keep its distance "from the sight and coast of Veracruz," although in the meantime, he ordered that the treasure be loaded onto a neutral ship, the *Minerva*, because "this would be the way to carry the silver to the point at which the British frigate was anchored, waiting for the transshipment."[85]

During the autumn of 1807 and the beginning of the following winter, there were two additional transfers of treasure to British warships, to the tune of more 1,500,000 silver pesos. (See Table 6.2) At the end of February 1808, another frigate, the *Diamond*, turned up at the anchorage of Anton Lizard, near to Veracruz, having come to pick up two million pesos on behalf of the Gordon & Murphy consortium, but the viceroy informed his superiors that he had scarcely a half of this sum available:

A million pesos were transferred on board and it (the *Diamond*) sailed on 25 February last, without waiting for the other million because its commander made clear that he could no longer delay his departure.... [86]

83 Ibid., f.137.

84 AGN, *Correspondencia de Virreyes*, vol. 233, exp. 1253, fs. 159–161.

85 AGN, *Correspondencia de Virreyes*, vol. 233, exp. 1362, f. 288.

86 AGN, *Correspondencia de Virreyes*, vol. 236, exp. 1510, fs. 133–134.

Table 6.2. *Remittances of Silver from Mexican Treasuries on Ships of British Navy, 1806–1808*

Date of Departure	Name of British Warship	Silver Remitted (in Pesos)
December 29, 1806/(contract with Gordon & Murphy)	*Resistance*	3,100,000
August 24, 1807/(contract with Hope house)	*Diana*	3,829,835
August 25, 1807/(contract with Gordon & Murphy)	*Thames*	2,000,000
February 25, 1808/(contract with Gordon & Murphy)	*Diamond*	1,000,000
August 30, 1808/(contract with Gordon & Murphy)	*Topaz*	1,000,000
November 25, 1808/(remittances for the Central Junta at Cádiz)	*Diamond*	1,696,344
	Melpomene	1,605,446
October 29, 1807(contract with Gordon & Murphy)	*Veteran*	551,641
February 3, 1808(contract with Gordon & Murphy)	*Adamant*	1,000,000

Sources: AGN, *Correspondencia de Virreyes*, vol. 233, exp. 1231, fs. 136–137; exp. 1326, fs. 244–245; exp. 1328, f. 247; vol. 236, exp. 1510, fs. 133–134; AGN, *Marina*, vol. 244, fs. 81–83; and Canga Argüelles, (1834), vol. 1, p. 162.

A few weeks later, another British frigate, the *Topaz*, arrived with the purpose of loading the remaining one million pesos that its twin ship, the *Diamond*, had not been able to take. At the end of March 1808 the loading was complete and the *Topaz* set sail for England.

The silver delivered to the *Topaz* was not the last silver cargo sent on British frigates, for in later years the colonial authorities in Mexico agreed on various occasions to send large sums to Spain in British naval vessels.[87] But, by then the situation had changed altogether. From July 1808, Great Britain was no longer the enemy of the Spanish crown and had become its principal ally in the struggle against the French armies which had invaded the Spanish peninsula.

In summary, it can be observed that during the last stages of the naval war between Spain and England (December 1806 to April 1808), British war frigates arrived in Veracruz on six opportunities on behalf of the Gordon & Murphy firm, loading a total of 8,651,641 silver pesos which were transported to England. (See Table 6.2.) These funds were of great importance for the British government in order to cover payments in silver to its allies in Europe fighting against Napoleon. They were also crucial to the Bank of England to maintain its metallic reserves and the East India Company to assure availability of silver for trade with India. The firm of Gordon Murphy received bills of exchange for these sums but we do not know exactly how the bulk of these bills were later transferred from England to the Spanish

87 For information about silver deliveries on British ships after 1808, see G. Jiménez Codinach, *Gran Bretaña y la independencia de México*, pp. 231–245.

royal treasury or to its several creditors, for there is difficulty in ascertaining the final destination of this large volume of Mexican funds, given the dispersed nature of the documentation in this time of war, contraband, and complex transatlantic transactions.[88]

The neutral trade conducted with Mexico was also of great importance to the British economy, as we have already argued. Some general estimates of the volume of this commerce can be obtained from contemporary reports, in particular those of the Veracruz Merchant Guild. A large number of local merchants were furious with the privileges obtained by foreign merchant houses and their local allies. The guild merchants calculated that neutral trade between 1805 and 1808 had allowed for the introduction of eighteen million pesos of foreign goods through Veracruz and the extraction of almost twenty-eight million silver pesos and four million pesos in Mexican commodities.[89] These large figures suggest that the Veracruz trade was among the most important and profitable of the entire transatlantic trade conducted during these years of Napoleonic wars.

The expeditions of neutral ships of the Hope/Baring and Gordon & Murphy merchant groups continued to arrive at the port of Veracruz during the first half of 1808, but were suspended in July owing to the invasion of the Iberian peninsula by the French army. In early 1808 the Napoleonic invasion of Spain produced a series of radical and profound changes in international alliances. The British government now threw its support to the Spanish patriot forces, struggling against the invading armies and the result was suspension of neutral trade since the British Navy henceforward allowed all Spanish vessels and warships clear passage across the Atlantic. Given the new circumstances, the Hope/Baring partnership no longer had an important role in the Veracruz trade after May 1808. But, surprisingly enough, the international merchant conglomerate headed by Gordon & Murphy continued to be active in Mexican–European trade for several more

88 At the same time as the treasure was being transferred to the British ships anchored near the port of Veracruz, a considerable quantity of precious metals was being loaded onto a French warship at the port of Acapulco. This surprising event can be explained taking into account (1) France was the ally of Spain at this time, and so agreements of mutual support existed; (2) in the Pacific, the British fleet did not have the same presence as in the Atlantic, making it easier for the French ships to operate with a certain freedom along the west coast of America. The French frigate had arrived from the Philippines, accompanying the Spanish galleon *Magallanes* on the Manila to Acapulco route. For its return to Manila, the viceroy authorized 2,670,387 pesos be sent in the French warship, of which a little more than a fifth were destined to sustain the military fort (*situado*) of the Philippines. It can be assumed that the French Navy would have instructions to transport the remainder of the silver from the Philippines to France to assist the Napoleonic navy and army. AGN, *Correspondencia de Virreyes*, vol. 233, exp. 1421, f. 363.

89 "Representación presentada por el Consulado de Veracruz a la Suprema Junta Central de España," AGN, *Consulado*, 252, exp. 5, fs. 6–7.

years – a fact that was due to their close ties to the Spanish patriot government that found shelter from late 1809 in the great port of Cádiz, the only major city in Spain that was not occupied by the Napoleonic armies.[90]

90 G. Jiménez Codinach, *Gran Bretaña y la independencia de México*, pp. 231–239, has collected a great amount of documentation which demonstrates that the Gordon & Murphy consortium was responsible for sending 42 ships to Veracruz between 1808 and 1811, the majority closely associated with the requirements of Spanish royal treasuries, including the transfer of bullion from Mexico to pay British troops fighting in Portugal against Napoleon under Wellington's command.

7

Mexican Silver for the Cortes of Cádiz and the War against Napoleon, 1808–1811

> Loans are only useful in two circumstances, that is: when governments are solidly established and in consequence have credit and good faith, or when the investors run similar risks as the government and can see no other way to save their life and fortune than by helping it with money. . . .
>
> Manuel Abad y Queipo, Bishop of Valladolid de Michoacán, May 30, 1810[1]

The French army's occupation of the Iberian Peninsula in 1808 was – to use a modern phrase – a huge external shock, which brought down the monarchy in the metropolis and threatened the Spanish administration in the colonies. Paradoxically, in the viceroyalty of New Spain as well as in other Spanish American territories, loyalty to the Crown and mother country was reinforced as news spread of the Napoleonic invasion. Colonial elites in Mexico and Peru, in particular, feared the possible disturbance of the status quo and of their traditional privileges, which might be disrupted by political crisis and social upheaval. Despite collapse at the center of empire, therefore, the most important and richest colonies did not interrupt silver shipments to the metropolis. On the contrary, royal officials and the higher clergy mobilized new and vigorous financial campaigns to collect donations and loans to send to the patriot forces combating in Spain, the greatest sums being gathered in Mexico.

French troops began to traverse the Iberian Peninsula in October of 1807 with the ostensible aim of occupying Portugal, but soon the Napoleonic forces installed themselves in cities in northern and central Spain. A rapid succession of military and political events between March and June 1808 (beginning with the mutiny of Aranjuez) led to the fall of Charles IV's government. Although Ferdinand VII, son of the Spanish monarch, briefly assumed the Crown and attempted to maintain the appearance of an autonomous, royal administration, he was destined to a quick failure.

1 A collection of Abad y Queipo's economic writings is included in the volume originally edited in 1837 by José María Luis Mora, *Crédito Público* (Mexico: UNAM, 1986), p. 151.

Napoleon seized upon the weakness of both son and father and shortly negotiated their departure and the subsequent *imprisonment* of Charles IV and Fernando VII in respective palaces in southern France. The establishment of a French administration in the Spanish capital, however, was not met without popular resistance. The famous rebellion of the Madrid populace against the invaders in early May 1808 (immortalized in one of Goya's most famous paintings) was bloodily repressed. It was not long, however, before a number of regional, patriotic juntas began to be formed in different regions of Spain, and soon the struggle against the French invaders gained strength. In Spanish America, most colonial elites expressed their sympathies with the patriotic juntas that had sprung up in different regions of the mother country. But, inevitably, considerable confusion reigned with respect to the future of monarchy and empire.

In the pages that follow, attention is focused on the loans and donations collected in colonial Mexico to assist the patriot forces in Spain in their struggle against Napoleon. The financial contributions were considerable. Between late 1808 and early 1811, over twenty-five million pesos in tax monies, loans, and donations were sent from New Spain to Cádiz, principal seat of patriot resistance in southern Spain. The Spanish American financial contributions to the treasury of the *Junta Central* in Seville and Cádiz in 1809 and the Cádiz Parliament in the years 1810–1812 underscore the significance of fiscal and financial contributions of Mexico and the other colonies to the struggle against Napoleon during this period and demonstrate that without the silver sent, the patriot resistance in southern Spain would have probably lacked the financial resources to resist the prolonged French siege of Cádiz.[2] The paradox was, therefore, that the colonies should have helped to defend the metropolis in its darkest hour.

The Importance of Spanish American Contributions to the Struggle against Napoleon and to the Cádiz Parliament, 1810–1812

The Napoleonic invasion created a deep fiscal and financial crisis in Spain. After the French occupation, the Spanish population had to support double taxation: that of the invading army as well as war taxes (in money and kind) imposed by patriotic armies in various regions. The French administration attempted to keep control over the old fiscal system in the occupied territories, but with mixed results. On May 19, 1808, the Minister of

2 A detailed evaluation of income data for the Cádiz Parliament is found in C. Marichal, "Beneficios y costes fiscales." However, Josep Fontana argues that the patriot resistance in the rest of Spain did not receive much support from the government at Cádiz but rather had to rely on local resources. See Josep Fontana, "La financiación de la guerra de la independencia," *Hacienda Pública Española*, 69, 1981, 209–217 and Josep Fontana and Ramón Garrabou, *Guerra y Hacienda: la Hacienda del gobierno central en los años de la guerra de independencia 1808–1814* (Alicante, Spain: Instituto Juan Gil Albert, 1986).

Finance Miguel Joseph Azanza (who could be described as a collaborationist) informed the chief of occupation forces, the Duc de Berg, that the peasants of the entire country were tired of providing supplies to the invading troops and that tax collection had dropped abruptly as a result of the "total strangulation of mercantile operations" in Spain.[3] Moreover, the ferocity of war in 1808 and 1809 did not allow the fighting forces complete control of the peninsula but rather a series of advances and retreats by both armies.[4] In the event, the gradual collapse of the old financial administration also affected the Spanish resistance.[5]

The various patriotic juntas, established from May 1808 onward in different Spanish regions, received support from the British government, including direct subsidies of monies as well as substantial quantities of military equipment. In June 1808, the first agents from the Spanish juntas arrived in London and negotiated a program of financial support with the Prime Minister George Canning. Most of the British aid was remitted to the juntas of Asturias, Coruña, Leon, Seville, and Cádiz, for a total of seventy million *reales* (three and a half million pesos or dollars) between June 1808 and early 1809.[6] At the same time, British authorities dispatched uniforms and provisions to Spain: Canga Arguelles (later minister of Finance at Cádiz in 1811) calculated that between August and November of 1808, there had been sent from Britain 2,300 muskets, 8,200 swords, 160,000 pairs of shoes, and 50,000 shirts (of varying quality) for the tens of thousands of Spanish soldiers fighting against the French.[7]

3 *Archives Nationales* (Paris) *AF IV*, 1608, B1, *Rapport du Ministre des Finances pour le Gran Duc de Berg*, May 19, 1808. Azanza added that it would be futile to ask for a loan from Holland to finance the invading army, and it would be socially dangerous to ask for more extraordinary contributions from the Spanish peasants; he recommended that Napoleon transfer financial resources to Spain for the subsistence of the French army during two to four months.

4 It should be emphasized that Napoleon financed his armies largely by "living off the land," taking cattle and cereals from villages and farms where they could be found, although this was not conducive to orderly taxation, but rather exploitation. For additional information, consult A. Fugier, *Napoleón et l'Espagne* and Florin Aftalion, "Le financement des guerres de la Révolution et de l'Émpire," in Erik Aerts and François Crouzet, eds., *Economic Effects of the French Revolutionary and Napoleonic Wars*, Proceedings 10th International Economic History Congress (Leuven: Leuven University Press, 1990), pp. 22–29.

5 J. Fontana, 'Financiación de la guerra de independencia' and J. Fontana and R. Garrabou, *Guerra y Hacienda* provide important information about this subject especially with reference to the resistance in Catalonia.

6 José Canga Arguelles, *Observaciones sobre la historia de la guerra de España que escribe en inglés el teniente coronel Napier* (Madrid: 1835–1836), vol. 1, p. 149 and vol. 2, p. 304, gives the distribution as the following: eighteen million *reales* to the junta of Asturias, twenty million each to the juntas of Seville and Coruña, and ten million to the junta of León. See J. H. Sherwig, *Guineas and Gunpowder*, p. 198 for data on the first series of subsidies paid between June and August 1808.

7 J. Canga Arguelles, *Observaciones sobre historia de la guerra*, vol. 1, doc. 57, pp. 253–257. J. H. Sherwig, *Guineas and Gunpowder*, pp. 199–200, 222, 227, 249, 251, provides additional information on British shipments of military supplies to the Iberian Peninsula.

In any case, after the spring of 1809 and during most of the two following years, English subsidies to the Spanish patriots were radically reduced, being limited henceforward to small shipments of provisions and arms to Cádiz which were paid for with drafts on the royal treasuries of Mexico.[8] In fact, from mid-1809, the bulk of subsidies sent from England for cooperation in the Peninsular War were redirected almost entirely to sustain the British army in Portugal under Wellington's command and to provide succor to Lisbon's population.[9] As a result, the patriot armies and juntas in war-torn Spain were obliged to seek alternative sources of income. In most of the country, there was imposed what the historian Joseph Fontana has called "immediate taxation."[10] The patriot forces had recourse to voluntary or forced provisions supplied by the local population in those areas where resistance continued, and this form of emergency war finance became key for the struggle against the French. In Galicia, Catalonia, and Valencia the war was basically financed with forced local taxes, collected by the provincial juntas and military commanders.

On the other hand, in Seville and Cádiz – seats of patriot government in 1809 and 1810–1812 – the most important tax resources were remittances of silver from Spanish America, at least until early 1811. An analysis of government finance at Seville in the year 1809 and of resources available to the armies of Andalusia and Extremadura reveals the critical importance of colonial silver remittances for the patriots in the war's initial phases. Vicente Alcalá Galiano, treasurer of the Supreme Governing Junta (*Junta Suprema Gubernativa*) in Seville, reported:

> The (financial) assistance from America make up the principal funds that have been applied to the provision, conservation and increase of our armies. The total amount coming from those dominions to the Royal Treasury reached the sum (from January to October 1809) of 295,901,816 *reales*. . . .[11]

8 The Spanish Minister of Finance, José Canga Arguelles, stated that letters of credit worth three million pesos were sent by the Duque del Infantado to be paid by the Mexican royal treasures and delivered in Veracruz to Admiral Cochrane: J. Canga Argüelles, *Observaciones sobre historia de la guerra*, vol. 2, p. 307. Lucas Alamán, *Historia de México*, vol. 1, p. 301, includes reference to the splendid reception for Cochrane on his arrival in Mexico in 1809 owing to his reputation as a distinguished British admiral, who had supported the Spanish cause.

9 J. Canga Argüelles, *Observaciones sobre historia de la guerra*, vol. 3, pp. 135–260 includes important commentaries and documents about this issue, which should be compared with J. H. Sherwig, *Guineas and Gunpowder*, pp. 199–250.

10 J. Fontana, "Financiación de la guerra de independencia," p. 216.

11 Vicente Alcalá Galiano, *Informe del Tesorero General en ejercicio Don Vicente Alcalá Galiano, sobre la representación que la Junta Superior de Valencia hizo en 15 de septiembre de este año a la Suprema Gubernativa del Reino, reclamando la real orden de 20 de agosto anterior, en que se reencargaba el cumplimiento de las reales instrucciones en la distribución de los caudales del erario* (México: reprinted at Casa de Arizpe, 1810), p. 6. The equivalent figure is 14.7 million silver pesos at the rate of exchange (20 *reales* = 1 silver peso) used by the minister of Finance, Canga Arguelles, in 1811.

The total income of the governing council and the Army of Andalusia in 1809 was registered at 388,505,075 *reales* and, of this sum, 75 percent was made up of silver remittances from the colonies in the Americas.

The Supreme Junta was soon forced to abandon Seville, as the political, military, and financial situation in southern Spain became increasingly precarious as a result of the advance of the French troops in late 1809 and early 1810. The Napoleonic forces inflicted successive defeats upon the Spanish troops and, inevitably, forced retreats: the principal divisions of the armies of Andalusia and Extremadura retired south, fighting a rearguard action. In late 1809, they finally abandoned Seville and marched to the port of Cádiz. This city, with its magnificent bay opening on the Atlantic and excellent military defenses, provided the necessary resources for the patriot government as well as army and navy to survive during the years 1810 and 1811 at a time when the Napoleonic occupation reached its zenith in much of the rest of Europe.

Indispensable to the continued resistance against the French armies was the alliance that had been signed with Great Britain in early 1809. Crucially important was the protection offered by the British fleet that anchored in the bay and port of Cádiz. The great concentration of cannon on numerous ships of the line and frigates stationed in the inner and outer bay impeded all attempts by the French forces to cross the extremely narrow peninsula that stretched from the mainland to the port city. Also of fundamental importance was the fact that the British warships facilitated the regular movement of Spanish merchant fleets and warships across the Atlantic, maintaining the vital connections with the colonies in the Americas. As a result, Cádiz remained a bustling trade entrepôt during the war years: British merchants and shippers carried on a great activity there, sending out cargos of manufactured goods – mainly on Spanish vessels – to the colonies and receiving in exchange large quantities of silver and tropical produce.

The alliance with Great Britain, therefore, made not only the military but also the commercial and fiscal circumstances in the port of Cádiz more auspicious than might have been expected, given the concentration of thousands of military and political refugees who arrived there in the first months of 1810. After fleeing from Seville to Cádiz, the members of the Supreme Junta agreed to dissolve as governing council since the military defeats had undermined their legitimacy. Sovereignty was transferred to a Regency Council, but this body was politically weak and did not control significant fiscal resources.[12] As a result, from January 1810, authority to collect taxes

12 The Regency Council was constituted by the Bishop of Orense Pedro de Quevedo the senior officials Francisco de Saavedra, Francisco Xavier de Castaños, and Antonio Escaño, and the cleric Miguel Lardizabal y Uribe (representative for America).

was transferred to the Cádiz Council (*Junta de Cádiz*) – composed of leading merchants – which effectively administered most public monies for the patriot forces until the end of the year.[13] The Regency and the Cádiz Council proceeded to issue a call for elections to a general representative government for Spain and America, which became known as the *Cortes de Cádiz* (Cádiz Parliament).

A considerable volume of funds were soon accumulated in the coffers of the Cádiz Council as a result of collection of duties on the brisk transatlantic trade but, above all, as a result of the arrival of large fiscal remittances and loans in silver coin sent by the Spanish American colonies. The Cádiz merchants (who were in charge of the fiscal receipts of the patriot government) assumed their responsibilities with enthusiasm as illustrated in the proclamation to Spanish American (*Proclama a la América española*), published at the beginning of 1810 by the Cádiz Parliament. In it the authors affirmed: "Here is the nerve of the war; here our union with the British nation has been forged."[14]

The Cádiz Council sent official notices to Spanish America, indicating that the Regency had called on all residents of Spain and its possessions to participate in a National Congress (the Cádiz Parliament to begin sessions in 1810) and underlined that this political enterprise would be facilitated by the fact that Cádiz had connections with virtually, "all places in America." The text also added that the patriots required as much financial assistance as Spanish Americans could provide.[15]

But exactly what was the level of financial resources or disposable income available to the patriot government in Cádiz during 1810? The Count of Toreno, deputy-elect in the parliament and a man well informed on public finance, made a summary of income:

The entries of the Cádiz Council (*Junta de Cádiz*) during that time (January-October 1810) reached *351 million reales*. Of these about 84 million came from duties collected in the district; in donations and extraordinary charges of the city,

13 The contract between the Regency and the *Junta Superior de Cádiz* was established on March 31, 1810. See the interesting document, *Real aprobación y decreto de S.M. sobre el Reglamento que la Junta Superior de Cádiz propuso, haciéndose cargo provisionalmente en su distrito de todas las rentas de la Corona y su Dirección* (Cádiz, reprinted in Mexico, 1810), 8-page pamphlet, copy in the Collection Lafragua, no. 182, Biblioteca Nacional (BN) (Mexico).

14 *Junta Superior de Cádiz a la América Española* (Cádiz: February 28, 1810), doc. 393, Collection Lafragua, BN (Mexico), p. 6.

15 Ibid., pp. 6–7: In the same document it was stated: "Cádiz calls on you (*os*), peoples of America and is confident its voices will be heard. . . . In which city, in which port, in what remote and hidden place does not Cádiz have a correspondent, a parent or a friend? Oh, Americans! You have to defend the same rights, the same king to liberate, the same injustices to correct. . . . "

17 million; in loans and other categories 54 million; and, lastly, *more than 195 million from the Americas*.[16]

The testimony of Toreno indicates that more than half of the funds which financed the Spanish government came from colonial remittances: 56 percent of the total income collected by the Cádiz Council (January–October 1810) came directly in the shape of remittances from the Indies.[17]

The year 1811 was possibly the most difficult of the entire war for the Spanish patriots as their military forces suffered a string of defeats by the French army. At the same time, the Cádiz government suffered a sharp fall in the income both because of a drop in trade and as a result of the steep reduction in tax remittances and loans from the colonies, caused by the outbreak of the wars of independence in several regions of Spanish America.[18] Again, according to the reports of the Count of Toreno, total government income in Cádiz in 1811 scarcely reached 200 million *reales*, of which 71 million came from taxes sent from the Americas, mostly from New Spain.[19] The Mexican tax silver was transported by the British warships, *Bulwark* and *Implacable*, which carried 62 million *reales*, having loaded the tax monies at the port of Veracruz in early December 1810 and arriving at Cádiz in February 1811.[20]

In summary, the total remittances sent by the state treasuries in Spanish America to Cádiz between the end of 1808 and beginning of 1811 reached almost 30 million silver pesos (around 600 million *reales*).[21] These funds

16 Conde de Toreno, *Historia del levantamiento, guerra y revolución de España* (first edition published in 1835), second edition. (Madrid: Biblioteca de Autores Españoles, 1953), p. 306. (The italics in the quote are mine.)

17 These proportions coincide with those of the historian Timothy Anna who noted that in the last two months of 1810, the treasury income at Cádiz amounted to 56.7 millions of reales, "of which 30.5 million, or 54 per cent, arrived from America." Timothy Anna, *España y la independencia de América*, (Mexico: Fondo de Cultura Económica, 1986), p. 111.

18 J. Fontana and R. Garrabou, *Guerra y Hacienda*, p. 81, state: "1811 was the worst year of the war" and affirm that fiscal situation entered a very grave crisis at this time but offer few figures regarding the evolution of taxes at this time.

19 T. Anna, *España y la independencia de América*, pp. 116–117, comments upon Toreno's estimates which are similar to those of Finance Minister José Canga Arguelles, *Memoria presentada a las Cortes Generales y Extraordinarias sobre las rentas y gastos de la Corona* (Cádiz: Imprenta Real, 1811). J. Fontana and R. Garrabou, *Guerra y Hacienda*, p. 80, write that in 1811 the Cádiz government received 83 millions of *reales* from America, 73 millions of *reales* in taxes, and 10 millions in letters of credit against Lima's treasury (caja): they calculate the Cádiz government's total income in that year was approximately 200 millions *reales*.

20 For a list of shipments arriving to Cádiz with tax silver from Spanish America, see Table 7.4.

21 The total of tax remittances that arrived from the Americas to Cádiz between January 1809 and the beginning of 1811, as registered by Canga Arguelles (see Table 7.4), reached 29,378,027 silver

consisted of tax monies and loans: 80 percent of the total came from New Spain, while the rest was made up of lesser contributions from Peru and other colonies. The clear preponderance of Mexico in silver remittances reinforces the argument previously advanced with regard to its role as a colonial *submetropolis*, even in this critical era, crisscrossed by Atlantic wars and revolutions.

In the pages that follow, we look at three aspects of the last great campaign undertaken in colonial Mexico to provide the metropolis with financial assistance. First, we explore how – despite the political crisis in New Spain between July and September 1808 – the viceregal government was able to launch a successful effort to collect donations from all social sectors of the viceroyalty in order to contribute financially to the struggle *against* Napoleon. Second, we analyze specifically why the richest groups of New Spain provided so great a number of loans and supplements for the patriot government at Cádiz in the years 1809–1811. Lastly, we evaluate how important the shipments of Mexican fiscal remittances and loans silver were in relation to the viceroyalty's regular income. These transfers – which amounted to around twenty-five million pesos – were of two types, consisting of approximately ten million pesos in donations and loans, and fifteen million pesos in tax funds. For such a huge sum to be sent in less than three years bespoke the persistence and power of the colonial administration, despite the extreme weakness of the metropolis.

The Coup against the Viceroy of Mexico in 1808 and the First Loans for the Spanish Patriots

The months of July to September 1808 marked a first moment of crisis for the colonial regime in New Spain, although not its downfall. From the beginning of July, different versions of events transpiring in the metropolis began to circulate in Mexico. Bitter disputes broke out regarding the supreme authority to which the viceroyalty was now subject, particularly as news of the imprisonment of Charles IV and Fernando VII and the installment of a French administration in Madrid awoke enormous concern. Soon after, reports on the establishment of patriotic juntas in different regions of Spain generated an unprecedented political effervescence in the cities of the viceroyalty, although there were as yet few channels for public expression in colonial society. In the summer of 1808, therefore, great confusion reigned with regard to the legitimacy of the different Spanish juntas since all declared themselves "sovereign." Subsequently, however,

pesos (equivalent to 587,560,544 *reales*), while the income for Seville's general treasury and Cádiz' treasury, registered as arriving from Americas, was 591.4 million *reales*. This close correspondence is indicative of the reliability of the data.

the panorama became gradually clearer: from October 1808, the viceregal authorities accepted the sovereign rule of the Supreme Junta at Seville; in late 1809, they recognized the rule of the Regency and from 1810 that of the Cádiz Parliament (*Cortes de Cádiz*).[22]

In any case, during the critical months of July and August 1808, uncertainty about events in the metropolis contributed to political and social agitation. The debates and struggles between the distinct factions of the governing elites in Mexico City culminated in a coup against Viceroy Iturrigaray on the night of September 15, 1808. The movement was financed and promoted by a group of leading Mexico City merchants, headed by the rich entrepreneur Gabriel de Yermo. Following the abrupt dismissal and imprisonment of Iturrigaray, General Pedro Garibay, was named viceroy – a fact that tended to lend tranquility to the hierarchy of the colonial administration and power elites in the capital city, despite a series of local rivalries and conflicts.

The story of this early (royalist) *coup d'etat* in Mexico is well known, but there are as yet few in-depth studies of the buildup of tensions between the viceregal government and the distinct factions of New Spain's elite, which reached their climax in the fall of 1808.[23] The viceroy's arrogance and his poor relations with the powerful merchant guilds of Mexico City and Veracruz between 1805 and 1808 had already caused his isolation from many of the wealthiest members of society.[24] To this should be added the uncertainty and effervescence caused by news of the violent events taking place in Spain in the spring and summer of 1808. Increasingly heated political discussions within the colony reached a new high point in the month of August when virtual autonomy from the metropolis began to be discussed.[25]

The proposals for autonomy from Spain were anathema to the leading members of the merchant elite of colonial Mexico. They insisted that it was necessary to send financial support to the patriot government at Seville. This position was made explicit in the important meetings of notables on August 29 and September 9 in Mexico City, which were the key antecedents to the coup against the viceroy, who was increasingly accused of wavering between

22 For details see L. Alamán, *Historia de México*, Chapters 4 and 5 and Lawrence Black, "Conflict among Elites: The Overthrow of Viceroy Iturrigaray, Mexico 1808," unpublished Ph.D. thesis, Tulane University, 1980.

23 The unpublished study by L. Black, "Conflict among Elites" is the best account of the 1808 coup.

24 L. Black, "Conflict among Elites" describes Iturrigaray's alliances with different sectors of the elite (particularly the rich mine owners) which are contrasted with his disputes with the merchants.

25 The classic account is that of L. Alamán, *Historia de México*, vol. 1, who describes the debates during August and the beginning of September between the viceroy, the municipal government, and the Court (Audiencia) and other notables on the convenience of convening a general congress or assembly to discuss the political destiny of the viceroyalty, step by step.

loyalty and treason to the Crown.[26] For the most powerful merchants of Mexico, isolation from the metropolis and/or a modification of the political, social, and economic status quo within the colony represented a grave danger to maintenance of their privileges, which were based on the commercial monopoly exercised by guild members.[27]

The debates about the convenience of remitting funds to the metropolis were not unassociated with the movement that ended with the dismissal of the viceroy. Proclamations of support for Ferdinand VII began to be published in the official *Gazeta de Mexico* from early August 1808 with offers to organize volunteer companies of militia to sail for Spain and join the struggle against Napoleon.[28] Among the first corporations that made haste to express its loyalty was the Mexico City Mining Tribunal (*Tribunal de Minería*). The wealthy miners offered to finance the casting of 100 cannon in Mexico to be sent to the Iberian Peninsula.[29] They also promised to cover the salaries of eight battalions of 80 soldiers each, including a set of noncommissioned officers, selected and trained from students at the famous Mexico City School of Mining.[30]

Almost simultaneously, the ecclesiastical hierarchy announced its intention of participating in the campaign to raise funds for the Spanish patriot armies. The archbishop and the Mexico City Cathedral Council donated 80,000 pesos in September, encouraging other prelates to offer large sums. On September 13, 1808, the Archbishop Francisco de Lizana publicly exhorted the inhabitants of the viceroyalty to combine patriotism and Catholicism to sustain the Spanish government in the struggle against Napoleon, who – he argued – intended to "subvert religion, monarch and laws" in the mother country.[31] Lizana encouraged Mexicans to contribute

26 Fray Servando de Mier, *Historia de la Revolución de Nueva España* (original edition, Londres, 1813), second edition. (Mexico: Fondo de Cultura Económica, 1986), books iii and iv. It was argued, on the one hand, that the viceroy was an ally of the French and, on the other, that he favored independence from Spain.

27 For an analysis of the privileges of the Mexico City Merchant Guild, see G. Valle Pavón, "Consulado de Comerciantes," passim.

28 *Gazeta de México*, August 3 and 6, 1808. It should be noted that these proclamations had already begun to be distributed in Cuba in mid July when the Capitan-General Marqués de Someruelos requested donations for Spain. See the pamphlet *Proclama. Habitantes de la Isla de Cuba, hijos dignos de la generosa nación española*, Havana, July 17, 1808, 4 pp., Fondo Reservado, 165/LAF, BN (Mexico).

29 E. Flores Clair, *Las deudas del Tribuna*, p. 15, notes that the Tribunal de Minería contributed 200,000 pesos for casting the canons.

30 A long article in the *Gazeta de México* (Supplement), August 6, 1808, xv, 74, 543–545, explains this proposal.

31 *Exhortación del ilustrísimo Sr. D. Francisco Xavier de Lizana y Beaumont en que se manifiesta la obligación de socorrer a la Nación Española en la actual guerra con la Francia* [*Exhortation of the Illustrious Sr. Don Francisco de Lizano and Beaumont in Which He Shows the Obligation to Aid the Spanish Nation in*

to the defense of the Catholic religion, stating that if the French were not expelled from the Peninsular, there could be untold consequences for New Spain itself:

> The humble Indian, who honors with a candle the Saint that defends his home, as well as the wealthy Mexican who enjoys using his wealth for sumptuous events dedicated to the Virgin of Guadalupe, ... will find themselves forced to submit to the martial spirit and philosophy ... (of the French invaders). ... [32]

The official proclamation requesting financial contributions from the Mexican population for the defense of the metropolis was only ratified after the Viceroy Iturrigaray had been deposed in early September 1808, and the struggle for political power in the capital settled with the victory of the wealthy guild merchants. In spite of the growing popular discontent caused by the political *coup* in the capital, the new Viceroy, General Pedro Garibay, began to collect a great quantity of funds, sending them to the metropolis. The explicit objective was to provide financial resources for the struggle of the patriots against the French armies and, at the same time, to shore up the shaky edifice of the Spanish imperial state.

Mexican Silver for Defense of the Metropolis: The Donation of 1808–1809

On October 4, 1808, Viceroy Garibay published an official petition addressed to the inhabitants of New Spain, asking them to provide resources to sustain the Spanish in their war against the French. His edict suggested that the money would be sent in the name of the king to Junta at Seville and ordered the formation of "associations of bodies, communities or guilds" to collect the funds. Initially, there was certain confusion about the specific nature of the first contribution, but it was soon confirmed to be a *universal donation*. From November 1808 onward, the *Gazeta de Mexico* regularly published lists of the donors and the amounts they had contributed. The majority of the initial contributors were from the capital city and surrounding zones. (See Table 7.1.)

By November, almost half a million pesos had been collected from different social groups and regions, and over the next two years, additional amounts were added in successive campaigns, resulting in a total donation of more than two million pesos.[33] The detailed lists sent to Mexico by

Its Current War with France], (México: September 13, 1808), 4-page pamphlet, Fondo Reservado, Colección Lafragua, BN (Mexico).

32 Ibid., p. 2.

33 The *Gazeta de México* published the lists daily between late 1808 and early 1811.

Table 7.1. *Donations Collected in Mexico City between October 12 and November 11, 1808*[a]

Contributors	Pesos
Illustrious Archbishop of Mexico	30,000
The Ecclesiastical Council of the Archbishopric	50,000
The Order of the Carmelites	6,000
The Judge (*Oidor*) Tomás Calderon	2,000
The Judge (*Oidor*) Tomás Aguirre	1,000
The Chief Administrator of the royal treasury Francisco Xavier Borbón	1,000
The Chief Legal Council to the Viceregal Government (*Asesor General*) Miguel Bachiller and his wife	1,000
Dr. Juan Josef Guereña, Priest of the Parish of San Miguel	500
The Royal Prosecutor Ciriaco González Carbajal.	1,000
The Count of Medina and Torres	1,000
The Royal Congregation of the Oratorio of San Felipe Neri	1,000
Don Juan Francisco Gallo	2,000
Don Diego de Agreda	12,000
Count de la Cortina	6,000
Officers of Urban Regiment of Mexico City Merchant Guild	25,000
The Royal Inquisition of Mexico	11,000
The Augustinian Order in this capital	4,000
The Royal Convent of Jesús María	4,000
D. Tomás Domingo de Acha, merchant of this city	6,000
D. Domingo Ignacio Lardizabal, treasurer of Royal Customs and his son, D. Manuel Joaquín	4,000
Merchants registered by the Tribunal of the Merchant Guild	65,160
D. Mariano de Zúñiga and Ontiveros	1,000
Captain of Militia Francisco Servando Muñoz	1,000
Marquis de Selva Nevada	1,000
Marquis de Santa Cruz de Inguanzo	4,000
The Royal Pontifical University	10,000

[a] This donation, to help in the Spanish struggle against the French armies, continued to be collected throughout 1809 and 1810, and the names of the principal and secondary donors published daily.
Source: Gazeta de México (October 28 and November 11, 1808).

the regional functionaries in charge of collecting monies demonstrate that all categories of colonial society contributed: merchants, mine owners, landowners, bureaucrats, military officers and soldiers, diverse sectors of urban society, and hundreds of Indian peasant communities, which made contributions through their communal funds.[34]

In December 1808, the Guadalajara Merchant Guild published a manifesto, urging the local population to donate to Spain, offering its services as collection agency and dispatcher. The rhetorical language utilized by

34 For more details about this donation, see details in Appendix III.1.

the Guadalajara merchants was intended to awaken both the fear and the generosity of contributors, denouncing the "monster Napoleon," who after usurping Spain's dominions had taken harsh measures against the patriots. A literary note was added to the manifesto to add to the alarm:

> He (Napoleon) has ordered his generals that one hundred thousand Spaniards be sent to him, tied two by two with iron rings on their wrists . . . and has threatened to exterminate with blood and fire all towns that resist the completion of so inhuman orders . . . [35]

But militant propaganda was not enough to create a climate appropriate for the collection of new donations. In order to win over converts to the cause of the struggle against Napoleon, the colonial government declared the definitive suspension of the Consolidation Fund in New Spain.[36] The viceroy, the judges of the Royal Tribunal (*Real Audiencia*), and other high officers debated this measure, making the decree public by the end of the month. This naturally produced a rapid improvement in government–Church relations and also alleviated the pressure on thousands of property owners who had debts with the Offices of Pious Works (*Juzgados de Obras Pías y Capellanías*).

The reconciliation between ecclesiastical and civil powers was manifest in the collection of the donation in 1808 and 1809. For example, in Puebla de los Angeles, the second largest city in the viceroyalty, the local bishop quickly offered to donate 50,000 pesos on October 11, 1808 for "the urgent needs of the Spanish Peninsula" and, on the same day, announced a contribution for the same amount from the Puebla Cathedral Council. During October and November the wealthier inhabitants of the city, above all merchants, contributed an additional 35,000 pesos.[37]

The campaign to collect the donation was soon extended the length and breadth of the viceroyalty. In Guanajuato, the Mining Delegation (*Diputación de Minería*) offered to donate a silver peso for each hundred pounds of mercury used in the work of the silver mines "for as long as the war lasted." At the same time, a group of forty of the wealthiest proprietors (mostly silver miners) of San Luis Potosí offered a donation of 10,000 pesos

35 Juan E. Hernández y Dávalos, *Historia de la guerra de independencia de México*, vol. 1 (Mexico: Instituto Nacional de la Revolución Mexicana, 1985), doc. 254, p. 641.

36 This measure had been announced by Iturrigaray at the end of June but, in practice, collections for the Consolidation continued for several more months. The order regarding the "absolute cessation of the Consolidation Fund from 26 December 1804 concerning expropriation of church and the surrender of mortgages (*fincas pías y redenciones de censos*) . . . " was published in the *Gaceta de México*, October 26, 1808, 823–824.

37 AGN, *Donativos y Préstamos*, vol. 11, exp. 5, fs. 51–68.

while the municipal council (*ayuntamiento*) contributed 2,021 pesos and merchants donated 3,268 pesos.[38]

As in previous donations, the financial campaign was also promoted in rural villages. Great numbers of documents and lists have been conserved of the donations sent by estate administrators, rural traders, and above all, by tax officials and priests who were responsible for the collection in the peasant communities. It should be noted, however, that while the donations of 1808–1810 were initially intended as voluntary contributions for the mother country, the application of coercive measures was common. Tax officials raided the community treasuries of hundreds of peasant towns, which were precisely those least prepared to contribute to the Crown. The drainage of funds left them at the mercy of the terrible, agrarian crisis, which devastated the countryside in 1809, and the consequent wave of lethal epidemics, which swept through Mexico during that year.[39]

Despite the misfortunes of hundreds (if not thousands) of Indian peasant villages, the tax officials continued their efforts to collect resources and insisted that contributors should explicitly declare their payments as voluntary.[40] This was the case in dozens of Indian peasant villages around Veracruz, as illustrated by the following extract from a letter sent by the subdelegate there on November 24, 1808:

> The governor of the town of San Miguel de Texistepeque, his republic and other Tlatoques (chiefs) say that . . . they freely, with thanks and spontaneously and without any advantage, contribute to our Sovereign by donation of all the funds in their ownership. . . .[41]

Detailed studies of the government fiscal offensive to appropriate peasant resources have been published by historians Marta Terán and Iván Franco on the Intendancy of Valladolid de Michoacán that demonstrate how fiscal demands intensified.[42] Iván Franco provides a precise account of the

38 The detailed lists of donations, 1808–1810, are to be found in various sections of AGN, *Donativos y Préstamos*; for example, for Guanajuato, vol. 12, fs. 207–215; for San Luis, vol. 4, exp. 38, fs. 137–144.

39 On the 1809 agrarian crisis, see Enrique Florescano and Victoria San Vicente, eds., *Fuentes para la historia de la crisis agrícola (1809–1811). Selección documental* (Mexico: UNAM, 1985). Also, there are important considerations in Brian Hamnett, *La política española en una época revolucionaria* (Mexico: Fondo de Cultura Económica, 1985), Chapter 4.

40 See L. A. Jáuregui, "La anatomía del fisco colonial," Chapter 6, pp. 246–248 for a synthesis of the formulas employed by finance officials to evaluate the sums available in the community treasuries.

41 AGN, *Donativos y Préstamos*, vol. 12, f. 66.

42 Marta Terán, "Muera el mal gobierno: las reformas borbónicas en los pueblos michoacanos y el levantamiento indígena de 1810," Ph.D. thesis, El Colegio de México, 1995 and I. Franco, "La Intendencia de Valladolid."

Table 7.2. *Donations Collected in the Intendencia de Valladolid (Michoacán) 1808–1809*

Contributors	Pesos	Percent
Bishop of Valladolid	80,000	38.5
Augustine Order	10, 000	4.8
149 Indian peasant communities in fifteen subdelegations	86,701	41.7
Neighbors of the city of Valladolid	17,176	8.3
Employees of the royal treasury	7,320	3.5
Valladolid City Council	5,556	2.7
Members of Regiment of Dragoons of town of Patzcuaro	1,229	0.6
TOTAL	207,892	100.0

Source: Iván Franco "La Intendencia de Valladolid de Michoacán, 1787–1809. El proceso de formación del poder civil en una región de la Nueva España," Master's thesis, El Colegio de Michoacán, 1995, p. 379.

contributions and donations which indicates that in Michoacán, during the years 1808–1809, 42 percent of the donated funds came from 149 Indian communities, followed by ecclesiastical institutions (38 percent), while the landed proprietors – Creoles and Spanish – scarcely contributed 8 percent of the 207,000 pesos collected in the region.[43] (See Table 7.2.)

That a great part of the funds should have been raised from peasant communities bespeaks the persistence of the power of the royal administration. But, paradoxically, as historian Marta Terán has noted in a detailed study, it was the richest and most productive peasant villages that suffered the greatest exactions since they had accumulated "surpluses" in their community funds.[44]

To Save Crown and Commerce: Merchant Loans from Mexico for the Spanish Patriots, 1809–1811

The financial demands of the metropolitan government, 1808–1811, weighed upon the entire society of colonial Mexico, but there were certain social sectors that participated enthusiastically. In particular, the wealthiest merchants of Mexico City and Veracruz lent large sums quickly and repeatedly between 1808 and 1810. This participation was clearly not a matter of coercion but of *collaboration* by the key sectors of New Spain's elite, almost certainly because of their desire to maintain secular political privileges and economic oligopolies.

43 I. Franco, "La Intendencia de Valladolid," p. 346.

44 "Los pueblos pobres, sin bienes o con pocos ... perdieron menos con esta política ... En cambio, a los pueblos más abundantes y de vida resuelta les fue mal. ... "; M. Terán, "Muera el mal gobierno," pp. 154–155.

It may be presumed that this enthusiasm reflected the fact that after the coup against Iturrigaray, the capital city's merchant elite had assumed the real power behind the viceregal throne. If we consider how important it was for the great Mexican merchants to maintain control of trade with the metropolis and, in particular, with Cádiz, the great entrepôt of colonial trade, then their willingness to collaborate with large sums of money in the official financial war campaigns can be readily explained. In fact, maintenance of this vital transatlantic connection was indispensable to the survival of much of their business activity and of the privileges of the merchant guilds, which as many old regime corporations assured control of key business opportunities. If the Spanish government should disappear as a result of the Napoleonic onslaught and if Mexican ports should be opened to free traffic from other countries – in particular from England and the United States – this would radically alter the status quo. It would probably lead to the end of the secular trading oligopolies that the rich Mexico City guild merchants had exercised for more than two centuries.[45]

There is, therefore, little mystery on the size of the financial contributions of the Mexican colonial plutocracy to the metropolis in the critical years of 1808–1810. Initially, however, loans made up only a small part of the remittances sent from Veracruz to Cádiz to help finance the war against France. Between August 1808 and August 1809 the astounding amount of over fourteen million pesos was shipped to Cádiz, but most of this sum consisted of accumulated tax reserves, plus a donation collected during that year and four million pesos from the offices of the Consolidated Fund in the viceroyalty.[46] Subsequently, however, as tax reserves became depleted, the largest contributions did come in the way of loans from the wealthy Mexican merchant oligarchy and silver miners. (See Table 7.3.)

In July 1809, the new Viceroy, Archbishop Lizana, received orders from the Spanish minister of finance "to send 3 million pesos to pay drafts owed to the British government."[47] These bills were receipts that the Regency in Seville had delivered to British diplomats in Spain in exchange for the money and arms supplied from London to the first Spanish juntas for their

45 For detailed analysis of the mercantile and fiscal privileges of the powerful merchant guild, see the doctoral thesis of G. Valle Pavón, "Consulado de Comerciantes."

46 The resumption of silver shipments to Spain in the English warships *Diamante* and *Melpómene* that left Veracruz in December 1808 were effected principally with funds from the Mexico City mint, although a part of the monies also came from the tobacco monopoly. See L. A. Jáuregui, "La anatomía del fisco colonial," pp. 250–251. Later, at the beginning of 1809, the warship *San Justo* set sail for Cádiz, loaded with funds of the Consolidation Fund: see A. Lavrin, "Execution of the Laws."

47 L. A. Jáuregui, "La anatomía del fisco colonial," p. 252, who cites the *Gazeta de México*, July 12, 1809.

Table 7.3. *Colonial Mexico: Donations and Loans for Spain, 1808–1810*

Donations and Loans	Years	Pesos	Interest Rate
Donation[a]	1808–1810	1,941,643	No interest
Patriotic loan	1809	3,176,835	6%
Patriotic loan[b]	December 1809	1,393,500	No interest
Patriotic loan	1810	2,010,000	6–8%
Patriotic loan[b]	July 1810	1,000,000	No interest
Patriotic loan[b]	December 1810	2,000,000	No interest
Patriotic loan[b]	March 1810	1,194,000	No interest

Note: See list of loans in Appendix III.2.

[a] The donation which commenced in October 1808 continued throughout 1809 and 1810.

[b] These so-called patriotic loans were non-interest-bearing advances requested from the wealthiest merchants of the viceroyalty in order to provide the silver to be borne by the warships arriving at Veracruz and bound on their return voyage for Cádiz.

struggle against Napoleon in the initial months of resistance. Historian Luis Jáuregui has described the negotiations:

> A few days later, the first agent of the British government sent to New Spain arrived at Veracruz. On July 22 (1809) Alexander Cochrane-Johnston (the English naval officer who arrived in Veracruz) began negotiations with the new viceroy Lizana "to receive the 3 million pesos that England had lent Spain during the first months of their alliance and with a license to export the silver destined for the English treasury."[48]

Given the scarcity of hard cash in the coffers of the royal treasury in Mexico City, Viceroy Lizana asked wealthy Mexicans for a loan by means of an edict published on August 5 which called upon the inhabitants of the viceroyalty to show their "patriotism, loyalty, love and virtuous sentiment" to help "the most sacred cause that any nation has been called on to defend until now."[49] It was a notable success. By the end of August, more than 3 million pesos (equal to 3 million dollars) had been collected as a patriotic loan, with the greatest amounts provided by the leading merchant houses of Mexico City. Among the wealthy contributors were Antonio Bassoco who loaned an impressive 200,000 pesos; the brothers Francisco and Alonso Terán with an equal amount; Tomás Domingo Acha for 150,000 pesos; Sebastian Heras, 100,000 pesos; Gabriel Yturbe, 100,000; the Count de la Cortina, 50,000; and Gabriel de Yermo, 50,000. Another fifty merchants contributed with amounts that ranged between 10,000 and 50,000 pesos, and dozens more

48 L. A. Jáuregui, "La anatomía del fisco colonial," p. 252.

49 The loan was authorized by the Seville Supreme Junta in March 1809, so we may suppose that the official instruction was received by the viceroy in June. The viceroy delayed its proclamation for unknown motives. AGN, *Donativos y Préstamos*, vol. 3, fs. 16–17.

with lesser contributions. Such large sums bespoke the great wealth of the Mexican oligarchy, which in terms of capital assets rivaled the largest contemporary mercantile fortunes in Europe.

The terms of this loan were favorable to the investors. In contrast to the donations that offered neither return of capital nor interest to contributors, this new transaction guaranteed a high return and security to the most opulent members of New Spain's society. The financial conditions set out in the edict of August 5, 1809 reveal the benefits clearly: the punctual payment of an annual 6 percent interest "under the secure endowment of the Tobacco Monopoly or a fiscal department that the Lender may choose specially. . . ."[50] To reassure creditors, the royal treasury soon began to effect several return payments on a part of these funds to the merchants who had lent monies.[51]

The close collaboration between the government and the mercantile elite was reconfirmed by the successful issue of various emergency loans requested in the months of December 1809, July 1810, and December 1810, on arrival of Spanish and British warships at Veracruz. The ships had come with the express purpose of transporting treasure to assist the Spanish patriot government in Cádiz. The loans were solicited because of temporary scarcity of tax funds in the Mexico City and Veracruz royal treasuries, but in these cases no interest payments were promised. The viceroy requested the great merchants to make short-term advances since they were the only individuals who had large quantities of precious metal at their immediate disposal.

The first of the emergency loans was requested in December 1809 on arrival at Veracruz of the Spanish war frigates *Asia* and *Algeciras*, which brought peremptory orders to load all the silver that was available in the royal treasuries. The viceroy called for a series of meetings "of the principal residents of this capital" to solicit their help in collecting one million and a half pesos in less than two weeks. The major contributors, as was customary, were members of the merchant guild of the capital, among them Antonio Bassoco (who again advanced 200,000 pesos and was awarded the title of Count of Bassoco), Gabriel Yturbe e Iraeta (100,000), Tomás Domingo de Acha (150,000), and the Count de la Cortina (50,000), followed by sixty-five individuals who provided amounts ranging between 2,000 and 20,000 pesos.[52] As investors, these merchants, however, were not risking their capital. The government promised that when tax funds arrived at the

50 For additional details, consult Appendix III.2 and the sources given there.

51 Lucas Alamán noted that on September 6,1809, an announcement was published by the treasury that investors who so preferred could have payments deposited at interest: L. Alamán, *Historia de México*, vol. 1, p. 306.

52 See *Gazeta de México*, December 2, 6, 9, and 13, 1809, for the complete list of contributors.

treasuries, they would be quickly reimbursed. This was confirmed three months later in an article published in the recently founded newspaper, the *Diario Mercantil de Veracruz*, which called all parties that had provided money for the interest-free loan to turn up on March 7 "at the offices of the royal treasury to receive the value of half the amount that each one had lent."[53]

Six months later, in July 1810, the viceroy again asked for a second emergency loan when the British warship, *Bulwark*, anchored in Veracruz. The captain Charles Fleming traveled by horse and carriage to Mexico City, carrying instructions from the Spanish Minister of Finance the Marquis de Hormazas authorizing him to load "whatever wealth, products and effects are ready for shipment and transfer them to this Peninsula."[54] On this occasion the sums collected for the loan were less substantial, amounting to 550,000 pesos, to which was added an important quantity of tax revenues accumulated in the capital city's treasury.[55]

Finally, at the end of November 1810, another British warship, the *Implacable*, arrived with instructions to load a million and a half pesos for the patriot government at Cádiz. The ship's captain George Cockburn insisted that Viceroy Venegas gather all possible treasure urgently in order to aid the Spanish and British armies waging battle at that very moment against Napoleon's troops.[56] The viceroy collected all the funds available including 900,000 pesos from the tobacco monopoly, 500,000 pesos from the Mexico City mint, and a relatively small donation of 88,000 pesos, collected between September and November.[57]

At the same time, the viceroy decided to approach the Mexico City Merchant Guild to contribute to another new short-term loan, emphasizing the "urgency of sending aid" to the Spanish patriot government. In fact, the correspondence of the viceroy reveals that his intention was not to ship the

53 The Merchant's Guild of Veracruz was responsible for the payments being liquidated "by presenting a guarantee in his favor (the moneylender) with a signed receipt on the reverse": *Diario Mercantil de Veracruz*, 6 de marzo de 1810, BN (Madrid), sección de raros, R/60136.

54 The correspondence on Fleming's visit to Puebla and Mexico City in AGN, *Archivo Histórico de Hacienda*, vol. 766, exp. 1.

55 After departing from Veracruz, the *Bulwark* called at Havana where it probably collected additional sums, arriving at Cádiz on December 19, 1810 with 1,566,244 pesos of American silver: J. Canga Argüelles, *Observaciones sobre la historia de la guerra*, vol. 1, p. 162.

56 In one of his letters to the viceroy, Cockburn called attention to the recent victory of Wellington over troops commanded by the French General Massena. It should be noted that the anxiety of the English captain to load more wealth was not disassociated from the fact that all British naval commanders usually charged between 1 and 2% commission on shipments of silver to Europe. For the correspondence of Cockburn with the viceroy, see AGN, *Marina*, vol. 144, fs. 254–255. For a discussion of the commissions, see G. Jiménez Codinach, *Gran Bretaña y la independencia de México*, Chapter 4.

57 Documentation about the origins of the funds sent in the *Implacable* is to be found in AGN, *Marina*, vol. 144, fs. 253–265.

money but to replenish the already depleted colonial treasury. Nonetheless, the wealthier merchants did not hesitate to cooperate. Not surprisingly, the biggest contributor was Antonio Bassoco, once again advancing the colossal individual sum of 200,000 pesos, although other merchants were not far behind, such as Ramón Fernández (100,000), the Count de la Cortina (100,000), Pedro Echeverría (100,000), and Tomás Acha (100,000). They were followed by another sixty merchants who contributed smaller amounts, for example Pedro Alles (25,000), the Marguis de Inguanzo (25,000), José Vicente Olloqui (20,000), and Diego de Agreda (30,000).[58]

In the case of short-term loans, it was assumed that the lenders would be reimbursed quite quickly. On the other hand, providing long-term credit in late colonial Mexico was more risky, which made investors wary and made it more difficult for the government to collect money with speed. This was the case of the enormous twenty million peso patriotic loan requested by the Central Junta of Spain on January 10, 1810. The first negotiations for this huge credit began in early May in Mexico City but collection was delayed for several months. The exorbitant loan was severely criticized by different members of the elite, in particular, Bishop Abad y Queipo who considered that the funds could only be obtained by exercising unheard-of pressure on the population.

Government officials in Mexico City, nevertheless, were confident that the great loan could be collected successfully "through the merchant guilds of Mexico, Guadalajara and Veracruz." To entice investors, higher interest rates were offered, and the merchant guilds were named as intermediaries to obtain subscriptions. (For details see Appendix III.2.) They were also offered receipts from an increase in sales tax (*alcabalas*) charged at Acapulco as well as other tax income. Two members of each merchant guild in the viceroyalty attended the first meeting on May 19, 1810, in Mexico City to discuss the loan: Gabriel de Yermo and the Count de la Cortina from the Mexico City guild, José Ignacio de la Torre and Pedro Miguel Echeverría from the Veracruz merchant guild, and Juan José Cambero and Eugenio Moreno de Texada, representing the Guadalajara guild. They agreed not to publish the proclamation until September 25, when the viceroy formally invited the three merchant guilds to proceed with the subscription. Nevertheless, investment was extremely slow. By the end of 1812, only 983,000 pesos had been raised, mainly subscribed by ecclesiastical corporations which contributed mostly silver ornaments, and individual investors, many of whom deposited family silverware in the government treasuries.[59] These

58 The complete lists were published in the *Gaceta de México*, December 7 and 11, 1810, and supplements.

59 The texts of the Royal Order and documents of the Council (*Junta*) are published in Juan E. Hernández y Dávalos, *Historia de la guerra de independencia*, vol.2, docs 14 and 15.

extraordinary contributions suggest the marked scarcity of hard currency which had begun to affect even the wealthiest sectors of Mexican society.

This last loan exhausted the patience of the propertied classes of New Spain and reduced possibilities of further contributions for the metropolis. The failure of the loan was confirmed by the testimony of Bishop Abad y Queipo, one of the most lucid and informed minds on colonial financial matters. Responding to the requests of the merchant guilds to lend money, the skeptical bishop remarked that he did not believe the twenty-million-peso patriotic loan could be paid back:

> it would seem impossible to me that it can be realized completely or in part. Not completely because there is not enough hard cash in the kingdom to cover it without taking all the silver from the churches and all the silverware that is the property of individuals, both of these dangerous methods in the critical circumstances in which we find ourselves.[60]

For Abad y Queipo, the Mexican economy simply could not provide more money to the state: the catastrophic agrarian crisis (1809) had caused a steep drop in agricultural production; trade was increasingly stagnant and money was becoming scarce in all regions. Except for "some ten or dozen mercantile houses in the cities of Mexico and Veracruz," traditional credit networks had been devastated:

> We see all commerce constrained, bills delayed, and nobody able to make the stipulated term payments on credits. . . . All this is the effect of the impolitic and ruinous contributions and other extraordinary extractions that have left the viceroyalty without savings and without the necessary cash for business and trade.[61]

The viceroyalty of New Spain, however, faced not only an economic recession but also an imminent political crisis. The outbreak of popular insurrection in Guanajuato in September 1810, led by the revolutionary priest Miguel Hidalgo, marked the start of ten years of violent and extensive conflict throughout Mexico, later known as the wars of independence. After the outbreak of domestic warfare, further attempts to seek financial support for the metropolis were bound to be much more difficult, as historian Luis Jáuregui has argued. The patriot subscription of March 1811 was the last used to exclusively support peninsular troops and hence forward, the colonial administration focused its efforts, financial and military, on defense of royalist positions within the viceroyalty itself.[62]

60 Cited in J. M. L. Mora, *Crédito Público*, p. 143.

61 Ibid., p. 143.

62 L. A. Jáuregui, "La anatomía del fisco colonial," p. 266. Nevertheless, it should be observed that L. Alamán, *Historia de México*, vol. 2, pp. 235–236, affirmed that the last loan for the peninsula was in August 1811.

The Importance of the Flows of Mexican Silver to Europe: A Recapitulation

While the remittance of tax funds and loans from Mexico was subsequently suspended, it is important not to underestimate the astounding volume of silver sent to Cádiz between late 1808 and early 1811. This fact has been largely ignored by traditional as well as most modern historiography. In the short period between October 1808 and February 1811, the value of official remittances to Spain from Mexico amounted to twenty-four million silver pesos, an average of almost one million pesos per month. (See Table 7.4.) This was approximately half of the total amount of silver minted in the viceroyalty, to which should be added the considerable sums exported on private account, especially by the great merchants of Mexico City and Veracruz who were desperate to recover their control of transatlantic trade.[63]

The official silver exported represented a significant drainage of resources, and therefore implied significant costs for the Mexican economy. On the other hand, from the perspective of the patriot government at Cádiz, the silver flows were a crucial lifeline. The enormous transfers of silver were critical for the financial sustenance of the Spanish patriot armies and administration in Andalusia as they struggled to contain the advance of Napoleon's troops. In this sense, the viceroyalty of New Spain performed a key role in defending the mother country against the French invaders. Without Mexican silver, neither the Regency nor the government of the Cortes of Cádiz could have survived the powerful offensive of the Napoleonic army, particularly during the terrible years of 1809–1811.[64]

The information presented here on the volume of Mexican silver remittances calls for a revision of the interpretation of such influential historians as Joseph Fontana who have argued that the Spanish American contribution was substantial but not decisive to the war effort of the patriots.[65] Fontana argues correctly that in Catalonia, Valencia, and northern Spain, patriot resistance against the French invaders was financed locally. However, the situation was different in Andalusia, where the seat of patriot government remained throughout the war. From the data we have presented in this

63 For details on royal remittances in these years, see Carlos Marichal "Beneficios y costes fiscales del colonialismo," pp. 490–505.

64 The issue is analyzed in C. Marichal, "Beneficios y costes fiscales."

65 J. Fontana and R. Garrabou, *Guerra y Hacienda*, p. 97, state that between 1809 and 1814 the patriot government collected some 1,500 million *reales*, of which around 600 million came from American remittances, abundant up to 1810 but in rapid decline after 1811. However, it is more pertinent to focus on the contrast between periods; in 1809–1811, total income was 1,000 million *reales*, of which 60% came from the Americas; while in 1812–1814, according to Fontana, income was 500 million, of which scarcely 5% were funds from the colonies.

Table 7.4. *Government Silver Remittances from Spanish America to Cádiz, 1808–1811*

Date of Arrival at Cádiz	Names of Ships	Port of Departure	Amounts of Silver Pesos Transported
December 24, 1808	British warship *Diamond*	Veracruz	1,696,344
December 24, 1808	British warship *Melpomene*	Veracruz	1,605,446
January 6, 1809	Spanish warship *San Lorenzo*	Havana	121,659
February 1, 1809	Spanish warship *San Justo*	Veracruz and Havana	6,753,133
August 6, 1809	Spanish warship *San Francisco de Paula*	Veracruz and Havana	3,361,869
August 10, 1809	Spanish brigantine *San Miguel*	Honduras	205,567
August 17, 1809	Spanish warship *San Fulgencio*	Callao de Lima	1,415,122
December 1, 1809	Spanish frigate *San Prueba*	Montevideo	152,959
December 22, 1809	Spanish warship *San. Ramon*	Veracruz	1,500,000
January 19, 1810	Spanish frigate *San Francisco de Borja*	Campeche	21
February 17 and 18, 1810	British warships *Undaunted* and *Ethalion*	Puerto Rico	2,369,971
March 12, 1810	Spanish corvette *Palomo*	Cartagena de Indias	44,636
March 16, 1810	Spanish frigate *Primera*	Callao de Lima	284,830
April 28, 1810	Spanish frigate *Joaquina*	Callao de Lima	310,235
May 2, 1810	Spanish warships *Asia* and *Algeciras*	Veracruz and Havana	4,146,189
May 4, 1810	Spanish brigantine *Alerta*	Cartagena de Indias	4,021
June 7, 1810	Spanish brigantine *Cazador*	Montevideo	24,904
June 24, 1810	Spanish corvette *Diamante*	Montevideo	13,182
June 24, 1810	Spanish frigate *Neptuno*	Callao de Lima	96,133
August 1, 1810	Spanish schooner *Correo Cármen*	Cartagena de Indias	638
August 7, 1810	Spanish frigate *Fuerte-hermosa*	Callao de Lima	230,518
August 25, 1810	Spanish brigantine *Catalina*	Veracruz	200
September 24, 1810	Spanish warship *Pedro de Alcántara*	Callao de Lima	1,726,016
October 6, 1810	Spanish frigate *Nicaragua*	Honduras	228,582
December 19, 1810	British warship *Bulwark*	Veracruz and Havana	1,566,244
February 18, 1811	British warship *Implacable*	Veracruz	1,530,000
February 22, 1811	Spanish warship *Astrea*	Callao de Lima	18,596
March 14, 1811	Spanish corvette *Nueva Atrevida*	Veracruz	1,000
		TOTAL	29,408,015

Source: José Canga Argüelles, *Diccionario de Hacienda*, vol. 1 (Madrid, 1833), p. 162.

chapter, it is clear that during the three years, 1809–1811, the treasuries of the patriot forces at Seville and Cádiz would have collapsed had it not been for the numerous shipments of silver from the colonies. These funds were successively destined to the sustenance of the Supreme Junta, the

Regency, and the Cádiz Parliament, as well as the armies of Andalusia and Extremadura. Without this transatlantic financial assistance, their destiny would have been highly in doubt.

At the same time, the Mexican silver shipments were of great significance for Great Britain, Spain's principal European ally against Napoleon. To begin with, the silver was required to assist Wellington's army in Portugal. Historians of British military strategy argue that, after naval defense, the Peninsular War was the most important priority in the struggle against Napoleon in Europe. The soldiers under Wellington were considered to be the ultimate bulwark of British influence on the continent. Nowhere else were so many troops of the regular British army and nowhere else were military expenditures so considerable. The latter were covered by sums authorized by the Parliament but a substantial portion came, indirectly, in the shape of Mexican silver: the British government taxed the colonial trades with Spanish America, and the Bank of England accumulated much silver on this account. These monetary resources were also indispensable to cover the numerous and large subsidies provided in cash to the allies of Great Britain in various parts of continental Europe engaged in war with France.[66]

These strategic interests also help explain the active role of the British Royal Navy in protecting both Spanish transatlantic shipping and the port of Cádiz during the Napoleonic onslaught. But there were also solid, commercial reasons for the participation of the navy in the Mexican silver shipments. During the war, British merchants took over much of Spanish American trade in Cádiz. English trading firms replaced most of their competitors in the supply of goods to be sent out to the Spanish American colonies and in exchange received most of the silver sent from the other side of the Atlantic to pay for these goods. As historians Francois Crouzet and Javier Cuenca have demonstrated in detailed studies, the British economy benefited markedly from the flexibility of its merchants in taking control of different international markets during the war years. The obstacles created by the continental blockade (set up by Napoleon) were overcome in good measure by contraband and new trading strategies, including the increasing control of the Spanish American commerce that went primarily through Cádiz. This allowed them to obtain a high percentage of silver and gold shipments which were indispensable to British military strategies but also for sustenance of the great trades with India and China. In this sense, providing naval protection for the port of Cádiz and the Spanish American fleets during the Napoleonic war proved to be one of the essential secrets of short- and long-term British economic and military success.

66 J. H. Sherwig, *Guineas and Gunpowder*, passim.

8

The Rebellion of 1810, Colonial Debts, and Bankruptcy of New Spain

In 1810, a few months before the outbreak of insurgency in Mexico, the erudite but pragmatic ecclesiastical administrator Manuel Abad y Queipo wrote to the Cádiz Parliament (*Cortes de Cádiz*): "Our American possessions and especially those of New Spain, are disposed to general insurrection if the wisdom of Your Excellencies does not prevent it." The enlightened bishop added that it would be necessary to abolish the tribute that weighed upon the Indian peasant towns and villages and smooth the other exactions that pressed upon the viceroyalty in order to partially remedy the effects of the "bad government of the reign of Don Carlos IV."[1] The parliamentary deputies at Cádiz took note of this and other reports arriving from the American colonies and proceeded to abolish the Indian tribute.[2] The remedy, however, was insufficient and came too late. Political discontent in the colonies had reached a boiling point and conflict was inevitable.

The collapse of the monarchy in Spain in 1808 and the birth of Liberal government at Cádiz in 1810 had pronounced repercussions across all of Spanish America. In most colonial territories the royalist authorities hung on to power, but insurgency spread rapidly, a clear sign that the days of the old colonial regime were numbered. The search for a new political order across the Hispanic world was unexpected and contradictory.[3] In several cities and regions in Spanish America where the colonial administration was relatively weak and local elites divorced from mercantilist policies, independence movements quickly triumphed. This was the case in Buenos Aires as well as in most of the rest of the viceroyalty of the Rio de la Plata,

1 Text of Manuel Abad y Queipo in José María Luis Mora, *Crédito Público*, pp. 146–147 [facsimile of the first edition of Mora's essays published at Paris, 1837].

2 The abolition was decreed by the *Cortes de Cádiz* on March 13, 1811, although it had been abolished previously in New Spain by Viceroy Venegas to arrest the massive insurrection led by Hidalgo from September 1810 on.

3 See the excellent account of the diverse revolutionary movements in John Lynch, *The Spanish American Revolutions, 1808–1826* (New York: W.W. Norton, 1973).

including Uruguay and Paraguay in the years 1810–1811. Similarly, in Chile, republican movements triumphed briefly between 1811 and 1814 although they were later repressed by royalist forces (sent by the viceroy of Peru), until in 1818 these forces were finally evicted and independence consolidated. Conservative forces and royalist military officers also stymied the initial success of insurgents in Caracas, leading to prolonged civil war in Venezuela and then in the neighboring viceroyalty of New Granada, where war between the royalist armies and insurgent forces, led by Simón Bolivar, ran for over a decade. In the silver-rich viceroyalty of Peru, on the other hand, the power equilibrium continued to be favorable to the colonial administration which was able to impose its will and impede insurgency for more than a decade.[4] From Quito to Lima and Potosí, royalists continued to govern until the early 1820s and, as a result, the traditional heart of Spanish administration in South America remained loyal to monarchy and empire.

In late colonial Mexico the royalist regime also held onto power until 1821, but it was confronted by extensive popular rebellions. The year 1810 signaled the outbreak of insurrection in Mexico, led by the soldier priests Miguel Hidalgo and José María Morelos, although colonial authorities and troops held sway in practically all cities for a decade. The revolts that broke out in central Mexico in September of 1810 were the prologue of an extended civil war (and, in many ways, also a class war), a conflict that confronted the viceregal administration and its allies (military officials, church hierarchy, and economic elites) with different rebel groups that enjoyed broad popular support.[5] The former kept control of the large colonial army and therefore the royalist administration remained in power, although forced to defend against extensive guerrilla warfare in the countryside.

During the years of domestic warfare, the great majority of the leading merchants, silver miners, and landowners of colonial Mexico remained closely identified with the traditional regime, with its hierarchic social and corporate order and its religious, political, social, and economic practices. Their interests lay in supporting the monarchy and the status quo, which explains why they were willing to finance the counterrevolutionary struggle.

4 On the counterrevolution in Mexico and Peru, see Brian Hamnett, *Revolución y contrarrevolución en México y el Perú: liberalismo, realeza y separatismo, 1800–1824* (México: Fondo de Cultura Económica, 1978).

5 Brian Hamnett, "Absolutismo ilustrado y crisis multidimensional en el período colonial tardío, 1760–1808," in Josefina Vázquez, ed., *Interpretaciones del siglo XVIII mexicano* (Mexico: Nueva Imagen, 1992), p. 78, points out that it would be tempting to postulate a polarization between Europeans and Americans (within the elite of New Spain) but that such an opposition never existed. The wealthy joined hands against the insurgents during the entire war. He argues that the polarization was propaganda invented by nationalists after independence.

Their loyalty to the Crown had been systematically demonstrated for decades and they continued to provide a series of smaller loans to the royalist forces that battled the insurgents within Mexico for another ten years. Yet both fiscal and financial resources of the colonial regime were already seriously depleted by 1810, and the wars only accentuated the growing insolvency.

Ten years of war caused the definitive bankruptcy of the viceroyalty of New Spain and help explain why the royalist administration collapsed so abruptly in 1821. But, as we have already seen in detail, the financial crisis had its roots in the prolonged drainage of tax funds and incessant demands for loans by the Spanish crown to pay for numerous international wars between 1780 and 1810. In previous chapters, we have provided estimates of the huge volume of tax remittances as well as loans raised in colonial Mexico. In this chapter, we provide estimates of total government debt outstanding in 1810 and years immediately following, distinguishing between creditor groups. These colonial debts increasingly became a source of grievances during the war years insofar as the royalist administration faced increasing difficulties in covering debt service. A provisional balance is presented of the different categories of debt as well as rough estimates of the capital depletion experienced by the privileged corporations, which participated in the royal loans up to 1810.

The Colonial Debt in 1810

While not underestimating the effects of aggressive tax policy of the Bourbon's administration, this book has devoted special attention to the colonial debt. Our study suggests that it is important to attempt to evaluate the impact of the government's debt policy on the society and the economy of Mexico, although there is a clear need for more research on its impact during the wars of independence and in the immediate postwar. The present study concludes with a more limited objective which consists in offering some quantitative estimates of the colonial debt by sector around 1810: here we summarize information on the loans, supplements, and donations studied in previous chapters.

On the basis of the abundant archival materials reviewed, it is possible to affirm that between 1780 and 1810 the royal administration in Mexico collected at least thirty million pesos from individuals and corporations in the shape of loans and five million pesos as donations, all of which were shipped abroad. These figures for total indebtedness are substantially lower than those of other historians, particularly Herbert Klein, who has suggested that the colonial public debt grew by leaps and bounds, particularly, after 1800. Klein's calculations of debt, however, are based on the annual treasury summaries (*cartas cuentas*), which should be disaggregated to avoid double counting and other accounting problems.[6] While our estimates of the government's colonial debt with the private sector are more modest, this does not imply that they did not have important economic consequences.

The argument made here is that one of the greatest disadvantages of the colonial debt was that the money lent (or donated) was not invested in Mexico itself but simply shipped abroad to pay for the military expenses and debts of the Spanish crown. The amounts lent were never returned by the principal debtor,the metropolitan treasury, which in fact required that both interest and principal be repaid to local investors by the treasuries of the viceroyalty. As a result, these colonial debts reduced capital assets in the economy and, at the same, increased the future tax burden of the inhabitants of New Spain. Their economic effects were altogether different from the adoption of a public debt policy in which government borrowing results in stimulus to the domestic economy by means of public expenditures. In contrast, the colonial debts were little more than a way of extracting private savings from New Spain's economy for transfer to the metropolis.[7]

A key issue then is to evaluate how important this debt was in terms of the principal sources of capital that colonial corporations, institutions, and individuals had available for investing in the economy.[8] To proceed with this discussion, it is useful to analyze the total amounts collected for the Crown by the various privileged corporations of colonial Mexico.

Among the most important contributions to the Crown were those realized by the wealthy members of the merchant guilds of Mexico City and Veracruz. Over the years the Mexico City Merchant Guild was responsible for the administration of seven interest-bearing loans between 1782 and

6 H. Klein, *Las finanzas americanas*, p. 112, affirmed that "loans and private subsidies reached 5.8 million pesos per year in the 1780s and 21.6 million pesos per year in the first decade of the new (19th) century." However, loans from the private sector to the Crown were actually much lower than these figures suggest as demonstrated by thorough analysis of the documents in the Archivo General de la Nación in branches such as "Préstamos y donativos" and "Consolidación." Nonetheless, further research is needed on the accumulated debts in specific branches of colonial treasuries, which should be treated separately from private loans. The considerable problems of double accounting from 1787 until the end of the colonial epoch are cited in P. Pérez Herrero, *Los beneficiarios del reformismo borbónico*, pp. 207–264, among other authors.

7 Abad y Queipo in J. M. L. Mora, *Crédito Público*, p. 129 wrote in 1810: "As the extraction of metallic currency from New Spain is without return and has exceeded annual minting, the lack of money in circulation is now felt and each day will be felt even more. . . . "

8 H. Klein, *Las finanzas americanas*, p. 150, argues "this tax on individual savings was in fact a tax on the local capital market." J. Coatsworth, "Obstacles to Economic Growth," 80–100, and E. Cárdenas, "Algunas cuestiones sobre la depresión mexicana," in E. Cárdenas, comp., *Historia económica de México*, pp. 27–56, refer to the problem of the impact of transfers (including the money for the loans) on New Spain's investment rate; nevertheless, in a later revision, J. Coatsworth, *Orígenes del atraso*, pp. 108–109, argues that he considers an increase in the availability of this capital would not have produced a substantial increase in investment.

Table 8.1. *Loans for the Spanish Crown Administered by the Mexico City Merchant Guild 1780–1811 (in Pesos)*

Year	Interest-Bearing Loans	Interest-Free Loans
1782	1,000,000	1,655,415
1790	100,000	
1793	1,000,000	
1794	1,000,000	
1795–1802[a]	3,100,000[b]	
1809	850,000	1,393,500
1810	983,000	2,500,000
1811		1,194,000
SUBTOTAL	8,033,000	6,742,915

Note: See Appendix III.2.

[a] The interest-bearing loans included subscriptions by a large range of investors. The interest-free loans were mainly advanced by the great merchant houses.

[b] The tobacco loan.

1810, in which investors subscribed more than eight millions pesos. (See Table 8.1.) Guild members contributed a considerable proportion of the relatively large loans with the silver assets which they habitually reserved for the import–export trade. When trade declined as a result of naval war, investing money in crown loans at a 5 percent interest rate could be considered a reasonable investment. But not all contributions came from the merchants since other social groups also invested significant amounts of money.

Somewhat different were the non-interest-bearing loans – called supplements – that were advanced to the Crown almost exclusively by the larger merchants of the viceroyalty in 1782, 1809, 1810, and 1811, for a grand sum of approximately of seven million pesos. While a portion of these funds were returned to the moneylenders, none of the funds borrowed by Crown in the last two years 1810 and 1811 were repaid, a fact which reduced confidence in official financial practice after the beginning of the insurgency.[9] As Guillermina del Valle has argued in a recent and detailed study, the late colonial emergency loans meant that:

> The merchant body changed from being a collector of capital from individuals and corporations that invested in order to receive a safe return, to operating as an instrument of the royal treasury to extract and withdraw from circulation money that Mexico City proprietors had put aside for periods of scarcity.[10]

9 The issue is analyzed in detail by G. Valle Pavón, "Consulado de Comerciantes," Chapter 7.

10 G. Valle Pavón, "Consulado de Comerciantes," p. 616.

Table 8.2. *Crown Loans and Donations Administered by the Mexico City Mining Tribunal, 1777–1810 (in Pesos)*

Year	Loans	Donations
1777		300,000[a]
1782	1,000,000	
1783		150,000[b]
1790		100,000[c]
1793	1,100,000	
1794	1,000,000	
1795–1802	3,700,000[d]	
1798		500,000
1805		300,000
1808		200,000
SUBTOTAL	6,800,000	1,550,000

Note: See Appendixes III.1 and III3.2.

[a] Donation for royal shipworks.

[b] Donation for the prince and princess of Asturias.

[c] Donation for the war with Algiers.

[d] Tobacco loan.

Another privileged corporation which operated as financial intermediary in the management and administration of royal loans was the Mining Tribunal of Mexico (*Tribunal de Minería de México*), representing the interests of the greatest mine owners in the viceroyalty. In toto, the Tribunal placed four loans for the Crown, raising 6,800,000 pesos (at a 5 percent interest rate) between 1782 and 1802, obtaining subscriptions from a broad range of investors, including silver miners, landowners, merchants, and ecclesiastical institutions. Later the mining association ceased to participate in new loans, although it continued to collaborate in various royal donations. (See Table 8.2.)

One of the most important objectives of the Mining Tribunal, when it was created in 1776, had been to promote silver production by facilitating credits to small, medium, and large miners in the viceroyalty. But the major part of the funds collected for capital accounts of the Tribunal (known as the *Fondo Dotal*) was not channeled to mining but rather went to crown loans and donations from 1782 on, as well as to cover interest payments and the amortization of the loans issued. Investors relied on both the Mining Tribunal and the royal treasury to guarantee the debt service.[11]

11 The Tribunal ensured that the royal treasury would pay the greater part of services on the credits they arranged as well as the return of part of the capital up to 1810, after which payments were notably reduced. For details, see E. Flores Clair, *Las deudas del Tribunal de Minería, 1777–1823*, passim.

An additional proof of the negative impact of the rise in government debt was the short duration of the remarkable initiative launched by the Mining Tribunal in 1784, the *Banco de Avío Minero* ("Bank for Mining Finance"), the first investment bank of the colonial period. Despite great initial hopes, the financial institution was quickly burdened with royal debts during its brief existence (1784–1787). As a result, the bank was not able to operate properly and suspended its credit operations with the miners. The distinguished director of the Mining College Fausto de Elhuyar later commented on the financial failure of the bank and the miners' association, arguing that their assets had become a resource for the government instead of a fund for the benefit of the miners.[12] This opinion has been confirmed by the recent research of historian Eduardo Flores Clair who writes:

> The mining guild considered itself obliged to mortgage its fund to cover the interest payments on the loans they had issued on behalf of the king.... The Tribunal's coffers were cleared out; the donation and loans (to the government) became yet another tax and a fetter for the mining industry.[13]

Among all New Spain's corporations it was the church that made the greatest contributions to the Crown's war loans and donations. An extremely diverse range of ecclesiastical institutions participated in eleven loans and five donations, although the respective contribution to the Crown of the different participants was variable. (See Table 8.3.) The largest were the tobacco loan collected between 1795 and 1802 and the Consolidation Fund, between 1805 and 1809.[14]

We have previously argued that the church loans for the monarchy weakened the most important network of credit in the viceroyalty. The large sums of money dispatched to Cádiz between 1781 and 1811 were never to return and therefore caused a depletion of capital available for lending and investment inside Mexico. In this instance, it would be appropriate to speak of displacement of private creditors by the Crown. The application of the Consolidation Fund (*Consolidación de vales reales*) led to disentaliment of many religious properties and to the impoverishment of a great number of religious financial entities in all regions of Mexico. Perhaps most serious was the fact that debt service to investors proved irregular before 1810 and discontinued afterward. Information about interest payments paid by the government to ecclesiastical institutions is scarce, but it is established that in the case of the more than ten million pesos ceded to the Consolidation Fund, the principal was never returned and interest payments

12 See Elhuyar's text in W. Howe, *Mining Guild*, p. 383.

13 E. Flores Clair, *Las deudas del Tribunal*, p. 34.

14 As argued in Chapter 4, the delivery of funds for the Consolidation amounted, in effect, to a gigantic loan, on which the Crown offered to pay 3% interest per year.

Table 8.3. *Loans and Donations of the Catholic Church in Mexico to the Crown, 1782–1810 (in Silver Pesos)*[a]

(a) *Loans for the Crown*

Year	Church Subscriptions	Total value of Loans	Church Subscriptions/ Total Loan (%)	Intermediaries
1782	353,000	1,000,000	35.3	Merchant guild
1782	226,000	1,000,000	22.6	Mining Tribunal
1783	460,000	523,376	88.0	Royal treasury
1793	1,320,000	1,559,000[b]	84.7	Royal treasury
1793	160,000	1,000,000	16.0	Merchant guild
1794	477,500	1,000,000	47.8	Merchant guild
1793–1802	3,526,000[c]	9,272,264[d]	38.0	Mining Tribunal and Merchant guild
1805–1808	9,571,800	10,321,800[e]	92.7	Royal treasury
1809	173,000	3,176,835	5.4	Merchant guild
1809	314,000[b]	1,393,500	22.5	Merchant guild
1810	997,300	2,010,000	49.6	Merchant guild
SUBTOTAL	17,578,600			

(b) *Donations for the Crown*

Year	Church Contribution	Total Donation	Church Contribution/ Total Donation (%)
1782–1784	39,643	843,474	4.7
1793	141,000	460,714	30.7
1795	299,000[f]	701,552	42.6
1798	413,000[f]	2,118,914	19.5
1805	100,000[f]	497,557	21.1

[a] In this chart, we include contributions by all the religious institutions, cathedral chapters, bishoprics, chaplaincies, pious works, convents, religious colleges, seminars, etc.

[b] Interest-free loans.

[c] This is an estimate of the church participation based on the 38 per cent of church participation in the interest-bearing loans of 1782–1794, which is clearly documented.

[d] This is the sum of the 1793 and 1794 loans administered by the Mining Tribunal and the tobacco loan of 1795–1803.

[e] The sum of the Consolidation loan also includes 750,000 pesos contributed by the Indian towns.

[f] Estimates based on sources in Appendix III.1.

Sources: See tables in Valle Pavón (1997) as well as sources cited in Appendix III.2. On the donation, see tables in Rodríguez Venegas (1996) and Appendix III.2.

were extremely meager.[15] The result was a virtual expropriation by the metropolitan treasury of many of the principal sources of capital and credit in the colonial economy.

What was the effect of the transfer of these funds on New Spain's finances and economy overall? This question is not easy to resolve, not least because reliable estimates of the stock of total investment and annual investment rates are not yet available. However, it would seem perverse to argue that the transfer of loan funds to the metropolis did not have an effect on the investment path of the economy of colonial Mexico.[16] Given the reduced size of financial markets in this period, thirty million pesos drained from elites and corporations cannot be considered a small sum.[17] Our hypothesis is that metropolitan financial demands debilitated the colonial economy – through the constant borrowing in the form of royal loans – and so depressed private investment.[18]

Until the end of the colonial period, there had existed an extensive credit system and a relatively complex (if not very deep) capital market in Mexico. This is attested by recent work on the financial operations of the merchant guilds of Mexico and Veracruz and the Mining Tribunal as well as by studies on the numerous loans and credit extended by religious and pious organizations to merchants, rentiers, landowners, and silver miners, all of which provide testimony on the vigor of credit and financial markets in New Spain.[19] When the royal administration contracted the Mexico City

15 In Spain the monies obtained from the Consolidation were never returned to the church. See the comments on unpaid debt service in J. Fontana, *La quiebra de la monarquía absoluta*, pp. 415–418.

16 J. Coatsworth, *Orígenes del atraso*, p. 109, considers that the reduced annual investment rate would have amounted to a million pesos per month, which according to his calculations represented about 5% of total annual investment. He discounts the cumulative effect of this figure over a thirty-year period, stating that the inflation would have minimized its economic contribution. Also see two articles by David Brading "Facts and Figments in Bourbon Mexico," *Bulletin of Latin American Research*, 4, 1 (1985), 61–64 and "Comments on 'The Economic Cycle" that advance similar arguments.

17 R. Garner and S. E. Stefanou, *Economic Growth and Change*, pp. 12–14, and Richard Salvucci, "Economic Growth and Change in Bourbon Mexico: A Review Essay," in *The Americas*, 51, 2 (1994), 219–231, estimate the gross product of New Spain at 200 million pesos. But, what was the size of the capital market? As yet there are no reliable estimates: contemporaries suggested that the total capital stock of religious foundations at the end of the eighteenth century was around 40 million pesos, although the majority was in the form of outstanding loans; to this should be added the funds administered by nonecclesiastical corporations (such as the merchant guilds) and investors.

18 Economists use the expression "crowding out" which is considered prejudicial when government expenditure refinances existing debt rather than making physical investments. Such was the case in New Spain, with funds transferred to cover metropolitan debts and not invested in the viceroyalty.

19 See, among others: P. Pérez Herrero, *Plata y libranzas*; G. Valle Pavón, "Consulado de Comerciantes"; M. Souto "Consulado de comercio"; G. Von Wobeser, *El crédito eclesiástico en Nueva España*; E. Flores Clair *Las deudas del Tribunal*; D. Ladd, *Mexican Nobility*; and L. Greenow, *Credit and Socioeconomic Change*.

Merchant Guild and Mining Tribunal as intermediaries for successive credit operations, it contributed to a process of change in these markets as a result of the introduction of new credit instruments and new practices for their purchase and sale.[20] The privileged corporations of New Spain, as well as many wealthy individuals, invested their funds because the interest rates were relatively attractive, although there were some exceptions as in the case of non-interest-bearing loans, issued on various occasions in wartime situations.

But since the viceroyalty's financial markets were neither broad nor deep, many of the government demands had a profoundly negative influence. This is documented in the extended protests against the Consolidation Fund by merchants, miners, landowners, and farmers, as we have seen in Chapter 4. The appropriation by the Crown of the loan capital of hundreds of religious institutions was a clear example of the disadvantages that the emergency financial policies of the Crown had for both entrepreneurs and the church. In sum, the principal defect of the colonial debt was that the collected monies were not spent in New Spain but were sent abroad. Royal debt policy extracted private capital stock which could have been invested productively, and – we may add – in Bourbon Mexico the number of actual and potential investment opportunities was not negligible before 1810.[21]

Finally, it is important to evaluate the impact of government debt on savings in the community funds (*cajas de comunidad*) of rural villages. The social groups which suffered most from the fiscal and financial demands of the Crown were precisely those least prepared to resist the impact, namely, the Indian peasant communities. Specific case studies confirm the exploitation. Studies by historian Dorothy Tanck and other colleagues illustrate how the functionaries of the royal treasuries progressively took control of the communal funds of peasant villages and towns throughout the viceroyalty. (See Table 8.4.)

The greater part of the monies extracted was used to cover financial demands of the monarchy in Spain.[22] In the case of Yucatan, over a period of thirty years, a total of 400,000 pesos was taken from Indian village

20 G. Valle Pavón, "Consulado de Comerciantes," provides the most detailed analysis.

21 Investment in mines, estates and sugar mills, roads (especially between Mexico and Veracruz), as well as the great program of public works and urban building at the end of the eighteenth century are outstanding examples. Both R. Garner and S. E. Stefanou, *Economic Growth and Change*, and C. Marichal, "La historiografía económica reciente" give full bibliographical references to useful studies on the evolution of different sectors in the Mexican economy during the eighteenth century.

22 D. Tanck, "Escuelas y cajas de comunidad," analyses this process in the Yucatan and M Terán,"Muera el mal gobierno" for Michoacán, examining the diverse ways by which, from 1780, the royal officials ("Intendentes" and Subdelegados) progressively took over the administration of the communal treasuries of the Indian towns.

Table 8.4. *Loans and Donations to the Crown by the Indian Towns of Mexico, 1780–1810 (in Pesos)*

Donations	
1780–1781	400,000[a]
1793–1802	616,659
1809–1810	300,000[b]
Loans	
For Banco de San Carlos (1783)	134,300
For Compañía de Filipinas	98,187
For royal War loans 1793–1801	707,803
For Royal Consolidation Fund	750,000
SUBTOTAL	2,698,918

[a] Rodríguez Venegas (1996) provides archival lists.
[b] Estimates based on Tank (1994) and Franco (1988).

funds: in 1790, royal officials used 50,000 pesos taken from these communal treasuries to buy stock of the Bank of San Carlos in Madrid; in 1796 another 80,000 pesos was loaned to the Crown (with the tobacco monopoly acting as guarantor); between 1807 and 1808 almost 200,000 pesos were sent from the Yucatan villages to the Consolidation Fund in Madrid; and in 1809 a donation of 32,000 pesos was made "for the mother country that has been invaded by the perfidious Napoleon."[23]

Throughout the viceroyalty the situation was similar. The Indian towns had already contributed heavily to the Crown decades before – as revealed by the more than 400,000 pesos they were forced to make to the universal donation in the years 1781–1783 – and to the donations and loans in 1793, 1795, and 1798, totaling more than 800,000 pesos.[24] And between 1805 and 1808 the Indian communities were forced to disburse to the *Juntas de Consolidación* the enormous sum of 670,000 pesos.[25] Such forced contributions undermined the foundations of rural community finance that

23 D. Tanck, "Escuelas y cajas de comunidad," pp. 430–436.

24 D. Tanck, "Protesta indígena al rey," p. 27, mentions that: "Between 1793 and 1801 the *cajas de comunidad* (of New Spain) bestowed several donations to the king: 50,072 pesos in 1793; 11,638 pesos in 1795; and 122,445 pesos in 1799. Donations totalled 184,155 pesos. Also, the communal funds lent 644,500 pesos to the government (during this period)." The author quotes as one of the most comprehensive sources, AGN, *Consolidación*, vol. 10, fs. 395 and 395.

25 D. Tanck, *Pueblos de indios*, Chapter 4, presents accurate figures on payments by the *cajas de comunidades* of the Indian republics. The amount was comparable to the total sum of funds contributed to the *Consolidación* by the entirety of nun convents, which were the religious institutions that had most capital and properties in New Spain. On the latter, see A. Lavrin, "Execution of the Laws," 41.

traditionally fulfilled many important economic functions and also provided monetary reserves for hundreds of thousands of peasants in Bourbon Mexico at times of agrarian crises.[26]

By late 1809, the ecclesiastical hierarchy began to express concern about the drain of resources from the peasant villages and protested to financial officials. Archbishop Manuel Vázquez de León criticized the measures decreed by the Royal Legal Counselor of the Indian Communities (*Real Fiscal Protector de Naturales*) Vicente Rebolledo, ordering that two-thirds of the monies in the communal funds of Indian towns should be used "as a donation during the War." The archbishop reminded Rebolledo that the Indian peasants had already made important contributions to the donation and had also " . . . ceded their stock of goods and even the capital and interest that belonged to them to the Consolidation Fund."[27]

Incredible as it may seem, the royal officials were not satisfied with the contributions obtained from the Indian peasant population but rather attempted to increase them by even more rigorous tax collection.[28] As Luis Jáuregui points out, Viceroy Lizana (formerly archbishop who on other occasions had expressed his concern for the Indians' fate) decided it was necessary to extract as much money as possible from the rural communities to comply with the demands of the royal purse. In March 1810, the viceroy requested the office of fiscal accounts (*Tribunal de Cuentas*) to apply an increase in the tribute rates. The officers replied that this measure was not possible but added that it might be possible to increase the number of taxpayers (*tributarios*) by an acceleration in reproduction rates of Indian peasant women. The argument was crudely disguised:

> An increase in tribute (can be obtained) by multiplying the number of Indians, blacks and free mulattos.... Increased income can come from multiplication of marriages which is the Catholic means for increasing the population . . . and brings the benefit of giving new life to people, injecting them with greater love for the government and invigorating the true strength of the State . . . [29]

26 Indian communities claimed more than once that the funds they had been forced to advance to the Banco de San Carlos did not yield interests in cash, but were only paid with *vales reales*, a kind of debt instrument that did not circulate in any significant quantities in New Spain. See the letter dated July 27, 1804, from Iturrigaray to Soler where he describes the misery of Indian communities. AGN, *Correspondencia de Virreyes, 1a serie*, vol. 219, file 533, f. 231.

27 Letter, November 6, 1809, AGN, *Donativos y Préstamos*, vol. 12, f. 17.

28 Margarita Menegus, "Los bienes de la comunidad y las reformas borbónicas, 1786–1814," in *Estructuras agrarias y reformismo ilustrado en la España del siglo XVIII* (Madrid: Ministerio de Agricultura, 1989), p. 389, points out that the the sum of monies from communal treasuries transferred to the Crown treasury in Mexico in 1809 was over 180,000 pesos.

29 Quoted in L. Jáuregui, *La real hacienda de la Nueva España*, p. 215.

In summary, the Crown's fiscal policy weighed unequally on New Spain's population, with traumatic effects on the peasant communities.[30] But it was precisely the most productive rural sectors – which had accumulated savings – that suffered the most and to such an extent that by 1810, the more prosperous Indian peasant towns no longer had much left in the way of communal monetary reserves.

Preliminary estimates allow us to conclude that the total amount contributed by Indian towns in colonial Mexico between 1780 and 1810 in the shape of loans and donations for the Crown reached almost 2.7 million pesos. Virtually no interest was ever paid on this large sum, and the principal was never returned to the owners. The approximately 4,500 Indian peasant villages depended on these resources for a variety of economic, political, religious, and educational needs, as described in previous chapters. The decapitalization of the extensive network of what may be described as the savings and loan system of the Mexican peasantry represented an extremely severe blow to a predominantly agrarian society.[31]

Colonial Debt in the Early Years of Insurgency: The Bankruptcy of the Viceroyalty

As a result of the outbreak of insurgency and war, the royal administration began progressively to suspend service on debts, which now constituted a major burden. The bulk of fiscal income was devoted to paying the loyalist military forces that struggled to contain numerous rebellions throughout the viceroyalty. The result was a growing tax crisis. In a thoughtful study on the gradual disintegration of New Spain's fiscal system, historian John TePaske has suggested that the war of independence was, in itself, the cause of a dramatic decline in the efficiency of tax policy and administration, reducing revenues as well as transfers between treasuries. Political and military conflicts spurred a centrifugal process that advanced with great rapidity, disarticulating the complex, fiscal and financial system of the Bourbon

30 The success of the donation was extraordinary as indicated by reports from the far-off province of New Mexico, more than 2,000 kilometres to the North of Mexico City. In this sparsely populated territory, the royal officials forced the traders and small cattlemen, as well as the Indian communities to contribute money and in-kind, resulting in 117 pesos in metal, together with 218 blankets (*sarapes*), 149 *fanegas* of corn, 52 tanned hides, 18 strings of chiles, and 32 garlic plants. In the case of Indian women from the village of San Felipe, it was reported that they were obliged to contribute apiece one peso of silver and one buffalo hide! See Marc Simmons, *Spanish Government in New Mexico* (Albuquerque: University of New Mexico Press, 1968), p. 93.

31 M. Terán, "Muera el mal gobierno," p. 177, argues that Bourbon policies led to the reduction of autonomous control of the Indian towns, including the loss of control over the communal treasury and the total loss of surplus monies. The consequence, she argues, was decapitalization of the towns.

regime.[32] As a result there was a steep fall in ordinary tax income of the royalist administration which never returned to the levels attained before 1810.[33] The information on total gross revenues of various regional treasuries is indicative of the dramatic decline in income, but much further research is required to clarify this fundamental issue in detail.[34]

The decentralization of income and expenditure – especially in these areas where there was most intense military conflict – led to a marked reduction in the transfer of funds from the silver-producing districts to the treasuries of Mexico and Veracruz. John TePaske argues: "Most significantly, though, the independence movement marked the end of remissions of tax receipts to Mexico City from the wealthy mining districts and other treasuries of the viceroyalty."[35] The immediate consequence was that there were no longer available funds for the remittances abroad (*situados*), which had traditionally been essential to the sustenance of the Spanish colonies in the greater Caribbean. The result was, inevitably, that after 1810 the viceroyalty began to cut its links to the rest of the empire as a result of the abrupt decline in shipments of tax monies abroad.

The reduction in tax income obliged the royalists to seek new methods of financing military obligations. The war against the insurgency gave birth to new forms of exactions which included not only extraordinary taxes but also expropriations and forced loans. However, these instruments were also applied by insurgent armies and, as a result, this gave rise to a system of "double taxation" which may be described as the coexistence of the traditional royalist tax administration with the emergency finance of the insurgent forces.

From 1810 onward, certain members of the colonial elite in Mexico expressed their concern with regard to the effects of war and debts on the administration's solvency and emphasized the difficulties in repressing the

32 John Jay TePaske, "The Financial Disintegration of the Royal Government of Mexico during the Epoch of Independence," in Jaime Rodríguez O., ed., *The Independence of Mexico and the Creation of the New Nation* (Los Angeles: University of California Press, 1989), pp. 63–84.

33 Important studies on the fiscal and financial crises during the wars of 1810–1820 include Luis Jáuregui, *La Real Hacienda de Nueva España*; Timothy Anna, *La caída del gobierno español en la ciudad de México* (Mexico: Fondo de Cultura Económica, 1981); John J. TePaske, "The Financial Disintegration of the Royal Government of Mexico" and "La crisis financiera del virreinato de Nueva España a fines de la colonia," *Secuencia*, 19 (1991), 123–140; G. Valle Pavón "Consulado de Comerciantes"; María Eugenia Romero Sotelo, *Minería y guerra: la economía de la Nueva España, 1810–1821* (Mexico: El Colegio de México, 1997).

34 Numerous tables on fiscal income are included in John J. TePaske, "The Financial Disintegration of the Royal Government of Mexico, in particular in pages 74–83. However, most of these use aggregate data. Future studies should carry out more detailed analysis in order to reach more definite and precise conclusions on the evolution of each of the major tax branches and the principal, regional trends during the wars of independence.

35 John J. TePaske, "The Financial Disintegration of the Royal Government of Mexico," p. 73.

insurgency and the economic effects of the interruption of much transport and commerce. Successive viceroys requested support to finance the fight the war against the insurgents and received considerable support from the wealthiest groups in colonial society. But progressively, the financial contributions decreased as many members of the colonial elite argued that the volume of loans and donations advanced in preceding years had drained their personal resources, and therefore did not allow them to provide more money for the royal administration.

The result was a financial crisis that was explicitly confirmed by the reports of a commission of financial experts in 1813 who evaluated the level of government debt and proposed remedies to attempt to maintain service payments in the midst of war. In the pages following, we comment these reports in some detail insofar as it is important to be aware of the opinion of those contemporaries who had the best information on the evolution of royal finances.

In 1813, Viceroy Calleja gave instructions for the organization of a special financial commission (*Junta Permanente de Arbitrios*) to analyze the fiscal and debt situation of the government.[36] Calleja wished to obtain greater financial stability for his government and to open up the possibility of new loans for military operations. But the trends of fiscal receipts were not encouraging. According to the decree of April 17, 1813: "The Public accounts are in agony . . . with a monthly deficit of 260,000 pesos, consuming all public funds and exhausting all ordinary and some extraordinary financial instruments. . . . "[37] To attempt a debt conversion would not be an easy task, since investors resented the suspension of debt service on an already long sequence of loans and donations collected before 1810 and, even more, the forced loans decreed since the outbreak of the insurgency. This was confirmed in a key report on the situation of the finances of the viceroyalty at the end of 1813. The collective authors were wealthy individuals and high-level functionaries with a profound knowledge of the economic status of the royal administration: the group included one of the wealthiest miners of Mexico José María Fagoaga, the director of the Mining College, Fausto de Elhuyar, the rich Veracruz merchant Tomás Murphy, the great landed proprietor José Martínez del Campo, and the knowledgeable

36 On the several debt commissions formed between 1810 and 1812, see L. Jáuregui, *La real hacienda de la Nueva España*, Chapter 6. The *Junta Permanente de Arbitrios*, constituted in 1813, was made up of the Intendant of Mexico, Ramón Gutiérrez del Mazo, an ecclesiastical representative, Andrés Fernández Madrid, a representative of mine owners, José María Fagoaga, two representatives from commerce, Antonio Bassoco and Tomás Murphy, the head of the royal treasury of Guadalajara, Antonio Medina, and the accountant of the Central Army (*Ejército del Centro*), Francisco Javier de Aramberri. L. Jáuregui, *La real hacienda de la Nueva España*, pp. 266–270, analyzes the activity of this commission in detail.

37 Cited by L. Jáuregui, *La real hacienda de la Nueva España*, p. 266.

and sophisticated treasury functionary Antonio Medina. Their report included a debt summary and an estimate of potential tax income, as well as numerous penetrating observations on the evolution of public and private finance during the war.[38]

The debt summary in this report was entitled, "Approximate state of the national debt up to the end of June, 1813" and showed that the cumulative debt incurred by the government with corporations and individuals amounted to 32 million silver pesos.[39] Of this total, 4.3 million pesos consisted of old debt (*juros antiguos*) as well as loans placed between 1782 and 1795, an additional 6.9 million pesos still outstanding from the tobacco loan (collected between 1795 and 1802), 10.5 million pesos from the Consolidation Fund (1805–1808), some 5 million pesos provided in loans to the patriot government in Seville and Cádiz in the years 1808–1811 for the struggle against Napoleon, and, finally, 5.4 million pesos in forced and voluntary loans to finance the war against New Spain's insurgents, between 1810 and 1813.

The members of the commission calculated that 1.2 million pesos were needed annually to meet debt service costs, a sum that could have been collected had it not been for the increase of military expenditures which had doubled since the outbreak of insurgency.[40] Owing to the reduction in available revenues, it was necessary to resort to credit to ensure that the royalist forces could advance in territory controlled by rebels and bandits and, eventually, reopen roads blocked by insurgents, a situation that had caused commercial and fiscal crises in those areas.[41]

As a result of the increase in military expenditures, remittances to Spain and to colonial garrisons in the Caribbean had been suspended from mid-1811. The Commission added that "there would be no funds for the Peninsula for many years." In spite of the suspension of tax remittances,

38 The reference is to *Memoria instructiva y documentada del estado comparativo de la Real Hacienda del año de 1809 anterior a la revolución, con el de 1812 en que estaban destruidas por ella el comercio, la agricultura, las artes y la minería*, *Biblioteca Nacional de México*, ms. 1282. This document was accompanied by a proposal for the consolidation of the debt of the government of New Spain, prepared by Antonio Medina. I wish to thank Guillermina del Valle for directing my attention to this document.

39 Ibid.: *Estado aproximado de la deuda nacional hasta fin de junio de 1813*. It is somewhat curious that the term "national" was used while making reference to the debt of the colonial administration. This showed the adoption of the same vocabulary used in the financial documents of the Cádiz Parliament of 1810–1812.

40 According to the Commission, the military and administrative domestic budget in a year of peace was around 5.5 million pesos, while during the war it was estimated to have increased to around 9 million pesos. However, the Commission did not have detailed income and expenditure documentation for each of the regional treasuries, 1810–1813. *Memoria instructiva* (1813), fs. 45–46.

41 See, in particular, the *Memoria instructiva* (1813), f. 31, which pointed out that "the general obstruction of the roads" made collection of the sales (*alcabalas*) and tobacco taxes difficult.

additional loans were needed by the royalist authorities in Mexico. Without them there was the possibility that the insurgents would paralyze the economy, provoking the final breakdown of business activities in New Spain.[42] In order to attract economic elites, the Commission advised that it would be necessary to guarantee debt service payments and the amortization of the original capital. They noted:

> Most borrowed sums have not been returned and a great and considerable amount of interest (in arrears) has not been paid.... Here is the origin of the public's lack of confidence and the reason that the government has exhausted its resources.[43]

Debt service payments had been maintained with a certain regularity until the outbreak of the rebellion, 1810, but subsequently became less punctual, to the point that it is possible to speak of a partial suspension of debt payments by the government. Numerous proprietors and wealthy taxpayers refused to continue supplying financial assistance to the administration. As historian Josefa Vega has argued in a study on the forced loan of 1812:

> Their arguments were almost always the same: the ruin of their estates and commerce by the insurrection and, above all, the failure to return their previous loans, the many patriotic subscriptions and the continuous requests for donations.[44]

With the hope of resolving this dilemma, the royal treasury official, Antonio Medina, proposed a plan in 1813 to consolidate the debt and ensure its service.[45] The idea was to imitate the British Treasury by establishing a sinking *fund* to which a series of fiscal incomes would be assigned: among them a portion of sales taxes (*alcabalas*), taxes on wax and cocoa, and some tobacco monopoly income. Medina suggested, as well, that a direct contribution on property would be helpful to stabilize the finances of New Spain. With these innovations, the treasury expert expected that the government could renew service on loans advanced by the merchant guilds and by the Mining Tribunal, and perhaps even have success in

42 The Commission noted that already before the war, the economic situation had worsened because of the heavy taxes for the Consolidation, just as the 1809–1810 loans brought a deep scarcity of precious metals "in the Kingdom because of the cash deficit needed by the political system" *Memoria instructiva* (1813), f. 25; the reference is clearly to the traditional policies of sending fiscal contributions (*situados*) to the Caribbean and remittances to the metropolis.

43 Ibid., f. 32.

44 Josefa Vega, "Los primeros préstamos de la guerra de independencia, 1809–1812," *Historia Mexicana*, xxxix, 4 [156] (1990), p. 930.

45 Antonio Medina was a finance official of the royal treasury in Guadalajara and was well known for his broad knowledge of finance. Later he would serve as the first Finance Minister during the government of Iturbide, 1821/1822, and as author of the first Ministry of Finance Report (*Memoria de Hacienda*) of the independent regime.

having the public debt securities circulate as means of payment or as credit instruments.[46]

But the intensification of guerilla warfare in many regions of Mexico condemned to failure Medina's projected consolidation. With the benefit of hindsight, it can only be characterized as utopian. Nevertheless, it should be noted that senior treasury officials had long kept up their hope of military improvements and an economic recovery, which might allow creditors to renew their previously substantial contributions to the government. A report on New Spain's debt in 1817 affirmed that: "the sum of 8,897,082 pesos has been paid to the capitalists on loans worth 22 million pesos issued since 1794, and now only 3.8 million pesos are owed in back interest."[47] Apparently the officials did not consider the partial default as definitive. But in fact there was no longer a real possibility of regaining the confidence of the propertied sectors that had long demonstrated their loyalty to the colonial regime.

The royalist troops in Mexico continued to fight the insurgents – essentially rural guerrillas – for several years until September 1821 when in a rather abrupt about-face, the officers of the colonial army, led by General Agustín Iturbide, decided to conclude the war and declare independence from Spain. It was clearly the war that finally undermined the royal administration, but the weakening of the fiscal and financial system was also a key factor. Increases in military expenditure reduced the capacity of the government to cover its debt service and – as we have argued – provoked a growing crisis in colonial financial markets and the despair of the wealthiest sectors of colonial society: they were soon engaged in capital flight to save a part of their fortunes. Perhaps the drama of the situation is best captured in the succinct words of one of the most knowledgeable experts of the viceroyalty's public and private finances, Manuel Abad y Queipo, who had foretold the bankruptcy as early as 1810:

> These facts and their consequences are demonstration enough that New Spain contributed more than it could. They show that the funds were not inexhaustible, as believed, but are actually exhausted.[48]

These circumstances would not be reversed. On the contrary, during the ten years of war (1810–1820), the fiscal and financial machinery of the colonial treasuries would be progressively weakened until their final collapse, sealing the fate of an imperial regime that had lasted for more than 300 years.

46 Ibid., fs. 33–35.

47 "*Sobre la deuda de la Real hacienda y medio de reestablecer su crédito*," México, 21 de febrero de 1817, *Biblioteca Nacional de Madrid*, ms. 19.702/23.

48 Abad y Queipo in J. M. L. Mora, *Crédito Público*, p. 96.

Conclusions: The Financial Collapse of Viceroyalty and Monarchy

The fiscal and financial crisis of New Spain's colonial administration after 1810 was not a singular event. It was part of a much broader debacle. The finances of other Spanish American viceroyalties were also crumbling, slowly but surely. As a result of the wars of independence (1810–1825), the Spanish empire progressively disintegrated into a multitude of fragments, eventually to reconstitute in an extraordinary mosaic of new and distinct nations. At the same time, the heart of the old monarchy, Spain itself, suffered military defeat and confronted the deepest bankruptcy.[1] There was thus a striking symbiosis in the prolonged collapse of colonial regime and metropolis. This would appear to be a frequent lesson of the downfall of imperial states through much of history, ancient and modern.

This study has called attention to the interlocking relationship between imperial wars and the incessant fiscal and financial exactions of the metropolitan state from its richest Spanish American colony during the half century spanning the decades 1760–1810. Even though these contributions to the Crown were sustained and large, they only could delay the final debacle. In the end, all financial expedients were vain. The silver obtained from New Spain through taxes, *donativos*, numerous loans, and the Consolidation Fund was absorbed by military expenditures and by the service on domestic and foreign debts taken by the Spanish government to pay for the international wars in which the Crown engaged almost incessantly. By 1810, the governments of both viceroyalty and monarchy were bankrupt.

This would seem to be a straightforward empirical conclusion. But are there any larger lessons to learn from our study of the fiscal and debt dynamics of the viceroyalty and of the Spanish empire in its final decades? More specifically, how does it contribute to a deeper understanding of the logic of imperial finance? Most important, our analysis illustrates the inextricable nature of many of the links between the different component parts of the imperial state. The Spanish empire was the most integrated of all European imperial states of the era. Metropolis and colonies were bound together by

1 The classic study is J. Fontana, *La quiebra de la monarquía absoluta*.

a web of administrative, military, fiscal, and financial relations that were inherent to survival. These bonds were reinforced by the demands of each successive Atlantic war, although military conflict certainly placed increasingly severe strains upon the colonies and, in particular, on the viceroyalty of New Spain because of the enormous volume of fiscal and financial resources transferred abroad.

The Fiscal and Financial Burden of Colonialism in New Spain

The demands of war finance gradually outstripped the tax base of the viceroyalty despite the extraordinary silver boom of the late colonial era. But prior to the wars of independence, there were few possibilities of modifying imperial tax or financial policies. The viceroy and other officials responsible for the colonial administration obeyed the orders of metropolitan government to their ultimate consequences. And since there were no elective legislatures in the viceroyalty, colonial taxpayers were simply obliged to contribute. Nonetheless, it is important to evaluate the overall economic and fiscal consequences of such policies. Our interpretation tends to underscore the negative effects of royal fiscal and financial practice on New Spain's economy and society.

During the last decades of the eighteenth century and the first of the nineteenth, increasing amounts of the colony's revenues and capital resources (collected from all of the inhabitants of the viceroyalty) were being exported to Spain. These transfers illustrate the remorseless fiscal logic of the Spanish imperial state. The policy stood in contrast to other European states that had never been able to obtain significant fiscal remittances from their colonies in the Americas but rather had been obliged to finance the greater part of the costs of their empires, with funds sent from the metropolis.

However successful the Bourbon tax reforms may be considered from an imperial perspective, they certainly proved to be a significant burden for New Spain. Indeed, some historians have argued that the aggressive tax and loan policies of the late Bourbon regime and those of the wars of independence not only drove the colonial administration into bankruptcy but also affected the future economic evolution of Mexico. Hebert Klein argues:

> The massive exploitation by the crown of the accounts of the colonial treasuries after 1780 – both for the increase for the colonial *situados* and the considerable increase of capital transfers to Spain through forced and voluntary loans – indicates that fiscal policies . . . were one of the most important factors in the economic decline of Mexico during the wars of independence.[2]

2 H. Klein, *Las finanzas americanas*, p. 174.

While it is not our purpose here to evaluate the postcolonial impact of these fiscal and financial policies, the present book certainly provides a general panorama of the long-term tax trends and estimates of the debt burden in the richest colony of the Spanish empire that can be useful for future debates on the costs of colonialism. Between 1760 and 1810, the tax records show that the treasuries of colonial Mexico transferred abroad the enormous sum of more than 250 million pesos, somewhat over 40 percent of total taxes collected in the viceroyalty. This was the effective *fiscal cost* of being a colony. Of this amount, approximately 100 million pesos were sent to other Spanish American colonies and the Philippines to help pay local costs of royal administrations there (as *situados*); the balance, 150 million pesos, was sent to the metropolis as a net fiscal transfer.[3] It can be calculated that New Spain's treasuries exported, on average, 8 million pesos of tax funds per annum during the three final decades (1780–1810) of colonial rule – a figure that bespeaks significant costs to the local economy and society since none of these monies were ever returned.

In a previous chapter, it was estimated that each inhabitant in New Spain paid in taxes approximately 3.6 silver pesos per year during this period. If the external transfers (tax transfers to the metropolis and to other Spanish American colonies) had not been realized, New Spain's annual tax burden would have been reduced by approximately 1.5 silver pesos per capita, on average, for the period 1780–1810.[4] If multiplied by 5, this would have implied that each Mexican family would have retained as their own income almost 8 silver pesos more per year. This income, in the hands of the taxpayers, would certainly have generated greater consumption, but might also have increased savings. According to Richard Salvucci, per capita subsistence income in 1800 was close to 34 pesos a year.[5] An increase of 4–5 percent in available income would have inevitably stimulated the expansion of the production of the most important commodities consumed by the

3 Calculations based on the series are found in C. Marichal and M. Souto, "Silver and Situados," 587–613, for the eighteenth century, plus the nine million peso estimate for transfers to the Caribbean from 1801 to 1809 by J. von Grafenstein, *Nueva España en el Circuncaribe*, pp. 315–317, plus the five million pesos sent to Philippines as *situados* between 1780 and 1804, plus the direct remittances to Spain and its official creditors in Europe between 1800 and 1810, which sum seventy million pesos, as seen in the information in Chapters 5–7.

4 The total population is estimated to be five million inhabitants in 1780 and close to six million in 1810. There were a small percentage of Bourbon Mexico's inhabitants who were not taxed because of exemptions or geographic isolation, including clergy, slaves, and isolated indigenous communities.

5 R. Salvucci, "Mexican National Income in the Era of Independence," p. 225, calculates an annual per capita subsistence income of 34 pesos: in this case an increase of 1.5 pesos in per capita consumption would have implied an increase of almost 3–4% per annum of total consumption.

colonial Mexican population: food and textiles.[6] With regard to savings, it may be presumed that wealthier groups would have increased their silver holdings or invested them in trade or enterprise.

Some authors, particularly John Coatsworth and David Brading, have claimed that an increase in silver available would have implied an expansion of the viceroyalty's monetary base and generated higher inflation than occurred; in such a case, the benefits of the fiscal saving might not have been significant.[7] These views, however, are not corroborated by the research of Richard Garner, who has provided the most detailed economic analysis of the period. Garner argues that in spite of the systematic increase in production and minting of silver coins (1.4 percent per year during the eighteenth century) there was only a slow rise in prices, especially of maize, the most important food product of the population of New Spain. The increase was not exceptional, averaging 0.5 percent per annum during the eighteenth century, with sharp peaks only at the time of serious agrarian crises.[8] In other words, it would appear that in the long run, relative price stability was maintained despite the enormous increase of silver produced and minted in the viceroyalty. At the very end of the colonial era, there was a significant shift upward in prices but also a decline in living conditions. In the most detailed study of consumption in this period, the historian Enriqueta Quiroz has demonstrated that in the decade 1800–1810 there is clear evidence of a sharp increase in food commodities in Mexico City and, simultaneously, a marked drop in consumption, particularly among the poor and working classes.[9]

Evidently, the economic and social analysis of the impact of the external transfer of an enormous accumulation of tax resources from colonial Mexico over various decades remains an open question. John Coatsworth

6 An increase in production would depend on avoiding supply bottlenecks of agricultural and textiles production, but most research on Mexico's economy for this period do not find evidence of such bottlenecks and demonstrate that there was a sustained increase in agricultural output and cattle products which surpassed population growth: R. Garner and S. E. Stefanou, *Economic Growth and Change*; J. C. Garavaglia and J. C. Grosso, "De Veracruz a Durango"; *Las alcabalas novohispanas, 1776–1821*, Mexico, AGN, 1987; and *Puebla desde una perspectiva microhistórica*; E. Van Young, *Hacienda and Market in Eighteenth Century Mexico* and Jorge Silva, "Producción agropecuaria y mercados regionales: el caso de Michoacán en el siglo XVIII," Ph.D. thesis, El Colegio de México, 1997.

7 David Brading, "Comments on 'the Economic Cycle in Bourbon Central Mexico," *Hispanic American Historical Review*, 69, 3 (1989), 531–538 and J. Coatsworth, *Orígenes del atraso*, pp. 108–109.

8 "Corn price levels only moved up slowly over the very long term. This suggests that inflation, as measured by corn was not much of a threat.... Indeed, it can be argued that over the long term corn prices were so low and supplies so ample that without making production more efficient a (large) producer had trouble earning a big enough profit to justify or encourage investing further in grain or food production." R. Garner, and S. E. Stefanou, *Economic Growth and Change*, pp. 28–29.

9 Enriqueta Quiroz, *Entre el lujo y la subsistencia: mercado, abastecimiento y prcios de la carne en la ciudad de México, 1750–1812* (México: El Colegio de México, Instituto Mora, 2005), p. 242.

has proposed estimates of the net exports of fiscal resources at somewhere between 5.0 and 7.5 percent of the annual gross annual product of the viceroyalty.[10] This is a big figure and the drainage of this wealth from New Spain would merit more research, especially if we consider that in *ancien regime* economies annual investment rates were extremely low. In any case, the funds sent abroad can be seen as a net export of capital without any compensation or return payment. On balance, a majority of historians believe this capital drain had a negative overall effect on New Spain's private economic activity. The following scenario may be a useful point for comparison: what would happen if an independent country had to contribute the equivalent value of 40 percent of its exports abroad without trading or financial recompense, as was the case for New Spain between 1790 and 1810? It does not seem possible that this would not have a depressing effect on the economy.[11] The economic historian Enrique Cárdenas has recently summed up the situation in a survey which argues that the Crown's appropriation of these resources severely prejudiced New Spain's economic performance in the first decades of the nineteenth century.[12]

The systematic and often coercive nature of the fiscal campaigns throughout Mexico during the final decades of the colonial regime has been a constant theme through this book. Yet the relative scarcity of tax revolts in Bourbon Mexico (with some localized exceptions) also raises many questions regarding the social impact of imperial tax policy and practice. The contrast with the great tax rebellions in the 1780s in the viceroyalties Peru and New Granada is striking. This is all the more surprising since the rigorous fiscal and financial policies applied in New Spain were the most extensive and efficacious in Spanish America in the second half of the eighteenth century. To all appearances, until the outbreak of rebellion in 1810, popular perceptions of tax pressures in New Spain did not radically conflict with the political and social consensus underlying this particular colonial society. In previous chapters, we have argued that such circumstance suggests that the majority of New Spain's population continued to accept the legitimacy of

10 J. Coatsworth, *Los orígenes del atraso* (México: Alianza Mexicana, 1990), pp. 85–87 and 108–109 and J. Coatsworth, "La independencia latinoamericana: hipotesis sobre los costes y beneficios," in Leandro Prados de la Escosura and S. Amaral, eds., *La independencia americana: sus consecuencias económicas* (Madrid: Alianza Universidad, 1993), pp. 20–21.

11 In this regard, it seems that the arguments of R. Garner, and S. E. Stefanou, *Economic Growth and Change*, Chapter 7, are conclusive.

12 With regard to exports of collected taxes and the possible effect on contemporary investment rates, E. Cárdenas, "Algunas cuestiones sobre la depresión mexicana del siglo XIX," in Enrique Cárdenas, comp., *Historia económica de México*, vol. 2 (Mexico: Fondo de Cultura Económica, 1990), p. 41, affirms: "These figures show fully the real size of the colonial tax burden imposed on New Spain. If a part of this net savings had been used in productive projects, such as transport facilities, Mexico's economic growth model would probably have been very distinct from the one that it experienced."

the viceregal government in an implicit agreement that may be called the "fiscal constitution" of the colonial regime.[13]

No one explanation, however, can account for the duration of fiscal consensus in increasingly difficult circumstances at the turn of the century. Consequently, it might be suggested that future research should concentrate on exploring various complementary approaches to construct an historically convincing interpretation of the considerable political and fiscal passivity in New Spain before 1810.[14] Future studies of the colonial tax system would do well to explore the intersection of three different levels – economic, social, and ideological/religious – that undoubtedly played an important role in popular opinion and perceptions in New Spain before the breakdown of consensus in 1810.

The extraordinarily complex mix of cultural and ideological factors that influenced the course of social discontent and insurrection between 1810 and 1820 has recently been studied in-depth by Eric Van Young: he suggests that the many internal conflicts that broke out in New Spain from 1810 must be understood in terms of a multicausal model in which the imperial crisis should be linked to the agrarian and fiscal crisis to explain the intensification of violent social tensions that finally expressed themselves in popular mobilizations on both political and military fronts.[15] Clearly, insurgency was not caused solely by the fiscal policies of previous decades, but the latter certainly played an important role in gradually undermining the legitimacy of the colonial regime.

Apart from taxes, understanding late colonial finance also requires analysis of the colonial debts imposed by the royal administration. Despite the fact that the fiscal screws were turned ever more harshly from the 1780s, this proved insufficient for the many, exacting metropolitan demands. As a result, treasury officials in Mexico looked with increasing frequency to the raising of donations and interest-free loans as well as to a succession of interest-paying loans in order to obtain additional funds. The funds obtained were sent almost in entirety to the metropolis but it was the colonial administration and taxpayers who were expected to pay the service and capital of these debts, which by 1812 surpassed thirty million pesos, a large sum for the time.

13 We have already referred to this point in Chapter 2. The issue is also raised in María del Refugio González, "La intervención del Estado en la economía y la sociedad en México: sus orígenes y desarrollo. Una propuesta de interpretación," *Mexican Studies*, 5, 1 (1988), 25–41.

14 E. Van Young, *La crisis del orden colonial*, pp. 9–15 and 335–428, makes a number of penetrating observations about the complex relationship between ideology and material conditions in his analysis of the origins of the rebellions that began in 1810.

15 Eric Van Young, *The Other Rebellion: Popular Violence, Ideology, and the Mexican Struggle for Independence, 1810–1821* (Stanford, CA: Stanford University Press, 2001).

Here we are confronted with a great paradox, which we have attempted to explain but must be reemphasized: while coercion was a frequently used instrument to obtain extraordinary resources from the viceroyalty, many wealthy individuals and privileged corporations in New Spain openly collaborated with enormous sums extended to the monarchy for its war efforts. Why they contributed remains an open question. We have suggested that there was clearly a *quid pro quo*, since loans to the Crown ensured the continuity of extraordinary privilege for the wealthy in a society with great swaths of impoverished social groups.[16] But is this an entirely adequate answer?

Our chapters analyzing the loans offered to the Crown by the great merchants, miners, and landowners suggest the enormous concentration of wealth in late colonial Mexico: there is no doubt that the rich, privileged corporations of the viceroyalty were intent on maintaining the status quo unchanged. Equally significant were the financial contributions of the Catholic Church, the great ally of the state for over three centuries of colonial rule. However, the application of so many extreme financial measures affecting religious foundations and especially the Consolidation Fund in 1805–1808 gradually undermined the alliance between the church and the Crown. It proved no surprise that many of the most severe critics of the late colonial regime were clerics nor that the rebellions that broke out against Spanish rule in 1810 were led by revolutionary parish priests like Miguel Hidalgo and José María Morelos. In any case, the information presented in this study on tax and debt policy provides a good deal of hard evidence which can be of use to future studies that propose to explore the enormous tensions and difficulties that the Mexican economy would subsequently confront in the transition from colony to independent nation.

But, again, let us broaden our perspectives by suggesting that the analysis of the finances of Bourbon Mexico is of interest for broader comparative purposes. For example, it is relevant to future comparative work on the finances of the other Spanish American colonies, with which New Spain had diverse and complex links. But it is also of considerable interest for the comprehension of the financial trajectory of the Spanish monarchy itself. In the final analysis, the deficits of the metropolitan government were the root and cause of the aggressive tax and financial campaigns applied in late colonial Mexico. The estimates we have presented in previous chapters clearly indicate the crucial importance of the colonial remittances in the midst of the gravest wars of the late Bourbon regime, although even such large transfers of Mexican silver were insufficient to save the Crown.

16 On this subject, also see Pedro Pérez Herrero, "Los beneficiarios del reformismo borbónico: metrópoli versus élites novohispanas," *Historia Mexicana*, xii, 2 [162] (1991), 207–264.

The Bankruptcy of the Spanish Monarchy and Its Consequences

The bankruptcy of the empire was even more pronounced at the core than in the periphery. Fiscal revenues in metropolitan Spain stagnated from the late 1790s as did expenditures and public debts which increased spectacularly. The financial crisis of the monarchy, already visible in the last years of the eighteenth century, would deepen with remarkable rapidity in the following decade. Studies on this subject by Pedro Tedde suggest that while the monarchy of Charles III (1759–1788) was able to successfully meet the challenges of reinforcement of empire, the finances of the Spanish state began to sink under Charles IV (1789–1808).[17] This collapse cannot be understood without taking into account the debilitating effects and enormous expense of waging successive wars in the Americas and in Europe. The Napoleonic invasion broke the back of the Spanish monarchy, but it was simply the most devastating culmination of this period of international military strife.

Regular tax revenues had gradually increased in Spain from the 1760s to the mid-1790s. Contributions in the shape of direct tax transfers from Spanish America – mainly Mexico and Peru – were considerable but did not generally surpass 15 percent of the ordinary income of the General Treasury in Spain. In other words, during this period the metropolitan government was able to pay for most of its own expenses: the main fiscal contribution of the colonies was to finance the empire. But from the 1790s, as the metropolitan government accumulated enormous deficits, colonial silver remittances became crucial to the Treasury at Madrid. It was particularly as a result of the war with the French Convention that expenditures and deficits exploded. To make matters worse, after the outbreak of the First Naval War with Britain in 1796, ordinary tax income collected in the metropolis dropped more than 40 percent and remained at this low plateau until 1808. The decline was compensated for in part by huge remittances of official silver from Mexico and the other Spanish American colonies: we have provided estimates of how crucial the remittances of American tax silver became. But even these faltered after the beginning of the Second Naval War with Britain in 1805 which caused a dramatic decline in transatlantic shipping with Spanish America.

Yet it was not only tax trends which underlay the eventual bankruptcy of the Crown; domestic debt policy and practice also failed in the first years of the new century. The metropolitan treasury was not able to guarantee the service on the huge volume of domestic debt securities, known as *vales reales*, issued to the tune of almost 2 billion *reales* (100 million silver pesos or dollars) between 1782 and 1807. These debt instruments helped

17 Pedro Tedde, "Crisis del Estado y deuda pública a comienzos del siglo XIX," *Hacienda Pública Española* 26 (1987), pp. 169–195.

pay for extraordinary military expenditures but – as we have seen – their market value fell markedly after 1797, with only a temporary recovery in 1802–1803.[18] As a result, each time the government of Charles IV sought emergency finance, it reaped less and less cash and yet was committed to pay higher interest payments.[19] Worse, the debt assumed by the government also implied a double burden since the issue of the *vales reales* obliged the state treasury to assume the mortgage on the great mass of properties of the Catholic Church that were disentailed between 1798 and 1808. As a result, by 1807, the total debt of the Consolidation Fund in Spain surpassed 3.3 billion *reales*.

In addition to this huge sum, it is necessary to add the 250-million *reales* (12.5 million silver pesos) of debts which we have calculated were due on the operations carried out by the Consolidation Fund in Spanish America. These were capital assets taken by the Crown from religious foundations in all the colonies, and disproportionately from Mexico, which provided some 80 percent of the funds exported from Spanish America on this account to Spain. These extortionate policies caused a virtual collapse of rural credit markets in the viceroyalty of New Spain. It was expected that the metropolitan treasury would return this sum eventually, but it never did so.

The treasury of Charles IV confronted less critical problems with the foreign debts, but again, this was due to the special financial contribution of colonial Mexico. The service on the bulk of the various loans issued in Holland from the 1780s until 1807 was covered basically with Mexican tax silver remittances. As may be observed in the majority of the Dutch loan contracts taken by the Spanish crown, it was specified that debt service would be guaranteed with bills on the Mexican royal treasuries. (See Appendix III.3.) After the Napoleonic invasion, however, debt service on these loans was interrupted, not to be renewed until the early 1820s.

War aggravated the financial problems of the Crown, particularly the external demands imposed upon Charles IV by his wartime allies, which included the expensive cooperation of the Spanish Navy with France (during several decades) as well as the subsidy payments demanded by Napoleon from October 1803 onward. The Spanish General Treasury was unable to cover the subsidy payments and, therefore – as we have seen – ingenious expedients were devised to obtain Mexican silver for their fulfillment. Once again, the richest colony was to save the metropolis from insolvency.

Finally, it is worthwhile commenting on the role of American tax and loan remittances to Spain after 1808, which have been described in Chapter 7.

18 The fluctuations in the quotations of the *vales reales* (see Figure 4.2) offer an instructive guide to the degree of confidence of investors in future payment by the government.

19 Furthermore, by the time of the Napoleonic invasion, less than 10% of the original *vales reales* had been amortized. See Miguel Artola, *La hacienda del Antiguo Régimen*, pp. 455–458.

The Napoleonic invasion implied the virtual defeat of the Spanish monarchy and the appropriation by the French of fiscal resources in most of the Iberian Peninsula. The patriot armies struggled bravely to resist but, in practice, had few domestic fiscal resources once forced into refuge in Cádiz. Nonetheless, the relation with the colonies across the Atlantic saved the Liberal government at Cádiz. Despite the cracks in the empire, the remittances of American treasure to the metropolis were not interrupted between 1808 and 1811 – a fact that reflected the continued vigor of the colonial treasuries. These shipments of American monies (the bulk from New Spain) were initially used in part to support the patriotic councils (*juntas patrióticas*) that sprang up in different Spanish regions from June 1808. Subsequently, in 1809, the silver was used to finance the three-man Regency as well as the Central Junta at Seville. And finally, when the Army of Andalusia was forced to beat a retreat and fall back to the southern port city of Cádiz, the colonial silver remittances served to finance both the defense of this last outpost of Spanish resistance and the ordinary expenses of the extraordinary experiment in Liberal government, known as the *Cortes of Cádiz* (Cádiz Parliament) of 1810–1812.

Spanish American silver remittances, nonetheless, would not continue indefinitely. The outbreak of rebellions in three of the viceroyalties (Buenos Aires, New Granada, and New Spain) from 1810 onward marked the beginning of the end for the integrated fiscal system of the Spanish imperial state. Combined with the financial crisis of the absolutist monarchy, this circumstance helps to explain the failure of the absolute monarch Ferdinand VII in his persistent attempts to recover the Americas after his return to power in Madrid in 1814. The Spanish state no longer had the military, naval, or fiscal strength to maintain a vast and far-flung empire. On several occasions, the absolutist regime sent the remains of its once important fleet and significant portions of its army to South America between 1815 and 1824 but failed in the bid to recover empire.

The bankruptcy of the metropolitan treasury of the monarchy implied that the costs of waging war against the insurgent movements in Spanish America during the years 1810–1824 had to be covered fundamentally by the respective colonial administrations. The royalist authorities in Mexico spent the bulk of their fiscal resources to finance the struggle against the rebel movements between 1810 and 1820 as did the royalists in upper and lower Peru during the war years of 1818–1824. But in the colonies – as in the metropolis – the cumulative burdens of more than thirty years of financing the wars of the Spanish crown had severely weakened the royal administration as well as the fiscal and financial structures on which it depended. The wars of independence would eventually destroy both.

The main objective of this book has been to emphasize the importance of the fiscal and financial *antecedents* of the final bankruptcy and breakdown of royal administration in late colonial Mexico. We have argued that the major cause of this bankruptcy – which clearly reached its apogee during the wars of independence in the years 1810–1820 – was generated, in good measure, by the previous and incessant metropolitan demands to cover the costs of war and of the debts of the monarchy, particularly in the decades of 1790–1810.

Was there any alternative to participation in the wars that swept Europe and the Atlantic or to the financial maelstrom in which the monarchy of Charles IV was engulfed? This remains an open question. In the event, by the time of the Napoleonic wars, Spain had become but a pawn of the more aggressive European powers and was soon subject to the most violent and prolonged invasion in its history. These events shook the Spanish empire to its roots. While the Spanish American colonies were not so directly affected by European military events, the fiscal and financial pressures continued to intensify as a result of war demands and skyrocketing royal debts. Imperial bankruptcy was the prelude to the wars of independence.

Appendixes

Appendix I

Monetary Equivalents in the Late Eighteenth Century

A silver peso in colonial Mexico was worth eight silver *reales* and each *real* was worth twelve *granos*.

In Spain one silver peso was equivalent to twenty reales de vellón, the monetary unit most common there.

For additional details on the Spanish monetary system at that time, see Bernardo García Martínez, "El sistema monetario de los últimos años del periodo novohispano," *Historia Mexicana*, xvii, 3 [67] (1968), 349–360.

Exchange Rates. From 1783:

One silver peso was equal to one silver dollar;
one silver *real* was worth the equivalent of twelve cents;
one *grano* was worth one penny.

Before 1776, there was a substantial difference in the trade value of these coins between England and its colonies. In England the Spanish milled dollar (silver peso) was worth anywhere between 4s. 3d. and 4s. 6d. st., up to 4s. 9d. st. In New York, however, the Spanish milled dollar was rated by custom at 8s., in Pennsylvania at 7s. 6d., and in Virginia it was worth 6s. 8d. by 1764. These variations were also common in other regions and markets around the world.

Generally speaking, at this time 1 silver peso was equivalent to approximately 5 francs and to 1.7 Dutch florins.

The prices of silver varied in relation to gold. The variation of silver against gold after 1760 was not trivial. The ratio of gold to silver in 1760–1769 was about 14.51:1.00. In 1780–1789, it was 14.45:1.00, and in 1781, it hit 13.33. In this sense, the Mexican silver boom of the late eighteenth century tended to erode the metal's purchasing power when converted to gold prices.

For details, see "The Real Exchange Rate of the Mexican Peso, 1762–1812: A Research Note and Estimate," *Journal of European Economic History*, 23, 1, (1994), 131–140.

Table I.1. *General Treasury of Spain, Income, 1763–1811 (in millions of reales[a])*

Years	Ordinary Tax Income from Spain	Income Sent from the Indies	Indies as Percentage of Total	TOTAL
1763	416,854	58,056	12.22	474,910
1764	396,633	55,923	12.36	452,556
1765	402,453	88,075	17.96	490,528
1766	377,455	63,635	14.43	441,090
1767	384,356	78,162	16.90	462,518
1768	382,340	65,593	14.64	447,933
1769	391,856	17,839	4.35	409,695
1770	350,147	109,487	23.82	459,634
1771	367,308	12,241	3.23	379,549
1772	349,468	94,688	21.32	444,156
1773	351,053	32,055	8.37	383,108
1774	352,702	134,503	27.61	487,205
1775	348,477	67,125	16.15	415,602
1776	361,752	80,021	18.11	441,773
1777	390,050	21,659	5.26	411,709
1778	408,797	123,970	23.27	532,767
1779	427,300	10,349	2.36	437,649
1780	706,776	5,329	0.75	712,105
1781	627,975	33,346	5.04	661,321
1782	709,885	4,826	0.68	714,711
1783	503,624	18,883	3.61	522,507
1784	515,720	79,903	13.42	595,623
1785	548,013	43,942	7.42	591,955
1786	519,586	77,143	12.93	596,729
1787	533,063	67,217	11.20	600,280
1788	572,371	85,152	12.95	657,523
1789	498,084	24,767	4.74	522,851
1790	515,963	100,768	16.34	616,731
1791	514,289	161,269	23.87	675,558
1792	499,275	130,331	20.70	629,606
1793	473,391	141,728	23.04	615,119
1794	509,316	195,718	27.76	705,034
1795	595,364	138,764	18.90	734,128
1796	698,473	236,896	25.33	935,369
1797	664,232	12,360	1.83	676,592
1798	516,480	131,800	20.33	648,280
1799	460,132	90,861	16.49	550,993
1800	436,576	1,326	0.30	437,902
1801	432,619	341	0.08	432,960
1802	485,817	350,195	41.89	836,012
1803	561,257	240,260	29.98	801,517
1804	689,239	291,200	29.70	980,439

Years	Ordinary Tax Income from Spain	Income Sent from the Indies	Percentage	TOTAL
1805	473,285	50,073	9.57	523,358
1806	499,508	40,820	7.55	540,328
1807	552,545	2,751	0.50	555,296
1808	n.i.	n.i.	n.i.	n.i.
1809	126,577	295,000	76.03	388,000
1810	150,500	250,500	62.47	401,000
1811	260,000	73,000	21.92	333,000

[a] The equivalency is one silver peso = twenty reales vellón.

n.i., no information.

Sources: José Patricio Merino, *Las cuentas de la Administración central española, 1750–1820* (Madrid: Instituto de Estudios Fiscales, 1987); Carlos Marichal, "Beneficios y costes fiscales del colonialismo: las remesas americanas a España, 1760–1814," *Revista de Historia Económica*, xv, 3 (1997), 475–505.

Table I.2. *Fiscal Transfers from New Spain to the Caribbean and Spain, 1720–1799 (Five-Year Totals)*

Five-Year Periods	Situados to Caribbean[a] (in Silver Pesos)	Remittances to Spain (in Silver Pesos)	TOTAL	Situados (%)	Spain (%)
1720–1724	4,499,062	3,234,788	7,733,850	58.17	41.83
1725–1729	3,085,054	3,059,482	6,144,536	50.21	49.79
1730–1734	4,197,179	5,106,367	9,303,546	45.11	54.89
1735–1739	4,656,450	4,373,282	9,029,732	51.57	48.43
1740–1744	6,912,558	1,690,717	8,603,275	80.35	19.65
1745–1749	8,959,912	4,532,150	13,492,062	66.41	33.59
1750–1754	5,617,366	4,988,090	10,605,456	52.97	47.03
1755–1759	10,287,737	7,186,906	17,474,643	58.87	41.13
1760–1764	12,490,166	4,375,698	16,865,864	74.06	25.94
1765–1769	12,415,397	1,962,393	14,377,790	86.35	13.65
1770–1774	15,239,170	5,895,231	21,134,401	72.11	27.89
1775–1779	19,299,632	8,455,391	27,755,023	69.54	30.46
1780–1784	39,182,777	6,644,404	45,827,181	85.50	14.50
1785–1789	22,466,573	9,911,646	32,378,219	69.39	30.61
1790–1794	23,185,235	24,323,787	47,509,022	48.80	51.20
1795–1799	24,118,964	18,850,747	42,969,711	56.13	43.87

[a] *Situados* were remittances to Spanish administration and military garrisons in Cuba, Puerto Rico, Santo Domingo, Trinidad, Florida, and Louisiana.

Source: J. J. TePaske and H. Klein, *Ingresos y egresos de la Real Hacienda de Nueva España*, 2 vols. (Mexico: Instituto Nacional de Antropología e Historia, Colección Fuentes, 1986–1988).

Table I.3. *Silver Coin Mintage and Remittances by the Royal Treasuries of New Spain*

Years	Remittances to Castille (Silver Pesos)	Remittances to Caribbean (Silver Pesos)	Total Remittances (Silver Pesos)	Mintage of New Spain Silver Production	
				Silver (Marks)	Silver (Pesos)
1720–1729	6,294,270	7,584,116	13,878,386	9,873,198	83,922,183
1730–1739	9,479,649	8,853,629	18,333,278	10,650,545	90,529,633
1740–1749	6,222,867	15,872,470	22,095,337	12,067,202	102,571,217
1750–1759	12,174,996	15,905,103	28,080,099	14,793,893	125,748,091
1760–1769	6,338,091	24,905,563	31,243,654	13,280,859	112,887,302
1770–1779	14,350,622	34,538,802	48,889,424	19,361,189	164,570,107
1780–1789	16,556,050	61,705,650	78,261,700	22,050,436	187,428,706
1790–1799	43,174,534	47,485,230	90,659,764	26,021,253	221,180,651

Note: 1 mark = 8.5 pesos.
Source: John J. Tepaske. and Herbert S. Klein, *Ingresos y egresos de la Real Hacienda de Nueva España*, 2 vols. (México: Instituto Nacional de Antropología e Historia, Colección Fuentes, 1986–1988). Alexander von Humboldt, *Ensayo político sobre el reino de la Nueva España*, Mexico, Ed. Porrúa, 1991. Richard Garner, Economic History Data Desk, that can be consulted in http://home.comcast.net/~richardgarner04/.

Table I.4. *Index Numbers*[a]

Years	Remittances to Castille	Remittances to Caribbean	Total Remittances	Mintage Silver (Pesos)
1720–1729	100	100	100	100
1730–1739	117	117	117	108
1740–1749	115	209	158	122
1750–1759	169	262	212	150
1760–1769	88	328	198	135
1770–1779	199	455	317	196
1780–1789	263	814	515	223
1790–1799	600	626	612	264

[a] These index numbers are based on date in Table 1.3.

Table I.5. *State Expenditures in Spain and Great Britain (1764–1793)*

	Spain						Great Britain					
Years	Spanish Net Public Expenditure ('000 Reales de Vellón)	Civil Government (%)	Army (%)	Navy (%)	Defense (%)	Debt (%)	British Net Public Expenditure ('000 Pounds)	Civil Government (%)	Army (%)	Navy (%)	Defense (%)	Debt (%)
1764–1768	486,438	46.4	33.8	16.1	49.9	3.7	10,360	8.4	19.1	21.0	42.8	47.0
1769–1773	434,293	30.5	43.0	20.8	63.9	5.7	10,180	11.4	14.9	20.0	38.0	46.3
1774–1778	484,071	29.3	40.7	26.1	66.8	3.9	13,435	10.1	26.3	21.8	52.2	35.2
1779–1783	693,273	24.5	32.3	28.6	60.9	14.7	24,175	4.3	30.1	28.9	64.7	28.1
1784–1788	611,921	30.2	31.1	25.8	56.9	12.9	19,775	7.4	11.7	29.0	43.6	46.6
1789–1793	650,871	33.1	34.2	25.9	60.1	6.9	17,478	9.9	14.6	15.7	33.8	53.4
AVERAGE	560,144	31.8	35.3	24.4	59.6	8.5	15,901	8.0	20.1	23.7	47.7	41.6

Source: Rafael Torres Sánchez, "Possibilities and Limits: Testing the Fiscal Military State in the Anglo-Spanish War of 1779–1783," Paper presented at *Session 69, xiv International Economic History Congress*, Helsinki, August 2006, p. 3; Spanish figures taken from José Patricio Merino, *Las cuentas de la Administración central española, 1750–1820* (Madrid: Instituto de Estudios Fiscales, 1987); British figures from Mitchell (1988), 578–580. The GB defense figures include Ordinance.

Table I.6. *Remittances from Spanish America and from New Spain to General Treasury of Spain, 1763–1811 (in silver pesos)*

Años	Total from all Spanish America	From New Spain	New Spain as percent of Spanish America
1763–1767	343,851	42,969	12.50
1768–1772	299,848	67,106	22.38
1773–1777	335,363	186,367	55.57
1778–1782	177,820	110,935	62.39
1783–1787	287,088	127,444	44.39
1788–1792	502,287	408,873	81.40
1793–1797	725,466	472,382	65.11
1798–1802	574,523	378,617	65.90
1803–1807	625,104	360,000	57.59
1808–1811	618,500	556,638	90.00
SUBTOTAL (1763–1811)	4,489,850	2,711,330	60.39

Sources: José Patricio Merino, *Las cuentas de la Administración central española, 1750–1820* (Madrid: Instituto de Estudios Fiscales, 1987); TePaske John J. and Herbert S. Klein, *Ingresos y egresos de la Real Hacienda de Nueva España*, 2 vols. (México: Instituto Nacional de Antropología e Historia, Colección Fuentes), 1986–1988; and Herbert S. Klein, *Royal Treasuries of the Spanish Empire in America, 1580–1825*, 3 vols. (Durham, N.C.: Duke University Press), 1982; *Diccionario de Hacienda*, Madrid, 1833–1834, vol. 1, p. 162.

Appendix II

Table II.1. *Alcabala (Sales Tax) Income in New Spain, 1777–1811 (in silver pesos)*

Años	Garavaglia and Grosso	Manuel Payno
1777	881,263	1,778,028
1778	1,933,989	2,535,302
1779	1,659,801	2,218,648
1780	1,790,904	2,421,281
1781	2,334,125	2,951,381
1782	2,168,769	3,197,260
1783	2,262,980	2,740,494
1784	2,458,639	3,671,521
1785	2,331,007	3,405,579
1786	1,923,789	2,863,327
1787	2,023,582	3,167,018
1788	2,097,508	2,753,568
1789	2,086,678	2,853,707
1790	2,004,316	3,112,557
1791	2,146,169	2,819,722
1792	2,052,570	2,538,449
1793	1,976,792	2,505,570
1794	2,042,094	2,481,194
1795	2,177,870	2,894,296
1796	2,126,351	2,659,414
1797	1,907,246	2,348,548
1798	1,920,894	2,263,669
1799	2,067,975	2,416,968
1800	2,169,764	2,497,986
1801	2,179,105	2,650,620
1802	2,150,003	2,822,665
1803	2,310,710	2,996,682
1804	2,245,079	3,038,030
1805	2,134,983	3,002,772
1806	2,126,861	2,426,001
1807	2,279,947	2,845,495
1808	2,196,637	2,969,329
1809	2,386,709	2,846,560
1810	1,800,051	2,943,989
1811	1,228,518	2,913,019

Source: Juan Carlos Garavaglia and Juan Carlos Grosso, *Las alcabalas novohispanas, 1776–1821* (Mexico: AGN, 1987) and table by Manuel Payno in Archivo General de la Nación (Mexico), *Historia*, vol. 660. f. 26.

Table II.2. *Pulque Tax Income in New Spain, 1765–1810 (in silver pesos)*

Años	Archivo General de Indias	Fonseca and Urrutia	Manuel Payno
1765	370,668	373,208	378,208
1766	342,248	352,123	352,123
1767	360,050	379,268	479,268
1768	329,763	340,099	340,699
1769	335,368	367,447	367,447
1770	323,441	361,254	361,254
1771	291,827	449,077	349,077
1772	330,514	376,407	376,407
1773	396,843	423,844	423,844
1774	398,442	433,154	433,154
1775	408,562	468,888	468,888
1776	450,370	488,053	488,053
1777	580,840	617,564	523,194
1778	564,154	709,252	734,387
1779	648,231	814,755	834,789
1780	676,106	818,470	861,710
1781	837,839	972,169	958,334
1782	827,876	951,013	996,010
1783	933,767	997,816	1,016,009
1784	904,933	985,659	1,047,221
1785	850,457	978,881	945,512
1786	376,494	693,456	712,651
1787	178,582	638,356	714,640
1788	606,387	893,815	877,815
1789	776,569	879,592	833,798
1790	619,677	745,331	879,093
1791	592,949		848,571
1792	619,134		870,040
1793	633,706		850,704
1794	557,779		801,001
1795	510,700		756,144
1796	550,071		826,835
1797	576,307		850,370
1798	532,077		833,031
1799	530,702		814,714
1800	550,014		835,348
1801			817,304
1802	498,531		752,812
1803	476,873		731,350
1804	488,775		708,899
1805	455,347		677,777
1806			677,749
1807			712,198
1808			680,306
1809	417,240		659,113
1810	372,024		561,509

Sources: José Jesús Hernández Palomo, *La renta del pulque en Nueva España, 1663–1810* (Seville: Escuela de Estudios Hispanoamericanos, 1980); Fabián de Fonseca and Carlos de Urrutia, *Historia general de la Real Hacienda*, vol. 1 (Mexico: Vicente G. Torres, 1845–1853); Manuel Payno in Archivo General de la Nación (Mexico), *Historia*, vol. 660. f. 26.

Table II.3. *Tobacco Monopoly in Colonial Mexico: Expenditures, Sales and Profits, 1767–1809*

Years	Expenses in Manufacture	Payments Tobacco leaf	Costs of Paper	Total Expenses	Net Profits	Total sales
1767				1,051,746	417,732	1,469,478
1768				724,912	807,382	1,532,294
1769				840,726	980,764	1,821,490
1770				1,211,865	816,093	2,027,958
1771				1,614,257	886,758	2,501,015
1772				1,899,680	959,588	2,859,268
1773				1,833,435	1,218,719	3,052,154
1774	1,149,519	775,092	25,963	1,950,574	1,241,537	3,192,111
1775	1,564,512	850,965	36,390	2,451,867	1,229,994	3,681,861
1776	1,554,118	718,558	58,274	2,330,950	1,514,792	3,845,742
1777	1,587,617	601,067	223,427	2,412,111	1,943,196	4,355,307
1778	1,861,383	682,426	117,401	2,661,210	2,433,152	5,094,362
1779	1,979,326	563,221	240,607	2,783,154	2,657,181	5,440,335
1780	2,073,514	533,701	75,675	2,682,890	2,985,217	5,668,107
1781	2,307,574	704,255	113,386	3,125,215	2,953,863	6,079,078
1782	2,044,177	895,222	209,193	3,148,592	3,240,930	6,389,522
1783	2,206,515	854,283	285,128	3,345,926	3,285,920	6,631,846
1784	2,172,207	874,381	301,062	3,347,650	3,357,846	6,705,496
1785	2,186,905	821,330	122,793	3,131,028	3,286,530	6,417,558
1786	2,068,417	622,070	42,864	2,733,351	3,091,645	5,824,996
1787	2,205,245	747,299	84,109	3,036,653	2,921,066	5,957,719
1788	2,175,454	1,083,845	77,641	3,336,940	2,906,242	6,243,182
1789	2,028,684	600,246	54,039	2,682,969	3,610,212	6,293,181
1790	2,057,482	755,462	24,403	2,837,347	3,397,967	6,235,314
1791	2,062,496	977,340	18,952	3,058,788	3,426,838	6,485,626
1792	2,040,141	890,840	60,020	2,991,001	3,714,634	6,705,635
1793	2,111,926	1,101,638	45,206	3,258,770	3,426,093	6,684,863
1794	2,197,917	1,159,326	60,295	3,417,538	3,108,813	6,526,351
1795	2,170,259	789,616	79,988	3,039,863	3,935,600	6,975,463
1796	2,374,554	971,174	54,583	3,400,311	3,936,228	7,336,539
1797	2,407,403	962,474	477,121	3,846,998	2,813,351	6,660,349
1798	1,882,869	903,269	925,638	3,711,776	4,539,798	8,251,574
1799	2,061,034	1,019,823	1,044,374	4,125,231	3,396,390	7,521,621
1800	2,356,307	538,658	1,125,592	4,020,557	3,412,602	7,433,159
1801	2,405,671	626,319	860,088	3,892,078	3,933,835	7,825,913
1802	2,412,633	594,229	587,342	3,594,204	4,092,630	7,686,834
1803	2,664,107	1,140,671	392,134	4,196,912	3,550,616	7,747,528
1804	2,685,134	1,338,957	101,655	4,125,746	3,784,973	7,910,719
1805	2,764,381	1,457,063	103,833	4,325,277	4,274,346	8,599,623
1806	2,662,072	1,508,271	1,084,721	5,255,064	3,861,328	9,116,392
1807	2,855,775	1,483,466	1,948,181	6,287,422	3,129,782	9,417,204
1808	2,831,605	1,329,587	452,789	4,613,981	4,447,487	9,061,468
1809	2,968,378	2,226,481	783,887	5,978,746	3,579,951	9,558,697

Sources: Lucas Alamán, *Historia de México*, Mexico, Fondo de Cultura Económica, 1985, vol. 5, appendix 1. Data in silver pesos.

Appendix III

III.1: List of *Donativos Universales*[1] Collected in New Spain, 1781–1810

Donativo of 1781–1784. Amount collected: 843,474 pesos.

On August 17, 1780, the Spanish monarch Charles III ordered that a *donativo* be collected from "his beloved vassals in the West Indies," with payments to be made to the Crown of "one peso by each freeman, including both Indians and the other castes that compose the People . . . and two pesos by each of the Spaniards and Nobles." Viceroy Mayorga, however, did not promulgate this royal instruction until March 16, 1781. The greater part of the *donativo* (almost 75 percent) was collected from Indians and castes. However, some wealthy individuals made large contributions, for example, the Count of Regla (28,865 pesos), the Count of Valenciana (25,000 pesos), and lesser sums by fifty-five rich proprietors, including miners, landowners, and merchants.

Sources: There are numerous references to this donativo in AGN, *Donativos y Préstamos*, vols. 10, 14, 17, 21, 24, and 26. For detailed lists of contributors, also see C. Rodriguéz (1995).

Donativo of 1793. Amount collected: 460,714 pesos.

By royal decree of March 27, 1793, Charles IV requested a *donativo* from the clergy in the Americans for expenses in the "Saintly War declared against the French." Subsequently, the Spanish Minister of Finance Diego de Gardoqui made this order extensive to the entire population of Spanish America, the instruction being applied in New Spain by Viceroy Revillagigedo. Almost half of the collections came from rural towns and villages, although in a lesser proportion than in the previous *donativo* of 1781–1784.

Sources: For lists of contributors and amounts collected, see AGN, *Histórico de Hacienda*, vol. 799, exp. (expediente) 4; AGN, *Donativos y Préstamos*, vol. 28, exp. 7, fs. (folios) 94–98, and exp. 8, fs. 122–125; and AGN, *Donativos y Préstamos*, vols. 1 and 26, passim.

Donativo of 1795. Amount collected: 701,552 pesos.

1 The *Donativos universales* were forced contributions levied by the Spanish crown upon the entire population of the viceroyalty. The largest volume of primary documents on the *donativos* can be found in the thirty-three volumes of the archival branch known as *Donativos y Préstamos* in the Archivo General de la Nación in Mexico City.

By royal orders of May 13 and June 24, 1795, a new *donativo* was applied by Viceroy Branciforte to assist in the war against France, with the object of raising one million pesos in New Spain.

Sources: Extensive correspondence can be found in AGN, *Donativos y Préstamos*, vols. 13, 23, 28, and 30; a series of important letters are in *Correspondencia de Virreyes*, 1a serie, vol. 180, fs. 504–511.

Donativo of 1798. Amount collected: 2,118,914 pesos.

By royal decree of May 27, 1798, the Spanish Minister of Finance Francisco Saavedra requested a voluntary *donativo* in Spain and the Americas. Viceroy Azanza promulgated this instruction in New Spain on October 28, 1798. Spaniards (whites) were to contribute 2 pesos per head of family, castes and mulatos 1 peso, and Indian peasants 4 silver *reales* (half a peso). In the years 1798–1800 the sum of 1,618,914 pesos was collected; in addition, the Tribunal de Mineria provided 500,000 pesos, although it was forced to ask for a loan from religious foundations to be able to do so.

Sources: For lists of individuals, see AGN, *Donativos y Préstamos*, vol. 32, exp. 8, fs. 55–57; vol. 2, fs. 230–231; and vol. 33, exp. 9, fs. 157–158; there is also much scattered information in AGN, *Donativos y Préstamos*, vols. 2, 14–16, 18–20, 25, and 27–28. On the donation of the Tribunal de Minería, see AGN, *Donativos y Préstamos*, vol. 33, exp. 3, fs. 123–126.

Donativo and Loan of 1805. Amount collected: 497,557 de pesos.

After the declaration of war against England on December 28, 1804, the Spanish crown requested financial assistance from "all the *provinces* of the empire." In New Spain, the collection of a *donativo* from April 1805 included contributions from the Tribunal de Mineria (300,000 pesos), from various bishops (100,000 pesos), and from the Mexico City Merchant Guild (50,000 pesos).

Sources: See lists in *Gaceta de México*, April 9, June 4, and July 15, 1805.

Donativo of 1805 (for the Widows and Orphans of the Naval Battle of Trafalgar). Amount collected: 23,764 pesos.

In New Spain, a *donativo* began to be collected from March 5, 1806, on behalf of the "the widows and orphans of the defenders of the nation who died in the naval combat of Trafalgar." Small sums were registered irregularly in the *Gaceta de México* during the years 1806 and 1807.

Sources: See *Gaceta de México*, from March 5, 1806 through August 26, 1807.

Donativo of 1808–1810 (for the War against Napoleon). Amount collected: 1,941,643 pesos.

On October 4, 1808, Viceroy Pedro Garibay published a request for a *donativo* to assist the Spanish patriot troops in their struggle against the French military forces that had invaded Spain. The lists of contributors began to be published in *Gaceta de México* from October 12, 1808, and in scarcely a month, 450,000 pesos were collected. The collection of this same *donativo* was continued for two more years until the outbreak of insurgency led by Miguel Hidalgo in Guanajuato in September 1810, which marked the first stage of the prolonged civil war in Mexico, known as the war of independence.

Sources: Fairly complete lists of contributors can be found in weekly *Gaceta de México* during the years 1808–1810; also see abundant correspondence scattered various volumes in AGN, *Donativos y Préstamos*: vols. 3–4, 6, 9, 11, 12, and 29.

Donativos *Requested in the Years 1810–1811.* Amounts collected: incomplete information.

On May 5, 1810, the Regency Council in Cádiz requested a new donativo for the struggle against the French troops. In the decree, the Council declared: "Vosotros (los americanos) pagais la deuda del Estado en plata y oro, ellos (los soldados españoles) en sangre. . . . " Subsequently, on September 22, 1810, the viceroy of New Spain Francisco Xavier Venegas gathered notables and upper clergy at the government palace in Mexico City to urge them to contribute. The official order for this so-called *tercer donativo* in New Spain was published on September 25, 1810. Among the large contributions were those by the Count of Regla (4,000 pesos) and Count Bassoco (25,000 pesos).

According to Lucas Alaman, additional donativos were requested in 1810 and 1811. For example, the Mexico City Merchant Guild organized one donativo of 300,000 pesos to pay for shoes and boots for the Spanish troops. Additional subscriptions were announced in support of the celebrated troops under the leadership of the Castilian guerilla leader known as *Empecinado* who had numerous successes against the French: in Mexico 43,000 pesos were raised for this purpose.

Sources: Hernández and Dávalos (1878), doc. 39; and Alamán (1985), pp.233–234. For correspondence on the *tercer donativo* of September 25, 1810, see AGN, *Donativos y Préstamos*, vol. 4, exp. 20, fs. 64–68, exp. 105. fs. 329–336; vol. 6, exp. 12, fs. 227–256; and vol. 11, exp. 7, fs. 78–80.

III.2: List of Loans Raised in New Spain to Finance Wars of the Spanish Crown, 1781–1811[2]

Loan of the Merchant Guilds of New Spain for the Spanish Crown, March 1781–March 1782. Amount requested: 1,655,415 pesos (non-interest-bearing loan).

This non-interest-bearing loan was an advance to be supplied by wealthy merchants of Mexico, Veracruz, and Xalapa for the Crown to pay for war expenses against Britain, particularly in the greater Caribbean. Contributors included forty-seven merchants from the city of Mexico, nineteen merchants from Xalapa, and fifteen from the port of Veracruz. The official documents indicated that repayment would be effected on presentation of certificates of the loan "resguardos correspondientes a cada prestamista," (AGN, *Consulado de México*, caja 306, exp.7). The correspondence of the viceroy with regard to this loan suggested that titles of nobility might be forthcoming as a result of major contributions. With time, such leading merchants of Mexico City as Antonio Bassoco and Pedro Alonso de Alles did receive titles, but this occurred only after contributing to various royal loans.

Sources: Abundant documents in AGN, *Consulado*, caja 306, exp. 7, fs. 7–10; *Donativos y Préstamos*, vol. 21, exp. 5, fs. 110–119; and in AGI, *Audiencia de México*, exp. 2348, letter of Viceroy Mayorga to the Spanish Minister José Gálvez, April 30, 1784.

Loan of the Mexico City Merchant Guild, August 1782. Amount requested: 1,000,000 pesos. *Interest*: 5 percent.

The viceroy of New Spain, Martín de Mayorga, requested the Mexico City Merchant Guild in August 1782 to provide a loan for the Crown to finance expenses of the war against Britain. The guild was authorized to collect a small percentage of the port tax, known as *avería*, to cover debt service. Among the leading lenders who subscribed to the loan were nine merchants, seven rentiers of the city of Mexico, and nine ecclesiastical corporations.

Sources: AGN, *Archivo Histórico de Hacienda*, legs. 683–626 and *Correspndencia de Virreyes*, vol. 131, exp. 1691, fs. 48–49 and exp. 1760, fs. 130–131. Guillermina del Valle (1997), Chapter 4 includes detailed information on individual contributions.

Loan of the Tribunal de Minería, August 1782. Amount requested: 1,000,000 pesos. *Interest*: 5 percent.

2 The largest volume of primary documents on the loans can be found in the thirty-three volumes of the archival branch known as *Donativos y Préstamos* in the Archivo General de la Nación in Mexico City.

In August 1782, Viceroy Mayorga requested the Mining Tribunal (run by the association of silver miners) to operate as financial intermediary for a one-million-peso loan to finance expenses of the war against Britain. The Tribunal would receive sums from the Mexico City mint to guarantee debt service. The Crown also promised not to allow for increase in the price of mercury during the duration of the loan. A total of eighteen individuals and corporations subscribed to the loan, with sums ranking between $3,000 and $200,000, including $110,000 from the Banco de Avió de la Minería and major contributions by the marquis of Castañiza (250,000 pesos), the merchant Francisco Martínez Cabezón (200,000 pesos), and merchants Vicente de las Heras and Antonio Bassoco (100,000 pesos apiece).

Sources: Lists of contributors can be found in AGN, *Minería*, vol. 63, ff. 145–146 and Howe (1949), pp.82–102. There is additional information in AGN, *Correspondencia de Virreyes*, 131, exp. 1691, fs. 48–49, and exp. 1760, fs. 130–131.

Tobacco Loan of 1783. Amount requested: 523,376 pesos. *Interest*: 5 percent.

By royal instruction of August 17, 1780, Charles III authorized royal financial officers to obtain loan monies for the war against Britain by allowing for the mortgage of funds in the Indies of the tax branches of tobacco and *alcabalas*, offering an annual return of 4 percent interest to those same tax branches while the monies were used for other purposes. This measure was not applied in New Spain until January of 1783 when Viceroy Mayorga promulgated it: he offered to pay 5 percent annual interest payments to the tobacco monopoly for the lending of its funds to the Crown for war expenses in Cuba. Apparently, most of the sums collected came from Durango and Guadalajara (461,657 pesos).

Sources: AGN, *Bandos*, vol. 12, exp. 42, fs. 146–148; AGN, *Impresos Oficiales*, vol. 49, exp. 38, fs. 398–399. Also documents in David Marley, AGN (1985), docs. XII and XIII and the essay by José Joaquín Real Diaz, titled "Martin de Mayorga" *Calderón Quijano* (1968), vol. 2, p. 147.

Loan of the Mexico City Merchant Guild, 1786. Amount requested: 150,000. *Interest*: 5 percent.

According to documents of the Mexico City Merchant Guild, the purpose of the loan was to alleviate the grave agrarian crisis of that year: "afligió al reino en el año de 1786 una hambre y carestía general de viveres que puso a todos en la mayor consternación . . . y el Gobierno . . . acudió a este Consulado, quien concurriendo por su parte al socorro de estas graves indigencias . . . 150,000 pesos." In practice, most of the funds were used to improve three principal roads to Mexico City in order to speed up the transport of corn and cereals.

Sources: AGN, *Archivo Histórico de Hacienda*, vol. 442, exp. 16, fs. 1–9.

Loan of the Mexico City Merchant Guild, 1790. Amount requested: 100,000 pesos. *Interest*: 5 percent.

This was a loan for the Crown to celebrate the end of the war with Algiers. The Mexico City Merchant Guild circulated the following declaration among its members: "En el año de 1790 en virtud de Real Orden del 6 de diciembre de 1785 se tomaron otros 100,000 a réditos sobre el mismo cuatro al millar para que este Consulado contribuyese por su parte a las paces celebradas con la Regencia de Argel."

Sources: AGN, *Archivo Histórico de Hacienda*, vol. 442, exp. 16, fs. 1–9. See list of subscribers in Guillermina del Valle (1997), Table III.6, p. 214.

Loan of 1793–1794. Amount requested: 1,559,000 pesos. *Interest*: no interest.

On December 6, 1792, Charles IV requested a loan from his vassals in the Americas to help finance the imminent war against France. The monarch instructed the viceroy of New Spain to send as quickly as possible "six to eight million pesos, or the largest sum possible." A non-interest-bearing loan was promoted by the colonial government in Mexico. By July 9, 1794, 1,559,000 pesos had been collected without interest and with only the promise of amortization by the royal treasuries in a period of two years. A series of promissory notes called "*libranzas*" were issued by the royal treasury to the lenders in exchange for the silver advanced.

Sources: See Guillermina del Valle (1997), Table IV-I, pp. 285–286, which includes a preliminary list of subscribers; see additional documents in AGN, *Donativos y Préstamos*, vol. 1, exps 1–45, 80, and 88 and vol. 28, fs. 3–17.

Loan of the Mexico City Merchant Guild, 1793. Amount requested: 1,000,000 pesos. *Interest*: 5 percent

In early 1793, Viceroy Revillagigedo asked the Mexico City Merchant Guild to help raise a loan for the war against revolutionary France. The merchant guild reported on February 23, 1793, that it had approved a loan for 1,000,000 pesos but against a guarantee of an increase of its percentage of receipts of the *averia* port tax. It immediately provided the royal treasury with an advance in silver of 350,000 pesos and by April 13 had collected 547,000 pesos, obtaining a number of additional subscriptions until it successfully completed collecting the million pesos promised by June 7, 1793. The merchant guild requested the authorities to publish the information on individual contributors in the official gazette, newspaper *Gazeta de México*, but the viceroy refused to do so.

Sources: AGN, *Donativos y Préstamos*, vol. 1, exp. 80, fs. 317–318, exp. 88, fs. 319–323; vol. 28, fs. 1–24. For a list of subscribers to the loan, see Guillermina del Valle (1997), Cuadro IV-2, pp. 287–288.

Loan of the Tribunal de Minería, 1793. Amount requested: 1,000,000 pesos. *Interest*: 5 percent. (Amount collected: 1,100,000 pesos.)

In early 1793, Viceroy Revillagigedo asked the Mining Tribunal to serve as financial intermediary for a one-million-peso loan to finance the war against France. The miners accepted and obtained the funds from diverse investors, including an extra 100,000 pesos from silver miners of Guanajuato. The sum of 3 *gramos* on each silver mark minted at the Mexico City mint was assigned for payment of debt service.

Sources: Howe (1949), pp. 375–377; AGN, *Correspondencia de Virreyes*, series II, vols. 17–170, doc. 616.

Loan of Tribunal de Minería, August 1794. Amount requested: 1,000,000 pesos. *Interest*: 5 percent.

Once again, the viceroy of New Spain requested the Mining Tribunal to serve as financial intermediary for another one-million-peso loan to finance the war against France. The miners' association accepted and soon raised the funds.

Source: Howe (1949), pp. 377–378.

Loan of the Mexico City Merchant Guild, August 1794. Amount requested: 1,000,000 pesos. *Interest*: 5 percent.

The viceroy asked the Mexico City Merchant Guild in August 1794 to serve as financial intermediary for another one-million-peso loan to finance the war against France. Six wealthy merchants contributed, including Antonio Bassoco who made the largest individual subscription to the tune of 200,000 pesos. A further thirteen individual investors and nineteen religious corporations also subscribed sums.

Source: Guillermina del Valle (1997), Table IV-3, pp. 289–290.

Tobacco Loan of 1795–1802. Amount requested nominal: 15,000,000 pesos. *Interest*: 5 percent. (Amount actually collected: 7,172,264 pesos.)

On December 12, 1794, the king Charles IV and his Finance Minister, Diego de Gardoqui, authorized the mortgage of funds of the tobacco monopoly in New Spain to guarantee a huge 15-million-peso loan at 5 percent interest. In April, 1795, the viceroy of New Spain, the marquis of Branciforte, asked the Mexico City Merchant Guild and the Mining

Tribunal to take charge of the subscription and to raise a minimum sum of 3 million pesos each. The receipts of the tobacco monopoly served as guarantee of debt service. Actually the loan was a much-extended operation, lasting almost eight years. According to one document from 1813, (Biblioteca Nacional, ms. 1282), 3.1 million pesos were collected by the Merchant Guild and 3.7 million pesos by the Tribunal de Minería.

Sources: On the loan contract, see AGN, *Correspondencia de Virreyes*, 1st series, vol. 213, exp. 57, f. 100 and AGN, *Consulado*, caja 312, exp. 8; also see *Correspondencia de Virreyes*, 1st series, vol. 180, exp. 337 and exp. 361. For some information on subscribers, see Guillermina del Valle (1997), Table IV-4, pp. 291–292.

Patriotic Loan of October 22, 1798. Amount requested: 500,000 pesos. *Interest*: non-interest-bearing loan. (Amount collected: 496,366 pesos.)

On May 27, 1798, the Spanish Minister of Finance, Francisco Saavedra, signed a royal decree requesting a donativo and a *préstamo patriótico* from the vassals of the king in the Americas in order to pay for expenses in the naval war against Britain. The loan was issued in the shape of bonds ("acciones") of 50 pesos each (1,000 *reales*) without interest, to be returned to subscribers ten years alter the end of the war. The lists of the contributors were to be published in the official gazettes in the Spanish American colonies.

Viceroy Azanza himself advanced a personal loan of 15,000 pesos but the largest individual contribution was that of the Veracruz Merchant Guild for 100,000 pesos. According to the documentation found, the total raised was 496,366 pesos, and there were 8,162 bonds issued, some of which evidently were worth more than 50 pesos.

Sources: For the royal instruction, see *Memoria de Hacienda* of Francisco de Saavedra, in J. Canga Arguelles, *Diccionario de Hacienda*, (1833–1834), vol. 2, p. 185. On individual subscribers, see lists regularly published in *Gazeta de México*, 1798–1799; also AGN, *Donativos y Préstamos*, vol. 32, exp. 14, fs. 198–200 and AGN, *Donativos y Préstamos*, vol. 2, exps. 12, 55–57.

Patriotic Loan of August 5, 1809. Amount requested: 3 million pesos. *Interest*: 6 percent. (Amount collected: 3,176,835 pesos.)

Viceroy Francisco Xavier de Lizana y Beaumont publicly notified the inhabitants of New Spain on August 5, 1809, that the Spanish minister of Finance had announced the request of a new loan for the struggle against Napoleón under the authority of Ferdinand VII, in order to obtain contributions from "los vasallos (de Fernando VII) en todos sus distantes y muy extensos dominios." The viceroy requested the merchant guilds of the cities of Mexico, Veracruz, and Guadalajara to collaborate as well as the royal treasury officials of New Spain. An exceptional 6 percent was offered as annual interest on the loan and five years for amortization. The loan was issued in the shape of a kind of bond ("escrituras de imposición") provided to all subscribers. Among the wealthy merchants who each invested more than 100,000 pesos were Antonio Bassoco, Gabriel Iturbe, Sebastian Heras, Tomás Domingo Acha, Francisco, and Antonio Alonso Terán. The other subscribers were also mainly merchants, fifty of whom invested 25,000 or more apiece. The Mexico City Merchant Guild found additional subscribers who placed 2,000–20,000 pesos per head.

The publication of the request for the loan was impelled by the arrival on July 26, 1809, of a British warship to Veracruz with admiral Cochrane on board. The admiral had been commissioned by the Supreme Junta of Seville to collect funds in Spanish America to cover debts due to the British government for support in the struggle against Napoleon.

Sources: Gazeta de México, vol. 16, nos 102 and 105 (August 11 and 23, 1809) pp. 761–764 and 787. Also see Alamán, vol. 1, pp. 304–305; AGN, *Donativos y Préstamos*, vol. 3, fs. 16–17; also see lists of subscribers in Guillermina del Valle (1997), Table IV-1, pp. 423–426.

Préstamo/Suplemento de Emergencia: Noviembre/Diciembre de 1809. Amount requested: 1 million pesos. *Interest*: no interest.

This non-interest-bearing loan was intended to fulfill royal orders to the effect that silver should be boarded on the warship *Asia* to leave Veracruz bound for Cádiz in December 1809 in order to assist the patriot troops fighting against the French invaders in Spain. The viceroy, archbishop Lizana, called together a series of meetings of the wealthiest residents of Mexico City. In less than one week, fifteen merchants, silver miners, and landowners contributed sums ranging between 20,000 and 200,000 pesos, while another sixty individuals contributed sums of less than 20,000 pesos each.

Sources: Gazeta de México, December 2, 1809, p. 1088 and December 6, 1809, pp. 1095–1096, which provide complete lists of lenders. Also see information in *Diario Mercantil de Veracruz*, March 6, 1810 (copy in Biblioteca Nacional, Madrid).

Patriotic Loan of January 10, 1810. Amount requested nominal: 20 million pesos. *Interest*: 6 percent. (Amount collected: 2,010,000 pesos.)

The Spanish Regency ratified a royal order on January 10, 1810, requesting a great loan of 20 million pesos to be raised in the Spanish American colonies to help finance the war against the French army in Spain. On September 25, 1810, Viceroy Venegas requested the merchant guilds of the cities of Mexico, Veracruz, and Guadalajara to begin subscription to this loan, offering tax branches as guarantee of debt service and amortization. The official proclamation indicated that the bonds ("acciones" o documentos entregadas a los prestamistas) "serán negociables o transmisibles por endosos de unos a otros. . . . " In other words, the intention was that these securities should be marketable.

Sources: The texts of the royal order and other relevant documents can be found in Hernández y Dávalos (1878), vol. 2, docs. 14 and 15; also see Alamán (1850), vol. 2, p. 233. For information on the subscription, see AGN, *Donativos y Préstamos*, vols. 4–6 and 11; and Guillermina del Valle (1997), Table VI.3, pp. 430–436.

Information on repayments on part of this loan is found in "Memoria instructiva y documentada del estado comparativo de los productos de la Real Hacienda del año de 1809," (México, 1813), Biblioteca Nacional, ms. 1282.

Emergency Patriotic Loan to Be Dispatched to Spain on the British Warship Bulwark, July 1810. Amount requested: 1 million pesos. *Interest*: no interest.

In the last two weeks of July, 1810, approximately one million pesos of a short-term loan ("empréstito gratuito y de corto plazo") were collected in Mexico City among wealthy merchants "para cargar en el buque de guerra inglés, el *Baluarte*, que salía con destino a Cádiz "para socorro de nuestra madre patria."

Sources: AGN, *Donativos y Préstamos*, vol. 1, leg. 1, exp. 7, July 19 and 21, 1810. For a complete list of contributors, see Guillermina del Valle (1997), Table VI.4, pp. 437–439.

Emergency Patriotic Loan to Be Dispatched to Spain on the British Warship Implacable, December 1810. Amount requested: 2,000,000 pesos. *Interest*: no interest. (Amount actually collected: 1,567,000 pesos.)

Lucas Alamán wrote that in 1810, despite the war against the insurgent forces in Mexico led by revolutionary priest Miguel Hidalgo, "los recursos no solo abundaban sino que todavía se continuaban haciendo remesas considerable de caudales a España, contribuyendo a este fin los acaudalados españoles. Así fue que el virrey en diciembre de 1810 resolvió mandar a Cádiz un pronto socorro de dos millones de pesos por el navío inglés *Implacable*, solicitando fondos de los comerciantes novohispanos. Una lista completa de los contribuyentes se publicó en la Gaceta, participando con gruesas sumas entre el 7 y 21 de diciembre la mayoría de los comerciantes del Consulado, españoles y criollos."

It should be noted, however, that the correspondence between Viceroy Venegas and George Cockburn, captain of the British warship *Implacable* (which was to take the silver to Cádiz), indicates that only 1,567,000 pesos were actually boarded, of which 87,000 pesos came from a previous donativo, 980,000 pesos from the tobacco monopoly, and 500,000 pesos from profits of the Mexico City mint.

Sources: Gazeta Extraordinaria de México, December 7, 11, and 21, 1810. Also see Alamán (1850), vol. 2, p. 232. For the correspondence between the viceroy and Cockburn, see AGN, *Marina*, vol. 244, fs. 253–265.

Emergency Patriotic Loan to Be dispatched to Spain on the Spanish Warship Miño, March 1810. Amount requested: 2,000,000 pesos. *Interest*: no interest. (Amount actually collected: 1,194,000 pesos.)

This was also an emergency loan the purpose of which was to send all possible silver to Cádiz to finance the war against the French. According to Guillermina del Valle (1997), pp. 415–416: "A fines de marzo de 1811, el virrey Venegas convocó a los sujetos más acaudalados de la capital con objeto de pedirle un empréstito más para socorrer a la 'Madre Patria' con una 'lúcida remesa' que no bajara de de dos millones de pesos, la cual se remitiría en el buque de guerra *Miño*. Con cierta dificultad, el Consulado logró se juntaran 742,000 pesos con aportaciones de sus miembros, a los que se agregaron otros 452,000 restantes del préstamo patriótico de 1810."

Source: For a complete list of subscribers, see Guillermina del Valle (1997), Table VI. 7, pp. 444–445.

III.3: Loans Taken in Holland by the Spanish Crown, 1770–1806 (with Debt Service Mainly in Mexican Silver)[3]

1779 *First Foreign Loan for the Imperial Canal of Aragón y Tauste* for a sum of 2,000,000 florins with annual interest payment of 3.5 percent and amortization in twenty years. Issued by the merchant bankers of Echenique, Sánchez & Cía. of Amsterdam.

1780 *Second Foreign Loan for the Imperial Canal of Aragón y Tauste* for a sum of 2,000,000 florins with annual interest payment of 3.5 percent and

3 The debt service of the majority of the Spanish loans issued in Holland was guaranteed by promissory notes (*libranzas*) to be paid in silver by the royal treasuries of Mexico. The principal sources of information on these loans are: Miguel Artola, *La hacienda del antiguo régimen* (1982), pp. 324, 387, 405, 413, 453, 454; Marten G. Buist, *At Spes Non Fracta: Hope and Company, 1770–1815* (La Haya: Martinus Nijhoff, 1974), Chapters 9–12; José Canga Argüelles, *Diccionario de Hacienda*, Madrid, 1833–1834 (1834), vol. I, 304–314, vol. II, 378–383; James C. Riley, *International Government Finance and the Amsterdam Capital Market, 1740–1815* (Cambridge: U.K.: Cambridge University Press, 1980), pp.165–173.

amortization in twenty years. Issued by the merchant bankers of Echenique, Sánchez & Cía. of Amsterdam.

1781 *Third Foreign Loan for the Imperial Canal of Aragón y Tauste* for a sum of 2,298,000 florins with annual interest payment of 3.5 percent and amortization in twenty years. Issued by the merchant bankers of Echenique, Sánchez & Cía. of Amsterdam. The contract specified that the Spanish government would establish a special sinking fund for payment of debt service and amortization.

1782 *Foreign loan of 3 million florins for the Spanish crown:* interest rate of 5 percent and negotiated by the Madrid merchant bank of Cabarrús y Lalanne with the Amsterdam merchant banks of Hope and Fitzeaux. Riley (1980), p. 168, affirms that the loan was paid off between 1789 and 1792 with remittances of Mexican silver pesos.

1792 *Foreign loan of 6 million florins for the Spanish crown:* interest rate of 4.5 percent. Amortization was to commence in 1798 and conclude in 1807. This loan was negotiated by the Madrid Gardoqui banking firm (headed by the brother of the Spanish Minister of Finance, Diego de Gardoqui) with the Ámsterdam banking firm of Hope & Co. The loan was guaranteed with the mortgage of the products of the customs receipts at the port of Cádiz.

1799 *Foreign loan of 3 million florins for the Spanish crown*: interest rate of 5 percent and amortization in eight years. Its purpose was to convert previous Spanish foreign loans issued at Amsterdam. It was issued by the new international banker to the Spanish crown at Amsterdam, the firm of Weduwe E. Croese & Cía. The guarantees of debt service were six promissory notes (*libranzas*) for 1,319,000 pesos on the royal treasuries of México.

1800 *Foreign loan of 2.5 million florins for the Spanish crown*: interest rate of 5 percent and amortization in eight years. Its purpose also was to convert previous Spanish foreign loans issued at Amsterdam. It was also issued by the banker to the Spanish crown at Ámsterdam, the firm of Weduwe E. Croese & Cía. The guarantees of debt service were promissory notes on the royal treasuries of México.

1801 *Foreign loan of 4.5 million florins for the Spanish crown:* interest rate of 5 percent and amortization in eight years. Its purpose was to convert previous Spanish foreign loans issued at Amsterdam. It was also issued by the banker to the Spanish crown at Ámsterdam, the firm of Weduwe E. Croese & Cía. The guarantees of debt service were promissory notes on the royal treasuries of México.

1805 *Foreign loan of 10 million florins for the Spanish crown*, issued by the Amsterdam banking firm of Hope & Co. The loan carried an interest rate of 5.5 percent and amortization to be completed in ten years. Guarantee of payment was covered with a series of promissory notes (*libranzas*) on the royal treasuries of Mexico worth 8,484,375 pesos, almost double the value of the loan.

1807 *Foreign loan of 22 million florins for the Spanish crown*, issued by the Amsterdam banking firm of Hope & Cía. With an interest rate of 6 percent and amortization to be completed in seven years. The bonds were sold at 90 percent of nominal value and the Hope bankers charged a commission of 7.5 percent due, presumably, to the high risks in European financial markets at this stage of the Napoleonic wars. As guarantee of payments on these securities, the Caja de Consolidación gave Hope & Co. promissory notes (*libranzas*) worth almost 28.5 million pesos to be cashed at Veracruz in case the Spanish government found itself unable to remit directly to Amsterdam. Half of this loan was to be used to convert previous Dutch loans to Spain and the rest for international obligations of the Spanish crown. In fact, Hope & Co. used some of the proceeds to pay 4,500,000 florins to the French Treasury to comply with the Spanish government's obligations under the Subsidy Treaty that Napoleon had forced Charles IV to sign in late 1803. As a result of the French invasion of Spain in 1808, the debt service of this loan was suspended for many years.

Bibliography

Primary Sources

Archives Nationales (Paris) [ANF].
ANF AF IV, vol. 1608, B1 and B2.
ANF AF IV, vols. 1082, 1087, and 1211.
Archivo General de la Nación (Mexico City) [AGN].
AGN Caja Matriz: Libro Manual de Cargo y Data de la Real Caja Veracruz, vols. 1758, 1791, and 1799.
AGN Consolidación de Vales Reales, vols. 5–7, 10, and 20.
AGN Consulado, vols. 252, 254, 266, 267, 276, 306, and 312.
AGN Correspondencia de Virreyes, 1a serie, vols. 180, 183, 213, 214, 219, 224, 229, 233, 236; 2a serie, vols. 44, 45, 47.
AGN Diezmos, vols. 21 and 22.
AGN Donativos y Préstamos, vols. 1, 2, 10, 13–18, 21, 27, and 28.
AGN Historia, vol. 660.
AGN Marina, vols. 142–147, 201–213, 216–218, 221–226, 229, 230, 232–234, and 238–248.
AGN Real Hacienda, vol. 229.
AGN Reales Cédulas Originales, vols. 192, 193, and 195–199.
AGN Temporalidades, vols. 4, 40, and 114.
Archivo de Indias (Seville) [AGI].
AGI Audiencia de México, vols. 2348 and 2358.
Archivo Histórico del Banco de España (Madrid) [AHBE].
Banco de San Carlos: Secretaría, vols. 187, 552, 569, 708, 784, and 1042.
Banco de San Carlos Junta de Gobierno, libro 187.
Archivo Histórico Nacional (Madrid) [AHN].
AHN Ministerio de Hacienda, serie general, leg. 5848.

Secondary Sources

Acerra, Martine and André Zysberg, *L'essor des marines de guerre européennes, 1680–1790*, Paris: Editions Sedes, 1997.
Acosta, Antonio and Juan Marchena, *La influencia de España en el Caribe, la Florida y la Luisiana, 1500–1800*, Madrid: Instituto de Cooperación Iberoamericana, 1983.
Aftalion, Florin, *L'Économie de la Révolution Française*, Paris: Hachette, 1987.
______, "Le financement des guerres de la Révolution et de l'Émpire," in Erik Aerts and Francois Crouzet, eds., *Economic Effects of the French Revolutionary and Napoleonic Wars*, Proceedings 10th International Economic History Congress, Leuven: Leuven University Press, 1990, pp. 22–29.

Alamán, Lucas, *Historia de México*, 5 vols., Mexico: Fondo de Cultura Económica/Instituto Cultural Helénico, 1985 [facsimile of the first edition of 1849–1852].

Alcalá Galiano, Vicente, *Informe del Tesorero General en ejercicio Don Vicente Alcalá Galiano, sobre la representación que la Junta Superior de Valencia hizo en 15 de septiembre de este año a la Suprema Gubernativa del Reino, reclamando la real orden de 20 de agosto anterior, en que se reencargaba el cumplimiento de las reales instrucciones en la distribución de los caudales del erario*, México: Reimpreso en Casa de Arizpe, 1810, 18-page pamphlet.

Alonso Álvarez, Luis, "Los problemas de Hacienda filipina y el estanco del tabaco, siglos XVI–XVIII," in Agustín González Enciso and Rafael Torres Sánchez, eds., *Tabaco y economía en el siglo XVIII*, Pamplona, Spain: EUNSA, 1999, pp. 89–112.

Alvarado, Manuel, "La ciudad de México ante la fundación de la Armada de Barlovento, 1635–1643," Ph.D. thesis, El Colegio de México, 1979.

Álvarez Nogal, Carlos, *El crédito de la monarquía hispánica en el reinado de Felipe IV*, Avila: Junta de Castilla y León, 1997.

Amaral, Samuel, "Public Expenditure Financing in the Colonial Treasury: An Analysis of the Real Caja de Buenos Aires Accounts, 1789–1791," *Hispanic American Historical Review* 64 (May 1984), 287–295.

Amaral, Samuel and Leandro Prados de la Escosura, eds., *La independencia americana: sus consecuencias económicas*, Madrid: Alianza Universidad, 1993.

Anderson, Fred, *Crucible of War: The Seven Years' War and the Fate of Empire in British North America, 1754–1766*, New York: Vintage, 2000.

Andrade Muñoz and Germán Luis "La búsqueda española de suministros, víveres y pertrechos navales en Nueva España (siglo XVIII). Los intereses coloniales frente a los problemas imperiales," Master's thesis, Instituto Mora, Mexico, 2002.

Anes, Gonzalo, *Las crisis agrarias en la España moderna, El antiguo régimen: los Borbones*, Madrid: Alianza/Alfaguara, 1975.

Anna, Timothy, *The Fall of the Royal Government in Peru*, Lincoln: University of Nebraska Press, 1978.

———, *La caída del gobierno español en la ciudad de México*, Mexico: Fondo de Cultura Económica, 1981.

———, *España y la independencia de América*, Mexico: Fondo de Cultura Económica, 1986.

Antolín Espino, María del Pilar, "El virrey marqués de Cruillas," in José Antonio Calderón Quijano, ed., *Los virreyes de Nueva España en el reinado de Carlos III. tomo I (1759–1779)*, Seville: Escuela de Estudios Hispanoamericanos, 1967–1968.

Archer, Christon, "Bourbon Finances and Military Policy in New Spain, 1759–1812," *The Americas*, xxxvii, 3 (1981), 315–350.

———, *El ejército en el México borbónico, 1760–1810*, Mexico: Fondo de Cultura Económica, 1983.

Arcila Farías, Eduardo, *Comercio entre México y Venezuela en los siglos XVI y XVII*, Mexico: IMCE, 1975.

———, *Historia de un monopolio. El estanco del tabaco en Venezuela (1779–1833)*, Caracas: Universidad Central de Venezuela, Instituto de Estudios Hispanoamericanos, Facultad de Humanidades y Educación, 1977.

Arnold, Linda, *Burocracia y burócratas en México, 1742–1835*, Mexico: Grijalbo/Consejo Nacional para la Cultura y las Artes, 1991.

Artola, Miguel, *La hacienda del antiguo régimen*, Madrid: Alianza, 1982.

Artola, Miguel and L. Bilbao, eds., *Estudios de Hacienda: de Ensenada a Mon*, Madrid: Instituto de Estudios Fiscales, 1984.

Ayala, Manuel Joseph, *Diccionario de gobierno y legislación de Indias*, Madrid: Quinto Centenario, 1988.

Aymes, J. R., *La guerra de independencia en España, 1808–1814*, Madrid: Siglo XXI, 1974.

Barbier, Jacques, "The Culmination of the Bourbon Reforms, 1787–1792," *Hispanic American Historical Review*, 57, 1 (February 1977), 51–68.

———, "Peninsular Finance and Colonial Trade: The Dilemma of Carlos IV's Spain," *Journal of Latin American Studies*, 12, 1 (1980), 21–37.

———, "Toward a New Chronology for Bourbon Colonialism: The 'Depositaría de Indias a Cádiz, 1722–1789'," *Ibero-Amerikanisches Archiv*, 6, 4 (1980), 335–353.

———, "Venezuelan Libranzas, 1788–1807: From Economic Nostrum to Fiscal Imperative," *The Americas*, xxxvii, 4 (1981), 457–479.

Barbier, Jacques and Herbert S. Klein, "Revolutionary Wars and Public Finance: The Madrid Treasury, 1784–1807," *The Journal of Economic History*, 41, 2 (1981), 315–339.

———, "Las prioridades de un rey ilustrado: el gasto público bajo el reinado de Carlos III," *Revista de Historia Económica*, 3, 3 (1986), 473–496.

Barbier, Jacques and Allan J. Kuethe, eds., *The North American Role in the Spanish Imperial Economy, 1760–1819*, Manchester: Manchester University, 1984.

Barro, Robert J. "Government Spending, Interest Rates, Prices and Budget Deficits in the United Kingdom," *Journal of Monetary Economics*, 20 (September 1987), 221–248.

Bauer, Arnold, "The Church in the Economy of Spanish America. Censos and Depósitos in the 18th and 19th Centuries," *Hispanic American Historical Review*, 63, 4 (1983), 707–733.

———, *La iglesia en la economía de América Latina, siglos xvi al xix*, Mexico: Instituto Nacional de Antropología e Historia, 1986.

Baugh, Daniel A., "Naval Power: What Gave the British Navy Superiority?" in Leandro Prados, ed., *Exceptionalism and Industrialisation: Britian and Its European Rivals, 1688–1815*, Cambridge, U.K.: Cambridge University Press, 2004, pp. 235–257.

Bauzon, Leslie, *Deficit Government: Mexico and the Philippine Situado, 1606–1804*, Tokyo: The Centre for East Asian Cultural Studies, 1981.

Becker, Robert, *Revolution, Reform and the Politics of American Taxation, 1763–1783*, New Orleans: Louisiana State University, 1980.

Beer, George, *British Colonial Policy, 1754–1765*, New York: Macmillan, 1922.

Beerman, Eric, *España y la independencia de Estados Unidos*, Madrid: MAPFRE, 1992.

Bergeron, Louis, *Banquiers, négociants et manufacturiers parisiens: du directoire á l'Empire*, Paris: Ecole des Hautes Etudes en Sciences Sociales/Mouton, 1978.

Bernal, Antonio Miguel, *La financiación de la Carrera de India (1492–1824): Dinero y crédito en el comercio colonial con América*, Seville: Fundación El Monte, 1992.

———, ed., *Dinero, moneda y crédito en la monarquía hispánica*, Madrid: Fundación ICO/Marcial Pons, 2000.

Bernal, Antonio Miguel and Antonio García Baquero, *Tres siglos de comercio sevillano (1598–1868): Cuestiones y problemas*, Seville: Cámara Oficial de Comercio, Industria y Navegación de Sevilla, 1973.

Bernstein, Harry, *Origins of Inter-American Interest, 1700–1812*, New York: Russell and Russell, 1946.

Berruezo, María Teresa, *La participación americana en las Cortes de Cádiz, 1810–1814*, Madrid: Centro de Estudios Constitucionales, 1986.

Black, Lawrence, "Conflict among Elites: The Overthrow of Viceroy Iturrigaray, Mexico 1808," unpublished Ph.D. thesis, Tulane University, 1980.

Blanning, T. C. W., *The Origins of the French Revolutionary Wars*, New York: Longmans, 1991.

Bobb, Bernard A., *The ViceRegency of Antonio María Bucareli in New Spain, 1771–1779*, Austin: University of Texas Press, 1962.

Bonnel, Ulane, *La France, les États Unis et la guerre de course, 1797–1815*, Paris: Nouvelles Editions Latines, 1961.
Bonnett Vélez, Diana, "Estancos y fiscalidad en la Nueva Granada, 1770–1800," unpublished manuscript, 1995.
Bonney, Richard, ed., *Economic Systems and State Finance*, Oxford: Oxford University Press/The European Science Foundation, 1995.
———,"What's New about the New French Fiscal History," *The Journal of Modern History*, 70, 3 (September 1998), 639–667.
———, ed., *The Rise of the Fiscal State in Europe, c. 1200–1800*, Oxford: Oxford University Press, 1999.
———, "Towards the Comparative Fiscal History of Britain and France during the Long Eighteenth Century," in Leandro Prados, ed., *Exceptionalism and Industrialisation: Britain and Its European Rivals, 1688–1815*, Cambridge, U.K.: Cambridge University Press, 2004, pp. 191–215.
Borah, Woodrow, *El Juzgado General de Indios en la Nueva España*, Mexico: Fondo de Cultura Económica, 1985.
———, "*La recolección de diezmos en el obispado de Oaxaca*," in Arnold Bauer, ed., *La iglesia en la economía de América Latina, siglos xvi al xix*, Mexico: Instituto Nacional de Antropología e Historia, 1986, pp. 61–100.
Borchart de Moreno, Cristina R., *Los mercaderes y el capitalismo en México, 1775–1778*, Mexico: Fondo de Cultura Económica, 1984.
Bordo, Michael and Roberto Cortes Conde, eds., *Transferring Wealth and Power from the Old to the New World: Monetary and Fiscal Institutions in the 17th through the 19th Centuries*, Cambridge, U.K.: Cambridge University Press, 2001.
Bordo, Michael and Eugene N. White, "A Tale of Two Currencies: British and French during the Napoleonic Wars," *The Journal of Economic History*, 51, 2 (1991), 303–316.
Bottin, Michel, *Histoire des Finances publiques*, Paris: Economica, 1997.
Bouvier, Jean, "A propos de la crise dite de 1805: les crisis économiques sous l'Empire," *Revue d'Histoire Moderne et Contemporaine*, xvii (July–September 1970), 506–513.
Boyer-Xambeau, Marie-Therese, Ghislain Deleplace, and Lucien Gillard, *Monnaie privée et pouvoir des princes*, Paris: Presse de la Fondation Nationale des Sciences Politiques, 1986.
———, "A la recherche d'un âge d'or des marchés financiers: intégration et efficence au xviiie siècle," *Cahiers d'Économie Politique*, 21 (1992), 33–65.
Brading, David, *Mineros y comerciantes en el México borbónico, 1763–1810*, Mexico: Fondo de Cultura Económica, 1975.
———,"Facts and Figments in Bourbon Mexico," *Bulletin of Latin American Research*, 4, 1 (1985), 61–64.
———, "Comments on 'The Economic Cycle in Bourbon Central Mexico," *Hispanic American Historical Review*, 69, 3 (1989), 531–538.
———, *The First America: The Spanish Monarchy, Creole Patriots and the Liberal State, 1492–1867*, Cambridge, U.K.: Cambridge University Press, 1991. [The Spanish translation is titled *Orbe indiano: de la monarquía católica a la republica criolla, 1492–1867*, Mexico: Fondo de Cultura Económica, 1993.]
———, *Una iglesia asediada: el obispado de Michoacán, 1749–1810*, Mexico: Fondo de Cultura Económica, 1994.
Braudel, Fernand, *La Méditerranée et le Monde Méditerranéan à l'Epque de Philippe II*, Paris: Armand Colin, 1949. (Also see the English translation of the revised edition published by Harper Torchbooks, 1972.)
Brewer, John, *The Sinews of Power: War, Money and the English State, 1688–1783*, London: Unwin Hyman, 1989.

Bribiesca Sumano, María Elena, *Catálogo de la serie Correspondencia de Virreyes: Marqués de Branciforte*, Mexico: Archivo General de la Nación, 1985.

Brown, V. L., "Contraband Trade. A Factor in the Decline of Spain's Empire in America," *Hispanic American Historical Review*, 8, 2 (1928), 178–189.

Bruchey, Stuart, *Robert Oliver, Merchant of Baltimore, 1783–1819*, Baltimore, Md.: Johns Hopkins Press, 1956.

Buist, Marten G., *At Spes Non Fracta: Hope and Company, 1770–1815. Merchant Bankers and Diplomats at Work*, The Hague, Holland: Martinus Nijhoff, 1974.

Cabat, Geoffrey A., "The Consolidation of 1803 in Guatemala," *The Americas*, xxviii, 1 (July 1971), 20–38.

Calabria, Antonio, *The Cost of Empire: The Finances of the Kingdom of Naples in the Time of Spanish Rule*, Cambridge, U.K.: Cambridge University Press, 1991.

Calderón Quijano, José Antonio, *Historia de las fortificaciones de Nueva España*, Seville: Escuela de Estudios Hispanoamericanos, 1953.

______, "El Banco de San Carlos y las comunidades de indios en la Nueva España," *Anuario de Estudios Americanos*, 19 (1962), 1–144.

______, *Los virreyes de la Nueva España durante el reinado de Carlos IV*, 2 vols. Seville: Escuela de Estudios Hispanoamericanos, 1972.

______, *Las fortificaciones españolas en América y Filipinas*, Madrid: MAPFRE, 1996.

Callahan, William, *Church, Politics and Society in Spain, 1750–1874*, Cambridge, Mass.: Harvard University Press, 1984.

Calvo, Thomas, "Los ingresos eclesiásticos en la diócesis de Guadalajara en 1708," in Pilar Martínez López-Cano, ed., *Iglesia, estado y economía, siglos xvi al xix*, Mexico: UNAM, 1995, pp. 47–59.

Campbell, Leon, *The Military and Society in Colonial Peru, 1750–1820*, Philadelphia, Pa.: The American Philosophical Society, 1978.

Campillo y Cosío, Joseph del, *Nuevo sistema de gobierno económico para la América*, Mexico: UNAM, 1993 [facsímile of the first edition of 1789; with a preliminary study of Rosa Cusminsky de Cedrero].

Canga Argüelles, José, *Memoria presentada a las Cortes Generales y Extraordinarias sobre las rentas y gastos de la Corona*, Cádiz: Imprenta Real, 1811.

______, *Diccionario de Hacienda*, 2 vols., Madrid: Imprenta de Don Marcelino Calero y Portocarrero, 1833–1834 [reprint facsimile by the Instituto de Estudios Fiscales, Madrid, 1984].

______, *Observaciones sobre la historia de la guerra de España que escribe en inglés el teniente coronel Napier*, Madrid, 1835–1836, 3 vols.

______, "Apuntes para la historia de la Hacienda Pública de España en el año de 1811 (Cádiz, 1813)," reprinted in Fabián Estapé, ed., *Textos olvidados*, Madrid: Instituto de Estudios Fiscales, 1991, pp. 21–76.

Cárdenas Sánchez, Enrique, *Cuando se originó el atraso económico de México: la economía mexicana en el largo siglo XIX, 1780–1920*, Madrid: Fundación Ortega y Gasset, 2003.

______, comp., "Algunas cuestiones sobre la depresión mexicana del siglo XIX," in *Historia económica de México*, vol. 2. Mexico: Fondo de Cultura Económica, 1990, pp. 27–56.

Casillero Calvo, Alfredo and Allan Kuethe, eds., *Historia General de América Latina*, vol. 3, Paris: UNESCO/Editorial Trotta, 2000.

Celaya Nández, Yolanda, "El costo fiscal en la defensa del Caribe: la Armada de Barlovento, 1702–1748," in Johanna Graffenstein and Carlos Marichal, comps., *Los nervios del imperio: los situados en la América española en el siglo XVIII*, Mexico: El Colegio de México/Instituto Mora, in press.

Cervantes Bello, Francisco, "La iglesia y la crisis del crédito colonial en Puebla, 1800–1814," in Leonor Ludlow and Carlos Marichal, eds., *Banca y poder en México, 1800–1925*, Mexico: Grijalbo, 1986, pp. 51–74.

______, "El crédito eclesiástico en Puebla, 1800–1856," Ph.D. thesis, El Colegio de México, 1993.

Céspedes del Castillo, Guillermo, *El tabaco en la Nueva España*, Madrid: Academia de la Historia, 1992.

Chamoux, Marie Noelle, et al., *Prestar y pedir prestado: relaciones sociales y crédito en México del siglo XVII al XX*, Mexico: Ciesas, 1993.

Chávez Orozco, Luis, ed., *Las cajas de comunidades indígenas de la Nueva España*, Mexico: Secretaría de Economía Nacional, 1934.

______, ed., *El comercio exterior y su influjo en la economía de la Nueva España*, Mexico: Banco Nacional del Comercio Exterior, 1960.

Chowning, Margaret, "The Consolidación de Vales Reales in the Bishopric of Michoacan," *Hispanic American Historical Review*, 3, 69 (1989), 451–478.

______, "The Contours of the Post-1810 Depression in Mexico: A Reappraisal from a Regional Perspective," *Latin American Research Review*, 27, 2 (1992), 119–150.

Cipolla, Carlo M., *The Economic Decline of Empires*, London: Methuen, 1970.

Coatsworth, John, "Obstacles to Economic Growth in Nineteenth Century Mexico," *American Historical Review*, 83, 1 (1978), 80–100.

______, "La historiografía económica de México," *Revista de Historia Económica*, 6, 2 (1988), 277–294.

______, *Los orígenes del atraso*, Mexico: Alianza Mexicana, 1990.

Collins B. James, *Classes, Estates and Order in Early Modern Britanny*, Cambridge, U.K.: Cambridge University Press, 1994.

Collins, Randall, *Macrohistory, Essays in Sociology of the Long Run*, Stanford, Calif.: Stanford University Press, 1999.

Comín, Francisco, *Hacienda y economía en la España contemporánea, 1800–1936*, Madrid, Ministerio de Hacienda, 2 vols., 1988.

Cordoncillo, José María, *Historia de la Real Lotería en Nueva España, 1770–1821*, Seville: Escuela de Estudios Hispanoamericanos, 1966.

Costeloe, Michael P., *Church Wealth in Mexico: A Study of the Juzgado de Capellanía in the Archbishopric of Mexico, 1800–1856*, Cambridge, U.K.: Cambridge University Press, 1967.

______, "La administración, recolección y distribución de los diezmos en el arzobispado de México, 1800–1860," in Arnold Bauer, ed., *La iglesia en la economía de América Latina, siglos xvi al xix*, Mexico: Instituto Nacional de Antropología e Historia, 1986, pp. 101–128.

______, *Response to Revolution: Imperial Spain and the Spanish American Revolutions, 1810–1840*, Cambridge, U.K.: Cambridge University Press, 1986.

Couturier, Edith, "The Philanthropic Activities of Pedro Romero de Terreros, First Count of Regla, 1753–1781," *The Americas*, xxxii, 1 (1975), 13–30.

Crespo, Horacio, ed., *Historia del azúcar en México*, vol. 1, Mexico: Fondo de Cultura Económica, 1988.

Crouzet, François, *L'Economie Britannique et le Blocus Continental (1806–1813)*, 2 vols., Paris: Presses Universitaires de France, 1958.

______, *La grande inflation: la monnaie en France de Louis XVI à Napoléon*, Paris: Fayard, 1993.

Cuella Martinelli, María Ángeles, *La renta de los naipes en la Nueva España*, Seville: Escuela de Estudios Hispanoamericanos, 1966.

Cuenca, Esteban Javier, "Ingresos netos del Estado español, 1788–1820," *Hacienda Pública Española*, 69 (1981), 183–208.

———, "Statistics of Spain's Colonial Trade, 1792–1820: Consular Duties, Cargo Inventories and Balance of Trade," *Hispanic American Historical Review*, 61, 3 (1981), 381–428.

———, "Comercio y hacienda en la caída del imperio español, 1776–1826," in J. Fontana, ed., *La economía española al final del antiguo Régimen, vol. 3 Comercio y colonias*, Madrid: Alianza y Banco de España: 1982, pp. 389–453.

———, "Of Nimble Arrows and Faulty Bows: A Call for Rigor. Commentaries on 'Public Expenditures Financing in the Colonial Treasury'," *Hispanic American Historical Review*, 64, 2 (1984), 297–303.

———, "Precios y cantidades en el comercio español con Francia y Gran Bretaña, 1797–1808: Coyuntura internacional y opciones imperiales," *Revista de Historia Económica*, 9, 1 (1991), 127–163.

———, "The British Balance of Payments, 1772–1820: India Transfers and War Finance," *Economic History Review*, liv, 1 (2001), 58–86.

———, "India's Contribution to the British Balance of Payments, 1757–1812," unpublished paper in *Session 106 of the XIV International Economic History Conference*, Helsinki, 2006.

Deans-Smith, Susan, *Bureaucrats, Planters and Workers: The Making of the Tobacco Monopoly in Bourbon Mexico*, Austin: University of Texas Press, 1992.

Delgado Ribas, Josep María, "Política ilustrada, industria española y mercado americano, 1720–1820," *Revista de Historia Moderna* (Pedralbes), 1, 3, 1983.

Dessert, Daniel, *Argent, pouvoir et société au Grand Siècle*, Paris: Fayard, 1984.

Díaz-Trechuelo, Ma. L., Ma. L. Rodríguez Baena, and C. Pajarón Parody, "Antonio Ma. Bucareli y Ursúa," in José Antonio Calderón Quijano, ed., *Los virreyes de Nueva España en el reinado de Carlos III* (1759–1779), vol. 1, Seville: Escuela de Estudios Hispanoamericanos, 1967.

Dickson, P. G. M., *The Financial Revolution in England. A Study in the Development of Public Credit, 1688–1756*, New York: Macmillan, 1967.

Dobado Gonzalez, Rafael, "El trabajo en las minas de Almadén, 1750–1855," Ph.D. thesis, 2 vols., Universidad Complutense de Madrid, 1989.

———, "El crecimiento guiado por la minería, el papel del Estado y el costo económico de la independencia," unpublished paper presented at El Colegio de Mexico, May 9, 2006.

Domínguez, Jorge, *Insurrección o lealtad: la desintegración del imperio español en América*, Mexico: Fondo de Cultura Económica, 1985.

Ehrenberg, Richard, *Das Haus Parish in Hamburg*, Jena: G. Fischer, 1925.

Elliott, John H., *Imperial Spain, 1469–1714*, New York: St. Martin's Press, 1963.

———, "A Europe of Composite Monarchies," *Past and Present*, 137 (1992), 48–71.

Ertman, Thomas, *Birth of Leviathan: Building States and Regimes in Medieval and Early Modern Europe*, Cambridge, U.K.: Cambridge University Press, 1997.

Esdaile, Charles, J., *The Duke of Wellington and the Command of the Spanish Army, 1812–1814*, New York: St. Martin's Press, 1990.

Farris, Nancy M., *Crown and Clergy in Colonial Mexico, 1759–1821. The Crisis of Ecclesiastical Privilege*, London: University of London, Althlone, 1968.

Ferguson, E. James, *The Power of the Purse: A History of American Public Finance, 1776–1790*, Chapel Hill: University of North Carolina Press, 1961.

Ferguson, Niall, *The Cash Nexus: Money and Power in the Modern World, 1700–2000*, New York: Basic Books, 2000.

———, *Empire: The Rise and Demise of the British World Order*, New York: Basic Books, 2002.

Fernández Albadalejo, Pablo, *Fragmentos de monarquía*, Madrid: Alianza, 1992.

Fisher, John, *Commercial Relations between Spain and Spanish America in the Era of Free Trade, 1778–1796*, Liverpool: University of Liverpool, Centre for Latin American Studies, 1985. (Monograph Series, 13.)

———, *El comercio entre España e Hispanoamérica, 1797–1820*, Madrid: Banco de España, 1993. (Estudios de Historia Económica, 27.)

Fisher, John, Allan J. Kuethe, and Anthony Mcfarlane, eds., *Reform and Insurrection in Bourbon New Granada and Peru*, Baton Rouge: Louisiana State University Press, 1990.

Fisher, Lillian Estelle, *The Background of the Revolution for Mexican Independence*, New York: Russell and Russell, 1971.

Flores Caballero, Romeo, "La Consolidación de Vales Reales en la economía, la sociedad y la política novohispanas," *Historia Mexicana*, xvii, 3 [71] (1969), 334–378.

Flores Clair, Eduardo, *Las deudas del Tribunal de Minería, 1777–1823*, Mexico: Instituto Nacional de Antropología e Historia, 1996.

Florescano, Enrique, *Fuentes para la historia de la crisis agrícola de 1785–1786*, 2 vols., Mexico: Instituto Nacional de Antropología e Historia, 1981.

———, *Precios del maíz y crisis agraria en México, 1708–1810*, Mexico: Era, 1986.

Florescano, Enrique and Isabel Gil, eds., *Descripciones económicas generales de Nueva España, 1784–1817*, Mexico: Secretaría de Educación Pública-Instituto Nacional de Antropología e Historia, 1973.

Florescano, Enrique and Rodolfo Pastor, comp., *La crisis agrícola de 1785–86. Selección documental*, Mexico: Archivo General de la Nación, 1981.

Florescano, Enrique and Victoria San Vicente, comps., *Fuentes para la historia de la crisis agrícola (1809–1811). Selección documental*, Mexico: UNAM, 1985.

Flynn, Dennis, O., "Fiscal Crisis and the Decline of Spain (Castile)," *The Journal of Economic History*, 42 (1982), 139–148.

Fonseca, Fabián de and Carlos de Urrutia, *Historia general de la Real Hacienda*, 6 vols., Mexico: Vicente G. Torres, 1845–1853.

Fontana, Josep, *La quiebra de la monarquía absoluta, 1814–1820: la crisis del Antiguo régimen en España*, Barcelona: Ariel, 1971.

———, *Hacienda y Estado en la crisis final del antiguo régimen español, 1823–1833*, Madrid: Instituto de Estudios Fiscales, 1973.

———, "La financiación de la guerra de la independencia," *Hacienda Pública Española*, 69 (1981), 209–217.

———, *La economía española al final del antiguo régimen: comercio y colonias*, Madrid: Alianza, 1982.

Fontana, Josep and Ramón Garrabou, *Guerra y Hacienda: la Hacienda del gobierno central en los años de la guerra de independencia 1808–1814*, Alicante, Spain: Instituto Juan Gil Albert, 1986.

Fradera, Josep M., *Filipinas, la colonia más peculiar: la hacienda pública en la definición de la política colonial, 1762–1868*, Madrid: CSIC, 1999.

Franco, Iván, "La Intendencia de Valladolid de Michoacán, 1787–1809. El proceso de formación del poder civil en una región de la Nueva España," Master's thesis, El Colegio de Michoacán, 1995.

Fugier, André, "Un financier diplomate: José Martínez de Hervas, chargé d'affaires d'Espagne à París, 1803–04," *Revue des Études Napoleoniennes*, 23 (1924), 81–102.

———, *Napoleón et l'Espagne, 1799–1808*, 2 vols., Paris: F. Alcan, 1930.

Galeana, Heladio, "La renta de correos como monopolio estatal en la Nueva España, 1766–1821," Master's thesis, Universidad Autónoma Metropolitana-Iztapalapa, 1998.

Garavaglia, Juan Carlos, "De Veracruz a Durango: un análisis regional de la Nueva España borbónica," *Siglo XIX*, 2, 4 (1987), 9–52.

———, *Las alcabalas novohispanas, 1776–1821*, Mexico: Archivo General de la Nación, 1987.

———, "Le regioni della Nueva España nel periodo borbónico: una analisis quantitativa, 1778–1809," *Rivista Storica Italiana*, xcix (1987), 718–753.

———, *Puebla desde una perspectiva microhistórica: Tepeaca y su entorno agrario: población, producción e intercambio, 1740–1870*, Mexico: Claves Latinoamericanas, 1994.

Garavaglia, Juan Carlos and Juan Carlos Grosso, "Estado borbónico y presión fiscal en la Nueva España, 1750–1821," in Antonio Anino, coord., *América Latina: del Estado colonial al Estado nación*, vol. 1, Turin: Franco Angeli Libri, pp. 78–97.

Garavaglia, Juan Carlos and Juan Marchena, *América Latina: De los orígenes a la independencia*, 2 vols., Barcelona: Crítica, 2005.

García Acosta, Virginia, *Los precios del trigo en la historia colonial de México*, Mexico: Ciesas, 1988.

García Ayluardo, Clara, "El comerciante y el crédito durante la época borbónica en la Nueva España," in Leonor Ludlow and Carlos Marichal, eds., *Banca y poder en México, 1800–1925*, Mexico: Grijalbo, 1986, pp. 27–50.

García Baquero, Antonio, *Comercio colonial y guerras revolucionarias: la decadencia económica de Cádiz a raíz de la emancipación americana*, Seville: Escuela de Estudios Hispanoamericanos, 1972.

García Martínez, Bernardo, "El sistema monetario de los últimos años del periodo novohispano," *Historia Mexicana*, xvii, 3 [67] (1968), 349–360.

García Peña, Ana Lidia, "El impacto popular de las reformas fiscales en la ciudad de México, 1780–1820," in C. Marichal and Daniela Marino, eds., *De colonia a nación*, México: Instituto Mora, 2001, pp. 85–133.

Garner, Richard, "Reformas borbónicas y operaciones hacendarias: La real caja de Zacatecas, 1750–1821," *Historia Mexicana*, xxvii, 4 [108] (1978), 542–587.

———, "Exportaciones de circulante en el siglo XVIII (1750–1810)," *Historia Mexicana*, xxxi, 4 [124] (1982), 544–598.

———, "Price Trends in Eighteenth Century Mexico," *Hispanic American Historical Review*, 65, 2 (1985), 279–325.

———, "Further Considerations of Facts and Figments in Bourbon Mexico," *Bulletin of Latin American Studies*, vi, 1 (1987), 55–63.

Garner, Richard and S. E. Stefanou, *Economic Growth and Change in Bourbon Mexico*, Gainesville: University of Florida Press, 1993.

Garner, Richard and William Taylor, eds., *Iberian Colonies, New World Societies: Essays in Memory of Charles Gibson*, Pennsylvania: State College, 1985.

Geggus, David Patrick, *Slavery, War and Revolution: The British Occupation of Saint Domingue, 1793–1798*, Oxford: Clarendon Press, 1982.

Glascock, Melvin, "New Spain and the War for America, 1779–1783," Ph.D. thesis, Louisiana State University and Agricultural and Mechanical College, 1969.

Glete, Jan, *Navies and Nations: Warships, Navies and State Building in Europe and America, 1500–1860*, 2 vols., Stockholm: Almquist and Wiksell International, 1993.

Goebel, Dorothy Buerne, "British Trade to the Spanish Colonies, 1796–1823," *American Historical Review*, 43, 2 (1938), 288–320.

Gómez Álvarez, Cristina, "El alto clero poblano y la revolución de independencia, 1808–1821," Ph.D. thesis, UNAM, México, 1993.

Gómez, Mónica, "El debate sobre el ingreso fiscal y la actividad económica. El caso de la Nueva España en el siglo XVIII," in C. Marichal and D. Marino, eds., *De colonia a nación*, México: Instituto Mora, 2001, pp. 115–134.

González Enciso, Agustín, "Las exportaciones norteamericanas a Cádiz, 1805–1813," *Moneda y Crédito*, 151 (1979), 51–78.

González, María del Refugio, "La intervención del Estado en la economía y la sociedad en México: sus orígenes y desarrollo. Una propuesta de interpretación," *Mexican Studies*, 5, 1 (1988), 25–41.

Gortari, Hira de and Guillermo Palacios, "El comercio novohispano a través de Veracruz (1802–1810)," *Historia Mexicana*, xvii, 3 [67] (1968), 427–454.

Grafenstein Gareis, Johanna von, "México y el Caribe durante los años de la emancipación, 1779–1808," Ph.D. thesis, UNAM, Mexico, 1994.

———, *Nueva España en el Circuncaribe, 1779–1808: revolución, competencia imperial y vínculos intercoloniales*, Mexico: UNAM, 1997.

Graffenstein, Johanna and Carlos Marichal, comps. *Los nervios del imperio: los situados en la América española en el siglo XVIII*, Mexico: El Colegio de México/Instituto Mora, in press.

Greenow, Linda, *Credit and Socioeconomic Change in Colonial Mexico: Loans and Mortgages in Guadalajara, 1720–1820*, Boulder, Colo.: Westview, 1983.

Gross, Jean-Pierre, "Progressive Taxation and Social Justice in 18th Century France," *Past and Present*, 140 (1993), 79–126.

Grosso, Juan Carlos, Jorge Silva Riquer, and Carmen Yuste, eds., *Circuitos mercantiles y mercados en Latinoamérica: siglos XVIII y XIX*, Mexico: Instituto de Investigaciones "Dr. José María Luis Mora," 1995.

Guedea, Virginia, *En busca de un gobierno alterno: los Guadalupes de México*, Mexico: UNAM, 1992.

Guerra, François-Xavier, *Modernidad e independencias: ensayos sobre las revoluciones hispánicas*, Mexico: Fondo de Cultura Económica/MAPFRE, 1992.

Guéry, Alain, "Les finances de la monarchie française sous l'Ancien Régime," *Annales, Economies, Sociétés, Civilisations*, 33, 2 (March–April 1978), 216–239.

Guimerá, Agustín, ed., *El reformismo borbónico*, Madrid: Alianza, 1996.

Gwyn, Julián, "British Government Spending and the North American Colonies, 1740–1775," *Journal of Imperial and Commonwealth History*, 8, 2 (1980), 74–84.

Hamilton, Earl, *American Treasure and the Price Revolution in Spain, 1551–1650*, Cambridge, Mass.: Harvard University Press, 1934.

Hamnett, Brian, "The Appropriation of Mexican Church Wealth by the Spanish Bourbon Government: The Consolidación de Vales Reales, 1805–1809," *Journal of Latin American Studies*, 1, 2 (1969), 85–113.

———, *Politics and Trade in Southern Mexico, 1750–1821*, Cambridge, U.K.: Cambridge University Press, 1971.

———, "Mercantile Rivalry and the Peninsular Division: The Consulados of New Spain and the Impact of the Bourbon Reforms, 1780–1824," *Ibero-Amerikanisches Archiv*, N.F. Jg. 2 (1976), 273–305.

———, *Revolución y contrarrevolución en México y el Perú: liberalismo, realeza y separatismo, 1800–1824*, Mexico: Fondo de Cultura Económica, 1978.

———, *La política española en una época revolucionaria*, Mexico: Fondo de Cultura Económica, 1985.

———, *Raíces de la insurgencia en México: historia regional, 1750–1824*, Mexico: Fondo de Cultura Económica, 1990.

———, "Absolutismo ilustrado y crisis multidimensional en el período colonial tardío, 1760–1808," in Josefina Vázquez, ed., *Interpretaciones del siglo XVIII mexicano*, Mexico: Nueva Imagen, 1992, pp. 67–108.

Harbron, John D., *Trafalgar and the Spanish Navy*, Annapolis, Md.: Naval Institute, 1988.

Harley H. Hinrichs, *A General Theory of Tax Structure Change during Economic Development*, Cambridge, Mass.: Harvard Law School, 1966.

Harris, Robert D., "French Finances and the American War, 1777–1783," *The Journal of Modern History*, 48, 2 (June 1976), 233–258.

Harris, Semour E., *The Assignats*, Cambridge, Mass.: Harvard University Press, 1930.

Hausberger, Bernd, *La Nueva España y sus metales preciosos: la industria minera colonial a través de los libros de cargo y data de la Real Hacienda, 1761–1767*, Berlín: Vervuert, Iberoamericana, 1997.

Hendrickson, David C. and Robert Tucker, *The Fall of the First British Empires: Origins of the War of American Independence*, Baltimore, Md.: Johns Hopkins Press, 1982.

Heredia Herrera, Antonio, *La renta del azogue en Nueva España, 1709–1751*, Seville: Escuela de Estudios Hispanoamericanos, 1978.

Hernández Palomo, José Jesús, *La renta del pulque en Nueva España, 1663–1810*, Seville: Escuela de Estudios Hispanoamericanos, 1980.

Hernández Silva, Cuauhtémoc, "Las élites regionales y la formación del Estado de Sonora, 1790–1831," Ph.D. thesis, El Colegio de México, 1995.

Hernández y Dávalos, Juan E., *Historia de la guerra de independencia de México*, 5 vols., Mexico: Instituto Nacional de la Revolución Mexicana, 1985.

Herr, Richard, "Hacia el derrumbe del antiguo régimen: crisis fiscal y desamortización bajo Carlos IV," *Moneda y Crédito*, 118 (1971), 37–100.

———, "La vente des propriétés de mainmorte en Espagne, 1798–1808," *Annales, Economies, Sociétés, Civilisations*, 44, 1 (1974), 215–228.

———, *Rural Change and Royal Finances in Spain at the end of the Old Regime*, Berkeley: University of California Press, 1989.

Herrera Canales, Inés, *El comercio exterior de México, 1821–1857*, Mexico: El Colegio de México, 1977.

Hidy, Ralph, *The House of Baring in American Trade and Finance. English Merchant Bankers at Work, 1763–1861*, Cambridge, Mass.: Harvard University Press, 1949.

Hoffman, Paul E., "El desarrollo de las defensas del Caribe. Siglo XVI y principios del siglo XVII," en Antonio Acosta and Juan Marchena, comps., *La influencia de España en el caribe, la Florida y la Luisiana, 1500–1800*, Madrid: Instituto de Cooperación Iberoamericana, 1983, pp. 15–35.

Hoffman, Philip T. and Jean-Laurent Rosenthal, "The Political Economy of Warfare and Taxation in Early Modern Europe," in John Nye and John Dorbak, eds., *Frontiers of of Research in Institutional Economics*, San Diego, Calif.: Academic Press, 1997.

Hoffman, Philip T. and Kathryn Norberg, eds., *Fiscal Crises, Liberty and Representative Government, 1450–1789*, Stanford, Calif.: Stanford University Press, 1994.

Hopkins, Anthony G., ed., *Globalization in World History*, New York: W.W. Norton & Co., 2002.

Howe, Walter, *The Mining Guild of New Spain and Its Tribunal General, 1770–1821*, Cambridge, Mass.: Harvard University Press, 1949.

Humboldt, Alexander von, *Ensayo político sobre la isla de Cuba*, La Habana: Archivo Nacional de Cuba, 1960. [Edition and introduction by Fernando Ortiz, who used the first translation to Spanish, dated 1827 and included notes from subsequent editions.]

———, "Tablas geográficas políticas del reino de Nueva España," text from the first edition from 1804, reproduced in Enrique Florescano and Isabel Gil, eds., *Descripciones económicas generales de Nueva España, 1784–1817*, Mexico: Secretaría de Educación Pública-Instituto Nacional de Antropología e Historia, 1973, pp. 128–230.

———, *Ensayo político sobre el reino de la Nueva España*, Mexico: Ed. Porrúa, 1991. [First published in Paris in 1807–1811; the first complete, Spanish translation is from 1822.]

Humphreys, Robin A., *Latin American History: A Guide to the Literature in English*, London: Oxford University Press, 1958.

Humphreys, Robin A. and John Lynch, eds., *The Origins of the Latin American Revolutions, 1808–1826*, New York: Alfred Knopf, 1965.

Ibarra, Antonio, "Mercado urbano y mercado regional en la Guadalajara colonial, 1790–1811," Ph.D. thesis, El Colegio de México, 1995.

Irigoin, Alexandra, "Bargaining for Absolutism: A Spanish Path to Nation State and Empire Building," unpublished manuscript, October 2005.

Israel, Jonathan, *The Dutch Republic and the Hispanic World, 1606–1661*, Oxford: Clarendon Press, 1982.

Izard, Miguel, "Metropolitanos, criollos y reformistas. La Nueva España de Revillagigedo, 1789–1794," *Boletín Americanista*, 22, 30 (1980), 181–222.

Jackson, John Alexander, "The Mexican Silver Schemes: Finance and Profiteering in the Napoleonic Era, 1796–1811," Ph.D. thesis, University of North Carolina, 1980.

Jacobsen, Nils and Hans Jurgen Puhle, eds., *The Economies of Mexico and Peru during the Late Colonial Period, 1760–1810*, Berlin: Colloquium Verlag, 1986.

Jara, Álvaro, "El financiamiento de la defensa en Cartagena de Indias: los excedentes de las Cajas de Bogotá y de Quito, 1761–1802," *Historia* (Santiago de Chile), 28 (1994), 117–182.

Jara, Álvaro and John J. TePaske, "El virreinato de Nueva Granada: la caja central de Santa Fé de Bogotá, ingresos y egresos, 1700–1808," unpublished paper, Universidad de Chile, 1994.

Jáuregui Frías, Luis Antonio, "La anatomía del fisco colonial: la real hacienda de la Nueva España, 1784–1821," Ph.D. thesis, El Colegio de México, 1994.

———, *La Real Hacienda de Nueva España: su administración en la época de los intendentes, 1786–1821*, México: UNAM, 1999.

———, "Vino viejo y odres nuevos. La historia fiscal en México," *Historia Mexicana*, iii, 3 (January–March 2003), 725–773.

Jiménez Codinach, Guadalupe, "An Atlantic Silver Entrepot: Veracruz and the House of Gordon and Murphy," paper presented in *Symposium on "Atlantic Port Cities, 1650–1850,"* Baltimore, Md.: Johns Hopkins University, 1986.

———, "Veracruz, almacén de plata en el Atlántico. La Casa de Gordon y Murphy, 1805–1824," *Historia Mexicana*, xxxviii, 2 [150] (1988), 325–388.

———, *La Gran Bretaña y la independencia de México, 1808–1821*, Mexico: Fondo de Cultura Económica, 1991.

Junta Superior de Cádiz a la América Española [Cádiz, February 28, 1810], doc. 393, Collection Lafragua, Biblioteca Nacional (Mexico), 10-page pamphlet.

Kennedy, Paul, *The Rise and Fall of British Naval Mastery*, London: Macmillan, 1983.

Kicza, John, *Empresarios coloniales: familias y negocios en la ciudad de México durante los Borbones*, Mexico: Fondo de Cultura Económica, 1986.

Klein, Herbert S., "Structure and Profitability of Royal Finance in the Viceroyalty of the Río de la Plata in 1790," *Hispanic American Historical Review*, 54 (August 1973), 440–469.

———, "La economía de la Nueva España, 1680–1809: Un análisis a partir de las cajas reales," *Historia Mexicana*, xxxiv, 4 [136] (1985), 561–609.

———, "Recent Trends in the Study of Spanish American Colonial Public Finance," *Latin American Research Review*, 23, 1 (1988), 35–62.

——— "Historia fiscal colonial: resultados y perspectivas," *Historia Mexicana*, xiii, 2 (1992), 261–308.

———, *Las finanzas americanas del imperio español, 1680–1809*, Mexico: Instituto de Investigaciones "Dr. José María Luis Mora"/Universidad Autónoma Metropolitana, 1995.

———, *The American Finances of the Spanish Empire: Royal Expenditures in Colonial Mexico, Peru and Bolivia, 1680–1809*, Albuquerque: University of New Mexico Press, 1998.

———, "Origin and Volume of Remission of Royal Tax Revenues from the Viceroyalties of Peru and Nueva España," in Antonio Miguel Bernal, ed., *Dinero, moneda y crédito en la monarquía hispánica*, Madrid: Fundación ICO/Marcial Pons, 2000, pp. 269–292.

Klein, Herbert S. and John TePaske, *Las cajas reales de la real hacienda de la América española (siglos xvi a principios del xix)* CD, Mexico: Asociación Mexicana de Historia Económica/El Colegio de México, 2004. [The historical series in this CD can also be consulted in the Web page, Historical Statistics of Mexico managed by El Colegio de México, www.colmex.mx.]

Koenigsberger, Helmut G., *La práctica del imperio*, Madrid: Alianza, 1969. [The first German edition dates from 1950.]

Kuethe, Allan J., *Military Reform and Society in New Granada, 1773–1808*, Gainesville: University of Florida Press, 1976.

———, *Cuba, 1753–1815, Crown, Military and Society*, Knoxville: University of Tennesese Press, 1986.

———, "La desregulación comercial y la reforma imperial en la época de Carlos III: los casos de Nueva España y Cuba," *Historia Mexicana* xii, 2 [162] (1991), 265–292.

Kuethe, Allan J. and Juan Marchena F., eds., *Soldados del Rey. El ejército borbónico en América colonial en vísperas de la Independencia*, Castellon, Spain: Universitat Jaume I, 2005. (Colección América, 4.)

Kuethe, Allan J. and G. Douglas Inglis, "Absolutism and Enlightened Reform: Charles III, the Establishment of the Alcabala and Commercial Reorganization in Cuba," *Past and Present*, 109 (1985), 118–143.

Kuethe, Allan J. and Lowell Blaisdell, "French Influences and the Origins of the Bourbon Colonial Reorganization," *Hispanic American Historical Review*, 71, 3 (August 1991), 579–607.

Labaree, Leonard W., *Royal Government in America: A Study of the British Colonial System Before 1783*, New York: F. Ungar, 1964.

Labouchere, G., "L'Annexion de la Louisiane aux États-Unis et les maisons Hope et Baring," *Revue d'Histoire Diplomatique*, 30, 3 (1916), 423–455.

Ladd, Doris, *The Mexican Nobility at Independence, 1780–1826*, Austin: University of Texas Press, 1976.

Laffer, Arthur, *The Economics of the Tax Revolt*, New York: Harcourt Brace, 1979.

Lafuente Ferrari, E., *El virrey Iturrigaray y los orígenes de la independencia de México*, Madrid: Consejo Superior de Investigación Científica/Instituto Gonzalo Fernández de Oviedo, 1941.

Laguardia, Jorge Mario, "Centroamérica en las Cortes de Cádiz," *Revista de Derecho Político*, 33 (1991), 367–389.

Lang, M. F., *El monopolio estatal del mercurio en el México colonial*, Mexico: Fondo de Cultura Económica, 1977.

Lavrin, Asunción, "The Execution of the Laws of Consolidación in New Spain: Economic Aims and Results," *Hispanic American Historical Review*, 53, 1 (1973), 27–49.

Le Riverend Brusone, Julio, *Historia económica de Cuba*, La Habana: Instituto Cubano del Libro, 1974.

Lerdo de Tejada, Miguel, *Comercio exterior de México desde la conquista hasta hoy*, Mexico: Rafael, 1853.

Lévy, Arthur, *Un grand profiteur de guerre sous la Révolution, l'Empire et la Restauration: G.J. Ouvrard*, Paris, 1929

Lewis, James A., "New Spain during the American Revolution, 1779–1783: A Viceroyalty at War," Ph.D. thesis, Duke University, 1975.

———, "Las damas de La Havana, el Precursor, and Francisco de Saavedra: A Note on Spanish Participation in the Battle of Yorktown," *The Americas*, xxxvii, 1 (July 1980), 83–98.

———, *The Final Campaign of the American Revolution: Rise and Fall of the Spanish Bahamas*, Charleston: University of South Carolina Press, 1991.

Liehr, Reinhart, "Statsverschuldung und privatkredit: die "consolidación de vales reales in Hispanoamerika," *Ibero-Amerikanishes Archiv*, N.F. Jg. 6, 2 (1980), 150–183.

Lindley, Richard, *Haciendas and Economic Development in Guadalajara, Mexico at Independence*, Austin: University of Texas Press, 1983.

Lira González, Andrés, "Aspecto fiscal de la Nueva España en la segunda mitad del siglo XVIII," *Historia Mexicana*, xvii, 3 [67] (1968), 361–394.

Liss, Peggy, *Atlantic Empires. The Network of Trade and Revolutions, 1713–1826*, Baltimore, Md.: Johns Hopkins Press, 1983. [The Spanish translation is *Los imperios trasatlánticos: las redes del comercio y de las revoluciones de Independencia*, Mexico: Fondo de Cultura Económica, 1989.]

Little, Marcela M., "Sales Taxes and Internal Commerce in Bourbon Mexico, 1754–1821," Ph.D. thesis, Duke University, 1985.

López Cancelada, Juan, *Defensa de la Nueva España*, Mexico: Miguel Ángel Porrúa Editores, 1989 [facsímile of 1811 edition].

López Godínez, María Elena, *Guía del Ramo de Donativos y Préstamos del Archivo General de la Nación, 1781–1820*, Mexico: Archivo General de la Nación, ms., 1986.

———, "Monografía de los donativos y préstamos en Nueva España, 1780–1815," B. A. thesis in history, tesis de licenciatura, Universidad del Claustro de Sor Juana, Mexico, 1993.

Lucena Giraldo, Manuel, ed., "Las tinieblas de la memoria: una reflexión sobre los imperios en la Edad moderna," *Debates y Perspectivas*, 2, 2 (special issue) (September 2002).

Ludlow, Leonor and Carlos Marichal, eds., *Banca y poder en México, 1800–1925*, México: Grijalbo, 1986.

Ludlow, Leonor, Carlos Marichal, and Silva, Jorge, eds., *Los negocios y las ganancias: de la Colonia al México moderno*, Mexico: Instituto de Investigaciones "Dr. José María Luis Mora"/UNAM, 1993.

Lynch, John, "British Policy and Spanish America, 1783–1808," *Journal of Latin American Studies*, 1, 1 (1969), 1–30.

———, *The Spanish American Revolutions, 1808–1826*, New York: W.W. Norton, 1973.

Mahan, Alfred T., *The Influence of Seapower upon the French Revolution and Empire, 1793–1812*, 2 vols., London: Sampson Low, Marston, 1892.

Malamud, Carlos D., "La Comisión de Reemplazos de Cádiz y la financiación de la reconquista americana," in *Andalucía y América en el siglo XIX: Actas de las V Jornadas*, Seville: Escuela de Estudio Hispano-Americanos, 1986, pp. 317–347.

———, "Acerca del concepto de Estado colonial en la América hispana," *Revista de Occidente*, 116, (January 1991), 116–127.

Marchena Fernández, Juan, "La financiación militar en Indias: introducción a su estudio," *Anuario de Estudios Americanos*, 36 (1979), 93–110.

———, "La defensa del Caribe en siglo XVII: Ingenieros, soldados y pesos" in Antonio Acosta y Juan Marchena, eds., *La influencia de España en el caribe, la Florida y la Luisiana, 1500–1800*, Madrid: Instituto de Cooperación Iberoamericana, 1983, pp. 37–59.

———, *Oficiales y soldados en el ejército de América*, Seville: CSIC, 1983.

———, "Financiación militar y situados," in Segundo Congreso de Historia Militar, *Temas de historia militar*, vol. 1, Madrid: Ediciones del Ministerio del Ejército, 1988, pp. 263–307.

Marichal, Carlos, "La Iglesia y la crisis financiera del virreinato, 1780–1808; apuntes sobre un tema viejo y nuevo," *Relaciones. Estudios de Historia y Sociedad*, 10, 40 (1989), 103–130.

———, "Las guerras imperiales y los préstamos novohispanos, 1781–1804," in *Historia Mexicana*, xxxix, 4 [156] (1990), 881–907.

———, "La historiografía económica reciente sobre el México borbónico: los estudios del comercio y las finanzas virreinales, 1760–1820," *Boletín del Instituto de Historia Argentina y Americana Dr. E. Ravignani (Buenos Aires)*, tercera serie, 2 (1990), 161–180.

———, "La Iglesia y la Corona: la bancarrota del gobierno de Carlos IV y la consolidación de Vales Reales en la Nueva España," in Pilar Martínez López-Cano, ed., *Iglesia, estado y economía, siglos xvi al xix*, Mexico: UNAM, 1995, pp. 241–262.

———, "Beneficios y costes fiscales del colonialismo: las remesas americanas a España, 1760–1814," *Revista de Historia Económica*, 15, 3 (1997), 475–505.

———, *La bancarrota del virreinato. Nueva España y las finanzas del imperio español, 1780–1810*, Mexico: Fondo de Cultura Económica and El Colegio de México/Fideicomiso Históricos de las Américas, 1999.

Marichal, Carlos and Daniel Marino, eds., *De colonia a nación: la transición fiscal en México, 1750–1850*, Mexico: El Colegio de México, 2001.

Marichal, Carlos, and Carlos Rodríguez Venegas, eds., *Boletín de Fuentes para la Historia Económica de México*, vols. 1–8, Mexico: El Colegio de México 1990–1992.

Marichal, Carlos, and Matilde Souto, "Silver and Situados: New Spain and the Financing of the Spanish Empire in the Caribbean in the Eighteenth Century," *Hispanic American Historical Review*, 74, 4 (1994), 587–613

Marley, Daniel, ed., *Documentos relativos a la guerra entre España e Inglaterra, 1779–1784*, Mexico: Archivo General de la Nación, 1985.

Martín Acosta, María Emelina, *El dinero americano y la política del imperio*, Madrid: MAPFRE, 1992.

Martínez López-Cano, Pilar, "Avances en los estudios sobre el crédito colonial," *Boletín del Instituto de Investigaciones Históricas de la UNAM*, Mexico: UNAM, 1994, pp. 34–45.

———, ed., *Iglesia, estado y economía, siglos xvi al xix*, Mexico: UNAM, 1995.

Martínez López-Cano, Pilar and Guillermina del Valle, eds., *El crédito en Nueva España*, Mexico: Instituto Mora/UNAM/El Colegio de México/El Colegio de Michoacán, 1998.

Mathias, Peter and Patrick O'Brien, "Taxation in Britain and France, 1715–1810. A Comparison of the Social and Economic Incidence of Taxes Collected for the Central Governments," *Journal of European Economic History*, 5, 3 (Winter 1976), 601–650.

Mahan, Alfred Thayer *The Influence of Sea Power upon the French Revolution and Empire, 1793–1812*, 2 vols., London: Sampson, Low and Co., 1893.

Mazín, Oscar, *Entre dos majestades. El obispo y la iglesia de Michoacán ante las reformas borbónicas, 1758–1772*, Zamora, Michoacán.: El Colegio de Michoacán, 1987.

———, ed., *México en el mundo hispánico*, 2 vols., Mexico: El Colegio Mexiquense, 2000.

McClelland, Peter D., "The Cost to America of British Imperial Policy" *American Economic Review*, lix, 2 (May 1969), 370–381.

McCusker, John J., *Money and Exchange in Europe and America, 1600–1775. A Handbook*, Kingsport: Tenn.: Macmillan Press, 1975.

McCusker, John J. and Russell R. Menard, *The Economy of British America, 1607–1789*, Chapel Hill, N.C.: Institute of Early American History, 1991.

McFarlane, Anthony, *El Reino Unido y América: la época colonial*, Madrid: MAPFRE, 1992.

Mcneill, John Robert, *Atlantic Empires of France and Spain, Louisbourg and Havana, 1700–1763*, Chapel Hill: University of North Carolina Press, 1985.

Mcneill, William H., *The Pursuit of Power: Technology, Armed Force and Society since a.d. 1000*, Chicago: University of Chicago Press, 1983.

Mcwatters, David Lorne, "The Royal Tobacco Monopoly in Bourbon Mexico, 1764–1810," M.A. thesis, University of Florida, 1979.

Medina Rubio, Arístides, *La iglesia y la producción agrícola en Puebla, 1540–1795*, Mexico: El Colegio de México, 1979.

Merino Navarro, José Patricio, *La armada española en el siglo XVIII*, Madrid: Fundación Universitaria Española, 1981.

———, "La Hacienda de Carlos IV," *Hacienda Pública Española*, 69 (1981), 139–181.

———, "1805: La crisis financiera internacional y deuda española," in M. Artola and L. Bilbao, eds., *Estudios de Hacienda: de Ensenada a Mon*, Madrid: Instituto de Estudios Fiscales, 1984, pp. 387–406.

———, *Las cuentas de la Administración central española, 1750–1820*, Madrid: Instituto de Estudios Fiscales, 1987.

Michaud, Claude, "Les Receveurs Généraux du Clergé de France aux XVIe et XVIe siècles," Ph.D. thesis, Université de París I, 1987.

Mier, Fray Servando de, *Historia de la Revolución de Nueva España*, 2 vols., México: Fondo de Cultura Económica, 1986 [facsímile of the original edition published at London, 1813].

Miño, Manuel, *Obrajes y tejedores de Nueva España, 1700–1810*, Madrid: Instituto de Estudios Fiscales, 1990.

———, "Estructura económica y crecimiento: la historiografía económica colonial mexicana," *Historia Mexicana*, xiii, 2 [166] (1992), 177–220.

Modelski, George and W. R. Thompson, *Sea Power in Global Politics, 1494–1943*, Seattle: University of Washington Press, 1988.

Mola, Marina Alfonso and Carlos Martínez Shaw, "Los astilleros de la América colonial," in Alfredo Casillero Calvo and Allan Kuethe, eds., *Historia General de América Latina*, vol. 3, Paris: UNESCO, 2000.

Mora, José María Luis, *Crédito Público*, Mexico: UNAM, 1986 [facsimile of the first edition published at París, 1837].

Morales, María Dolores, "La distribución de la propiedad en la ciudad de México entre 1813 y 1848" *Historias*, 12 (1986), 81–90.

Morgan, Edmund S. and Helen M. Morgan, *The Stamp Act: Prologue to Revolution*, New York: Collier, 1963.

Morin, Claude, *Michoacán en la Nueva España del siglo XVIII: crecimiento y desigualdad en una economía colonial*, Mexico: Fondo de Cultura Económica, 1979.

Morineau, Michel, *Incroyables gazettes et fabuleux métaux: les retours des trésors americains d'après les gazettes hollandaises, xvie-xviiie siècles*, Paris/London: University of Cambridge Press/Maison des Sciences de l'Homme, 1985.

———, "Budgets de l'état et gestion des finances royales en France au dix-huitième siècle," *Revue historique*, 264, 2, (1986), 289–336.

Mut Calafell, Antonio, "Inventario de los documentos de Secretaría del Archivo del Banco de España," *Archivo Histórico del Banco de España*, 1984.

Nater, Laura, "El tabaco y las finanzas del imperio español: Nueva España y la metrópoli, 1760–1810," Ph.D. thesis, El Colegio de México, 1998.

Neal, Larry, *The Rise of Financial Capitalism: International Capital Markets in the Age of Reason*, Cambridge, U.K.: Cambridge University Press, 1990.

Nester, William R., *The First Global War: Britain, France, and the Fate of North America, 1756–1775*, Westport, Conn.: Praeger, 2000.

Nolte, Vincent, *Fifty Years in Both Hemispheres: Reminscences of the Life of a Former Merchant*, New York, 1854.

North, Douglass C. and Barry R. Weingast, "Constitutions and Commitment: The Evolution of Institutions Governing Public Choice in Seventeenth Century England," *The Journal of Economic History*, 44, 4 (December 1989), 803–832.

O' Brien, Patrick K., "The Political Economy of British Taxation, 1600–1815," *Economic History Review*, 2nd series, 41 (1988), 1–32.

———, "Public Finance in the Wars with France, 1793–1815," in H. T. Dickinson, ed., *Britain and the French Revolution, 1789–1815*, New York: St. Martin's Press, 1989, pp. 165–187.

———, *Fiscal Exceptionalism: Great Britain and Its European Rivals from Civil War to Triumph at Trafalgar and Waterloo*, Working Paper No. 65/01, London School of Economics, 2001.

O'Phelan Godoy, Scarlett, *Un siglo de rebelioners anticoloniales. Perú y Bolivia, 1700–1783*, Cuzco, Peru: Centro Bartolomé de las Casas, 1988.

Ortiz de la Tabla, Javier, *Comercio exterior de Veracruz, 1778–1821: crisis de dependencia*, Seville: Escuela de Estudio Hispano-Americanos, 1978.

———, *Cádiz y el Atlántico, 1717–1778*, 2 vols., Cádiz, Spain: Diputación Provincial de Cádiz, 1988.

Ortiz Escamilla, Juan, ed., *Fuerzas militares en Iberoamérica, siglos xviii y xix*, Mexico: El Colegio de México, 2005.

Ouvrard, Gabriel Julien, *Mémoires*, 3 vols., Paris, 1826–1828.

Ouweneel, Arij and Catrien J. H. Bijleveld, "The Economic Cycle in Bourbon Central Mexico: A Critique of the Recaudación del diezmo líquido en pesos," *Hispanic American Historical Review*, 69, 3 (1989), 479–530.

Pacheco, Argelia, "Una estrategia imperial española. El situado a Puerto Rico, 1765–1815," Master's thesis, Instituto "Doctor José María Luis Mora," Mexico, 2002.

Pagden, Anthony, *Lords of All the World: Ideologies of Empire in Spain, Britain and France, c.1500–c.1800*, New Haven, Conn.: Yale University Press, 1995.

Parker, Geoffrey *The Army of Flanders and the Spanish Road, 1569–1659: The Logistics of Spanish Victory and Defeat in the Low Countries' Wars*, Cambridge, U.K.: Cambridge University Press, 1972.

Pastor, Rodolfo, *Campesinos y reformas: La mixteca, 1700–1856*, Mexico: El Colegio de México, 1987.

Payard, Maurice, *Le financier G.J. Ouvrard (1770–1846)*, Paris: Academie Nationale de Reims, 1958.

Peña, José F. de la, *Oligarquía y propiedad en Nueva España, 1550–1624*, Mexico: Fondo de Cultura Económica, 1983.

Pérez Herrero, Pedro, "I principi politici del riformismo borbonico americano. Considerazione storiografiche," *Rivista Storica Italiana*, xcix, 3 (1987), 696–717.

———, *Plata y libranzas: la circulación mercantil en el México borbónico*, Mexico: El Colegio de México, 1988.

———, "El crecimiento económico novohispano durante el siglo XVIII: una revisión," *Revista de Historia Económica*, 5, 1 (1989), 69–110.

———, "Los beneficiarios del reformismo borbónico: metrópoli versus élites novohispanas," *Historia Mexicana*, xii, 2 [162] (1991), 207–264.

———, "El México borbónico: un éxito fracasado?," in Josefina Vázquez, ed., *Interpretaciones del siglo XVIII mexicano*, Mexico: Nueva Imagen, 1992, pp. 109–152.

Pérez Herrero, Pedro and Pedro Vives, "Perfil bibliográfico de la América de Carlos III," *Cuadernos Hispanoamericanos* ["Los Complementarios"], 2 (1988), 251–273.

Phelan, John L., *The People and the King: The Comunero Revolution in Colombia, 1781*, Madison: University of Wisconsin Press, 1978.

Pieper, Renate, *La Real Hacienda bajo Fernando VI y Carlos III, 1753–1788*, Madrid: Instituto de Estudios Fiscales, 1992.

Pietschmann, Horst, "Consideraciones en torno al protoliberalismo, reformas borbónicas y revolución. La Nueva España en el último tercio del siglo XVIII," *Historia Mexicana*, xii, 2 [162] (1991), 167–206.

———, *Mexico zwischen Reform und Revolution: Vom bourbonischen Zeitalter zur Unabhängigkeit*, Stuttgart, Germany: Franz Steiner Verlag, 2000.

———, ed., *Atlantic History: History of the Atlantic System, 1580–1830*, Gottingen, Germany: Vandehoek & Ruprecht, 2002.

Pinto, Sonia, *El financiamiento extraordinario de la Real Hacienda en el virreinato peruano, Cuzco, 1575–1650*, Santiago: Universidad de Chile, 1981.

Piqueras, José A., ed., *Las Antillas en la era de las Luces y la Revolución*, Madrid: Siglo XXI, 2005.

Potter, Marc and Jean Laurent Rosenthal, "Politics and Public Finance in France: The Estates of Burgundy, 1660–1790," *The Journal of Interdisciplinary History*, 27, 4 (Spring 1997), 577–612.

Prados de la Escosura, Leandro, "La pérdida del imperio y sus consecuencias económicas," in L. Prados de la Escosura and S. Amaral, eds., *La independencia americana: sus consecuencias económicas*, Madrid: Alianza Universidad, 1993, pp. 253–300.

———, ed., *Exceptionalism and Industrialisation: Britain and Its European Rivals, 1688–1815*, Cambridge, U.K.: Cambridge University Press, 2004.

Priestley, Herbert Ingram, *José de Gálvez, Visitor-General of New Spain 1765–1771*, Philadelphia, Pa.: Porcupine Press, 1963.

Quirós, José María, *Guía de negociantes: compendio de la legislación mercantil de España e Indias*, Mexico: UNAM, 1986.

Quiroz, Alfonso W., *Deudas olvidadas: instrumentos de crédito en la economía colonial peruana, 1750–1820*, Lima: Pontificia Universidad Católica del Perú, 1993.

———, "Reassessing the Role of Credit in Late Colonial Peru: Censos, Escrituras and Imposiciones," *Hispanic American Historical Review*, 74, 2 (1994), 193–230.

———, "Crédito de origen eclesiástico y deuda pública colonial en el Perú, 1750–1820," in Pilar Martínez López-Cano, ed., *Iglesia, estado y economía, siglos xvi al xix*, Mexico: UNAM, 1995, pp. 275–288.

Quiroz, Enriqueta, *Entre el lujo y la subsistencia: mercado, abastecimiento y prcios de la carne en la ciudad de México, 1750–1812*, Mexico: El Colegio de México, Instituto Mora, 2005.

Raymond E. Callahan, *The East India Company and Army Reform, 1783–1798*, Cambridge, Mass.: Harvard University Press, 1972.

Renaut, Francis Paul, *Le pacte de famille et l'Amérique: la politique coloniale franco-espagnole, de 1760 à 1792*, Paris: Leroux, 1922.

Riley, James C., *International Government Finance and the Amsterdam Capital Market, 1740–1815*, Cambridge, U.K.: Cambridge University Press, 1980.

———, *The Seven Years War and the Old Regime in France: The Economic and Financial Toll*, Princeton, N.J.: Princeton University Press, 1986.

———, "French Finances, 1727–1768," *The Journal of Modern History*, 59 (1987), 209–243.

Rodger, N. A., "Recent Books on the Royal Navy of the Eighteenth Century," *The Journal of Military History*, 63, 3 (July, 1999), 683–703.

Rodríguez García, Vicente, *El fiscal de Real Hacienda en Nueva España, Ramón de Posada y Soto, 1781–1793*, Oviedo: Universidad de Oviedo, 1985.

Rodríguez Gordillo, José Manuel, *La creación del estanco del tabaco en España*, Seville: Fundación Altadis, 2002.

Rodríguez O., Jaime, ed., *The Independence of Mexico and the Creation of the New Nation*, Los Angeles: University of California Press, 1989.

———, *La independencia de la América española*, Mexico: Fondo de Cultura Económica, 1996.

Rodríguez Venegas, Carlos, "La sociedad novohispana y las guerras imperiales a la luz del donativo y préstamos de 1781," B.A. thesis, UNAM, Mexico, 1996.

Romero Sotelo, María Eugenia, *Minería y guerra: la economía de la Nueva España, 1810–1821*, Mexico: El Colegio de México, 1997.

Root, Hilton L., *The Fountain of Privilege: Political Foundations of Markets in Old Regime France and England*, Berkeley: University of California Press, 1993.

———, *La constuction de l'Etat moderne en Europe: La France et l'Angleterre*, Paris: PUF, 1994.

Rubio Mañé, J. Ignacio, "Movimientos marítimos entre Veracruz y Campeche, 1801–1810," *Boletín del Archivo General de la Nación*, 1a serie, 24, 4 (1953), 595–676; 25, 1 (1954), 91–146.

———, "Egresos de caudales por el puerto de Veracruz, 1784–1804," *Boletín del Archivo General de la Nación*, 25, 3 (1954), 469–518; 26, 1 (1955), 93–144; 26, 2 (1955), 259–292; 26, 3 (1955), 457–486; and 27, 1 (1956), 101–164.

Rydjord, John, *Foreign Interest in the Independence of New Spain*, Durham: North Carolina, 1935.

———, "Napoleon and Mexican Silver," *The Southwestern Social Science Quarterly*, 19, 2 (1938), 171–182.

Saavedra de Sangronis, Francisco de, *Journal of Don Francisco Saavedra de Sangronis during the commission which he had in his charge, 1780–1783*, Gainesville: University of Florida Press, 1989 [Edición a cargo de Francisco Morales Padrón, traducción de Aileen Topping].

Sagra, Ramón de la, *Historia económico-política y estadística de la isla de Cuba*, La Habana: Imprenta de las Viudas de Arazosa y Soler. 1831.

Salvucci, Linda, "Costumbres viejas, 'hombres nuevos': José de Gálvez y la burocracia fiscal novo-hispana (1754–1800)," *Historia Mexicana*, xxxiii, 2 (1983), 224–264.

———, "Atlantic Intersections: Early American Commerce and the Rise of the Spanish West Indies (Cuba)," *Business History Review*, 79 (Winter 2005), 781–800.

Salvucci, Richard, *Textiles and Capitalism in Mexico: An Economic History of the Obrajes, 1539–1840*, Princeton, N.J.: Princeton University Press, 1987.

———, "Economic Growth and Change in Bourbon Mexico: A Review Essay," *The Americas*, li, 2 (1994), 219–231.

———, "The Real Exchange Rate of the Mexican Peso, 1762–1812: A Research Note and Estimate," *Journal of European Economic History*, 23, 1 (1994), 131–140.

———, "Mexican National Income in the Era of Independence, 1800–1840," in S. Haber, ed., *How Latin America Fell Behind: Essays on the Economic Histories of Brazil and Mexico, 1800–1914*, Stanford, Calif.: Stanford University Press, 1997, pp. 216–242.

Sánchez Maldonado, Maria Isabel, *Diezmos y crédito eclesiástico: el diezmatorio de Acámbaro, 1724–1771*, Zamora, Michoacán: El Colegio de Michoacán, 1994.

Sánchez Santiró, Ernest, Luis Jáuregui, and Antonio Ibarra, *Finanzas y política en el mundo iberoamericano. Del antiguo régimen a la independencia*, Mexico: Universidad Autónoma de Morelos/Instituto Mora/UNAM, 2001.

Schom, Alan, *Trafalgar: Countdown to Battle, 1803–1805*, New York, London: Joseph, 1990.

Schwaller, John Fredrick, *Origins of Church Wealth in Mexico. Ecclesiastical Revenues and Church Finances, 1523–1600*, Albuquerque: University of New Mexico Press, 1985.

Seijas y Lobera, Francisco, *Gobierno militar y político del Reino Imperial de la Nueva España (1702)*, edition prepared by Pablo Emilio Pérez Mallaína Bueno, Mexico: UNAM, 1986.

Sempat Assadourian, Carlos, *El sistema de la economía colonial: el mercado interior. Regiones y espacio económico*, Mexico: Grijalbo, 1983.

Serrano Álvarez, José Manuel, *Fortificaciones y tropas. El gasto militar en Tierra Firme, 1700–1788*, Seville: Universidad de Sevilla/CSIS/Diputación de Sevilla, 2004.

Shepherd, James F. and Walton, Gary, *Shipping, Maritime Trade and Economic Development of North America*, London, U.K.: Cambridge University Press, 1972.

Sherwig, John H., *Guineas and Gunpowder. British Foreign Aid in the Wars with France, 1793–1815*, Cambridge, Mass.: Harvard University Press, 1969.

Silva Prada, Natalia, "Contribución de la población indígena novohispana al erario real: el donativo gracioso de 1781," unpublished manuscript, 1995.

Silva Ricquer, Jorge, "La Consolidación de vales reales en el obispado de Michoacán, 1804–1809," in Virginia Gudea and J. Rodríguez, eds., *Cinco siglos de historia de México* vol. 2, México: Instituto de Investigaciones "Dr. José María Luis Mora," 1992, pp. 65–81.

———, *La administración de alcabalas y pulques de Michoacán, 1776–1821*, Mexico: Instituto de Investigaciones "Dr. José María Luis Mora," 1993.

———, "Producción agropecuaria y mercados regionales: el caso de Michoacán en el siglo XVIII," Ph.D. thesis, El Colegio de México, 1997.

Simmons, Marc, *Spanish Government in New Mexico*, Albuquerque: University of New Mexico Press, 1968.

Slicher van Bath, B. H., *Real Hacienda y economía en Hispanoamerica, 1541–1820*, Amsterdam: CEDLA, 1989.

Smith, Adam, *An Inquiry into the Nature and Causes of the Wealth of Nations*, fifth edition, London: Methuen and Co. Ltd., 1904 [first edition published in 1776].

Smith, Robert S., "Shipping in the Port of Veracruz, 1790–1821," *Hispanic American Historical Review*, 23, 1 (1943), 5–20.

———, "José María Quirós: Balanza del comercio marítimo de Veracruz e ideas económicas," *Trimestre Económico*, 13 (1947), 680–711.

———, "Sales Taxes in New Spain, 1575–1770," *Hispanic American Historical Review*, 28, 1 (February 1948), 2–37.

Solís, Ramón, *El Cádiz de las Cortes: la vida en la ciudad en los años de 1810 a 1813*, Madrid: Alianza, 1969.

Soria, Víctor M., *La Casa de Moneda bajo la administración borbónica, 1733–1821*, Mexico: Universidad Autónoma Metropolitana, 1994.

Souto Mantecón, Matilde, "El Consulado de comercio de Veracruz, 1796–1821," Ph.D. thesis, El Colegio de México, 1996.

Stasavage, David, *Public Debt and the Birth of the Democratic State: France and Great Britain, 1688–1789*, New York: Cambridge University Press, 2003.

Stein, Barbara H. and Stanley J. Stein, *Apogee of Empire: Spain and New Spain in the Age of Charles III, 1759–1788*, Baltimore, Md.: Johns Hopkins Press, 2003.

Stein, Stanley J., "Crisis metropolitana, comercio atlántico y descapitalización colonial: España y Nueva España, 1804–1808," in, *Congreso bicentenerario de Simón Bolivar*, vol. iv, Caracas: Academia Nacional de Historia, 1985, pp. 152–218.

———, "Prelude to Upheaval in Spain and New Spain, 1800–1808: Trust Funds, Spanish Finance and Colonial Silver," in Richard Garner and William Taylor, eds., *Iberian Colonies, New World Societies: Essays in Memory of Charles Gibson*, Pennsylvania: State College, 1985, pp. 185–202.

———, "Caribbean Counterpoint: Veracruz vs. Havana. War and Neutral Trade, 1797–1799," in Jeanne Chase, ed., *Geographie du capital marchand, 1760–1860*, Paris: L' Ecole des Hautes Etudes en Sciences Sociales, 1987.

———, "Un raudal de oro y plata que corría sin cesar de España a Francia: Spanish Mercantile Policy and trade with France under Charles III," paper presented at *Congreso Internacional "Carlos III y la Ilustración,"* Madrid, 1988.

Stone, Lawrence, ed., *An Imperial State at War: Britain from 1689 to 1815*, London: Routledge, 1994.

Sugawara, Masae, *La deuda pública de España y la economía novohispana*, Mexico: Instituto Nacional de Antropología e Historia, 1976. (Colección Científica, 28).

———, "Los antecedentes coloniales de la deuda pública en México. 1) España: los Vales Reales, orígenes y desarrollo de 1784 a 1804," in *Boletín del Archivo General de la Nación*, 2a serie, 8, 1–2 (1967), 129–402.

Tanck de Estrada, Dorothy, "Escuelas y cajas de comunidad en Yucatán al final de la colonial," *Historia Mexicana*, xiii, 3 [171] (1994), 401–449.

———, "Protesta indígena al rey en contra de las cajas de comunidad, 1793–1806. Cultura política en torno a los reglamentos para los pueblos de indios," unpublished paper, 1995.

———, *Pueblos de indios y educación en el México colonial, 1750–1821*, Mexico: El Colegio de México, 1998.

———, *Atlas ilustrado de los pueblos de indios: Nueva España, 1800*, Mexico: El Colegio de México, 2005.

Tedde, Pedro, "Comerciantes y banqueros madrileños al final del Antiguo Régimen," in *Historia económica y pensamiento social: Estudios en Homenaje a Diego Mateo del Peral*, Madrid: Alianza, 1983, pp. 283–300.

———, "Crisis del Estado y deuda pública a comienzos del siglo XIX," *Hacienda Pública Española* 1987, 81, 169–195.

———, "Los negocios de Cabarrus con la Real Hacienda, 1780–1783," *Revista de Historia Económica*, 5, 3 (1987), 527–551.

———, *El Banco de San Carlos, 1782–1829*, Madrid: Banco de España/Editorial Alianza, 1988.

———, "Política financiera y política comercial en el reinado de Carlos III," in *Actas del Congreso Internacional sobre Carlos III y la Ilustración*, vol. 2, Madrid: Ministerio de Cultura, 1989, pp. 139–217.

Tenenbaum, Barbara, *The Politics of Penury: Debts and Taxes in Mexico, 1821–1856*, Albuquerque: University of New Mexico Press, 1986.

TePaske, John J., "La política española en el Caribe durante los siglos XVII y XVIII" en Antonio Acosta y Juan Marchena, comps., *La influencia de España en el caribe, la Florida y la Luisiana, 1500–1800*, Madrid: Instituto de Cooperación Iberoamericana, 1983, pp. 61–87.

———, "New World Silver, Castile and the Far East (1590–1750)," in John F. Richards, *Precious Metals in the Later Medieval and Early Modern Worlds*, Durham, N.C.: Duke University Press, 1983, pp. 425–445.

———, "Economic Cycles in New Spain in the Eighteenth Century: The View from the Public Sector," in Richard Garner and William Taylor, eds., *Iberian Colonies, New World Societies: Essays in Memory of Charles Gibson*, Pennsylvania: State College, 1985, pp. 119–142.

———, "General Tendencies and Secular Trends in the Economies of Mexico and Peru, 1750–1810: The View from the Cajas of Mexico and Lima," in Nils Jacobsen and and Hans Jurgen Puhle, eds., *The Economies of Mexico and Peru during the Late Colonial Period, 1760–1810*, Berlin: Colloquium Verlag, 1986, pp. 316–339.

———, "The Financial Disintegration of the Royal Government of Mexico during the Epoch of Independence," in Jaime E. Rodríguez O., ed., *The Independence of Mexico and the Creation of the New Nation*, Los Angeles: University of California Press 1989, pp. 63–84.

———, "La crisis financiera del virreinato de Nueva España a fines de la colonia," *Secuencia*, 19 (1991), 123–140.

———, "Los registros de la contaduría real: problemas y trampas," *Boletín de Fuentes para la Historia Económica de México*, 7 (1992), 9–16.

TePaske, John J. and Herbert S. Klein, *Royal Treasuries of the Spanish Empire in America, 1580–1825*, 3 vols., Durham, N.C.: Duke University Press, 1982.

———, *Ingresos y egresos de la Real Hacienda de Nueva España*, Mexico: Instituto Nacional de Antropología e Historia, 1986–1988. (Colección Fuentes, 2 vols.).

TePaske, John J. and José Hernández Palomo y María Luz, *La Real Hacienda de Nueva España: La real Caja de México, 1576–1816*, Mexico: Instituto Nacional de Antropología e Historia, 1976. (Colección Científica, 41.)

Terán, Marta, "Muera el mal gobierno: las reformas borbónicas en los pueblos michoacanos y el levantamiento indígena de 1810," Ph.D. thesis, El Colegio de México, 1995.

Teresa de Mier, Fray Servando, *Historia de la revolución de Nueva España*, Mexico: Fondo de Cultura Económica, 1986 [facsimile of the edition published in 1813].

Thomas, Peter, "The Cost of the British Army in North America, 1763–1775," *William and Mary Quarterly*, 45 (1988), 510–516.

Thomas, Robert Paul, "A Quantitative Approach to the Study of the Effects of British Imperial Policy upon Colonial Welfare," *The Journal of Economic History*, 25, 4 (1965), 615–638.

Thomson, Buchanan P., *Spain: Forgotten Ally of the American Revolution*, North Quincy, Mass.: Christopher, 1976.

Tilly, Charles, *The Formation of Nation States in Western Europe*, Princeton, N.J.: Princeton University Press, 1975.

______, *Coercion, Capital and European States,* A.D. *900–1990*, Cambridge, U.K.: Basil Blackwell, 1990.

Torales Pacheco., Maria. Cristina, Tarsico García Díaz, Carmen Yuste, *La compañía de comercio de Francisco Ignacio de Yraeta (1767–1797)*, 2 vols., Mexico: Instituto Mexicano de Comercio Exterior, 1985.

Toreno, Conde de, *Historia del levantamiento, guerra y revolución de España*, second edition, Madrid: Biblioteca de Autores Españoles, 1953 [first edition published in 1835].

Torre Villar, Ernesto de la, ed., *El contrabando y el comercio exterior en la Nueva España*, Mexico: Banco Nacional de Comercio Exterior 1967.

Torres Ramírez, Bibiano, *La Armada de Barlovento*, Seville: Escuela de Estudios Hispanoamericanos, 1981.

Torres Sánchez, Rafael "Possibilities and Limits: Testing the Fiscal Military State in the Anglo-Spanish War of 1779–1783," paper presented at *Session 69, XIV International Economic History Congress*, Helsinki, August 2006.

Tortella Casares, Teresa, *Índice de los primeros accionistas del Banco Nacional de San Carlos*, Madrid: Banco de España, 1986.

Tovar Pinzón, Hermes, "Remesas, situados y real hacienda en el siglo XVII," in Antonio Miguel Bernal, ed., *Dinero, moneda y crédito en la monarquía hispánica*, Madrid: Fundación ICO/Marcial Pons, 2000, pp. 241–267.

Tulard, Jean, *Dictionnaire Napoleón*, Paris: Fayard, 1987.

Valdés Lakowsky, Vera, *De las minas al mar: historia de la plata mexicana en Asia, 1563–1834*, Mexico: Fondo de Cultura Económica, 1987.

Valle Pavón, Guillermina del, "Las corporaciones religiosas en los empréstitos negociados por el Consulado de México a fines del siglo xviii," in Pilar Martínez López-Cano, ed., *Iglesia, estado y economía, siglos xvi al xix*, Mexico: UNAM, 1995, pp. 225–240.

______, "El Consulado de Comerciantes de la Ciudad de México y las finanzas novohispanas, 1592–1827," Ph.D. thesis, El Colegio de México, 1997.

______, "El apoyo financiero del Consulado de Comerciantes a las guerras españolas del siglo XVIII," in Pilar Martínez López-Cano and Guillermina del Valle, eds., *El crédito en Nueva* España, Mexico: Instituto Mora, 1998, pp. 131–150.

______, "Historia financiera de la Nueva España en el siglo XVIII y principios del XIX, una revisión crítica," *Historia Mexicana*, iii, 3 (January–March 2003), 649–675.

Van Young, Eric, *Hacienda and Market in Eighteenth Century Mexico: The Rural Economy of the Guadalajara Region, 1675–1820*, Berkeley: University of California Press, 1981.

———, "Recent Aglophone Scholarship on Mexico and Central America in the Age of Revolution (1750–1850)," *Hispanic American Historical Review*, 65 (1985), 725–748.

———, *La crisis del orden colonial: Estructura agraria y rebeliones populares de la Nueva España, 1750–1821*, Mexico: Alianza Mexicana, 1992.

———, *The Other Rebellion: Popular Violence, Ideology, and the Mexican Struggle for Independence, 1810–1821*. Stanford, Calif.: Stanford University Press, 2001.

Vargas-Lobsinger, María, "El ascenso social y económico de los inmigrantes españoles: el caso de Francisco Valdivielso (1683–1743)," *Historia Mexicana*, xxxv, 4 [140] (1986), 601–619.

Vega, Josefa, "Los primeros préstamos de la guerra de independencia, 1809–1812," *Historia Mexicana*, xxxix, 4 [156] (1990), 909–932.

Velasco Ceballos, Rómulo, *La administración de D. Frey Antonio María de Bucareli y Ursúa, cuadregésimo sexto virrey de México*, 2 vols., Mexico: Archivo General de la Nación, 1936.

Velde, Francois R. and David R. Weir, "The Financial Market and Government Debt Policy in France, 1746–1793," *The Journal of Economic History*, 52, 1 (1992), 1–39.

Villanova, Manuel, "Economía y civismo" *Revista Cubana*, xvi (1892), 157–190 [reprinted in the Habana by the Ministry of Education in 1945].

Villar Ortiz, Covadonga, *La renta de la pólvora en Nueva España, 1569–1767*, Seville: Escuela de Estudios Hispanoamericanos, 1988.

Villiers, Patrick, *Marine royale, corsaires et trafic dans l'Atlantique: de Louis XIV a Louis XVI*, Dunkerque, France: Société Dunkerquoise d'Histoire et d'Archéologie, 1991.

Vizcarra Catalina and Richard Sicotte, "El control del contrabando en el Perú colonial: el caso del monopolio del tabaco, 1752–1813," in Carlos Contreras and Manuel Glave, eds., *Estado y mercado en la historia del Perú*, Lima: Pontificia Universidad Católica, 2002, pp. 184–211.

Walker, Geoffrey, *Política española y comercio colonial*, Barcelona: Ariel, 1979.

Wallerstein, Immanuel and Christopher Chase-Dunn, *Rise and Demise: Comparing World Systems*, Boulder, Colo.: Westview Press, 1997.

Walters, P. G., "The American Career of David Parish," *The Journal of Economic History*, 4, 2 (1944), 149–166.

Weir, David R., "Tontines, Public Finance and Revolution in France and England, 1688–1789," *The Journal of Economic History*, 49 (1989), 1–28.

———, "Les crises économiques et les origines de la révolution française," *Annales, Economies, Sociétés, Civilisations*, 4 (1991), 917–947.

Whitaker, A. P., *The United States and the Independence of Latin America, 1800–1830*, Baltimore: Johns Hopkins Press, 1941.

White, Eugene N., "Fueron inflacionarias las finanzas estatales en el siglo XVIII?: una nueva interpretación de los vales reales," *Revista de Historia Económica*, 5, 3 (1987), 509–526.

———, "Was There a Solution to the Ancien Regime's Financial Dilemma?" *The Journal of Economic History*, 49, 3 (1989), 545–568.

———, "The French Revolution and the Politics of Government Finance, 1770–1815," *The Journal of Economic History*, 55, 2 (June 1995), 227–255.

Wobeser, Gisela von, "Mecanismos crediticios en la Nueva España. El uso del censo consignativo," *Mexican Studies. Estudios Mexicanos*, 5, 1 (1989), 1–23.

———, "La inquisición como institución crediticia en el siglo XVIII," *Historia Mexicana*, xxxix, 4 [156] (1990), 849–880.

———, *El crédito eclesiástico en la Nueva España: siglo XVIII*, Mexico: UNAM, 1994.

———, *Dominación colonial: La Consolidación de vales reales, 1804–1812*, Mexico: UNAM, 2003.

Wolf, Otto, *Ouvrard, Speculator of Genius, 1770–1846*, New York: Barrie and Rockliff 1962.

Wortman, Miles, "Rentas públicas y tendencias económicas en Centroamérica, 1787–1819," *Hispanic American Historical Review*, 4, 2 (May 1975), 251–286.

———, *Government and Society in Central America, 1680–1840*, New York: Columbia University Press, 1982.

Yañez Ruiz, Manuel, *El problema fiscal en México*, 6 vols., Mexico: SHCP, 1958.

Zylberberg, Michel, *Une si douce domination. Les milieux d'affaires français et l'Espagne vers 1780–1808*, Paris: Comité pour l'histoire économique et financière de la France, 1993.

Index

Other Books in the Series (continued from page iii)

16. *Conflicts and Conspiracies: Brazil and Portugal, 1750–1808*, Kenneth Maxwell
17. *Marriage, Class and Colour in Nineteenth-Century Cuba: A Study of Racial Attitudes and Sexual Values in a Slave Society*, Verena Stolcke
18. *Politics, Economics and Society in Argentina in the Revolutionary Period*, Tulio Halperín Donghi
19. *Politics in Argentina, 1890–1930: The Rise and Fall of Radicalism*, David Rock
20. *Studies in the Colonial History of Spanish America*, Mario Góngora
21. *Chilean Rural Society from the Spanish Conquest to 1930*, Arnold J. Bauer
22. *Letters and People of the Spanish Indies: Sixteenth Century*, James Lockhart and Enrique Otte, eds.
23. *The African Experience in Spanish America, 1502 to the Present Day*, Leslie B. Rout, Jr.
24. *The Cristero Rebellion: The Mexican People between Church and State, 1926–1929*, Jean A. Meyer
25. *Allende's Chile: The Political Economy of the Rise and Fall of the Unidad Popular*, Stefan de Vylder
26. *Land and Labour in Latin America: Essays on the Development of Agrarian Capitalism in the Nineteenth and Twentieth Centuries*, Kenneth Duncan and Ian Rutledge, eds.
27. *A History of the Bolivian Labour Movement, 1848–1971*, Guillermo Lora
28. *Coronelismo: The Municipality and Representative Government in Brazil*, Victor Nunes Leal
29. *Drought and Irrigation in North-east Brazil*, Anthony L. Hall
30. *The Merchants of Buenos Aires, 1778–1810: Family and Commerce*, Susan Migden Socolow
31. *Foreign Immigrants in Early Bourbon Mexico, 1700–1760*, Charles F. Nunn
32. *Haciendas and Ranchos in the Mexican Bajío, Léon, 1700–1860*, D. A. Brading
33. *Modernization in a Mexican Ejido: A Study in Economic Adaptation*, Billie R. DeWalt
34. *From Dessalines to Duvalier: Race, Colour and National Independence in Haiti*, David Nicholls
35. *A Socioeconomic History of Argentina, 1776–1860*, Jonathan C. Brown
36. *Coffee in Colombia, 1850–1970: An Economic, Social and Political History*, Marco Palacios
37. *Odious Commerce: Britain, Spain and the Abolition of the Cuban Slave Trade*, David Murray
38. *Caudillo and Peasant in the Mexican Revolution*, D. A. Brading, ed.
39. *The Struggle for Land: A Political Economy of the Pioneer Frontier in Brazil from 1930 to the Present Day*, J. Foweraker

40. *Oil and Politics in Latin America, Nationalist Movements and State Companies*, George Philip
41. *Demographic Collapse: Indian Peru, 1520–1620*, Noble David Cook
42. *Revolution from Without: Yucatán, Mexico, and the United States, 1880–1924*, Gilbert M. Joseph
43. *Juan Vicente Gómez and the Oil Companies in Venezuela, 1908–1935*, B. S. McBeth
44. Law and Politics in Aztec Texcoco, Jerome A. Offner
45. *Brazil's State-Owned Enterprises: A Case Study of the State as Entrepreneur*, Thomas J. Trebat
46. *Early Latin America: A History of Colonial Spanish America and Brazil*, James Lockhart and Stuart B. Schwartz
47. *Capitalist Development and the Peasant Economy in Peru*, Adolfo Figueroa
48. *Miners, Peasants and Entrepreneurs: Regional Development in the Central Highlands of Peru*, Norman Long and Bryan Roberts
49. *Unions and Politics in Mexico: The Case of the Automobile Industry*, Ian Roxborough
50. *Housing, the State, and the Poor: Policy and Practice in Three Latin American Cities*, Alan Gilbert and Peter M. Ward
51. *Tobacco on the Periphery: A Case Study in Cuban Labour History, 1860–1958*, Jean Stubbs
52. *Sugar Plantations in the Formation of Brazilian Society: Bahia, 1550–1835*, Stuart B. Schwartz
53. *The Province of Buenos Aires and Argentine Politics, 1912–1943*, Richard J. Walter
54. *The Mexican Revolution, Volume 1: Porfirians, Liberals, and Peasants*, Alan Knight
55. *The Mexican Revolution, Volume 2: Counter-Revolution and Reconstruction*, Alan Knight
56. *Pre-Revolutionary Caracas: Politics, Economy, and Society 1777–1811*, P. Michael McKinley
57. *Catholic Colonialism: A Parish History of Guatemala, 1524–1821*, Adriaan C. van Oss
58. *The Agrarian Question and the Peasant Movement in Colombia: Struggles of the National Peasant Association, 1967–1981*, Leon Zamosc
59. *Roots of Insurgency: Mexican Regions, 1750–1824*, Brian R. Hamnett
60. *Latin America and the Comintern, 1919–1943*, Manuel Caballero
61. *Ambivalent Conquests: Maya and Spaniard in Yucatan, 1517–1570, Second Edition*, Inga Clendinnen
62. *A Tropical Belle Epoque: Elite Culture and Society in Turn-of-the-Century Rio de Janeiro*, Jeffrey D. Needell
63. *The Political Economy of Central America since 1920*, Victor Bulmer-Thomas

64. *Resistance and Integration: Peronism and the Argentine Working Class, 1946–1976*, Daniel James
65. *South America and the First World War: The Impact of the War on Brazil, Argentina, Peru and Chile*, Bill Albert
66. *The Politics of Coalition Rule in Colombia*, Jonathan Hartlyn
67. *The Demography of Inequality in Brazil*, Charles H. Wood and José Alberto Magno de Carvalho
68. *House and Street: The Domestic World of Servants and Masters in Nineteenth-Century Rio de Janeiro*, Sandra Lauderdale Graham
69. *Power and the Ruling Classes in Northeast Brazil: Juazeiro and Petrolina in Transition*, Ronald H. Chilcote
70. *The Politics of Memory: Native Historical Interpretation in the Colombian Andes*, Joanne Rappaport
71. *Native Society and Disease in Colonial Ecuador*, Suzanne Austin Alchon
72. *Negotiating Democracy: Politicians and Generals in Uruguay*, Charles Guy Gillespie
73. *The Central Republic in Mexico, 1835–1846: "Hombres de Bien" in the Age of Santa Anna*, Michael P. Costeloe
74. *Politics and Urban Growth in Buenos Aires, 1910–1942*, Richard J. Walter
75. *Colombia before Independence: Economy, Society and Politics under Bourbon Rule*, Anthony McFarlane
76. *Power and Violence in the Colonial City: Oruro from the Mining Renaissance to the Rebellion of Tupac Amaru (1740–1782)*, Oscar Cornblit
77. *The Economic History of Latin America since Independence, Second Edition*, Victor Bulmer-Thomas
78. *Business Interest Groups in Nineteenth-Century Brazil*, Eugene Ridings
79. *The Cuban Slave Market, 1790–1880*, Laird W. Bergad, Fe Iglesias García, and María del Carmen Barcia
80. *The Kingdom of Quito, 1690–1830: The State and Regional Development*, Kenneth J. Andrien
81. *The Revolutionary Mission: American Enterprise in Latin America, 1900–1945*, Thomas F. O'Brien
82. *A History of Chile, 1808–2002, Second Edition*, Simon Collier and William F. Sater
83. *The Rise of Capitalism on the Pampas: The Estancias of Buenos Aires, 1785–1870*, Samuel Amaral
84. *The Independence of Spanish America*, Jaime E. Rodríguez
85. *Slavery and the Demographic and Economic History of Minas Gerais, Brazil, 1720–1888*, Laird W. Bergad
86. *Between Revolution and the Ballot Box: The Origins of the Argentine Radical Party in the 1890s*, Paula Alonso
87. *Andrés Bello: Scholarship and Nation-Building in Nineteenth-Century Latin America*, Ivan Jaksic

88. *Deference and Defiance in Monterrey: Workers, Paternalism, and Revolution in Mexico, 1890–1950*, Michael Snodgrass
89. *Chile: The Making of a Republic, 1830–1865: Politics and Ideas*, Simon Collier
90. *Shadows of Empire: The Indian Nobility of Cusco, 1750–1825*, David T. Garrett

www.ingramcontent.com/pod-product-compliance
Lightning Source LLC
LaVergne TN
LVHW090308210926
848480LV00001B/174
9780521142359